Sleep and its spaces in Middle English literature

Manchester University Press

Series editors: Anke Bernau, David Matthews and James Paz

Series founded by: J. J. Anderson and Gail Ashton

Advisory board: Ruth Evans, Patricia C. Ingham, Andrew James Johnston, Chris Jones, Catherine Karkov, Nicola McDonald, Haruko Momma, Susan Phillips, Sarah Salih, Larry Scanlon, Stephanie Trigg and Matthew Vernon

Manchester Medieval Literature and Culture publishes monographs and essay collections comprising new research informed by current critical methodologies on the literary cultures of the Middle Ages. We are interested in all periods, from the early Middle Ages through to the late, and we include post-medieval engagements with and representations of the medieval period (or 'medievalism'). 'Literature' is taken in a broad sense, to include the many different medieval genres: imaginative, historical, political, scientific, religious. While we welcome contributions on the diverse cultures of medieval Britain and are happy to receive submissions on Anglo-Norman, Anglo-Latin and Celtic writings, we are also open to work on the Middle Ages in Europe more widely, and beyond.

Titles available in the series

34. *Northern memories and the English Middle Ages*
    Tim William Machan

35. *Harley manuscript geographies: Literary history and the medieval miscellany*
    Daniel Birkholz

36. *Play time: Gender, anti-Semitism and temporality in medieval biblical drama*
    Daisy Black

37. *Transfiguring medievalism: Poetry, attention and the mysteries of the body*
    Cary Howie

38. *Objects of affection: The book and the household in late-medieval England*
    Myra Seaman

39. *The gift of narrative in medieval England*
    Nicholas Perkins

40. *Sleep and its spaces in Middle English literature: Emotions, ethics, dreams*
    Megan G. Leitch

Sleep and its spaces in Middle English literature

Emotions, ethics, dreams

Megan G. Leitch

MANCHESTER UNIVERSITY PRESS

Copyright © Megan G. Leitch 2021

The right of Megan G. Leitch to be identified as the author of this work has been asserted by them in accordance with the Copyright, Designs and Patents Act 1988.

Published by Manchester University Press
Oxford Road, Manchester, M13 9PL

www.manchesteruniversitypress.co.uk

British Library Cataloguing-in-Publication Data
A catalogue record for this book is available from the British Library

ISBN 978 1 5261 5110 0 hardback
ISBN 978 1 5261 7159 7 paperback

First published 2021
Paperback published 2023

The publisher has no responsibility for the persistence or accuracy of URLs for any external or third-party internet websites referred to in this book, and does not guarantee that any content on such websites is, or will remain, accurate or appropriate.

Typeset
by Sunrise Setting Ltd, Brixham

Contents

Acknowledgements	vi
Introduction: remarkable sleep	1
1 Emotions, epistemology and the nature of sleep	47
2 Ethics, appetite and the dangers of sleep	91
3 Sleeping spaces and the circumscription of desire	151
4 The hermeneutics of sleep in Chaucer's dream poems	198
Coda: 'all good letters were layde a slepe': medieval sleep and early modern heirs	242
Bibliography	255
Index	281

Acknowledgements

I'm fortunate to have written this book with the support of kind colleagues at Cardiff University, and within a wider medievalist community of brilliant and convivial romance scholars, Arthurians, Chaucerians and historians. For particular suggestions and conversations germane to this project, I'm grateful to Elizabeth Archibald, Laura Ashe, Richard Beadle, Jo Bellis, Neil Cartlidge, Sasha Handley, Jessica Henderson, Amy Kaufman, Phil Knox, Carolyne Larrington, Ben Pohl, Ad Putter, Raluca Radulescu, Samantha Rayner, Cory Rushton, Sarah Salih, Corinne Saunders, Ceri Sullivan, Leah Tether, Usha Vishnuvajjala, Dan Wakelin, Kevin Whetter and Nicky Zeeman, as well as the audiences of talks at Bristol, Cambridge, Durham, the London Old and Middle English Research Seminar, Oxford and Swansea. I'd especially like to thank stalwart friends whose invaluable input included reading chapters – Ben Barootes, Sophie Battell, Venetia Bridges, Aisling Byrne, Helen Cooper, Derek Dunne, Marcel Elias, Vicky Flood and Shazia Jagot – and expert assistance with Latin – Jess Lockhart and Venetia Bridges. Any errors are, of course, my own.

Anke Bernau and Meredith Carroll at Manchester University Press have been fantastic to work with, and the generous and insightful feedback from the press's two anonymous readers has made this a better book. A term as a visiting research fellow at St Catherine's College in Oxford in 2015, and a Cardiff University Research Leave Fellowship for 2018–19, helped with research and writing. Parts of Chapters 2 and 3 appeared in earlier form in *Arthurian Literature* (2011), *Parergon* (2015) and *Sexual Culture in the Literature of Medieval Britain* (Boydell and Brewer, 2014); I am grateful to the publishers for permission to develop this material here.

Introduction: remarkable sleep

> Sir Launcelot rested hym longe with play and game, and than he thought hymself to preve in straunge adventures, and bade his nevew Sir Lyonell for to make hym redy, 'for we too muste go seke adventures'. So they mounted on theire horses, armed at all ryghtes, and rode into a depe foreste and so into a playne.
>
> So the wedir was hote aboute noone, and *Sir Launcelot had grete luste to slepe*. Than Sir Lyonell aspyed a grete appyll-tre that stoode by an hedge, and seyde, 'Sir, yondir is a fayre shadow, there may we reste us and oure horsys.'
>
> 'Hit is trouthe,' seyde Sir Launcelot, 'for *this seven yere I was not so slepy as I am nowe.*'
>
> So there they alyted and tyed there horsys unto sondry treis and Sir Launcelot layde hym downe undir this appyll tre, and his helmet undir his hede. [...] So *Sir Launcelot slepte passyng faste.*[1]

When Malory's Launcelot goes riding through the forest in search of adventure, the first thing he encounters is an overpowering desire to sleep. Although he has 'rested hym longe' before setting out, Launcelot, King Arthur's pre-eminent knight, succumbs to a 'grete luste to slepe' after, it seems, merely a morning's ride. The consequences of this sudden lethargy are dire: while Launcelot is asleep, Lionel is captured by another knight. Launcelot not only fails in his chivalric duty to protect his friend and nephew; he too is captured, detained against his will by four queens who seek to make him their lover and to corrupt his loyalty to Arthur and Guenevere. Being 'armed at all ryghtes' and a redoubtable fighter is no protection while unconscious; in surrendering to his desire to sleep, Launcelot also surrenders to an enemy abduction and endures an unwanted seduction attempt. In re-shaping earlier Arthurian narrative material to write his *Morte Darthur* (1470), Thomas Malory not only selectively jettisons Launcelot's earlier backstory in order to begin Launcelot's own tale with this particular episode. Malory also alters the implications of Launcelot's act of falling asleep, figuring it not (as in his thirteenth-century French source) as an appropriate or expedient response to weariness and heat,[2] but rather as a lack of temperance, in a way that foregrounds ethical responsibility. In the conduct manuals esteemed by late medieval readers of romance – the aristocratic, gentry and aspiring middle classes[3] – midday and post-prandial sleep is explicitly frowned upon, seen not only as unhealthy, but also as socially and spiritually insalubrious. As Gilbert Kymer's early fifteenth-century dietary for King Henry V's brother, Humphrey Duke of Gloucester, exhorts, 'you ought to avoid sleeping in the day after noon […], and you should not sleep in the middle [of the day] after any meal or during one'.[4] When Launcelot and Lionel alight in the 'playne' at the forest's edge, then, midday sleep occupies a semantic field that includes sloth, excess, illness and irresponsibility, hedged about by more tangible dangers. For a knight like Malory's Launcelot, for whom the forest of romance is a space of adventure,[5] sleep takes place at the edge of the genre's vital undertakings: on the verge between knightly endeavour and chivalric undoing.

A 'lust' or appetite for sleep similarly shapes Geoffrey Chaucer's *Book of the Duchess*, written a century before Malory finished his Arthuriad, in which the narrator declares that he has 'such a lust […] to slepe' when he falls asleep to dream of the Man in Black and his lament for his lost beloved.[6] In the lengthy prologue to the dream, for Chaucer's insomniac, possibly lovelorn narrator, and for the figures he reads and dreams about, sleep both is, and stands in for, the object of desire. Here in his first sustained narrative poem, Chaucer – like Malory – foregrounds an interest in sleep in terms that mark a departure from the French sources to which he is in other ways much indebted. For Chaucer's dream vision narrator, unlike for Malory's Launcelot, sleep is not a failure in ethical conduct or a dangerous lapse of bodily decorum; nor does it signify, as it often can in medieval mentalities, sloth or a lack of spiritual perception. Here, sleep is not idleness, but an antidote to idleness; it is a long-awaited respite from melancholic inertia, vital for the poem's pursuit of consolation for a lost beloved and restoration of productive imagination. And just as the *Book of the Duchess* foregrounds questions about interpreting the narrator's dream, so too does it pose hermeneutic questions about the cause of his sleep. Sleep, then, for both Chaucerian dreamer and Arthurian knight, is a bodily appetite; it is an embodied performance, and one that invites interpretation. And while the connotations of sleep with which these representations engage are varied and complex, they also form part of a wider, and consistent, set of contemporary habits – and habits of thinking – about sleep.

This book explores what it means for literary characters such as Malory's Launcelot and Chaucer's narrator, among many others, to have a 'lust' for sleep. As an object of desire in Middle English literature, sleep is also a generative subject. Representations of figures who long for or are overcome by sleep abound in a range of Middle English genres, from popular romances to Ricardian dream visions, from fabliaux to saints' lives and biblical drama. Literary sleep has sometimes been seen as merely a pause in the plot, a mundane necessity, or a platform for other significant experiences: it can be a euphemism for intimate encounters, or the prelude to visionary experience. In these terms, literary sleep might seem simply a concomitant of action: an accompanying absence, a moment of inactivity rather than an act, a form of punctuation that is essential but unremarkable. Yet one of the most remarkable things about sleep in Middle English textual culture is the extent to which it is remarked upon, in a wide variety of genres, and in ways that bespeak attentiveness to both its performance and its interpretation. Malory's Launcelot is not only sleepy; he also comments on his desire to sleep, declaring that 'this seven yere I was not so slepy as I am nowe' (an assertion not found in Malory's French source),[7] and signalling that his 'passyng faste' sleep (as an event unparalleled in seven years) is remarkable or extra-ordinary. Sleepers whose experiences are both remarked-upon and remarkable, in these ways and others, sprawl across the pages of Middle English literature: drowsy knights and kings neglecting their duties, vulnerable damsels and queens, dreamers and visionaries, cuckolds, saints and fickle figures in need of correction among them. Sleep enters discourse as a highly charged focus of narrative, conversation, commentary, regulation and interpretation. The performance of literary sleep animates ethical codes and emotive scripts, and in the ways that it provokes interpretation (both diegetic and exegetic), it is inherently epistemological: it contributes to what and how characters and readers know, and desire to know.

This book, then, takes as its starting point the ways in which characters and contemporaries themselves assert that sleep is significant, in order to show how Middle English literature registers intimate concerns with sleep and the spaces in which it takes place. These concerns have been overlooked by studies more concerned with what sleep sometimes enables (dreams and dream poetry), or with what sleep sometimes stands in for or supersedes (sex). This book concentrates particularly on Middle English literature of the fourteenth and fifteenth centuries, but it also attends to a *longue durée*, in the literature and ideas about sleep circulating from the twelfth century to the early seventeenth. It focuses on continuities (cultural, scientific, social, spiritual, spatial) across this span, without neglecting shifts and developments.[8] From the twelfth-century *Peterborough Chronicle*'s comment that during the civil war between Stephen and Matilda, people said that 'Christ and his saints slept', to Shakespeare's Queen Elizabeth Woodville's lament that God must have been sleeping when her two little boys were murdered in the Tower, literary sleep marks crises of perception and conduct in culturally specific ways.[9] And although I am primarily concerned with literal sleep, I also consider metaphorical sleep, since, as these evaluative comments from the *Peterborough Chronicle* and *Richard III* show, figurative sleep shares some discursive implications with physiological sleep.

In analysing how an appetite for sleep shapes different medieval narrative genres, I argue that there are specific cultural resonances, as well as particular generic ones, that distinguish late medieval English literary engagements with sleep. Sleep, that is, mediates thematic concerns and questions in ways that carry specific ethical, affective and epistemic implications in the late medieval English cultural imagination, and that also offer defining contributions to different Middle English genres: romance, dream vision, biblical drama and fabliau. Sleep does have comparable ideological implications in non-narrative genres such as lyrics and carols;[10] and other Middle English texts which this book does not have the scope to address in full, but in which sleep has complementary connotations to those discussed here, range from Margery Kempe's autobiographical visions to ballads about sleeping in the lap of a woman.[11] Sleep's polysemous implications can be both positive and negative, and this book explores the ways in which the spiritual significances of sleep intersect with sleep's medical and social dimensions.

Performing and interpreting sleep in Middle English literature

In the medieval English imagination, sleep is an embodied and culturally determined act, both performed and interpreted; both subject to a particular habitus, and understood through particular, and pervasive, hermeneutic lenses. Sleep, here, is something that overpowers, but also something that can be prepared for; however, in neither case can sleep be effected by an act of will. Representations of sleepers in Middle English literature engage with varied yet overlapping contemporary ideas of the dangers of sleep, from the supernatural noon-day demon sometimes thought to prey upon unwary sleepers, to condemnations of idleness as a sin, and to the instructions in conduct manuals and medical tracts that readers should not sleep during the day for fear of the damage it could do to their social reputations as well as their bodily health. Given that an appetite for sleep in Middle English literature often yields to sex, snoring, sloth and other forms of intemperance, sleep is an experience to which the language of desire and surrender, as well as of regulation and censure, inheres. Yet representations of sleep are also shaped by the *locus amoenus* tradition, the idea of a pleasant outdoors space conducive to peaceful slumber. In addition, medieval literary sleep has desirable medical dimensions, since sleep was widely understood as beneficial for health and well-being, both physical and mental; a natural and necessary process which required preparation and proper practice, and could ward off or alleviate disease or emotional distemper. Sleep's epistemological dimensions include the ways in which sleep enabled contemplation and enlightenment by leading to dreams and other revelations of truth and knowledge;[12] and yet sleep could also, on the other hand, constitute a lack of perception.[13] In this complex cultural grammar of sleep, place, or space, matters too: the spaces in which literary characters are overpowered by sleep – whether outside under an apple tree, in a bedchamber, or in the bottom of a boat, a church, or the middle of a public hall – carry different connotations, expectations, possibilities and perils.

This book's focus complements recent trends situating Middle English literature, or individual authors such as Chaucer, more in relation to continental European literature and thought.[14] Where sleep is concerned, in recognising the transmission and translation of, and profound engagement with, literary and medical texts from the continent, we can also gain greater recognition of English or insular innovations. While some of the connotations of sleep certainly pertain to other medieval cultures too, late medieval English literary culture's engagements with sleep are distinguished by both the pervasiveness and the particularities of its investment in sleep as an embodied performance with specific and recognisable ethical, affective, medical and epistemological implications. This sort of argument for cultural specificity might invite some accusations of special pleading, but it is an argument that is sustained by the accretion of detailed readings of literary texts across the span of this book. When Middle English literary texts engage with sleep, they often offer marked departures from their sources, versions of these narratives written in other times and places. The fact that many, though certainly not all, of the English literary works addressed here are (partly) translations from other medieval languages (especially French) in no way diminishes their cultural specificity; rather, this gives us a means of deepening our understanding of medieval English literary concerns. Middle English literature's concerted interest in sleep can be seen in what this literary culture borrows from other cultures, as well as in what it alters and expands, or generates itself. The act of translation is an act of cultural encounter and transformation: as Sif Rikhardsdottir observes, a translation offers 'evidence of the impressions of the receiving culture', and can be seen as 'an independent work representative of the social and literary context from which it [the translation itself] originates'.[15] A similar approach informs my study of the cultural translation of (French and Latin) texts into Middle English.

When Middle English texts that are translations or that incorporate translated elements – such as Malory's *Morte Darthur*, the prose and verse *Melusine* romances, and Chaucer's *Book of the Duchess* – move from one cultural context to another, small alterations can convey significant shifts in meaning. These English texts' emphases on sleep are often added to, expanded or altered from what is found in their sources. One particularly pervasive type of altered emphasis occurs when Middle English texts emphasise ethical rather than erotic implications of sleep, as, for instance, when the opening sequence of the fourteenth-century *Ywain and Gawain* offers a conspicuous departure from its source, Chrétien de Troyes' *Yvain* (discussed in Chapter 2). And yet Middle English narrative genres also offer distinctive ways of discussing and negotiating sexual encounters – often (as addressed in Chapter 3) by dwelling on the spaces of sleep, rather than on bodies. Significantly, English translations and adaptations develop emphases on sleep that they share with Middle English texts that have no (extant) narrative sources, such as *Sir Orfeo*, *Sir Gawain and the Green Knight* and *Mankind*, suggesting that these emphases reflect the concerns of Middle English writers and their readerships. This study, then, aims to add to our awareness of the capacious horizons of medieval English literary culture in its learned adaptations, its inventiveness and its self-reflexivity; and, also, to illuminate Chaucer's underappreciated debts to English traditions alongside his more celebrated debts to continental ones.

Some aspects of the medieval English interest in sleep make striking contributions to different genres' approaches to ethics, emotions and epistemology. Sleepers' performance of unconsciousness in romance and dream visions, even when ill-advised, is usually decorous, whereas in fabliau, allegory and drama, sleep is often marked by scatological features such as snoring and slobbering. Representations of sleep not only *conform* to different genres; sleep (and insomnia) are deployed to *communicate*, and are read and analysed, both diegetically and extra-diegetically. Sleep, for instance, inscribes and interrogates conduct in relation to the ethical expectations that inhere, respectively, to popular romances or morality plays, to chivalric duty or Christian labour. Several hitherto unrecognised motifs in Middle English romance are shaped by untimely, outdoor sleep. And while fabliau is not of course a moralising genre, it is nevertheless invested in moral expectations; Chaucer's fabliaux deploy the ethical implications of sleep (and snoring) to underscore class commentaries, enable tricksters' stratagems and construct comedy. Different spaces accommodate and influence sleep in different genres, and various emotions – especially anger and sorrow – cause, and/or are mediated by, sleep, in romance, cycle plays and dream visions. In dream visions, sleeping outdoors during the day (for instance, in *Pearl* and *Piers Plowman*) is more likely to be associated with the *locus amoenus* tradition than with the courtesy books' condemnation of daytime naps and commentaries on the dangers of unhealthy outdoor vapours, or with the dangers of attack and abduction that shape romance. However, in the *Prologue* to the *Legend of Good Women*, although Chaucer's narrator muses on the daisy outdoors during the day, he then conscientiously defers his sleep until night-time, and falls asleep not in the field, but in the home (if in a sort of constructed *locus amoenus* space rather than a regular bed). In this temporal deferral, the poem deploys the (un)ethical legibility of daytime sleep, as per the courtesy books, as a commentary on Chaucer's need for self-regulation: he needs to regulate not only his corporeal habits, but also his compositional ones, in order to write more positively about women. Moreover, the sleep of dream vision narrators in Langland's *Piers Plowman* and poems in the Plowman tradition, even in its emotional inflections, often foregrounds ethical (or unethical) implications, in ways that further these works' admonitory or corrective instruction. By contrast, in Chaucer's *Book of the Duchess* and *Parliament of Fowls*, emotions engender sleep and the dream visions that sleep contains in ways that emphasise sleep's implications for mental health and the embodiment of inspiration; sleep, that is, offers a term for lived experience that balances the authority of old books, and that intervenes in Chaucerian debates about consolation and the composition of poetry.

Given the cultural legibility of where, when, how and why medieval people slept (or were unable to sleep), and the ways in which sleep interacts with the inward wits, the sleep of dream vision narrators is not just the necessary precondition for visionary experience; it also contributes to the implications of their dreams. In dream poetry, sleep is a way of knowing, a way of seeing. Medieval writers and readers were aware of how sleep could reset the balance of the humours (as discussed below), and correspondingly, strong emotions are shown to cause sleep in a variety of genres, including dream visions. Yet dream vision criticism has not taken account of the science of sleep, even though we find strong emotions causing not just sleep, but also dreams, and often together. The dream poems under discussion here are primarily literary dreams where multiple theories of the origins and meaning of dreams are themselves under discussion, both explicitly and implicitly, as in Chaucer's dream visions. This book argues that Chaucer's deployment of the science of sleep, especially in the *Book of the Duchess* and the *Parliament of Fowls*, invokes Aristotelian theories of dreams (which value dreams generated by humoral disposition) alongside the more well-studied Macrobian theories of dreams (in which only visions really matter). This is one way in which this book seeks to move away from seeing (Ricardian) dream visions as only, or primarily, intelligible in relation to Macrobius's classification of dreams.[16]

In the ways that representations of sleep shape dreams, this book is interested in reading dreams or visions that are components of longer works alongside dream vision texts that are traditionally considered a genre unto themselves, as well as in observing differences. Categories certainly matter, in relation to different types of dream as well as in relation to different types of dream-text, but connections have not received enough attention. I observe distinctions between, on the one hand, dreams which originate within the dreamer (resulting from waking preoccupations, from humoral or emotional imbalance), and, on the other hand, dreams which originate outside the dreamer (visions containing spiritual or prophetic truth). In the way that the conditions of sleep in Middle English literature often tell us about the state (emotional and/or ethical) of a character when s/he falls asleep, for the first type of dream (generated from the dreamer's lived experience), the sleep can illuminate the cause of the dream. And for the second type of dream (a vision of some external truth), the conditions of sleep often emphasise the purpose of the dream: when, for instance, there is a need for doctrinal enlightenment (in *Piers Plowman*) and/or a corrective for despair (in *Pearl*). However, focusing on the role of sleep in such dream poems also allows a greater recognition of the sometimes overlapping or overdetermined ways in which dreams are described – as in *Piers Plowman*, where the visions certainly contain spiritual truth, but when (for instance) Will falls asleep due to his woe and wrath, his humoral imbalance also shapes his dream-filled sleep. Or as in *Pearl*, where the narrator dreams about the focus of his melancholy and also gains spiritual enlightenment and a doctrinal commentary on his despair, evincing elements of both (broadly defined) types of dream. In these ways and others, this book considers how representations of secular sleep and spiritual sleep, while (often, but not always) concentrating on different implications, are shaped by the same cultural understanding of the possibilities of sleep.

* * *

This is the first book to address the scope and significance of Middle English literature's engagements with sleep, and the possibilities and crises that sleep mediates in this literary culture. While premodern sleep remains an understudied topic, it is beginning to receive more sustained attention, particularly from historians. Alongside the well-known view of inappropriate sleep as part of the deadly sin of sloth in medieval Christian Europe,[17] recent work by historians of science such as William Maclehose has explored the nuances of the Galenic medical understanding of sleep, which shaped western European thought from its introduction via Arabic medicine in the twelfth century through to the early seventeenth century.[18] Cultural historians including Jean Verdon, Roger Ekirch and Sasha Handley have addressed the distinctiveness of premodern sleeping habits and have analysed the contributions sleep makes to medieval and/or early modern society,[19] and an interdisciplinary study by Hollie Morgan has illuminated late medieval views of beds and bedchambers (including these objects' and spaces' roles in other important life events and practices such as childbirth, death and devotion, as well as sleep).[20] However, while Morgan's study does productively, if briefly, consider some literary representations of beds and chambers, the ways in which these spaces and a variety of others host sleep and mediate the expectations of sleep in literature have not received sustained attention. My analysis of the spaces of sleep is informed by the work of spatial theorists from Henri Lefebvre to Jeff Malpas who explore space and/or place in terms of 'the possibilities that it enables and the demands that it imposes', and by recent work on space in Middle English literature by scholars such as Matthew Boyd Goldie and Jan Shaw.[21]

More broadly, sleep's emotional, ethical and epistemological implications in Middle English literature invite more attention. The scholarship on Middle English dream visions is, of course, extensive;[22] rarely, however, have such studies focused on the sleep itself in dream poetry,[23] and what work there has been in this area has not attended to the ways in which the sleep of English dream visions intersects with either scientific paradigms or representations of sleep in other Middle English genres, leaving unaddressed the rich ethical, emotional and oneiric implications of how, when, where and why dream vision narrators fall asleep, and/or wake up. Nor have Middle English representations of sleep received much attention in other genres;[24] sustained attention to sleep in early modern English literature[25] has not yet been paralleled for Middle English literature. Recent work in the medical humanities has attended to premodern emotions and their embodiment in relation to topics such as swooning, illness and sloth,[26] in ways that invite parallel analysis of sleep as an embodied act with emotional dimensions. As Julie Orlemanski has demonstrated, the lexis of medicine, or 'termes of phisik', offered a recognisable discourse that Middle English literature deployed as part of an 'etiological imagination' in which 'symptomatic subjects [...] try to gloss and construe their own bodily conditions';[27] the language of sleep, I contend, participates in this glossing and construing in a variety of literary genres. Popular romance, dream vision, fabliau and drama are not often addressed together in a sustained fashion, but the way in which this book does so, in relation to the performance and interpretation of sleep, also affords new insights into how these Middle English genres both intersect and diverge. Thus, while this is a book about sleep, it is also a book that seeks to foster more sustained cross-genre study. Moreover, these medieval genres establish a set of conventions for signifying through sleep that some later writers continue to employ and rework.

This book responds both to Roger Ekirch's observation that 'sleep in pre-industrial communities remains largely understudied, for only the subject of dreams has drawn sustained scrutiny',[28] and to Garrett A. Sullivan's call for more critical attention to the 'neglected topic' of 'sleep's literary and cultural significance'.[29] Perhaps it is the quotidian nature of sleep that has caused it to receive relatively little scholarly attention until recently; however, to recognise the implications of late medieval literary sleep is to pay heed to the role of recognition itself. Literary representations of sleep, that is, make meaning through their recognisability, or their cultural intelligibility. This book argues that sleep in this textual culture communicates through a rich interplay between literature and life, between imagination and practice. Sleep in late medieval England – as it was performed, imagined and interpreted – was both biologically defined and culturally determined. This sort of approach to the study of sleep has gained traction recently; as Handley puts it, sleep is 'an embodied process with unique sensory dimensions and cultural meanings'.[30] Late medieval interest in sleep is insistently about interpreting and/or influencing how it is done, and about doing so in relation to contemporary ideas about what sleep means – for one's health, one's place in society and one's soul.

This study of sleep's vital implications for fashioning, reading and regulating the premodern subject, then, elucidates a mode of moulding somatic and social behaviour that shapes medieval and early modern literary texts, and the continuities between them. Later medieval insular representations of sleep draw upon biblical discourses and classical culture,[31] and adapt material from medieval continental literature, but also transform these inheritances in ways that are significant both in themselves and in their implications for their early modern successors. Literary scholars have attended to some aspects of the rich use of sleep by Shakespeare and other early modern writers,[32] but have not addressed the ways in which early modern representations drew upon medieval traditions. Whereas Garrett A. Sullivan locates the sources of early modern interest in literary sleep in classical traditions stemming from the writings of Plato and Aristotle, one of the aims of my book is to show how Middle English literature also shapes some aspects of the early modern interest in sleep. In tracing things forward, this study allows a complementary view of early modern English literature's 'sleep debts', especially with regard to the way in which sleep poses a 'challenge [...] to bodily self-regulation'.[33] Such continuities testify to the *longue durée* of the premodern investment in sleep. In *Cultural Reformations*, Brian Cummings and James Simpson observe that 'to continue to exist politely on either side' of the division between medieval and renaissance 'is to ignore the way that the works we study, and the way in which we study them, are implicated in [...] that terminology'.[34] By contrast, to use 'premodern' as an umbrella term, following David Wallace's *Premodern Places*, is to continue to rethink the relationship between medieval and early modern literature and culture. Wallace's thought-provoking work and other recent studies by Simpson and Helen Cooper exemplify a growing awareness of the need to reconsider this periodisation in order to deepen our understanding of the culture of these centuries.[35]

From the twelfth century to the early seventeenth – from the birth of the romance genre through to its use by Spenser and Shakespeare, who belonged to the last generation 'brought up on an extended range of medieval romances in more or less their original forms'[36] – sleep had distinctive scientific, spatial, social and spiritual parameters and expectations, and these attitudes about sleep shaped the literary genres that are also distinctive to these centuries. Across these five centuries, humoral theory informed the prevailing science of the body, and sleep played an important role in this paradigm of physical and emotional health. From the twelfth century onwards, beds and bedchambers, though still relatively scarce and protected, became more common (at least for the relatively wealthy literate classes),[37] creating spatial possibilities and expectations regarding sleep and sleeping arrangements that were exploited in literature as well as in life. The narrative genres of romance, fabliau, drama and dream vision flourished during this span, and these genres – not coincidentally – rely on and deploy the spatial logistics and legibilities of beds and bowers. This is also the age of courtly culture, and of English readerships whose values were shaped by conduct manuals and dietaries which encouraged careful attention to the undertaking and regulation of sleep as part of the pursuit of the prized virtues of courtesy and temperance. Ideas about the performance and interpretation of sleep also adhered to prevailing spiritual values in relation to sloth and idleness. And while this habitus of sleep was largely shared across north-western Europe, premodern English literature manifests a strong and distinctive hermeneutic focus on this habitus, engaging intently with sleep's implications for the fashioning of individual and communal identities.

Ricardian poems and Middle English romances were written at the same time as, and shared some horizons of expectation with, what has been called 'a remarkable upsurge in medical writing' in England between the Black Death in the mid-fourteenth century and the late fifteenth century, during which period 'thousands of discrete medical texts were copied, translated, or composed, the large majority for readers without university degrees'.[38] In Galenic medicine, which entered Western Europe c.1070–1300 via Arabic medicine and, despite challenges, persisted as the central medical paradigm until the mid-seventeenth century, sleep was considered one of the six 'non-natural' influences on the body, alongside food and drink, air, inanition and repletion, exercise and rest, and the passions or emotions.[39] Significantly, in this paradigm, the benefits of sleep included aiding digestion, or, more specifically, enabling the restorative transformation of food into the four humours – blood, phlegm, black bile and yellow bile – necessary for health and for a balanced temperament. Given that emotions were understood as imbalances in the humours – for instance, anger indicating a predominance of yellow bile, sorrow or melancholy a predominance of black bile – this way in which sleep acts to restore the balance between the humours makes sleep a direct response to a strong or uncomfortable emotion. Here, sleep seems to serve as a way of pressing the 'reset button'. As Marlowe's Dr Faustus would put it, it is a way to 'Confound these passions with a quiet sleep'; and Galenic medicine was still the prevailing scientific paradigm within which to interpret the passions, or emotions, when Marlowe was writing in the late sixteenth century.[40] We might refer to an angry person as in an 'ill humour'; however, whereas today this would be a metaphorical way of speaking, in late medieval and early modern mentalities, such a description would be firmly grounded in a literal understanding of physiology. From the holistic perspectives of Galenic medicine and of pre-Cartesian views of the interrelations between mind and body,[41] sleep serves to return strong or unhealthy emotions – and perhaps especially emotions produced by mental stress – to equilibrium. This medical, affective function of sleep has significant implications for understanding the aetiology and aims of premodern sleep, and of the dreams sleep facilitates, in popular romances and in Chaucer's and Langland's dream visions.

Late medieval society also had distinctive spatial expectations for the conduct of sleep. Because beds and bedrooms were much more scarce in premodern Europe than they are today, even those fortunate enough to occupy these privileged sleeping spaces, rather than a communal space such a hall, usually had to share – and not only, or not always, *with* someone, but rather, *alongside* someone, or multiple someones. Conduct books offer instructions on 'how to be a good bedfellow', admonishing sleepers to keep their limbs to themselves, to be polite and not to keep their bedfellows awake with endless chatter or by stealing the bedcovers.[42] Sleeping together in the Middle Ages, then, does not necessarily imply sex. However, the phrase 'to sleep with' as a long-lived euphemism for sex certainly held currency in the Middle Ages; for instance, in John Trevisa's 1387 translation of Ranulph Higden's mid-fourteenth-century *Polychronicon* – a text that, in Trevisa's English version, was popular through the fifteenth and early sixteenth centuries, and was printed by William Caxton in 1480 – Trevisa writes that 'A clerk of þe court hadde i-sleped wiþ hire', paralleling Higden's Latin ('clericus quidam de curia cum illa [...] dormitasset').[43] That sleeping together can readily imply sex is also manifest in Sir Thopas's dream (or, as we might term it today, his pipe dream) that 'An elf-queene shal my lemman be / And slepe under my goore [cloak].'[44] I am certainly not claiming that this metaphor was invented in late medieval England or was specific to Middle English;[45] rather, I am interested in the implications the late medieval currency of such a euphemism has for how Middle English literature imagines sleep. In the metaphor 'i-sleped wiþ hire', figurative sleep is about desire (and its fulfilment); a shared bed – a chance to, quite literally, sleep alongside someone – could enable a sexual encounter that might not otherwise be possible in a society with limited opportunities for privacy. That medieval people perceived sharing a bed as encouraging lust is visible in injunctions that boys and girls over the age of seven:

> schule no lengere lygge I-fere,
> Leste they by-twynne hem brede
> The lykynge of that fowle dede.[46]

This warning, in John Mirk's late fourteenth- or early fifteenth-century manual of tenets for priests to pass on to their parishioners, bears witness to fears about shared beds as 'the breeding ground of desire'.[47] Spatial expectations for the conduct of sleep, when not concerned with bedfellows, also included how a sleeper was supposed to lie, with clear instructions about the postures conducive to healthy sleep – that is, sleep that best encourages proper digestion (and the emotional well-being digestion fosters).

While focusing on literary sleep, this book also analyses other forms of textual evidence, and questions the distinctions we can (or should) make between literature and medical tracts, conduct books and sermons – between imagination and practice. As Kathleen Ashley and Robert Clark observe, conduct literature 'systematiz[ed…]

society's codes of behavior' and 'provided a guide for literate readers to negotiate new sets of social possibilities'.[48] Alongside the non-literary tracts or manuals more readily categorised as conduct literature, the ways in which late medieval and early modern people sometimes read literary texts such as romances, saints' lives and drama *as* conduct literature have also been recognised.[49] Equally, however, prescription and practice are not always synonymous. While conduct books have often been read as prescriptive (and indeed, do offer prescriptions – and proscriptions), we can allow for 'a more fluid notion of conduct beyond simply such options as resistance, compliance, or subversion. In practice, one could perform some combination of these options, creating new subject positions and new forms of conduct in the process.'[50] Though their instructions about sleep have received little attention, late medieval conduct texts, including dietaries, courtesy books and penitential manuals, often focus on what *not* to do with regard to sleep, instructing their readers not to sleep too long, not to sleep at the wrong time, in the wrong place, or in the wrong posture. These instructions form part of the late medieval habitus for performing, and hermeneutic for interpreting, sleep. Strenuous injunctions against (for instance) daytime sleep suggest that, while many medieval people were aware that daytime sleep was perceived as unhygienic and also ethically problematic, nonetheless some of them did indulge, as did literary characters like Malory's Launcelot and *Sir Orfeo*'s Queen Heurodis.

Sleep's ethical implications and dangers were gendered, in both literary texts and conduct literature, but not exclusively so. The intended readers of late medieval conduct literature are often youthful, with titles such as 'How the Wise Man Taught His Sonne' and 'How the Good Wijf Taughte Hir Doughtir' signalling the wisdom of the older generation to be passed on to the new in instructions with overlaps as well as gender-specific dimensions. Male readers were often the target audience of dietaries or regimens of health, but this does not mean that the tenets they contained were unknown to, or not applicable to, female readers. As Glenn Burger observes, 'the issue of lay female conduct' was a 'widespread, pan-European phenomenon' by the later Middle Ages; medieval conduct literature for women living worldly lives was written for and read by aristocratic, gentry and bourgeois women.[51] In tension with medieval antifeminist traditions, late medieval conduct texts for secular women – such as *Le*

Livre du chevalier de la Tour Landry (translated and printed by William Caxton in 1484 as *The Book of the Knight of the Tower*) – instead emphasised that women were 'inherently capable of self-improvement', and that reading was itself a way of developing a more ethical subject position for women, as it was for men.[52] Claire Sponsler and Mary Flannery have argued that where men's conduct literature anticipates that male readers' bodies are already disciplined, women's conduct literature instead emphasises that women's bodies are more in need of disciplining, via self-surveillance.[53] However, where the performance of sleep is concerned, late medieval conduct literature indicates that both men and women must exercise constant vigilance and self-surveillance, and continually discipline their bodily appetites, in order to maintain bodily decorum. Yet an overindulgence in sleep or an untimely or uncouth sleep contributes to dangers that are also sometimes gendered, and shaped by conceptions of honour and reputation that are gender-specific.

In the Middle English narrative genres addressed in this book, sleeping protagonists are, of course, often male: romance knights, fabliau cuckolds and dream vision narrators necessarily receive sustained attention here. Yet this book also explores how sleep illuminates performances and paradigms of female embodiment, in relation to figures such as *Sir Orfeo*'s Heurodis, Chaucer's Malkin, Caxton's Lucrece, the Wife of Pilate in the York Cycle Plays, Margery Kempe and Merlin's mother in the Prose *Merlin*. Where male (chivalric) honour is maintained by active duty, by displaying martial prowess and offering protection incommensurate with sleep, female honour is maintained by enacting 'hypervigilance' against threats to chastity and bodily integrity – threats that cannot be guarded against when sleeping. Yet for Malory's Launcelot, sleeping out of doors and under a tree renders the unconscious knight vulnerable to both forms of 'raptus' – abduction and rape – just as Heurodis, in *Sir Orfeo*, the anonymous early fourteenth-century Middle English retelling of the myth of Orpheus and Eurydice, is subject to raptus when she sleeps outside under a tree in the middle of the day. For male sleepers, particularly in romance, sleep's unethical implications are also *inter*personal, while some dangers of sleep, such as incubi, pertain only to women. Middle English literature often focuses on the problems that arise for both male and female characters who sleep when and where they should not; for both genders, untimely sleep or sleep in a vulnerable place can have personal consequences, blurring the boundaries between the dangers of different types of lack of bodily decorum.

To sleep, then, was to avail oneself of its benefits for physical and mental health while simultaneously becoming vulnerable to a range of perils (from unhealthy vapours to assault, abduction and incubi); it was also to become an object, available to view. Depictions of sleepers in medieval visual culture were abundant, including those in church windows and wall hangings as well as manuscript illuminations. With notable exceptions such as the illustration of the Lady's approach to Gawain's bed at Hautdesert in MS Cotton Nero A.x, a sexually charged variation on the couple-in-bed motif, medieval English literary manuscripts do not as often include complex narrative illustrations such as those of couples in bed together which feature in French manuscripts.[54] However, more common are psalter illuminations, for instance showing the soldiers asleep outside Christ's empty tomb, emblematising a reprehensible lack of vigilance as well as symbolising failures in spiritual perception.[55] Although a treatment of visual representations in their own right is beyond the remit of this book, the ways in which sleepers in textual culture are sometimes visually described and/or looked at invite interpretation in relation to the politics of the gaze.[56] Like the sleepers at the tomb of Christ, sleepers such as Malory's Launcelot in the presence of the Grail, or Tristram and Isolde sleeping in a tableau-like scene with a sword between them in the woods, are subject to the judgement of those who witness them. Expectations that the possibility of surveillance will condition personal self-regulation inform conduct manuals' instructions, for instance that those who cannot resist a midday nap should only sleep standing leaning against a cupboard, or sitting upright in a chair, in order to not only exercise, but also visibly display, a measure of temperance to maintain their social reputation (as discussed in Chapter 2). In these ways and others, to fall asleep in late medieval England, or to have difficulty falling asleep, is to become available for interpretation.

While the death of Shakespeare in 1616 provides a convenient *terminus ad quem* for this study of premodern English literary sleep, this date is used here as a shorthand for the scientific, literary and social transformations of the seventeenth century,[57] which altered perceptions of sleep's cultural and cognitive importance. Although English Protestants largely shared their medieval Catholic forebears' attitudes towards sleep, from the seventeenth century onward, the practice of 'radically restricting sleep, forgoing it entirely for a time, or rising very early [...] was very widespread amongst earnest Protestants', as those living in the world were encouraged to aspire to the sleeping habits that had previously pertained only to those in monastic positions or with ascetic dispositions.[58] More significantly, there was growing scepticism about Galenic humoral theory from the seventeenth century onward, when 'Galenism as a "science" waned'.[59] For Sasha Handley, the eighteenth-century concept of sensibility (as embodied by Jane Austen's Marianne Dashwood, in Handley's apt example) gave troubled sleep a form of social or moral capital, as an inability to sleep properly became prized as a symptom of refined sentiment.[60] Yet from the twelfth century onwards, notwithstanding widespread appreciation of the value of sleep, insomnia also offered a not entirely dissimilar form of capital as a symptom of lovesickness, itself pathologised (as arising from a predominance of melancholy) and exploited in the portrayal of *fin' amors* and in the genre of *dits amoreux* on which Chaucer drew, and in the genre of dream visions to which Chaucer made distinctive contributions. In my view, the seventeenth-century shift in attitudes to sleep is not one in which sleep was increasingly medicalised, but rather, one in which sleep was medicalised differently.[61] The founding of the Royal Society in 1660 contributed to changing scientific paradigms, and during the late seventeenth and eighteenth centuries, sleep's significance for digestion began to receive less attention than sleep's connections to the brain and nerves, with sensibility understood as a neurological condition.[62] The interplay between sleep and the emotions in the premodern period was rooted in bodily processes, rather than neurological ones, but this interplay also shapes some of the strong connections between mind and body that were foregrounded in the medieval period, more so than after Cartesian dualism took hold in the mid-seventeenth century, and in ways that modern science is now rediscovering.[63]

Linguistic and critical parameters

My approach to the emotions as culturally constructed – both socially coded and biologically defined – follows two decades of sustained work on medieval emotions by both historians and literary scholars.[64] Recent work on the late medieval period in particular has persuasively moved beyond the views of medieval emotions as simplistic and childlike that had been popularised by Norbert Elias's otherwise useful theory of the civilising process and Johan Huizinga's outdated views of the waning of the Middle Ages.[65] Like others in the growing field of the history of medieval and early modern emotions, I analyse 'emotions' while acknowledging that the word itself was not in use until the nineteenth century; 'passions' was instead the term for the feelings that comprised one of the six non-natural influences on the body.[66] In the Middle Ages, these emotions or passions were understood as embodied, occurring 'through the movements of the vital spirit and natural heat, produced in the heart and travelling through the arteries'.[67] Sleep was a similarly embodied process, induced by the movement of natural heat and the balance of the humours in interconnected ways. And in literature, of course, emotions, like cases of sleep, are 'discursive constructions' shaped 'not only by social and cultural rules, as products of a particular social or cultural context, but also by generic and discursive traditions of emotional representation'.[68] To analyse medieval literary emotions, Rikhardsdottir adapts the term 'emotive scripts' from Sylvan Tomkin's 'emotion script',[69] and others have observed the communal and social, as well as individual, dimensions of medieval (literary) emotions.[70] While the term 'affect' is also employed in some studies of the history of the emotions, and is sometimes, following Tomkins, used to distinguish the biological dimension of emotion, I follow scholars such as Rosenwein, Rikhardsdottir and Mary Flannery who recognise the critical contributions of affect studies but focus on reading medieval emotions *on* their own terms, if not always *in* their own terms.[71]

Like emotion, some other terms that did not have currency in Middle English also frame this book's analysis in ways that aim to elucidate, rather than distort, premodern attitudes. In this study, the term 'ethical' is used for the sphere of the practical pursuit of a moral life in order to distinguish it from morality as doctrine, though of course the two overlap.[72] To read for the ethics of sleep is to read in a way familiar and available to medieval and early modern readers from their courtesy books, dietaries and chivalric literature. It offers a way of appreciating how such texts 'encod[e ...] social practice',[73] of recognising the elements contributing to a culturally determined *habitus* for performing and interpreting sleep. For Pierre Bourdieu, habitus is anchored in the body, and mediated by language, but only secondarily, and is not necessarily conscious; Katharine Breen views (medieval) habitus as more conscious. Aspects of both unconscious habit, and conscious formation and regulation, are relevant here, as is the way in which a habitus can be collective as well as individual.[74] The concept of *mentalité*, or mental attitude, is similarly invoked here because it foregrounds what any person has in common with other people of a given period and place; as attitudes 'governing the immediate perceptions of social subjects', mentalities are necessarily collective.[75] The idea of a medieval English habitus of sleep conceptualises the way in which sleep's particular ethical, emotional, physical and spatial dimensions form a set of embodied practices and mental habits that are shared and societal.[76] Although sleep is something that subjects cannot control, it can nonetheless be understood as 'performed' behaviour because medieval people were expected to regulate their sleeping in many ways – when, where, for how long, wearing what and, significantly, in what postures: both at night (one side and then the other) and in any unavoidable daytime naps (as upright as possible). Medieval people were, in effect, expected to be very conscious of their habits when becoming unconscious. The literary manifestations of these habits – as employed by Ricardian poetry and popular romance, and inherited by renaissance drama – are epistemological in that they offer ways of knowing more about the sleeping subject, and also about cultural values and (perceived) external truths.

On the other hand, 'slepe' itself is decidedly Middle English, and the widespread use of the lexis of sleep in Middle English literature, in dialogue, narrative and commentaries, undergirds this book's focus. Middle English 'slepe' is derived from the Old English word, as is much – though not all – of the Middle English vocabulary of dreaming: Old English words for dreaming, 'swevan' and 'maettan', are familiar from Chaucer's references to 'swevens' and to what he 'mette' (dreamed).[77] The words themselves matter, as when Middle English texts alter their (predominantly French) sources in order to focus on sleep in ways or in moments where their sources do not. The examples with which this book began, of Malory's Launcelot and Chaucer's narrator in the *Book of the Duchess*, are representative of the ways in which Middle English authors invest episodes of literary sleep with meanings that depart from those of their sources. Significantly, Middle English authors also often focus on the ethical or emotional ramifications of sleep where their sources do not mention sleep at all (or where they do not have sources). For instance, the Middle English romance *Melusine*, a late fifteenth-century translation of a late fourteenth-century French source, has the fairy Melusine criticise the knightly protagonist Raymond for his failures of perception and activity by saying that 'he semeth to be asleep', rather than (as in the French version) that he seems to be 'pensif' (thoughtful).[78] And all four of the *Gawain*-poet's relatively independent late fourteenth-century works – including romance, dream vision and devotional literature – show a concerted interest in sleep, both lexically and thematically. Middle English literature manifests a widespread emphasis on the state or idea of sleep as an embodiment and communicator of moral value and cultural capital, or their opposites. That is, the Middle English lexical emphasis on 'sleep' is matched by a conceptual emphasis on the significance of slumber, and this includes metaphorical sleep, as well as literal. Middle English metaphorical sleep is often about lack or absence: a lack of perception or oversight, or even a neglect of duties, undesirable and destructive. Here sleep is (or can be) a mode of criticism, commenting on a lack of expected or desired activity or agency (whether human or divine).[79] 'Slepe', then, embodies and gives expression to English cultural concerns.

While this cultural specificity is shaped by linguistic specificity, I am not implying that the former is synonymous with the latter, nor that the literary culture(s) on which I am focusing should be considered homogenous or monolithic. This study acknowledges the pluralism of literary cultures in medieval England while contending that a variety of genres across several centuries are, as it were, speaking a common language with regard to sleep. Englishness, here, is a distinction in some ways more cultural than linguistic. To discuss either Englishness or insular cultural specificity in relation to the (later) Middle Ages is of course to recognise the trilingual culture of post-conquest medieval England, in which texts in Anglo-Norman French and Latin circulated alongside those in English.[80] This book focuses primarily, but not exclusively, on texts written in English; it also includes within its remit texts such as Chardri's thirteenth-century Anglo-Norman saints' lives, and Gilbert Kymer's

Introduction: remarkable sleep

early fifteenth-century Latin regimen of health for an English beneficiary, Humphrey Duke of Gloucester.

Moreover, to say that sleep takes on particular significance in insular or Middle English literature is not to say that sleep is insignificant in Old English literature. While the specificity of Middle English concerns with sleep has yet to be recognised, there has been some attention to the distinctive ways in which Old English literature engages with sleep. Paul Battles has addressed how Old English literature often departs from its sources to focus less on the sexual implications of sleep and more on the ethical dangers of sleeping in feasting contexts. Battles' work productively suggests that some of the concerns that I address here already carried an English cultural resonance even before their concerted development during the later Middle Ages.[81] However, since the Old English literary tradition is informed by cultural norms and intellectual traditions that are rather different from those of Middle English literary culture – preceding, for instance, the reception of Galenic medical ideas in north-western Europe, or the codes of chivalry and courtesy and the literary modes and expectations of romance, late medieval dream visions, cycle plays and morality plays – my study begins not with pre-conquest English literature but after the Norman Conquest, with the twelfth-century resurgence of literature written in English.

Once the medieval habitus of sleep had begun to be dramatically inflected by Galenic medicine in the twelfth century, it was shared, but not entirely homogenous, across western Europe.[82] On the whole, geographical differences were less significant than differentiations between those living secular, worldly lives, and those who, following a monastic rule, would be expected to rise to sing Matins in the middle of the night, and thus to regulate their sleep differently.[83] In addition to the regimenal expectations and medical possibilities of sleep, the potential for critique invested in metaphorical sleep was also shared across medieval European cultures, following influential views such as that expressed in Gregory the Great's *Pastoral Care* (c.590):

> it is well said, 'Give not sleep to your eyes, nor let your eyelids slumber [Proverbs 6:4]', for indeed to give sleep to the eyes is to cease from earnestness, so as to neglect altogether the care of our subordinates. But the eyelids slumber when our thoughts, weighed down by sloth, connive at what they know ought to be reproved.[84]

Here, sloth, as part of the deadly sin *acedia*, and failures in spiritual perception, are both expressed by sleep, in this seminal text for western medieval European culture. Moreover, in his commentary on St Paul's Letter to the Romans, Thomas Aquinas addresses the different significances of sleep acknowledged across western medieval Europe. Aquinas writes of six types of sleep: the sleep of nature (sleep as death); the sleep of vital powers (sleep as rest and restoration); the sleep of eternal glory (sleep as salvation); the sleep of contemplation (sleep as visionary experience); the sleep of sin (sleep as a cessation of living in a state of good grace); and the sleep of negligence (sleep as sloth, or failure to do good works).[85]

Continental medieval literature, like medieval insular literature, certainly employed the idea of sleep as a metaphor for vulnerability or absence, as in Boccaccio's *De casibus virorum illustrium*, where, in the preface, great men are said to be 'so attracted to vice and debauchery' that they think they have 'put Fortune perpetually to sleep'.[86] Although this study focuses on how Middle English literature engages with, and develops specific opportunities for exploring, the implications of sleep, it would also be illuminating to read the emotional dimensions of sleep discussed in Chapters One and Four in relation to a text such as Dante's *Divine Comedy*.[87] Medieval French representations of sleep are discussed in some detail in the following chapters where they have provided source material for Middle English texts; yet as Chapter 4 shows, although sleep and insomnia certainly feature in French dream visions and *dits amoreux*, Chaucer's dream visions pursue the medical and poetic implications and applications of sleep much more intensely. Sleep is linked to composition in medieval thought – as Bernard of Clairvaux and others foregrounded in their interpretation of *Song of Songs* 5:2, 'Ego dormio, et cor meum vigilat' ('I sleep, but my heart is awake')[88] – and English writers such as Chaucer explore this linkage in its fullest sense. My interest here, then, is the ways in which sleep is a theme to which Middle English literature turns with increasing frequency, and which it turns into a cultural grammar with particular ethical, emotive and poetic conventions.

Of course, there is also a temporal shift accompanying the linguistic and cultural shifts. That is, Middle English literary adaptations were generally written significantly later than their continental sources. This may seem a statement of the obvious, but since the difference in composition is often a matter of at least a century or two, Middle English thematisations of sleep (especially of the fourteenth and fifteenth centuries) were written at a time when western European society was more saturated with the tenets of the medical treatises and conduct manuals that were circulating in the medieval West by the twelfth century, but which were more readily available and familiar from the fourteenth century onwards. This provides a context for, though not a full explanation of, Middle English culture's distinctive focus on sleep. While Chaucer's dream visions engage with sleep in ways that his earlier French sources do not, so too does the English *Melusine* engage with sleep in ways its French source – which Jean d'Arras wrote at the same time Chaucer was writing – does not.

A salient precedent for Middle English literature's explorations of the emotional and ethical implications of sleep is the sleep of the disciples after the Last Supper, when Jesus has been praying and had instructed his disciplines to accompany him in prayer, but instead 'he found them sleeping for sorrow. / And he said to them: Why sleep you? Arise: pray: lest you enter into temptation.'[89] This sense in which sleep encapsulates the opposite of prayer and virtuous endeavour is developed in a range of Middle English texts, such as *Piers Plowman* and *Mankind*. Moreover, that the disciples sleep 'for sorrow', and that their problematic sleep takes place after a meal (and such a significant meal as the Last Supper), are both resonant precursors for Middle English genres from romance to Ricardian dream visions, as discussed in Chapters One and Two. The ways in which sleep becomes central to late medieval English literary culture, and endures to influence early modern English literary deployments of sleep, bear witness to distinctive ethical and emotional communities and economies. In a commentary on chivalric duty in the 1484 *Book of the Ordre of Chyualry* (printed on the cusp of the Tudor dynasty, just before the battle of Bosworth in 1485), William Caxton used his printer's epilogue to critique contemporary knighthood, admonishing 'O ye knyghtes of Englond where is the custome and vsage of noble chyualry that was vsed in those dayes […] Allas what doo ye/but *slepe* & take ease/and ar al disordred from chyualry.'[90] Here as elsewhere in Middle English literature, figurative sleep, like physical sleep, signifies concerns with secular ethics as well as spiritual behaviour. To counteract this perceived decline in the conduct of the 'knyghtes of Englond',[91] Caxton prescribes reading romances of Launcelot and of Gawain: romances which offer ethical instruction, and in which sleep similarly features as a warning about improper chivalric conduct.

Modern connections

Sleep is as urgent a topic for the twenty-first century as it was for the twelfth to seventeenth centuries. Sleep, we all know, is a good thing: we need it, we appreciate it, it sustains us. When we think about sleep, it is usually in terms of wanting more of it, thanks to the complications of modern life: alongside age-old adversaries of restful sleep such as illness, alcohol and caring responsibilities, modern factors such as high stress levels, shift work, jet lag, caffeine, screen time and non-natural light have all dramatically deepened our collective societal sleep debt. In the sleep stakes, industrialisaton has a lot to answer for. Popular science books addressing sleep have proliferated, focusing on how to sleep most effectively, and how to get the most from your sleep, whether at night or during a daytime nap. Yet, partly due to the availability and prevalence of electric light and stimulants, the 24/7 modern culture prioritises constant productivity and alertness at the cost of sleep.[92] As a result, some sleep scientists, along with the World Health Organization (WHO), have stated that all industrialised countries are living through a potentially catastrophic 'sleep loss epidemic', and have detailed the benefits of sleep for physical and mental health.[93] We are, as it were, waking up to the urgency of getting enough sleep, and even the productivity paradigm has shifted to adduce the benefits of sleep, with some writers seeking to debunk 'the myth that presenteeism and productivity are the same thing', in ways that might help to counter the insidious expectations of expanding workloads.[94]

Since the early twentieth century in particular, people have been sleeping increasingly less[95] – a trend we might wish to reverse – but in the premodern world, sleep was prized yet fraught in ways that both overlap with and differ from today's pressures. While today there are social pressures to cut sleep to unhealthily low levels, in the medieval world, there were pressures not to sleep to excess (rather than to curtail sleep much further), but with especial emphasis on not sleeping at the wrong time or in the wrong place. Where the modern impetus to sleep less serves the productivity paradigm, the medieval encouragement to sleep less (or not sleep too much) aims to counter slothfulness. There is an overlap, in that the premodern imperative to eschew idleness, to avoid sloth, is partly about 'being productive'; however, the value of premodern productivity is an embodied subjectivity that aligns more with the social capital derived (nowadays) from being a person with a strong work ethic than with today's emphasis on the products of continual labour.

Greater attention to sleep across a variety of disciplines and historical perspectives seems vital in light of the sleep loss epidemic declared by the WHO, and increasing recognition of the crucial benefits of sleep. Modern sleep science, although emerging from a different medical paradigm to the one that prevailed in premodern Europe, shares with Galenic science its view of the importance of sleep to physical and mental health, memory, dreams and the processing of traumatic emotions.[96] In this book I am not seeking to understand sleep's past through the prism of the present: I do not focus on examining how, for instance, Malory's Launcelot, when subjected to an irresistible daytime desire to sleep (several times in the *Morte*), seems as though he might be suffering from the sudden onset of a sleep disorder such as narcolepsy; or how the sleep deprivation of Chaucer's *Book of the Duchess* narrator would presumably tip the balance of his sleep away from deep (non-REM) sleep towards dream-filled REM sleep when he does finally nod off.[97] Yet bearing modern sleep science and sleep crises in mind when analysing sleep's past may, on the other hand, be useful for better understanding sleep's present and future. Some recent theories of the role of sleep in restoring balance to the emotions look remarkably like humoral theories on the same subject – in terms of the effects, if not the operations, ascribed to sleep.[98] For instance, modern sleep science, like medieval sleep science, recognises that there is a complex relationship between sleep and mental health, mood and emotions,[99] and that poor sleep increases the likelihood of depression, anxiety and stress.[100] At a time when psychologists are recognising that 'mental health issues can be signalled by problems with sleep, and sleep disturbances seem to predict and lead to a range of difficulties with mental health',[101] we might glean something for our own time from the ways in which writers such as Chaucer, Malory, Langland

and the *Gawain*-poet attended to similar problems. My main focus here, however, is on illuminating medieval literary sleep in relation to its own contemporary contexts.

Chapters

In taking the Middle English matter of sleep as its subject, this book attends to where, when, how and why sleep takes place (or does not take place) in order to uncover a set of epistemic attitudes towards sleep – a complex intertwining of the ethical, affective and visionary possibilities of sleep. In addressing romance, drama, fabliau and dream vision together, this book asks: how does the performance of sleep in these genres negotiate the frameworks for interpreting sleep in late medieval England? And what is sleep's role among the embodied endeavours of protagonists and those whom they encounter in Middle English literature, fundamental to explorations of (if sometimes in tension with) their duties and desires? The first three main chapters take a comparative approach, both reading across, and analysing differences between, the narrative genres under scrutiny here, while the fourth chapter offers a more in-depth case study. Chapters 1, 2 and 3 explore, respectively, the emotional, ethical and spatial dimensions of sleep in Middle English literature. Following these comparative chapters, Chapter 4 turns to a detailed analysis of the implications of sleep in Chaucer's dream visions, in which the epistemic expectations of sleep are both deployed and deliberated. Attending to the emotional, ethical and spatial dimensions of sleep in Chaucer's dream poetry sheds new light on both the dream theories, and the English literary traditions, with which Chaucer engages in these poems. While some of the ways in which early modern English literature continues this medieval mode of signifying through sleep are adumbrated throughout the book, the Coda concentrates on Shakespeare's sleepers to further explore the implications of this rich literary inheritance.

Chapter 1 begins by exploring the operations and implications of sleep in medieval science, focusing on sleep's medical and emotional benefits in particular. In the humoral theory of the body, in which health and well-being were determined by an individual's fluctuating economy of liquids with emotional attributes, sleep had a powerful role to play in generating balance by transforming food into the four humours during digestion. Thus, while sleep was important for physical health, it was also significant for mental health, offering relief from the 'unhealthful' humours of melancholy and choler in ways that are distinctively realised in Middle English literature. While medieval mentalities did not distinguish mental health from physical health in the same terms we do today, in pre-Cartesian conceptions of the interrelations of mind and body, holistic views of health meant that the implications of a bodily act such as sleep for emotional well-being were well recognised. In a similar fashion to the way in which swooning often signifies a strong emotion (whether sorrow or joy) in medieval literature, the sudden onset of sleep recognisably follows manifestations of powerful sorrow and anger. Sleep, moreover, not only marks these 'unhealthful' emotions, it also helps to mediate them. As a form of sorrow-making and anger management, sleep shapes subjectivities and judgements in romances, cycle plays and dream visions. Attending to the ways in which sleep parallels, as well as differs from, swooning as an expression of strong emotion in medieval English representations helps to deepen our understanding of the emotive scripts to which these two forms of unconsciousness contribute. Here, sleep bodies forth truths about individuals that are culturally determined.

This chapter also considers other aspects of sleep's relationship with truth and knowledge; in sustaining dreams, for instance, sleep is a way of knowing more about both the sleeping subject, and perceptions of external truths. Although wakefulness is often aligned with vigilance, perception and truth (today as in medieval mentalities, in, for instance, the idea of a religious or political awakening),[102] at other times it is sleep that offers modes of perception and access to truth. By considering medieval writers' and readers' knowledge of Aristotelian theories of dreams as well as the (more well-known today) Macrobian theories of dreams, this chapter concludes by suggesting that ideas about dreams caused by individuals' waking preoccupations – dreams generated from lived experience and humoral imbalances – have more to tell us about late medieval English dream visions than has been recognised.

To practise sleep was to profit from the benefits of sleep, but also to become vulnerable to its dangers. Sleep's nurturing nature, alleviating unhealthy emotions and ameliorating mental health through its role in digestion, was in tension with sleep's problematic connections to excess, to immoral indulgence in food and other appetites. Chapter 2 focuses on the dangers of sleep, exploring how the prescriptions and proscriptions regarding sleeping practices in conduct manuals – especially the strenuous injunctions against daytime sleep – illuminate literary representations of sleep. In Middle English romances, fabliaux, dream visions and drama, untimely sleep is dangerous, with risks to reputation and/or well-being. These genres share their interest in untimely sleep as a mode of admonition, but generic expectations also shape the consequences in distinctive ways. Across these genres, an appetite for sleep, especially when linked to other appetites – for food, for drinking to excess, for sex or sloth – marks a neglect of duties (ranging from chivalric endeavour to Christian labour and prayer), a lack of perception (of right conduct or religious truths) or a lack of vigilance (against attacks or abduction).

English romances often depart from their sources in order to figure sleeping (at the wrong time or in the wrong place) as the antithesis of courtesy and ethical conduct. In these departures, representations of sleep both contribute to, and challenge, the ways in which Middle English romance has been seen to differ from the interests of earlier French romance. The untimely, appetite-driven sleep of knights and kings, and that of ladies and queens, I suggest, both constitute motifs of Middle English romance that engage with gendered conceptions of honour. Other Middle English genres also negotiate the politics and problems of daytime sleep in relation to discourses of appetite and acts of intemperance. Untimely sleep, then, has some characteristics which cross genres; however, in a range of texts including Chaucer's fabliaux, Langland's allegory, the York cycle plays and the non-romance works of the *Gawain*-poet, untimely sleep is also accompanied by a more churlish or scatological embodiment than that of romance protagonists, and more often induced by drunkenness. Representations of snoring across these genres (apart from romance) are frequent, and mark sinful behaviour in ways that align with condemnations of snoring and drunken stupor as animal-like and subhuman. Here, sleep is a culturally coded way of communicating about and evaluating the conduct and aspirations of characters and contemporary readers. Moments where characters sink into untimely sleep shape their identities and reputations, offering readers reminders of what not to do, and exempla of the dangers of transgressing expectations.

The spaces of sleep raise certain expectations, and these expectations or connotations shape literary texts. The spaces associated with literary sleep – where sleep occurs, or is expected to occur – include not only purpose-built bedrooms (chambers or bowers) and beds, with the possibilities of privacy they sometimes offer, but also more public sleeping spaces such as the castle hall in which Malory's Gareth prepares himself for sleep and hopes to 'sleep with' Lyonesse, and a variety of outdoor sleeping spaces: under trees and in gardens, by the banks of rivers, or in the Malvern Hills, with various attendant dangers and possibilities. Given that, as spatial theorists such as Henri Lefebvre have observed, certain conduct is expected in certain spaces and 'space embodies social relationships' as well as relationships with and between objects and products,[103] a spatial analysis informs this book's exploration of the concerns convened by literary sleep.

Chapter 3, in particular, examines the literary implications of how, in a society in which beds and bedchambers were relatively scarce and protected, sleeping either in such specialised sleeping spaces, or elsewhere, entailed navigating various pleasures and dangers such as desire, detection, abduction and disease – as well as dreams. As with sleep itself, my interest in the spaces of sleep particularly concerns the ways in which they become the focus of narrative commentary and diegetic conversation. Spaces – owned or occupied, infiltrated or loaned – contribute to the implications or value of the sleep that takes place in them. In addition, bedrooms with doors that might be shut and locked, and inviting beds, are strategically deployed by those seeking to engineer or prevent sexual situations. Intriguingly, when negotiating the possibility of sex in Middle English romances, it is often the spaces of sleep, rather than bodies themselves, that receive textual attention. Beds and other sleeping spaces sometimes serve as contested liminal environments in which gendered roles can become destabilised, and the spaces of sleep (like sleep itself) also stimulate diegetic interpretations of character and conduct, as when bloody bedsheets lead to accusations of adultery in Arthurian literature. Yet the desires convened by the spaces of sleep include, not least, desires for sleep itself – ordinary desires with sometimes extraordinary implications, mediated by genre and by the signifying power of place, as when characters fall asleep in church, or in the *loci amoeni* spaces of dream visions.

Another of the contributions this book makes is to offer a new way of understanding Middle English dream poetry. While dream visions by Chaucer, Langland and the *Pearl*-poet have been well studied, the sleep in these poems has not. Reading late medieval English dream visions alongside sleep in other contemporary genres illuminates the connotations of the specific ways and places in which dream vision sleep occurs. Sleep encodes (for instance) the dreamer's ethical and affective state, shaping the dreams that follow; representations of the physiology of sleep also offer interventions in contemporary discourses about the origins, nature and interpretation of dreams, and foreground the embodiment of poetic inspiration. While dream visions are addressed in each of the main chapters of this book, Chapter 4 scrutinises the sleep in Chaucer's dream visions in light of this study's broader analysis of sleep. How Chaucer writes about sleep in the *Book of the Duchess*, the *Parliament of Fowls* and the *Prologue* to the *Legend of Good Women* participates in Middle English literary culture's pronounced interest in thematising the ethics and affect of sleep's causation and consequences, and in deploying the connotations of its spaces; rarely, however, has it been observed that Chaucer navigates debts to English literary traditions, alongside French and Italian ones, in his dream visions.

Focusing on the *Book of the Duchess* in particular, Chapter 4 rediscovers Chaucer's interest in the mind–body connections that sleep foregrounds through sleep's role in digestion, in the balancing of the humours and passions, and in the generation of dreams in the inward wits. It argues that Chaucer's dream poetry medicalises sleep in ways that invite analysis in relation to Galenic science, and that in turn illuminate the embodied endeavour of the medieval poet, especially through Chaucer's consideration of Aristotelian (alongside the more commonly invoked Macrobian) theories of dreams. Chaucer's *Book of the Duchess* foregrounds sleep – proper sleep – as an object of desire whose present absence embodies the sorrow not only of the narrator and Alcyone, the poem's first two pining lovers, but also of the Man in Black. Chaucer characterises troubled relationships to sleep through medically informed explorations of the physiology of sleep that link the narrator with the Man in Black and that register sleep's multifaceted relevance to the poem's concerns with consolation. In addition, Chaucer's concerted emphases on sleep, in their insistence on the embodiment of the poet, highlight the embodiment of poetic inspiration. Sleep, that is, offers a term for the role of experience – alongside Chaucer's more high-profile explorations of the role of old books – as inspiration for poetry. Such reflections on the role of experience in generating ideas for poetry are also, I suggest – especially because the medium of sleep through which they are conveyed is an established English literary interest – a way in which Chaucer reflects on his debts to English literary traditions, perhaps with less condescension than his otherwise similar reflections on English literary traditions in the 'Tale of Sir Thopas'.

Together, the four main chapters of this book show how Middle English literary culture develops (whether independently of any known sources, or as departures from extant sources) a widespread emphasis on the epistemic possibilities of sleep. As the Coda explores, Shakespeare inherits this medieval cultural understanding of sleep, and it in turn shapes his representations of the fates of, and guilty consciences inspired by, heirs in *Macbeth* and *Richard III*. Shakespeare's Macbeth may 'murder sleep', but he does so as the spawn of medieval conventions for signifying through sleep. And two hundred years after Chaucer's Symkin the Miller is cuckolded while 'as an hors he fnorteth in his sleep' in the bawdy 'Reeve's Tale', Shakespeare's Falstaff, a figure not incommensurate with the medieval genre of fabliau, is found onstage 'Fast asleep / [...] and snorting like a horse.'[104] For modern critics as for Shakespeare's Hamlet, dreams are the loci to which thoughts about sleep lead: 'To sleep, perchance to dream. Ay, there's the rub.'[105] Yet as this book shows, we can gain a better understanding of dreams and dream visions by attending to the sleep that enables them, and there is also much more to the premodern English imagination's engagements with sleep than a critical focus solely on dreams can encompass.

Notes

1 Thomas Malory, *Le Morte Darthur*, ed. P. J. C. Field, 2 vols (Cambridge: D. S. Brewer, 2013), I, 190.19–191.4. All italics and translations are mine unless otherwise stated.

2 Compare *Lancelot: Roman en prose du XIIIe siècle*, ed. Alexandre Micha, 9 vols (Genève: Droz, 1978–83), vol. 4, p. 166: 'si furent si las et si travillié qu'il *les couvint* a reposer tant que li chauz fust trespassez' ('they were so weary that it *befitted them* to rest until the heat passed'). In Malory's *Morte*, any implied temptation to read Launcelot's overpowering desire to sleep as the result of an enchantment is ruled out by the following narrative: the four queens are not expecting to find Launcelot, and it is only when they discover the already 'slepynge knyght' (so sound asleep that he does not wake when four queens and four attendant knights ride up to him) that Morgan casts 'an inchauntement uppon hym that he shall nat awake of all this seven owres, and than I woll lede hym away unto my castell' (Malory, *Morte Darthur*, p. 193.15–23). That this enchantment prolongs rather than establishes Launcelot's unconsciousness underscores the fact that the onset of this sleep, and the vulnerability it engenders, has a natural rather than supernatural cause.

3 Richard Firth Green, *Poets and Princepleasers: Literature and the English Court in the Late Middle Ages* (Toronto: University of Toronto Press, 1980), pp. 9–10; Roberta L. Krueger, 'Introduction: Teach Your Children Well: Medieval Conduct Guides for Youths', in Mark D. Johnston (ed.), *Medieval Conduct Literature: An Anthology of Vernacular Guides to Behaviour for Youths, with English Translations* (Toronto: University of Toronto Press, 2009), pp. ix–xxxiii (p. xii); Mark Addison Amos, '"For Manners Make Man": Bourdieu, de Certeau, and the Common Appropriation of Noble Manners in the *Book of Courtesy*', in Kathleen Ashley and Robert A. Clark (eds), *Medieval Conduct* (Minneapolis, MN: University of Minnesota Press, 2001), pp. 23–48 (pp. 45–6).

4 'Fugere debetis de die sompnum meridianum [...], et non dormiatis in mediate post aliquam refectionem quin inter ipsam at soporem': Gilbert Kymer, *Dietarium de sanitatis custodia*, British Library MS Sloane 4, fol. 63r-104r (fol. 86v). This detailed yet brisk handbook for health, written in Latin and as yet unedited, survives in a fifteenth-century miscellany.

5 Corinne Saunders, *The Forest of Romance: Avernus, Broceliande, Arden* (Cambridge: D. S. Brewer, 1993).

6 Geoffrey Chaucer, *The Book of the Duchess*, in *The Riverside Chaucer*, ed. Larry D. Benson, 3rd edn (Boston, MA: Houghton Mifflin, 1987), ll. 273–4. All references to Chaucer's works are to this edition.

7 Eugène Vinaver, *Commentary*, in *The Works of Sir Thomas Malory*, ed. Eugène Vinaver, 3rd edn, rev. by P. J. C. Field, 3 vols (Oxford: Clarendon Press, 1990), III, 1414.

8 The Reformations, of course, alter the frameworks for devotions and exhortations; however, the sense of sleep as a reprehensible lack of

perception or active agency – for both human and divine subjects – remains.

9 *The Peterborough Chronicle, 1070–1154*, ed. Cecily Clark (Oxford: Clarendon Press, 1970), p. 56.55–6; William Shakespeare, *The Tragedy of King Richard the Third*, in *The Norton Shakespeare*, ed. Stephen Greenblatt et al., 2nd edn (London: Norton, 2008), 4.iv.22–4. This discourse also follows biblical commentary, as in Psalms 44:23: 'Arise, why sleepest thou, O Lord? Arise, and cast us not off to the end' (all references to the bible are to *The Vulgate Bible: Douay–Rheims Translation*, ed. Swift Edgar and Angela M. Kinney (Cambridge, MA: Harvard University Press, 2010)). Elsewhere in the Old Testament, 'YHWH's competence as a guardian is affirmed by stressing that he stays awake on the job (Ps 121.3–4). On the other [hand], severe difficulties may suggest divine sleep, whether YHWH's (Pss 35.22–3; 44.24–5; 59.5b-6; 78.65) or Baal's (1 Kgs 18.27)': see Thomas H. McAlpine, *Sleep, Divine and Human, in the Old Testament* (Sheffield: Sheffield Academic Press, 1987), pp. 19–20.

10 In one Middle English carol, inspired by the Advent epistle (Rom. 13), 'Brethren, it is time to awake out of sleep; for now is our salvation nearer than we believed', sleep features as both a lack of perception and a slothful lack of activity: 'Owt of your slepe aryse and wake / For God mankynd nowe hath ytake / Al of a maide without eny make': in *A Selection of English Carols*, ed. Richard Greene (Oxford: Clarendon Press, 1962), no. 11, pp. 64–5; see also Douglas Gray, *Themes and Images in Medieval English Religious Lyric* (London: Routledge, 1972), pp. 96–8. Although this carol celebrates divine providence, it does so in the same language of sleep that the *Peterborough Chronicle* and Shakespeare's Elizabeth Woodville use to lament a lack of a providential intervention.

11 Margery Kempe is briefly discussed in Chapters 1 and 3. For sleep in ballads, see, for instance, 'Judas', in *Fourteenth Century Verse and Prose*, ed. Kenneth Sisam (Oxford: Clarendon Press, 1925), pp. 168–9.

12 As per the Song of Songs: 'I sleep, and my heart watcheth' (Canticles, 5:2).

13 As discussed further below, figuring sleep as a lack of (spiritual) perception follows Gregory the Great's influential *Pastoral Care* and medieval compline texts, which exhort those attending the final church service before night to be vigilant against the devil's incursions (1 Peter 5:8–9).

14 As exemplified recently by, for instance, Marion Turner, *Chaucer: A European Life* (Princeton, NJ: Princeton University Press, 2019); Joanna Bellis, *The Hundred Years War in Literature: 1337–1600* (Cambridge: D. S. Brewer, 2016); Jonathan Hsy, *Trading Tongues: Merchants,*

Multilingualism, and Medieval Literature (Columbus, OH: Ohio State University Press, 2013); and Ardis Butterfield, *The Familiar Enemy: Chaucer, Language, and Nation in the Hundred Years War* (Oxford: Oxford University Press, 2009).
15 Sif Rikhardsdottir, *Medieval Translations and Cultural Discourse: The Movement of Texts in England, France and Scandinavia* (Cambridge: D. S. Brewer, 2012), pp. 22 and 2.
16 This move follows Stephen F. Kruger, *Dreaming in the Middle Ages* (Cambridge: Cambridge University Press, 1992), and Tanya S. Lenz, *Dreams, Medicine, and Literary Practice: Exploring the Western Literary Tradition through Chaucer* (Turnhout: Brepols, 2014).
17 Jean Delumeau, *Sin and Fear: The Emergence of a Western Guilt Culture, 13th–18th Centuries*, trans. Eric Nicholson (1983; New York: St Martin's Press, 1990).
18 William F. MacLehose, 'Fear, Fantasy and Sleep in Medieval Medicine', in Elena Carrera (ed.), *Emotions and Health, 1200–1700* (Leiden: Brill, 2013), pp. 67–94; see also Pedro Gil Sotres, 'The Regimens of Health', in Mirko D. Grmek (ed.), *Western Medical Thought from Antiquity to the Middle Ages* (Cambridge, MA: Harvard University Press, 1998), pp. 291–318, and Karl H. Dannenfeldt, 'Sleep: Theory and Practice in the Late Renaissance', *Journal of the History of Medicine and Allied Sciences*, 41 (1986), 415–41.
19 Jean Verdon, *Night in the Middle Ages*, trans. George Holoch (Notre Dame, IN: University of Notre Dame Press, 2002); A. Roger Ekirch, *At Day's Close: A History of Nighttime* (London: Weidenfeld & Nicolson, 2005); Sasha Handley, *Sleep in Early Modern England* (London: Yale University Press, 2016).
20 Hollie L. S. Morgan, *Beds and Chambers in Late Medieval England: Readings, Representations and Realities* (Woodbridge: York Medieval Press, 2017); see also Michelle Perrot, *The Bedroom: An Intimate History*, trans. Lauren Elkin (New Haven, CT: Yale University Press, 2018).
21 Jeff Malpas, 'Place and Singularity', in Jeff Malpas (ed.), *The Intelligence of Place: Topographies and Poetics* (London: Bloomsbury, 2015), pp. 65–92 (p. 79); see also Henri Lefebvre, *The Production of Space*, trans. Donald Nicholson-Smith (Oxford: Blackwell, 1991), Molly Martin, *Castles and Space in Malory's 'Morte Darthur'* (Cambridge: D. S. Brewer, 2019), Matthew Boyd Goldie, *Scribes of Space: Place in Middle English Literature and Late Medieval Science* (Ithaca, NY: Cornell University Press, 2019), and Jan Shaw, *Space, Gender and Memory in Middle English Romance: Architectures of Wonder in Melusine* (New York: Palgrave Macmillan, 2016).

22 Seminal studies include Peter Brown, 'On the Borders of Middle English Dream Visions', in Peter Brown (ed.), *Reading Dreams: The Interpretation of Dreams from Chaucer to Shakespeare* (Oxford: Oxford University Press, 1999), pp. 22–50; J. Stephen Russell, *The English Dream Vision: Anatomy of a Form* (Columbus, OH: Ohio State University Press, 1988); Kathryn L. Lynch, *The High Medieval Dream Vision: Poetry, Philosophy, and Literary Form* (Stanford, CA: Stanford University Press, 1988); and A. C. Spearing, *Medieval Dream Poetry* (Cambridge: Cambridge University Press, 1976). Scholarship on Middle English dream visions is discussed more extensively in Chapter 4.

23 Notable exceptions include Rebecca Davis, '"Noon other werke": The Work of Sleep in Chaucer's *Book of the Duchess*', in Jamie C. Fumo (ed.), *Chaucer's* Book of the Duchess*: Contexts and Interpretations* (Cambridge: D. S. Brewer, 2018), pp. 51–69; Michael Raby, 'Sleep and the Transformation of Sense in Late Medieval Literature', *Studies in the Age of Chaucer*, 39 (2017), 191–224; David F. Johnson, '*In Somnium, In Visionem*: The Figurative Significance of Sleep in *Piers Plowman*', in L. A. J. R. Houwen and A. A. MacDonald (eds), *Loyal Letters: Studies on Mediaeval Alliterative Poetry & Prose* (Groningen: Egbert Forsten, 1994), pp. 240–5; and Lisa J. Kiser, 'Sleep, Dreams, and Poetry in Chaucer's *Book of the Duchess*', *Papers on Language & Literature*, 19 (1983), 3–12.

24 See, however, the discussion of the Seven Sleepers of Ephesus in Carolyn Dinshaw, *How Soon Is Now? Medieval Texts, Amateur Readers, and the Queerness of Time* (London: Duke University Press, 2012), pp. 55–9.

25 Garrett A. Sullivan, *Sleep, Romance and Human Embodiment: Vitality from Spenser to Milton* (Cambridge: Cambridge University Press, 2012).

26 See, for instance, Holly A. Crocker and Glenn Burger (eds), *Medieval Affect, Feeling, and Emotion* (Cambridge University Press, 2019); Virginia Langum, *Medicine and the Seven Deadly Sins in Late Medieval Literature and Culture* (New York: Palgrave Macmillan, 2016); Andrew Lynch, 'Positive Emotions in Arthurian Romance: Introduction', *Journal of the International Arthurian Society*, 4.1 (2016), 53–7; Corinne Saunders, 'Mind, Body and Affect in Medieval English Arthurian Romance', in Frank Brandsma, Carolyne Larrington, and Corinne Saunders (eds), *Emotions in Medieval Arthurian Literature: Body, Mind, Voice* (Cambridge: D. S. Brewer, 2015), pp. 31–46; and Corinne Saunders, 'Bodily Narratives: Illness, Medicine and Healing in Medieval Romance', in Neil Cartlidge (ed.), *Boundaries in Medieval Romance* (Cambridge: D. S. Brewer, 2008), pp. 175–90.

27 Chaucer, *Troilus and Criseyde*, II.1038; Julie Orlemanski, *Symptomatic Subjects: Bodies, Medicine, and Causation in the Literature of Late*

Medieval England (Philadelphia, PA: University of Pennsylvania Press, 2019), pp. 1–3.
28 Ekirch, *A History of Nighttime*, p. 262.
29 Sullivan, *Sleep, Romance and Human Embodiment*, p. 19.
30 Handley, *Sleep in Early Modern England*, p. 3.
31 Hebrew proverbs in the Old Testament bible connect sleep and sloth: for instance, 'Slothfulness casteth into a deep sleep; and an idle soul shall suffer hunger' [19:15]. See Delumeau, *Sin and Fear*, p. 230, and Thomas McAlpine's lexical study, which explores how sleep features in the Old Testament, for instance as an 'occasion of vulnerability', as the basis for dreams, and as a state that is mutually exclusive with most activities including 'notably work': *Sleep, Divine and Human*, pp. 15–18. These implications of sleep are continued in medieval literature, as are those of sleep in the New Testament, discussed further below. In addition, Middle English authors such as Gower and Chaucer draw especially upon Ovid's *Metamorphoses* as a fruitful source for representations of sleep, but use sleep to emphasise ethical failures where this classical source did not.
32 Sullivan, *Sleep, Romance and Human Embodiment*; Simon C. Estok, *Ecocriticism and Shakespeare: Reading Ecophobia* (New York: Palgrave Macmillan, 2011); Rebecca Totaro, 'Securing Sleep in Hamlet', *Studies in English Literature, 1500–1900*, 50.2 (2010), 407–26; William H. Sherman, 'Shakespearean Somniloquy: Sleep and Transformation in The Tempest', in Margaret Healy and Thomas Healy (eds), *Renaissance Transformations: The Making of English Writing (1500–1650)* (Edinburgh: Edinburgh University Press, 2009), pp. 177–91; David Roberts, 'Sleeping Beauties: Shakespeare, Sleep and the Stage', *The Cambridge Quarterly*, 35.3 (2006), 231–54; Ronald Hall, 'Sleeping Through Shakespeare', *Shakespeare in Southern Africa*, 12 (2000), 24–32; David Bevington, 'Asleep onstage', in John A. Alford (ed.), *From Page to Performance: Essays in Early English Drama* (East Lansing, MI: Michigan State University Press, 1995), pp. 51–83.
33 Sullivan, *Sleep, Romance and Human Embodiment*, p. 40.
34 Brian Cummings and James Simpson, 'Introduction', in Cummings and Simpson (eds), *Cultural Reformations: Medieval and Renaissance in Literary History* (Oxford: Oxford University Press, 2010), p. 4.
35 David Wallace, *Premodern Places: Calais to Surinam, Chaucer to Aphra Behn* (Oxford: Blackwell, 2004); Helen Cooper, *Shakespeare and the Medieval World* (London: Methuen Drama, 2010); James Simpson, *Reform and Cultural Revolution: 1350–1547* (Oxford: Oxford University Press, 2002).
36 Helen Cooper, *The English Romance in Time: Transforming Motifs from Geoffrey of Monmouth to the Death of Shakespeare* (Oxford:

Oxford University Press, 2004), p. 23. While the romance genre is primarily a medieval one, its popularity and the production of new texts, as well as the printing of old ones, continued through the sixteenth century: see Alex Davis, *Chivalry and Romance in the English Renaissance* (Cambridge: D. S. Brewer, 2003), esp. pp. 28–31, and Andrew King, *The Faerie Queene and Middle English Romance: The Matter of Just Memory* (Oxford: Clarendon Press, 2000), esp. p. 31.

37 Diana Webb, *Privacy and Solitude in the Middle Ages* (London: Hambledon Continuum, 2007), p. 98; Michael Thompson, *The Medieval Hall: The Basis of Secular Domestic Life, 600–1600 AD* (Aldershot: Scolar Press, 1995), p. 117; John Blair, 'Hall and Chamber: English Domestic Planning 1000–1250', in Gwyn Meirion-Jones and Michael Jones (eds), *Manorial Domestic Buildings in England and Northern France* (London: Society of Antiquaries of London, 1991), pp. 1–21 (p. 15).

38 Orlemanski, *Symptomatic Subjects*, pp. 1–2.

39 Dannenfeldt, 'Sleep: Theory and Practice in the Late Renaissance', pp. 415–16; Nancy G. Siraisi, *Medieval and Early Renaissance Medicine: An Introduction to Knowledge and Practice* (Chicago, IL: University of Chicago Press, 1990), p. 101, and *Avicenna in Renaissance Italy: The Canon and Medical Teaching in Italian Universities after 1500* (Princeton, NJ: Princeton University Press, 1987); Owsei Temkin, *Galenism: Rise and Decline of a Medical Philosophy* (Ithaca, NY: Cornell University Press, 1973).

40 Christopher Marlowe, *Dr Faustus*, ed. David Scott Kastan (New York: Norton, 2005), A-text 4.1.135 and B-text 4.4.25. Other recent studies of Galenic medicine's influence on medieval and early modern English literature include those collected in Jennifer C. Vaught (ed.), *Rhetorics of Bodily Disease and Health in Medieval and Early Modern England* (Farnham: Ashgate, 2010), which explores 'the vast extent to which rhetorics of bodily disease and health leave their imprint on medieval and early modern literature, religion, science, and medicine in England and its surrounding European context' (Vaught, p. 3). See also Elena Carrera (ed.), *Emotions and Health, 1200–1700* (Leiden: Brill, 2013).

41 Carole Rawcliffe, 'The Concept of Health in Late Medieval Society', in *Le interazioni fra economia e ambiente biologico nell'Europa preindustriale secc. XIII–XVIII* (Firenze: Firenza University Press, 2010), pp. 317–34. On the medieval 'mind-body continuum' and its manifestations in literature, see Saunders, 'Bodily Narratives: Illness, Medicine and Healing in Medieval Romance', esp. p. 177, and also Saunders, 'Mind, Body and Affect in Medieval English Arthurian Romance'; on this idea of the embodied mind in the early modern period, see, for instance, Gail Kern Paster, *Humoring the Body: Emotions and the*

Shakespearean Stage (Chicago, IL: University of Chicago Press, 2004), and Michael C. Schoenfeldt, *Bodies and Selves in Early Modern England: Physiology and Inwardness in Spenser, Shakespeare, Herbert, and Milton* (Cambridge: Cambridge University Press, 1999). As Saunders observes, modern medicine has moved away from Cartesian disassociations and is now looking afresh at connections between body and mind, as, for instance, in Antonio Damasio, *Looking for Spinoza: Joy, Sorrow and the Feeling Brain* (London: Harcourt, 2003).

42 Ekirch, *A History of Nighttime*, p. 279.

43 *John Trevisa's Translation of the Polychronicon of Ranulph Higden, Book VI*, ed. and trans. Ronald Waldron (Heidelberg: Universitätsverlag Winter, 2004), p. 133 (with Higden's Latin on the same page).

44 Chaucer, 'Tale of Sir Thopas', in the *Canterbury Tales*, VII.788–9.

45 Earlier examples of this euphemism are found in both Old English and Latin. For example, 'hire mid slaepe' (sleeps with her): Aelfred, Einleitung, 29, in Felix Liebermann, *Die Gesetze der Angelsachsen* (Halle: M. Niemeyer, 1898–1912; Aalen: Scientia, 1960), I, 38; cf. 'dormierit cum ea' (Vulgate, Exodus 22:16).

46 John Mirk, *Instructions for Parish Priests*, ed. Edward Peacock, OS 31 (London: Early English Text Society, 1868), p. 51.

47 Carolyn Dinshaw, *Getting Medieval: Sexualities and Communities, Pre- and Postmodern* (London: Duke University Press, 1999), p. 3; see also Simon Kemp, *Medieval Psychology* (New York: Greenwood Press, 1990), p. 160.

48 Kathleen Ashley and Robert L. A. Clark, 'Medieval Conduct: Texts, Theories, Practices,' in Kathleen Ashley and Robert L. A. Clark (eds), *Medieval Conduct* (Minneapolis, MN: University of Minnesota Press, 2001), pp. viii–xx (p. x).

49 Jonathan W. Nicholls, *The Matter of Courtesy: A Study of Medieval Courtesy Books and the Gawain-Poet* (Cambridge: D. S. Brewer, 1985); Ad Putter, *'Sir Gawain and the Green Knight' and French Arthurian Romance* (Oxford: Clarendon Press, 1995), esp. pp. 51–139.

50 Ashley and Clark, 'Medieval Conduct', pp. x and xvi.

51 Glenn D. Burger, *Conduct Becoming: Good Wives and Husbands in the Later Middle Ages* (Philadelphia, PA: University of Pennsylvania Press, 2018), p. 2. See also Holly A. Crocker, *The Matter of Virtue: Women's Ethical Action from Chaucer to Shakespeare* (Philadelphia, PA: University of Pennsylvania Press, 2019).

52 Burger, *Conduct Becoming*, p. 15.

53 Claire Sponsler, *Drama and Resistance: Bodies, Goods, and Theatricality in Late Medieval England* (Minneapolis, MN: University of Minnesota Press, 1997), pp. 59 and 61; Mary C. Flannery, *Practising*

Shame: Female Honour in Later Medieval England (Manchester: Manchester University Press, 2019), pp. 74–5.
54 For an overview of visual depictions of sleep and sex in continental medieval manuscripts, see Michael Camille, 'Manuscript Illumination and the Art of Copulation', in Karma Lochrie, Peggy McCracken, and James A. Schultz (eds), *Constructing Medieval Sexuality* (Minneapolis, MN: University of Minnesota Press, 1997), pp. 58–90. For instance, in medieval French or Italian texts, illuminators sometimes 'painted a couple in the euphemistic, post-coital act of "sleeping together"' in a bed with parted curtains (p. 70).
55 See, for instance, the Winchester Psalter, BL Cotton Nero C.IV, fol. 23.
56 See Michel Foucault, *Discipline and Punish: The Birth of the Prison*, trans. Alan Sheridan (New York: Pantheon, 1977), and Marita Sturken and Lisa Cartwright, *Practices of Looking: An Introduction to Visual Culture* (Oxford: Oxford University Press, 2012).
57 See Cooper, *Shakespeare and the Medieval World*, pp. 7–8.
58 Alec Ryrie, 'Sleeping, Waking and Dreaming in Protestant Piety', in Jessica Martin and Alec Ryrie (eds), *Private and Domestic Devotion in Early Modern Britain* (Farnham: Ashgate, 2012), pp. 73–92 (p. 76).
59 Stephen Pender, 'Subventing Disease: Anger, Passions, and the Non-Naturals', in *Rhetorics of Bodily Disease and Health in Medieval and Early Modern England*, pp. 193–218 (p. 195).
60 Handley, *Sleep in Early Modern England*, pp. 181–2.
61 On the medicalisation of sleep from the thirteenth through sixteenth centuries, see, as discussed above and in Chapter 1, Sotres, 'The Regimens of Health'; Siraisi, *Medieval and Early Renaissance Medicine*; Maclehose, 'Fear, Fantasy and Sleep in Medieval Medicine'; and Dannenfeldt, 'Sleep: Theory and Practice in the Late Renaissance'.
62 Handley, *Sleep in Early Modern England*.
63 Frank Brandsma, Carolyne Larrington, and Corinne Saunders, 'Introduction', in *Emotions in Medieval Arthurian Literature*, pp. 1–10 (p. 6).
64 See, for instance, Barbara Rosenwein, *Anger's Past: The Social Uses of an Emotion in the Middle Ages* (Ithaca, NY: Cornell University Press, 1998) and *Emotional Communities in the Early Middle Ages* (Ithaca, NY: Cornell University Press, 2006); Sarah McNamer, in *Affective Meditation and the Invention of Medieval Compassion* (Philadelphia, PA: University of Pennsylvania Press, 2010); Brandsma, Larrington, and Saunders (eds), *Emotions in Medieval Arthurian Literature: Body, Mind, Voice*; Mary C. Flannery, 'Personification and Embodied Emotional Practice in Middle English Literature', *Literature Compass*, 13 (2016), 351–61; Sif Rikhardsdottir, *Emotion in Old Norse*

Literature: Translations, Voices, Contexts (Cambridge: Boydell and Brewer, 2017); and Damien Boquet and Piroska Nagy, *Medieval Sensibilities: A History of Emotions in the Middle Ages*, trans. Robert Shaw (Cambridge: Polity Press, 2018). See also Rom Harré (ed.), *The Social Construction of Emotion* (Oxford: Blackwell, 1988); Rom Harré and W. Gerrod Parrott (eds), *The Emotions: Social, Cultural and Biological Dimensions* (London: Sage Publications, 1996).

65 See especially Boquet and Nagy, *Medieval Sensibilities: A History of Emotions in the Middle Ages*, pp. 3–5, updating Norbert Elias, *The Civilizing Process* (Oxford: Blackwell, 2000), and Johan Huizinga, *The Autumn of the Middle Ages*, trans. R. J. Payton and U. Mammitzch (Chicago, IL: University of Chicago Press, 1997).

66 Thomas Dixon, *From Passions to Emotions: The Creation of a Secular Psychological Category* (Cambridge: Cambridge University Press, 2003); see also Paster, *Emotions and the Shakespearean Stage*.

67 Saunders, 'Mind, Body and Affect in Medieval English Arthurian Romance', in *Emotions in Medieval Arthurian Literature*, pp. 31–46 (p. 34).

68 Rikhardsdottir, *Emotion in Old Norse Literature*, p. 11.

69 Sylvan Tomkin, 'Script Theory: Differential Magnification of Affects', in Herbert E. Howe and Richard A. Dienstbier (eds), *Nebraska Symposium on Motivation 1978*, vol. 26 (Lincoln, NE: University of Nebraska Press, 1979), pp. 201–36.

70 See especially Rosenwein, *Emotional Communities in the Early Middle Ages*, and Andrew Lynch, 'Malory and Emotion', in Megan G. Leitch and Cory James Rushton (eds), *A New Companion to Malory* (Cambridge: D. S. Brewer, 2019), pp. 177–90.

71 Melissa Gregg and Gregory J. Seigworth (eds), *The Affect Theory Reader* (Durham, NC: Duke University Press, 2010); see further Stephanie Trigg, 'Introduction: Emotional Histories – Beyond the Personalization of the Past and the Abstraction of Affect Theory', *Exemplaria*, 26 (2014), 3–15, and Flannery, *Practising Shame*.

72 See: J. Allan Mitchell, *Ethics and Exemplary Narrative in Chaucer and Gower* (Cambridge: D. S. Brewer, 2004), pp. 13–14; Alcuin Blamires, *Chaucer, Ethics, and Gender* (Oxford: Oxford University Press, 2006), p. 8.

73 Ashley and Clark, 'Medieval Conduct: Texts, Theories, Practices', pp. ix–xx.

74 See Pierre Bourdieu, *Outline of a Theory of Practice*, trans. Richard Nice (Cambridge: Cambridge University Press, 1977), esp. p. 94; and Katharine Breen, *Imagining an English Reading Public, 1150–1400* (Cambridge: Cambridge University Press, 2010), pp. 5–8. On the

medievalist roots of the term 'habitus', see Bruce Holsinger, 'Indigeneity: Panofsky, Bourdieu, and the Archaeology of the *Habitus*', in Holsinger, *The Premodern Condition: Medievalism and the Making of Theory* (Chicago, IL: University of Chicago Press, 2005), pp. 94–113.

75 Roger Chartier, 'Histoire des mentalités', in Lawrence D. Kritzman (ed.), *The Columbia History of Twentieth-Century French Thought* (New York: Columbia University Press, 2006), pp. 54–8 (p. 55).

76 See also Monique Scheer, 'Are Emotions a Kind of Practice (and Is That What Makes Them Have a History)? A Bourdieuian Approach to Understanding Emotion', *History and Theory*, 51.2 (2012), 193–230.

77 See, for instance, Chaucer, *The Book of the Duchess*, 276, and *The House of Fame*, 119; and, for Old English 'slepe', *Beowulf*, 'Sigon þa to slæpe' (*Beowulf: A Dual-Language Edition*, ed. and trans Howell D. Chickering (New York: Random House, 2006), 1251). However, 'dreame' or 'drem' (*House of Fame*, 62), while of Germanic origin, meant joy or music in Old English.

78 *Melusine*, ed. A. K. Donald, Early English Text Society (EETS) ES 68 (London: Paul, Trench, Trübner, 1895), p. 28.25–6; Jean d'Arras, *Mélusine*, ed. M. C. Brunet (Paris: Jannet, 1854), pp. 36–7.

79 The language of sleep also features in discussions of death in medieval and early modern English literature, from the *Pricke of Conscience* to Shakespeare's *Hamlet*; this figurative vein is discussed in Chapter 1.

80 On medieval England's multilingualism, see, for instance, Butterfield, *The Familiar Enemy*; Venetia Bridges, *Medieval Narratives of Alexander the Great: Transnational Texts in England and France* (Cambridge: D. S. Brewer, 2018); and Laura Ashe, *The Oxford English Literary History, Volume I, 1000–1350: Conquest and Transformation* (Oxford: Oxford University Press, 2017), esp. p. 376. On 'insular' medieval culture, and in relation to English romance in particular, Rosalind Field offers a reminder of 'the deeply bilingual nature of fourteenth-century literature': 'Patterns of Availability and Demand in Middle English Translations *de romanz*', in Laura Ashe, Ivana Djordjevic and Judith Weiss (eds), *Exploitations of Medieval Romance* (Cambridge: D. S. Brewer, 2010), pp. 73–89 (p. 89). Yet, as Field also acknowledges, many Middle English popular romances, such as *Emaré*, are not translations from French or Anglo-Norman romance, and the romances produced in England in the later Middle Ages were increasingly in English as the genre developed and audiences shifted to include more who spoke and read English as a native language.

81 See Paul Battles, 'Dying for a Drink: "Sleeping after the Feast" Scenes in *Beowulf*, *Andreas*, and the Old English Poetic Tradition', *Modern Philology*, 112.3 (2015), 435–57.

82 In the siesta cultures of the warmer mediterranean south, midday naps were expected rather than denounced. 'Siesta' is derived from the Latin 'hora sexta', and resting at the sixth hour of the day (at midday) follows a Roman practice. In the Old Testament (the product of a warm climate), siestas are likewise condoned: 'one sleeps when it is too dark or too hot' (McAlpine, *Sleep, Divine and Human*, p. 111). Nonetheless, although the medical and scientific tracts that reached later medieval north-western Europe were generally translated and transmitted from Arabic texts of medieval Spain, they decried midday naps as unhealthy and socially inappropriate.

83 Verdon, *Night in the Middle Ages*, pp. 207–12; C. H. Lawrence, *Medieval Monasticism: Forms of Religious Life in Western Europe in the Middle Ages* (London: Longman, 1984), pp. 112–14; Andrew Hughes, *Medieval Manuscripts for Mass and Office: A Guide to Their Organization and Terminology* (Toronto: University of Toronto Press, 1995), pp. 14–18.

84 Gregory the Great, *Pastoral Care*, ed. and trans. Henry Davis (Maryland, MD: Newman Press, 1950), iii. 4.

85 Thomas Aquinas, *Commentary on the Letter of St Paul to the Romans*, ed. John Mortensen (Lander, WY: Aquinas Institute for the Study of Sacred Doctrine, 2012). These types of sleep inform a range of Middle English genres, though presumably not, in most cases, as a result of direct engagement with Aquinas.

86 Readers are also urged to avoid being carried off by 'a deadly sleep': Giovanni Boccaccio, *The Fates of Illustrius Men*, trans. Louis Brewer Hall (New York: Frederick Ungar, 1965), p. 227.

87 Dante's opus is sufficiently concerned with sleep that it has led at least one scientist to posit that Dante must himself have suffered from narcolepsy: Giuseppe Plazzi, 'Dante's Description of Narcolepsy', *Sleep Medicine*, 14.11 (2013), 1221–3.

88 See Bernard of Clairvaux, *On the Song of Songs*, trans. Kilian Walsh, 4 vols (Kalamazoo, MI: Cistercian Institute Publications, 1983); for discussion, see Mary Carruthers, '"The Mystery of the Bed Chamber": Mnemotechnique and Vision in Chaucer's *Book of the Duchess*', in John M. Hill and Deborah M. Sinnreich-Levi (eds), *The Rhetorical Poetics of the Middle Ages: Reconstructive Polyphony: Essays in Honor of Robert O. Payne* (Madison, NJ: Fairleigh Dickinson University Press, 2000), pp. 67–87 (esp. p. 73).

89 Luke 22:45–6.

90 William Caxton, *The Book of the Ordre of Chyvalry*, ed. Alfred T. P. Byles, EETS OS 168 (London: Oxford University Press, 1926), pp. 122.8–123.10.

91 This book is interested in 'Englishness' as a cultural umbrella, rather than a nationalistic construction. However, comments such as Caxton's use here of the language of sleep to interpellate the knights of England as a collective in need of reform do connect language, literature and national identity along the lines of what Thorlac Turville-Petre describes (for an earlier period) in *England the Nation: Language, Literature, and National Identity, 1290–1340* (Oxford: Clarendon Press, 1996).
92 Jonathan Crary, *24/7: Late Capitalism and the Ends of Sleep* (London: Verso, 2013).
93 Matthew Walker, *Why We Sleep: The New Science of Sleep and Dreams* (London: Allen Lane, 2017), p. 4. See also Alice Gregory, *Nodding Off: The Science of Sleep from Cradle to Grave* (London: Bloomsbury, 2018).
94 Vicki Culpin, *The Business of Sleep: How Sleeping Better Can Transform Your Career* (London: Bloomsbury, 2018), p. ix; J. Pilcher and A. Huffcut, 'Effects of Sleep Deprivation on Performance: A Meta-Analysis', *Sleep*, 19 (1996), 318–26.
95 Walker, *Why We Sleep*, p. 4.
96 Walker, *Why We Sleep*; Gregory, *Nodding Off*.
97 'Sleep deprivation due to inadequate total hours of sleep may lead to an absolute reduction in the time spent in REM, but the percentage of the night in REM sleep may actually increase', www.verywellhealth.com/dream-deprivation-how-loss-of-rem-sleep-impacts-health-4159540 (accessed 4 March 2019).
98 Matthew Walker and E. van der Helm, 'Overnight Therapy? The Role of Sleep in Emotional Brain Processing', *Psychological Bulletin*, 135 (2009), 731–48.
99 See, for instance, A. Steptoe, K. O'Donnell, M. Marmot and J. Wardle, 'Positive Affect, Psychological Well-Being and Good Sleep', *Journal of Psychosomatic Research*, 64 (2008), 409–15; D. Tempesta, A. Couyoumdjian, G. Curcio, F. Moroni, C. Marzano, L. De Gennaro, and M. Ferrara, 'Lack of Sleep Affects the Evaluation of Emotional Stimuli', *Brain Research Bulletin*, 82 (2010), 194–208; Culpin, *The Business of Sleep*, pp. 69–77.
100 K. Barnett and N. Cooper, 'The Effects of a Poor Night's Sleep on Mood, Cognitive, Autonomic and Electrophysiological Measures', *Journal of Integrative Neuroscience*, 7 (2008), 405–20.
101 Gregory, *Nodding Off*, p. 150; see also P. K. Alvaro, R. M. Roberts, and J. K. Harris, 'A Systematic Review Assessing Bidirectionality between Sleep Disturbances, Anxiety, and Depression', *Sleep*, 36 (2013), 1059–68; and D. Freeman, B. Sheaves, G. M. Goodwin et al.,

'The Effects of Improving Sleep on Mental Health (OASIS): A Randomised Controlled Trial with Mediation Analysis', *Lancet Psychiatry*, 4 (2017), 749–58.
102 See also Crary, *24/7*, p. 23.
103 Lefebvre, *The Production of Space*, pp. 83 and 27. See also Gaston Bachelard, *The Poetics of Space*, trans. Maria Jolas (Boston, MA: Beacon Press, 1994; first published in English 1964).
104 Geoffrey Chaucer, 'Reeve's Tale', I.4163; Shakespeare, *Henry IV Part I*, 2.5.483–4.
105 Shakespeare, *Hamlet*, 3.i.67.

1

Emotions, epistemology and the nature of sleep

Chardri's thirteenth-century Anglo-Norman *Life of the Seven Sleepers* offers a striking focus on how emotions engender sleep. In Chardri's description, when the Seven Sleepers of Ephesus fall asleep in the cave in which they are hiding from their persecutors, their emotions play a causal role:

> Ke par dolur, ke par penser
> Endormirent li set bacheler.
> Kar ceo avent, sachez, suvent
> Ke gent, quant il sunt trop dolent
> Par pesance de lur penser,
> Lur cuvent tost sumiller.[1]
>
> (Whether out of distress or out of worry, the seven young men went to sleep – for it often happens, you know, that when people are very sad on account of the weight of their worries, it is natural that they are prompt to slumber.)

This is an extraordinary sleep: a sleep from which the Seven will not wake for three centuries. Their sleep is a miracle demonstrating God's power, and a story reproduced in hagiographical collections across the later Middle Ages, including in William Caxton's 1483 *Golden Legend*, an English translation of Jacobus de Varagine's thirteenth-century *Legenda aurea*.[2] Chardri's aside, however, emphasises that how or why they fall asleep is more ordinary, even expected: it is something that 'often happens, you know' ('avent, sachez, suvent'). This commentary on sleep as a fitting response to a strong, distressing emotion is not paralleled in Chardri's Latin source, but is also found in Chardri's other saint's life, Josaphaz.[3] Chardri wrote at a time when knowledge of Galenic medicine had recently spread through Western Europe to England via medical tracts translated from Arabic.[4] Chardri's insular saints' lives – in Anglo-Norman, directed towards English audiences[5] – speak to an understanding of sleep as a natural or appropriate response ('lur cuvent tost sumiller') to uncomfortable emotions such as sorrow or anxiety. Sleep is not just a reaction, it is also a renewal: in the prevailing Galenic theory, where an imbalance in the humours signified a strong emotion – black bile indicating melancholy or sorrow, yellow bile indicating choler or anger – sleep, by facilitating the transformation of food into the four humours, could restore the balance between the humours that was necessary for good health. And as Chardri shows, a strong imbalance in the humours was, additionally, believed to be able to generate sleep: this culturally specific construction of the emotions was also explicated in medieval medical paradigms and manuals of health, and with widespread implications for understanding premodern literature.

In medieval English culture, representations of sleep are shaped by its multifaceted relationship to nature and ideas of the natural. Sleep, here, is a form of medicine – a natural, appropriate and beneficial response to a matter of mental health.[6] Medicine, as a branch of natural philosophy (or science),[7] was sometimes called 'magyk natureel', as in Chaucer's Portrait of the Physician in the 'General Prologue' to the *Canterbury Tales*; medicine was 'concerned with unlocking the secrets of nature, both in diagnosis and in treatment and remedies.'[8] Although sleep, according to the principles of Galenic medicine, was understood as one of the six 'non-naturals', bodily processes seen as beneficial for well-being (as opposed to the 'naturals', which inhered to the body itself), it was also seen as a natural and necessary process. Describing sleep as a 'kyndeliche disposicioun', John Trevisa's late fourteenth-century translation of Bartholomæus Anglicus's proto-encyclopedic *De Proprietatibus Rerum* (*On the Properties of Things*) devotes two chapters to sleep, propounding sleep's importance for physiological and psychological well-being.[9] As I show here, both senses of the Middle English word 'kynde' – natural and benevolent[10] – pertain not only to this particular discussion of sleep, but also to insular representations of sleep and of sleep's implications for health more broadly.

This chapter explores how this medical understanding of sleep illuminates emotionally charged acts of falling asleep, particularly in Middle English romances, cycle plays and dream visions. It analyses the ways in which a range of writers, from Chardri to Chaucer, from Langland to Malory, negotiated prevailing views of the nature of sleep to communicate the consequences of embodied emotions. When characters get so sad or angry that they fall asleep, unconsciousness serves as a form of making emotion recognisable, of externalising the authenticity of affect, in ways that have partial parallels with, as well as differences from, swooning (a better-studied form of sudden-onset unconsciousness). In addition, in mediating 'unhealthful' emotions,[11] in helping to relieve sorrow and manage anger, sleep plays an important role in supporting both mental and physical health. Sleep, then, is a way of knowing more about the sleeping subject in premodern English culture, as is insomnia – an affliction affecting romance lovers, melancholic dream vision narrators and uneasy heads that wear the crown. Sleep also offers ways of learning about matters beyond the well-being of the sleeper: desires for sleep are often entwined with desires for truth, in ways that include, but are not limited to, the epistemological implications of dreams and visions. Through this chapter's identification and analysis of how Middle English literary representations of sleep engage with the thinking of Aristotle, Galen, Avicenna and Aquinas (among others), sleep emerges both with wide-ranging implications for the study of emotions in medieval English culture, and as more integral to the formation and content of dreams and dream visions than has been recognised.

'profite þat is in slepe': medicine and mental health

What, then, is sleep? What knowledge did premodern writers and readers have about it, and what attitudes did they have towards it? In the late Middle Ages, when sleep was widely understood as necessary and beneficial, its benefits – both physiological and psychological – originated in sleep's vital role in digestion. In medical tracts and dietaries, sleep's profitability is poised alongside discussions of the perils of oversleeping, or of sleeping at the wrong time or place, or in the wrong way. Sleep was not uniform, but it was universal, and (like death, for which it, despite its beneficial role, sometimes rhetorically substitutes) its functions and legibilities affected everyone, from prince to pauper. As Gilbert Hay remarks of Alexander the Great succumbing to sleep at a moment of uncertainty in the fifteenth-century *Buik of Alexander*, 'Than slepit he, [as] all man-kynd man do.'[12] This section explores how the sleep of humanity features in views of health and of the embodiment of the emotions in medieval English mentalities.

Sleep's importance for physical and mental health was emphasised in the medical tradition originating with the Greek physicians Hippocrates (c.460–370 BCE) and Galen (129–c.210 CE), medical authorities familiar in later medieval England and name-dropped by Chaucer's Man in Black in the *Book of the Duchess* and in the Portrait of the Physician in the *Canterbury Tales*. In lamenting that not even the great physicians 'Ypocras ne Galyen' could cure what ails him, the Man in Black asserts the strength of his grief for his beloved (whom no medicine, after all, could restore to life), but also speaks to contemporary respect for the medical expertise of these familiar authorities.[13] Galen was educated in Alexandria, where his medical learning included the works of Hippocrates, Aristotle and physicians writing in the intervening centuries whose works have not survived. Galen's own influential medical tracts were re-copied and respected for over a millennium and a half, but he is certainly not the only medical authority known during the later Middle Ages, as catalogues of physicians such as the one in Chaucer's Physician's Portrait show:

> Wel knew he the olde Esculapius,
> And Deyscorides, and eek Rufus,
> Olde Ypocras, Haly, and Galyen,
> Serapion, Razis, and Avycen,
> Averrois, Damascien, and Constantyn,
> Bernard, and Gatesden, and Gilbertyn.[14]

Classical and Arabic authorities stand alongside more recent thirteenth- and fourteenth-century French and English medical writers here, and similar lists circulated in regimenal texts such as the *Gouvernayle of Helthe*, and in Trevisa's *On the Properties of Things*.[15] However, Galen's name has become synonymous with the scientific and medical paradigm that prevailed in western Europe from the twelfth century to the early seventeenth. Because Galenic medicine centres on the body's fluctuating economy of humoral liquids, which underpin emotional dispositions, sleep, through its contribution to digestion in this medical paradigm, through helping to restore the balance between the humours, has a powerful role to play in the embodiment of the emotions and the emotions' implications for health (both physical and mental). This is a role that, I argue, is foregrounded and manipulated in medieval and early modern English literature from Chaucer's dream visions to Shakespearean drama, and from morality plays to Malory's *Morte Darthur*.

Galen's work was preserved in Arabic medical texts across the early and central Middle Ages, and when Arabic medicine became known in western Europe between 1070 and 1300, this shaped western awareness of a discourse on sleep – a discourse in which sleep has bodily and moral implications.[16] Galen's writings studied in the Middle Ages included *On the Affected Parts (De locis affectis)*, composed after 192 CE, and *Hygieina*, a treatise synthesising Hippocratic ideas on hygiene with Aristotelianism and Hellenistic science that was known in the Middle Ages as *De regimine sanitatis* or *De custodia sanitatis* through two Latin translations made in Italy in the thirteenth and fourteenth centuries.[17] The Persian polymaths responsible for copying Galen's and Hippocrates' texts, such as (to give the names by which they were known to the medieval west) Avicenna and Haly Abbas,[18] also enriched the medical writings transmitted to the later medieval west with new commentaries and syntheses, particularly concerning mental processes and the emotions, or accidents of the soul.[19] From the thirteenth century onwards, with the rise of universities and the proliferation of regimens of health, the Greek and Arabic tradition became more widely known in the Christian west, and alongside that of Galen, western medieval writers especially invoked the authority of Avicenna, whose early thirteenth-century 'Canon of Medicine' was translated in mid-twelfth-century Castilian Toledo. This medical tradition centred on a holistic theory of hygienic treatments and on the study of individual complexion; it posits that health is affected both by internal causes, and by external causes. The internal causes, or 'things natural', were comprised of 'the human body, what it is made of, and how it works', and six external causes became canonical in Galenic medicine as the 'non-natural' influences on health.[20] Galen describes the six non-naturals as 'all the necessary factors which alter the body'; they are air (which needed to be as pure as possible), food and drink, inanition and repletion, rest and exercise, sleep and waking, and the passions or emotions.[21] As suggested by the way in which several of these six non-naturals are pairings of opposite states or dispositions, balance is important for health; the proper performance or consumption of these six non-naturals required care. Sleeping and waking, then, are conjoined yet distinct, and maintaining a balance between them was necessary.

Advice on the six non-naturals took account of a number of variables pertaining to individuals and their environment, and sleep is no exception here. Galen wrote that people of different ages and complexions would need different amounts of sleep, but for each type, there is a 'perfect balance'.[22] An individual's complexion (or temperament) and thus his or her health depended on the balance of the four humours in his or her body, and – because the humours were either moist or dry, and either hot or cold – on the individual's state of moist/dry and hot/cold.[23] Men were thought to be more hot and dry, and women to be more cold and wet; an individual's complexion changed with age, so Galen's advice varies according to the four ages of man.[24] An individual's balance of the humours was also in flux diurnally, as different humours dominated at different times of day: anger predominated between six in the morning and noon; melancholy predominated from noon to six in the evening; from six in the evening until midnight, phlegm was ascendant; and midnight until six in the morning was the time when blood (or a sanguine temper) dominated. A different humour dominated each season, too: sanguine in spring, choleric (yellow bile) in summer, melancholy (black bile) in autumn, and phlegmatic in winter. The Galenic concentration on individual hygiene shaped regiminal treatises designed to guard against disease.[25] These treatises included specific advice about how (and how much) to sleep, and were often aimed towards men of elevated rank, such as Gilbert Kymer's early fifteenth-century regimen produced for the use of Humphrey, Duke of Gloucester, the brother of Henry V and uncle of Henry VI who cultivated interest in humanism in England in the first half of the fifteenth century.[26] However, especially in the later Middle Ages, in dietaries written by Lydgate and printed by William Caxton for example, the tenets of these regiminal texts also reached wider readerships.

Medieval and early modern English authors such as Chaucer and Shakespeare wrote about disease and strong emotions in ways that engage with this intellectual tradition; medicine is a form of cultural knowledge that would have been familiar, to a greater or lesser extent, to those educated enough to read and write.[27] Chaucer's writing, as Carol Falvo Heffernan puts it, 'indicates considerable medical knowledge, the kind one would expect to find in a university-educated physician […] as well as the humbler kind of knowledge exemplified in a popular work like Chaucer's own *Treatise on the Astrolabe*'.[28] An expectation that readers would understand the role of the four humours in medicine and health shapes Chaucer's Portrait of the Physician in the *Canterbury Tales*, who, we are told,

> knew the cause of everich maladye,
> Were it of hoot, or coold, or moyste or drye,
> And where they engendred, and of what humour.[29]

Medieval readers would also have understood the way in which the humours were coextensive with the emotions or passions – for instance, how choler or anger corresponds to (and is produced by) a preponderance of yellow bile. Popular Middle English texts such as the Arthurian romances *Ywain and Gawain*, *Sir Gawain and the Green Knight* and Malory's *Morte Darthur* do not explicitly articulate precise medical knowledge as often as Chaucer does, but, like Chaucer, they draw on 'the notion of a mind-body continuum' animated by humoral theory 'that is so central to medieval being in the world',[30] and humoral theory shapes their deployments of sleep, as the next section of this chapter explores.

The Galenic classification of people and their health needs according to complexions is particularly pertinent to the science and benefits of sleep. Sleep is discussed 'consistently and prominently' in regimens of health from the thirteenth century onward, and such regiminal texts are extant in ever greater numbers through to the fifteenth century,[31] bearing witness to wider audiences' engagement with medical tenets about sleep and their practical applications. In Galenic science, sleep facilitates concoction, which is the digestion of food via cooking – both during the first digestion, in the stomach, and during the second digestion, in the liver.[32] Physiologically, then, sleeping replenished the body by enabling the transformation of food into the four humours, most importantly into blood, which was 'used up' as it reached the body's extremities, but also phlegm, black bile and yellow bile.[33] Therefore, sleep restored balance to the body's liquids and the emotional imbalances to which it might be subjected while waking, such as melancholy or anger. This belief forms part of the premodern interest in 'materialist explanations of mental and emotional states'.[34] Thus, as Chaucer puts it in the 'Squire's Tale', 'sleep' is 'the norice of digestioun'.[35] What medieval people ate and digested was important not only for enabling exertion, but also for determining and regulating emotional disposition, and sleep was an essential part of this digestive process, helping to maintain health and emotional balance.

Sleep was thought to result from the movement of heat from the extremities to the core, causing moist vapours in the stomach to rise to the brain; this followed both the writings of Aristotle and later commentaries by writers such as Avicenna, Augustine and Aquinas, available in England in Latin.[36] This understanding of sleep as generated by movement of heat and moisture circulated in Middle English too, for instance in John Trevisa's statement that 'In slepe þe inner partyes hetiþ and þe vtter partyes keliþ and so whanne þe hete is depe wiþinne, þe lyme of þe comoun witte is ibounde.'[37] Aristotle wrote three treatises on sleep and dreams that formed part of a collection known in the Middle Ages, from the late thirteenth century onwards, as the *Parva Naturalia*.[38] Aristotle's *De Somno et Vigilia*, *De Insomniis*, and *De Divinatione per Somnum* together 'constitute the first systematic study of the phenomenon of sleep in ancient philosophy'.[39] In *De Somno et Vigilia*, Aristotle defines sleep as the opposite – and the absence – of wakefulness. Wakefulness is 'nothing other than the capacity to sense-perceive'; sleep, then, by contrast, is a lack or absence of the 'faculty of sensibility',[40] or 'a paralysis of the organs of sense perception', due to the moisture generated by digestive concoction rising to the brain, where these vapours cause condensation and obstruct the passages through which spirits are conveyed to the sensory and motor organs when awake.[41] Yet sleep is not only 'lack or absence of activity but rather contraction, densification, and force of compression'.[42] Sleep also distinguishes animals from plants, because it gives rest to sensory functions (the *virtutes animales*) that plants do not possess, while 'activating the *virtutes naturales*, especially those of digestion and retention'.[43] And during sleep, as digestion occurred, disease and unhealthful emotions could be alleviated.[44] The emotions were, of course, themselves one of the six non-natural influences on health and well-being, alongside sleep, but sleep could mediate and regulate the emotions. Thomas Aquinas, citing Augustine, also argues that sleep (and other bodily remedies) can assuage sorrow, and explicitly counters the objection that 'sorrow is in the soul: whereas sleep and baths regard the body' by observing that soul and body affect one another, and specifying that 'sorrow, by reason of its specific nature, is repugnant to the vital movement of the body; and consequently whatever restores the bodily nature to its due state of vital movement, is opposed to sorrow and assuages it.'[45] Especially because of the ways in which body and mind were thought to relate to each other more closely before Cartesian dualism took hold in the mid-seventeenth century, then, sleep played an important role in emotional health via its role in digestion.

Notwithstanding the currency of this understanding of sleep as a 'non-natural' influence on health, sleep in late medieval England was in other ways understood as thoroughly natural in its benefits. In his translation of Bartholomæus Anglicus' *De Proprietatibus Rerum*, John Trevisa addresses sleep's scientific workings and benefits, citing the views of a variety of medical authorities on the subject, including Aristotle, Augustine and Avicenna. Trevisa (c.1340–1402), Chaucer's direct contemporary, finished his translation of this lengthy protoencyclopedia at Berkley, Gloucester, in 1399, and his tract's wide circulation is attested by its eight extant fifteenth-century manuscript copies; it was also printed by Wynkyn de Worde, c.1495.[46] Trevisa's discussion of sleep, fittingly, follows a chapter on supper, 'De cena', which concludes by foregrounding sleep's connection to digestion: 'as Constaninus seiþ, whanne smoke of mete comeþ into the brayn we slepiþ eþeliche.'[47] The two chapters on sleep contribute to Book Six's consideration of daily health and hygiene. Trevisa cites Aristotle and Augustine on the nature of sleep as a cessation of 'þe vertues of felinge and of meuynge', stressing that 'in slep is best digestioun.'[48] Sleep, that is, is not merely the absence of wakefulness and the binding or cessation of the actions and perceptions available to a waking person, because

> slepe helpiþ and comfortiþ kinde, and is kyndeliche as waking is kindeliche also. Also the soule haþ no lykynge in priuacioun and haþ likynge in sleep, and so slepe is not priuacion but it is a kyndelich disposicioun.[49]

Here, sleep, as a 'kyndelich disposicioun', is a natural, necessary and beneficial process. Elaborating on the digestive function of sleep, Trevisa explains why labourers might sleep more deeply than others: 'Kynde slepe is a3einturnynge of þe spirites from depnes and fastnesse þat mete and drinke may be defied [digested], as it farith in þe slepe of trauailinge men. In hem slepe is depe and faste for superfluyte of resolucyoun of spiritis.'[50] This suggests a class dimension to sleep, which I shall return to in Chapter 2. Trevisa emphasises that above all, for everyone, the profitability of sleep should be recognised:

> men schal namelich take hede of profite þat is in slepe, for if þe slepe is kinde and temperat, it doþ to þe body ful mony profitis and fele, [...] and nameliche for þanne is good digestioun and purid þing departid from þing þat is vnpured.[51]

In addition to digestion and purification, sleep also has other benefits:

> if it is temperat in qualite and in quantite it releueþ a seke man, and bodeþ þat kinde schal haue þe victorie and maistrie of þe euel, and good turnynge and changinge.[52]

Sleep, here, is linked not only to physical health – relief for the sick – but also to the triumph of good over evil. This combination of medical and moral properties shapes sleep's implications in Middle English literary texts as well as in medical and regimenal tracts.

Medieval English readers encountered explicit instructions about sleep in regiminal texts: conduct manuals such as dietaries (treatises on general hygiene designed to help readers live healthily) and courtesy books (conduct texts which combine instructions about healthy living with instructions about how to perform civilised behaviour in relation to bodily necessities such as eating and sleeping). For instance, John Lydgate wrote a poetic *Dietary* that addresses how and when one should and should not sleep (in relation to mealtimes); in addition, the *Gouernayle of Helthe*, a simplified version of the *Regimen Sanitatis Salernitanum* (which circulated in England in Latin from the fourteenth century), circulated in English from the early fifteenth century, and was printed by William Caxton in the late fifteenth century – as discussed in more detail in Chapter 2. The dietary that Gilbert Kymer wrote for Humphrey of Gloucester in 1423 includes specific attention to Humphrey's bad habits (especially admonishing him on the deleterious effects of his sexual appetite, and the dangers of staying up too late), but it also, across its twenty-six chapters, addresses the Galenic tenets of hygienic living more generally. Kymer devotes Chapter 21 of his dietary to the regulation of sleep and waking, focusing on how the health benefits of sleep can be achieved by sleeping at the 'natural' time. As Kymer asserts, 'nichil sit ad corpus nutriendum sompno res iuvancior' ('nothing is a more helpful matter for the nourishment of the body than sleep').[53] Kymer's specifies the timing and duration of sleep most conducive to balancing the humours:

> Tempus vero didi naturalis quo corpus habundancius et salubrius nutritur est a nona post meridiem usque ad sextam de mane in quibus amicabiliores naturales humores viz flenma et sanguis multiplicantur.[54]
>
> (The natural time to be devoted [to sleep] by which the body is nourished more abundantly and beneficially is from nine hours after noon to six in the morning, in which the more amicable natural humours, namely phlegm and blood, are multiplied.)

These instructions about how to sleep are presented as though they are natural truths, rather than cultural constructs. Sleeping at night is natural and beneficial especially because it encourages the production of the 'more amicable natural humours', or the more 'healthful' ones, conducive to phlegmatic (pensive) and sanguine temperaments. Kymer advises that one should aim for nine hours of sleep a night, but also observes that the amount of sleep varies with the seasons, the climate of a given region, the size of one's supper and the amount of daytime exercise.[55] Deep sleep in the hours before dawn is especially prized, called golden sleep ('sompnus aureus dicitur') because of its humoral benefits: it 'bonum sanguinem auro longe meliorem quam sompnus alterius temporis exuberancius multiplicat' ('multiplies good blood more abundantly than sleep of another time does').[56]

This perspective on the benefits of sleep is shared by other dietaries circulating in medieval England, and resonates with Trevisa's focus on the 'profite þat is in slepe'. Early modern dietaries such as Thomas Cogan's *The Haven of Health* (1588) similarly stress sleep's importance for concoction, health and humoral balance.[57] Sleep, according to William Vaughan in 1607, 'strengthenth all the spirits', 'comforteth the body' and has the power to assuage melancholy and anger: sleep 'taketh away sorrow' and 'asswageth furie of the mind'.[58] The benefits of sleep are also voiced in premodern literature, as when Gawain arrives at Hautdesert after his journey through the wilderness in *Sir Gawain and the Green Knight*, and

Bertilak tells him, 'ʒe arn not wel waryst / Nauþer of sostnaunce ne of slepe':[59] here, the lord of Hautdesert's statement about what is needed to be 'wel waryst', or to recover and regain health, focuses on food and sleep together – fittingly, since the benefits of the former can only be properly achieved through the latter. As Chapter 2 demonstrates, this emphasis on proper sleep as sustaining and necessary for health in *Sir Gawain and the Green Knight* is in tension with the romance's focus on the dangers of problematic or improper sleep, just as the beneficial nature of sleep foregrounded by regimenal texts is in tension with their injunctions against sleeping too much or at the wrong time.

'Sorow-makynge' and anger management in Middle English literature

This understanding of the profitability of sleep, particularly in relation to the emotions and mental health, shapes how Middle English literature represents and resolves 'unhealthful' emotions, especially where displays of melancholy or choler are connected to textual concerns with love, loss, or learning. As in the example of Chardri's Seven Sleepers, where emotions are the embodied cause of sleep, sleep can, in turn, restore balance to the humours or emotions. Romances, cycle plays and dream visions draw upon this way in which sleep marks and mediates expressions of sorrow and anger as an embodied language with communicative possibilities that parallel those of swooning. Biblical and literary precedents inform this emphasis, not least when the disciples 'sleep[…] for sorrow' after the Last Supper,[60] but as Chardri's Anglo-Norman saints' lives do, Middle English literary texts often depart from their sources or independently develop a distinctive emphasis on the emotional and epistemological possibilities of sleep. Sleep gives clues to emotional states that are read diegetically (as well as glossed by narrators and in commentaries). For instance, in *Ywain and Gawain*, a maiden interprets Ywain's sleep as a sign of his sorrowful state of mind, commenting that 'Sorow will meng a mans blode / And make him forto wax wode'; in this comment, this early fourteenth-century Middle English romance departs from its source, Chrétien de Troyes' *Yvain*, by adding the detail that sorrow disturbs the blood, thereby explicitly emphasising the humoral, medical understanding of this display of strong emotion and how it engenders sleep.[61]

Sleep offers a means of managing these strong, unhealthy emotions in a way that constitutes a distinctive literary convention, as well as (and underpinned by the way in which it is) a recognisable medical response to a predominance of either yellow or black bile. The fifteenth-century York Cycle of mystery plays offers a demonstration of Chardri's maxim, that 'the weight of worries' or emotions prompts people to slumber, in Pageant 13, 'Joseph's Trouble about Mary'. Joseph is distraught that Mary is having a child that cannot be his; she will only say that it is his and God's, and she, like her ever-present maids, says there is no other man whose child it could have been. Joseph goes for a walk, and his emotional distress culminates in sleep:

> Joseph: Bot or I passe þis hill,
> Do with me what God will,
> Owther more or lesse;
> Here bus me bide full stille
> Till I haue slepid my fille,
> Myn hert so heuy it is.[62]

Here, Joseph says he needs to sleep due to a heavy heart – his emotions, the weight of his cares produce sleep, and sleep in turn (along with a corrective vision from an angel) helps him to regain humoral equilibrium. Strong emotions also precipitate the visionary sleep of Margery Kempe, as when 'sche lay stille [...], wepyng and mornyng for hir synnys, sodeynly sche was in a maner of slep. And anon sche saw, wyth hir gostly eye, owr Lordys body.'[63]

Dream visions also engage with the causal relationship between the emotions and sleep, configuring sleep as not just a simple reflection of the generic necessity for slumber. For instance, the narrator of Chaucer's *Parliament of Fowls* describes his process of falling asleep:

> Berafte me my bok for lak of lyght,
> And to my bed I gan me for to dresse,
> Fulfyld of thought and busy hevynesse;
> For both I hadde thyng which that I nolde,
> And ek I ne hadde that thyng that I wolde.
> But fynally my spirit at the laste,
> For wery of my labour al the day,
> Tok reste, that made me to slepe faste.[64]

Here, by specifying that this narrator falls asleep not only after reading,[65] but, moreover, when he is also 'Fulfyld of thought and busy hevynesse' (as is similarly the case in other Chaucerian dream visions such as the *Book of the Duchess*), Chaucer suggests an affective dimension. 'Hevyness' can of course mean simply 'drowsiness' or 'weight', but this 'thought and busy hevynesse', like Joseph's 'heuy' heart and Chardri's Seven Sleepers' 'pesance' ('heaviness') when they are 'trop dolent' ('very sad'), suggests the word's more affective implications of sorrow, anxiety, or annoyance.[66]

Significantly, then, sleep, like swooning, can be generated as a sudden-onset response to a strong emotion. Critical focus on swooning as a response to emotions in Middle English literature has commonly been on swoons produced by love or other elevated emotions,[67] but recent articles by Judith Weiss and Barry Windeatt have broadened the focus to include swoons generated by less desirable emotions such as sadness and shame.[68] Attending to the ways in which sleep parallels, as well as differs from, swooning as an expression of strong emotion in Middle English literature can deepen our understanding of the emotive scripts to which these two forms of unconsciousness contribute.[69] To fall into a 'swoghe' or to 'swoon' in Middle English can mean either to faint, or to fall asleep, as in the *Gawain*-poet's *Patience*, where Jonah effectively swoons into sleep: 'He swowed and slept sadly al ny3t.'[70] John Capgrave's mid-fifteenth-century *The Life of St Katherine* similarly testifies to the close links between sleep and swooning when specifying that 'Adam slepte in a swow.'[71] While sleep and swooning are conceptually contiguous as embodied means of communicating strong emotions in medieval literature, they were understood to have different scientific causes. Physiologically, swooning was thought to have a variety of possible causes, some of which implicate the swooning subject's affective and ethical state. John Trevisa's *On the Properties of Things* points out that swooning sometimes has mundane causes such as either 'grete replecioun of mete and of drinke' or excessive fasting, but could be caused by emotions such as 'drede that closith the herte swithe', or 'grete ioye other of wrathe that openeth the herte to swithe'.[72] Thus, like sleep, swooning was a recognisable, readable result of strong emotion in medieval medicine.

Malory's capacious *Morte Darthur* offers a useful case study for analysing the distinctive ways in which swooning and sleep mark uncomfortable emotional states in Middle English literature. For instance, when Malory's Guenevere reproaches Launcelot for sleeping with Elaine (a second time), the narrator reports that Launcelot

> toke suche an hartely sorow at her wordys that he felle downe to the floure in a sowne. [...] And whan Sir Launcelot awooke oute of hys swoghe, he lepte oute at a bay wyndow into a gardyne, [...] and so he ranne furth he knew nat whothir, and was as wylde woode as ever was man.[73]

Here, although conscious (if crazed) perambulation is the more prolonged outcome, Launcelot's overwhelming sorrow has its more immediate manifestation in unconsciousness, in the form of a swoon. Similarly, when Guenevere is put in her coffin and Launcelot swoons, a hermit construes the swoon as an indication of unbearable emotion:

> And whan she was put in th'erth Syr Launcelot swouned, and laye longe stylle, whyle the hermyte came and awaked hym, and sayd, 'Ye be to blame, for ye dysplese God with suche maner of sorow-makyng.'
>
> 'Truly,' sayd Syr Launcelot, 'I trust I do not dysplese God, for He knoweth myn entente, for my sorow was not, nor is not, for ony rejoysyng of synne. But my sorow may never have ende.'[74]

Launcelot hastens to inform the hermit that his swooning – his 'sorow-makyng' – is not for the loss of his relationship with Guenevere, which would be sinful; rather, it is for the loss of Arthur and Guenevere together, as a sign of Launcelot's proper, undying loyalty to his sovereigns. However, the hermit's diegetic reading of Launcelot's swoon as a sign of strong emotional response still holds; hermits are, after all, usually good at interpreting. As Barry Windeatt has demonstrated, Malory increases the frequency and intensity of swooning in the final two tales of the *Morte* – *The Book of Launcelot and Guenevere*, and *The Death of Arthur*.[75] For instance, while in Malory's French source, Arthur weeps (but does not swoon) at the death of Gawain – and, in the Alliterative *Morte Arthure*, with which Malory was familiar as the source for his earlier Tale II, Arthur's sorrow at his nephew's death results in one swoon – in Malory's *Morte*, Arthur swoons not once but thrice: 'The kynge made greate sorow oute of mesure, and toke Sir Gawayne in hys armys, and thryse he there sowned.'[76] Here and elsewhere in the final two tales, as Windeatt puts it, 'Malory seems intent on out-swooning his sources'; and while such 'serial swooning' may seem 'comically improbable in "real" life', here in literature it 'betokens and accords value to an estimable intensity of feeling, whether in suffering or joy, love or loss'.[77]

Malory also highlights ethical predicaments through his alterations to representations of swooning and sleep, in ways that show his text's pronounced interest in embodying ideological commentaries. For instance, whereas Malory's English source for the final two tales, the Stanzaic *Morte Arthur*, shows the brother of the knight poisoned by the apple swooning over his sibling's tomb, Malory instead gives Guenevere a swoon when she is accused of having murdered the poisoned knight: here, Guenevere is 'so abaysshed that she cowde none otherwayes do but wepte so hartely that she felle on a swowghe'.[78] As Windeatt sensibly remarks, this is not a gendered translation in Malory's *Morte*; it is, rather, a way of making a swoon serve as an ethical marker as well as an emotional one, since it registers Guenevere's innocence.[79] This also offers a more broadly applicable reminder: where Middle English literary sleep is concerned, emotions and ethics often cannot be easily separated (a point worth emphasising despite the way in which this book necessarily concentrates on emotions and ethics in separate chapters).

Among the variety of significant moments in which sleep, rather than swooning, renders a character's emotional and ethical state legible in the *Morte*, perhaps the most famous is Launcelot's sleep in the 'Tale of the Sankgreal' when the grail makes an appearance. Here, after attempting but failing to enter a chapel, Launcelot is 'passyng hevy and dysmayed' and falls asleep outdoors: 'And so he felle on slepe, and half wakyng and half slepynge he saw [...] the holy vessell of the Sankgreall.'[80] The narrator does mention that 'All thys [vision] Sir Launcelot sye and behylde hit, for he slepte nat veryly', but nonetheless, Launcelot's inability to entirely extricate himself from this sleep is narrated as a sign of his sin: 'he was overtakyn with synne, that he had no power to ryse agayne the holy vessell. Wherefore aftir that many men seyde hym shame.'[81] While elsewhere sleep can facilitate visionary experience, here sleep impedes it. Other characters corroborate a diegetic reading of Launcelot's sleep – a sleep preceded by uncomfortable emotions and dismay – as a sign of his negative ethical state: that is, an indication that Launcelot 'dwellith in som dedly synne' or 'ys unhappy' (unfortunate).[82] In this way, Malorian emotions and ethics are repeatedly made manifest through sleep.[83]

In the Tristram section of Malory's *Morte Darthur*, strong emotion again produces sleep. Launcelot reads a copy of a letter in which King Mark slanders Launcelot and Guenevere, revealing their adulterous affair to Arthur: 'And when he [Launcelot] wyste the entente of the letter he was so wrothe that he layde hym downe on his bed to slepe.'[84] Here, powerful anger – in humoral terms, yellow bile, or a choleric temperament – generates a sleep that makes Lancelot's (un)ethical and affective state legible to both characters and readers. A strong emotion, that is, marks the need for pressing the humoral reset button that sleep entails; sleep offers a form of redress, a way of restoring a more balanced mind. Malory's Launcelot, having earlier in the *Morte* succumbed to the 'grete luste to slepe' that resulted in both himself and his companion being captured by their enemies, seems particularly susceptible to overpowering urges to sleep that reflect on his character. Yet the ways in which Launcelot sleeps, and the ways in which his sleep is read, are also paralleled across Middle English literary genres. One notable difference between Launcelot's sleep here and the moment when he has 'grete luste to slepe' is that, here in his anger-induced sleep, Launcelot sleeps in his bed, rather than outdoors. A bed is, of course, the proper place for sleep, while sleeping outside under a tree was considered dangerous – according to Galenic medicine, and as witnessed elsewhere in romance by the ghastly fate that awaits Heurodis when she falls asleep outside under a tree in *Sir Orfeo*.[85]

However, Malory specifies that this letter is read after morning mass: 'as the kynge and the quene was at masse the varlet cam wyth the lettyrs, and whan masse was done the kynge and the quene opened the lettirs prevayly', and then Guenevere 'sente the lettir unto Sir Launcelot'.[86] Given the great number of events, encounters and jousts that occur in the *Morte* without temporal tags, this seems a telling detail. It notifies the reader that, when Launcelot's anger prompts him to sleep in his bed, it does so in the middle of the day – just as when Launcelot and Heurodis fall asleep outdoors. From a humoral perspective, the fact that it is in the morning that choler dominates correlates with Launcelot's morning surrender to anger-induced sleep. Yet in conduct manuals and dietaries for medieval readers, daytime sleep was explicitly condemned. Kymer's regimen of health offers a typical warning against daytime sleep, instructing its noble addressee that 'fugere debetis de die sompnum meridianum [...], et non dormiatis in mediate post aliquam refectionem' ('you ought to avoid sleeping in the day after noon [...], and you should not sleep in the middle of the day after any meal').[87] As discussed in more detail in Chapter 2, regiminal texts produced for medieval English readers, as well as sermons on idleness, often emphasise that daytime and post-prandial sleep is problematic, making it clear that even if Launcelot sleeps in the proper place when angry, he does not sleep at the proper time. Yet midday sleep may still be seen as helpful for Launcelot here from a medical perspective (if not from a moral one), since his sleep resets his emotions, providing a form of anger management that is healthy for him (and presumably also healthy for others, since he does not resort to violence).[88]

Malory's Arthur, meanwhile, also falls asleep because of his cares in a way that similarly suggests an intertwining of affect and ethics. This occurs when Arthur is out hunting and witnesses the passing of the questing beast:

> therewith the beeste departed with a grete noyse, whereof the kynge had grete mervayle. And so he was in a grete thought, and therewith he felle on slepe.
>
> Ryght so there com a knyght on foote unto Arthure, and seyde, 'Knyght full of thought and slepy, telle me if thou saw any straunge beeste passe thys way.'[89]

While the characteristically indeterminate parataxis of Malory's 'and so' here does not firmly locate the cause of the 'grete thought' that produces Arthur's sleep, the narrator presents two apposite circumstances. The most proximate is Arthur's sight of the questing beast, at which Arthur 'had grete mervayle'; however, we are also told that this hunting trip occurs the morning after Arthur has had a disturbing dream of 'gryffens and serpentes' that do 'grete harme' both to Arthur's people and to Arthur himself.[90] This dream in turn directly follows the incestuous conception of Mordred when Arthur sleeps with his half-sister Morgause, and it is because Arthur is 'passynge hevy of hys dreme' that he decides to go hunting.[91] Thus, Arthur's midday, outdoor sleep brought on by worry or thought seems a testament to his ethical state following this adulterous union. Unlike Launcelot, Arthur is unaware of the extent of the sinfulness of his own adultery (since he does not yet know Morgause is his

Emotions, epistemology and the nature of sleep 65

sister). However, both moments – when a letter reminds Launcelot of the reprehensibility of his affair with Guenevere, and this scene in which Merlin appears to tell Arthur of his true identity and thus the way in which, for Arthur's incestuous adultery, 'hit ys Goddis wylle that youre body sholde be punysshed for your fowle dedis' – are marked by a similar sort of emotion-induced sleep.[92] Moreover, in Malory's French source, *La Suite du Merlin*, Arthur does not fall asleep here; the French Arthur is, instead, merely pensive.[93] Malory, then, creates Arthur's sorrowful sleep, in a way that points up the parallels with Launcelot's angry sleep elsewhere.

Thus, in a romance such as Malory's *Morte*, the implications of sleep and swooning due to uncomfortable emotions are certainly not simple or unidirectional, but attention to the cultural discourses informing contemporary interpretation of such losses of consciousness can enrich our understanding of some of the ways in which both emotions and ethics are anchored in the body.[94] That this discourse often occurs in relation to Launcelot and Arthur, Malory's pre-eminent knight and king, and that Malory increases emphasis on both sleep and swooning relative to his sources, demonstrates that sleep and swooning are central to the *Morte*'s interest in valorising and/or condemning chivalric conduct. Launcelot's swoon at Arthur's and Guenevere's tomb registers his emotion in a way that testifies to his ethical state: he performs the proper response to the loss of his king and queen. Arguably, his earlier swoon when Guenevere reprimands him for his infidelity also reads on an ethical level, as a sign of his proper shame when his misconduct is brought home to him. However, Launcelot's sleep-inducing anger when he reads Mark's revelatory letter reflects less positively on Launcelot; it does not seem to offer an indication of repentance for his adultery, but rather resentment that it has been revealed (by the spiteful King Mark). Equally, Arthur's and Launcelot's troubled sleeps after the conception of Mordred and during the Grail Quest, respectively, occur when they have yet to acknowledge or repent their sins. When the emotional input provoking a bodily response is sorrow, swooning more often seems to register positive ethical states – or moral, remorseful responses to misconduct; while sleep, as a response to either sorrow or anger, more often marks negative ethical states.

Sleep offers a similarly multivalent commentary on moments of distress in *Piers Plowman* and other dream visions in the Plowman tradition. For Langland as for Malory, when emotions such as sorrow and anger produce sleep, sleep can mark a negative ethical state as well as constituting a healthy, beneficial process. Significantly, one of the dream visions in *Piers Plowman* is prompted by Will's affect when

> Scripture scorned me and a skile tolde,
> And lakked me in Latyn and light by me sette,
> And seide, '*Multi multa sciunt et seipsos nesciunt.*'
> Tho wepte I for wo and wraþe of hir speche
> And in a wynkynge worþ til I was aslepe.[95]

Here, when he is rebuked by Scripture for his moral failure, Will's combined sadness and anger seem to precipitate his sleep. That this sleep will be a contemplative sleep containing a dream with positive spiritual connotations does not detract from the fact that the sleep occurs when (and because) Will is in a condition where he could benefit from such a corrective vision. But this makes it all the more remarkable when Will falls asleep due to woe and wrath: as for the York play's Joseph or Malory's Arthur (or the *Pearl* dreamer, as discussed in Chapter 2), to a medieval reader, this affect-induced sleep shows all the more strongly that Will is in need of a corrective. Indeed, the medical 'correction' that sleep offers for an imbalance of the humours parallels the moral corrective that the dream entails. Sleeping, not waking, is when Will can learn what 'Dowel' is. In *Mum and the Sothsegger*, unhappy emotion – in this case, vexation – again seems to prompt the slumber that contains the dream. The narrator lies down in a field, thinks on the state of the world and

> nought the neer by a note *this noyed me ofte*
> That thorough construyng of clercz that knewe alle bokes
> That Mvm shuld be maister moste vppon erthe.
> And ere I were ware, a wynke me assailled,
> That I slepte sadly seuene houres large.
> Thenne mette I of mervailles mo thanne me luste
> To telle or to talke of, til I se tyme.[96]

This poem is, like *Piers Plowman*, about the wrongs of the world, but – unlike *Piers Plowman* – its narrator is not in the wrong (not, for example, deserving of Scripture's scorn). Where the emotion-induced sleep of Langland's dreamer is intertwined with his ethical state, here in *Mum and the Sothsegger* by contrast, the vexation and unhappiness that produces the dreamer's sleep is a testament to the unethical conduct of society at large.

In these various examples – from Will's sorrowful sleep to Joseph's distressed doze and Launcelot's soporific rage – sleep itself is shown to be a good thing, conducive to mental health, even though needing to sleep is often not a positive. While modern criticism may not customarily read Malorian romance in parallel with Ricardian dream visions and mystery plays, the negotiation of sleep's scientific, social and spiritual legibilities across these genres testifies to sleep's broader resonance in the medieval English cultural imagination. The performance of sleep generates ideological commentaries and subjectivities. Sleep is, of course, particularly generative when it features a dream: in the Piers Plowman tradition, sleep convenes moral instruction (as discussed further in Chapter 2), whereas for Chaucer's dream vision narrators, the way in which sleep mediates unhappy emotions shapes the matter of poetry (see Chapter 4).

Desiring sleep, desiring truth

What does it mean to desire sleep in Middle English literature? And how does sleep relate to desires for truth? Lulled to sleep on a grassy bank by a stream on a sunny summer's day, Langland's dreamer approaches truth. Desiring sleep in this *locus amoenus*, Will has his first vision of Truth, inhabiting the 'tour on a toft' and representing God the Father; slightly later in the poem, truth is also re-articulated as the code of conduct for the chivalric classes, who ought 'to serven truthe ever'.[97] Yet it is not only in relation to dreams that sleep poses questions about knowledge and veracity, and how they are apprehended. This section considers some of the other ways in which the question of accessing sleep, and the question of what can be accessed through sleep, are both inherently epistemological.

Sleep and insomnia both reveal 'truths' about the body that performs them. While sleep often features in Middle English literature as a beneficial, embodied mediation of strong emotions, depictions of insomnia foreground how the restoration sleep promises is desired but not always easy to obtain. Insomnia offers culturally coded insights into the sleep-desiring subject just as sleep itself does, bodying forth emotional states, implicated consciences or diseases that cannot be concealed or disguised. In medieval medical texts, while sleeping to excess is physiologically and socially insalubrious, insomnia is also unhealthy and lamentable. In the ways that sleep is natural, insomnia is unnatural. In regimenal texts, being unable to sleep at night, or replacing nocturnal sleep with waking activities to a significant degree, is also seen as deleterious and problematic. As Kymer puts it:

> de vigiliar*is* instanciis et nocturnis inco*n*gruis nut*ricionem* impedientibus quibus nocte*m* vertitis in die*m* qu*ia* si illas celerus no*n* dimisert*is* amara defelebit*is* inco*m*moda senectutis.[98]
>
> (concerning wakefulness that is persistent and incongruous with night-time due to the fostering of hindrances by which you turn the night into day, if you do not dismiss them swiftly, you will weep the bitter inconveniences of old age.)

Lack of night-time sleep, that is, can make one less healthy and less strong. Kymer's advice here – seeking to counter drinking and sexual appetites in particular – focuses on the problems that arise when sleep is passed over in favour of other desires. Regimenal texts also focus on the problems experienced by those who wish to sleep, but cannot. Among the more mundane, external causes of insomnia were restless bedfellows, or noises such as passing watchmen in cities.[99] Trevisa's chapter 'De vigilia', on waking (as the other component of the 'non-natural' to which sleep belongs), observes that an excess of waking at night is problematic for health, and can be caused by internal disturbances such as anxiety, madness, sorrow, or overindulgence.[100] As a result of insomnia, Trevisa cautions, 'ful yuele sikenes brediþ in þe body':

> Wakynge ouer mesure is defaute of myȝt to slepe and is an yuel of þe brayne contrary to litargye. And þis euel comeþ of to grete meuynge of þe brayne and drynes of reed colera oþir blake, of inteperat hete, and of to salte humours. Of alle þis comeþ inordinat wakinge, and agwisch folowiþ, colour changiþ, and besy þouȝtis encresiþ and rauynge and vnresonable suspeciouns.[101]

Sleep deprivation, then, is both caused by, and can lead to, mental disturbances. That insomnia was itself a form of suffering is highlighted by the way in which sleep deprivation was figured as one of the torments endured by Christ during the Passion.[102] In medieval medical literature, insomnia, as involuntary wakefulness, features as a disease of sleep, and can also be caused by fevers and lovesickness.[103] It is the dryness of melancholy that can induce insomnia, as sleep requires moist vapours rising to the brain.[104] Thus, while the previous sections have explored how strong emotions (sorrow, anger) can produce sleep (for Malory's Launcelot and Chardri's Seven Sleepers), strong emotions can also produce insomnia (in Chaucer's *Book of the Duchess*, and other explorations of melancholy or lovesickness).

Ideas of nature and the natural are explicitly intertwined with sleep and insomnia, with when one should sleep (but cannot), in medieval and early modern English literary texts as in medical ones. For instance, in the *Book of the Duchess*, Chaucer's narrator figures his insomnia or 'defaute of slep' as contrary to nature:

> And wel ye woot, agaynes kynde
> Hyt were to lyven in thys wyse,
> For nature wolde nat suffyse
> To noon erthly creature
> Nat longe tyme to endure
> Withoute slep and be in sorwe.
> And I ne may, ne nyght ne morwe,
> Slepe.[105]

Similarly, when Shakespeare's King Henry IV wishes he were better acquainted with sleep, apostrophising it as 'O sleep, O gentle sleep', he describes sleep as 'nature's soft nurse'.[106] Here, King Henry's commentary on his anxiety-induced insomnia – 'uneasy lies the head that wears a crown'[107] – is shaped by the same medical understanding of sleep as natural and nurturing as in late medieval English treatments of sleep.[108] Thomas Cogan's *The Haven of Health*, published in 1588, declares that 'We must follow the course of nature', and nature decrees that it is right 'to wake in the day, and sleepe in the night'.[109] The Doctor calls Lady Macbeth's sleepwalking – her habit of waking while sleeping – 'A great perturbation in nature, to receive at once the benefit of sleep and do the effects of watching.'[110] As discussed in more detail in the Coda, in *Macbeth* sleep is the natural, normative state that is ruptured by the disorder and transgressive actions of the Macbeths; sleep is an object of desire, representing peace (both personal and societal). In Galenic medicine, sleepwalking was explained as 'sleep fighting', an active phenomenon that was caused by a smokiness of the humours and an imbalance that excited the imagination.[111] The 'nature' that is perturbed by Lady Macbeth's actions (her ruptured sleep, and her regicide) is the nature of both the humoral body and the body politic.

Nocturnal waking, however, is also sometimes depicted as natural, at least for birds and courtly lovers. The 'General Prologue' to the *Canterbury Tales*, of course, begins by stating that

> smale foweles maken melodye
> That slepen al the nyght with open ye
> So Priketh hem Nature in hir corages.[112]

To sleep as little as a bird is to sleep in a way that is normal for creatures in tune with nature; they are by disposition prone to sleep less or more lightly. Chaucer's Squire, meanwhile, is said to sleep as little as the nightingale:

> So hoote he lovede that by nyghtertale
> He sleep namoore than dooth a nyghtyngale.[113]

This suggests that it is natural for lovers to be awake during the night. However, in the way that lovesickness was sometimes seen as a disease, it also shaped pathological descriptions of debilitating insomnia such as the representations of Chaucer's pining lovers Arcite and Troilus. In the 'Knight's Tale', when the disease of lovesickness renders Arcite's appearance and voice unrecognisable, Chaucer specifies that amongst his symptoms, 'His slep, his mete, his drynke, is hym biraft,/That lene he wex and drye as is a shaft'.[114] Lovesick insomnia becomes a tableau later in the 'Knight's Tale' in the ekphrastic description of the temple of Venus, where 'maystow se/Wroght on the wal, ful pitous to biholde,/The broken slepes and the sykes colde'.[115] Those unable to sleep are rendered available for the gaze as a pitiable sight; the acts and appearance of insomniacs are truthful, visual clues to their own emotions, and cues for the emotions they ought to elicit.

Sleep has other epistemic relationships with truth, as literary deployments of sleep – especially metaphorical sleep – also arbitrate desires to discover external truths. Sleep can be the enemy of truth, but it can also be the means of accessing, or displaying, truth. In some (biblical) traditions, sleep prevents perception, since sleep represents a lack of vigilance (as per Gregory the Great's *Pastoral*

Care),[116] and since sleep is the state from which one must 'awaken' in order to perceive doctrinal truths. For instance, in the Wakefield *Prima Pastorum* play, when the shepherds awake from their sleep, they find they are able to quote prophecies previously unknown to them, including Virgil's messianic Eclogue. Although this invokes a motif of 'awakening to the incarnation', the Wakefield example suggests that the shepherds have gained knowledge through their sleep, not (only) after it; sleep features as a state of enlightenment. As a discourse of critique, figurative sleep can also shape analysis or lamentation of the absence of loyalty or love, of social order or of divine providence. For example, in Peter Idley's *Instructions to His Son*, anxieties about the lack of social stability in Wars of the Roses England are expressed by the idea that truth is asleep:

> lawe must nedis be kepte
> Or ellis the londe were soone ouerthrowe;
> Awake trouthe that longe hath slepte.[117]

Truth, of course, has many guises in late medieval England: intellectual (or factual) and legal, but more importantly, theological and – here – ethical, in the sense of integrity.[118] Similarly, in the fifteenth-century political poem 'Take Good Heed', an admonition to Yorkist leaders to beware promises of good faith made by their enemies deploys the language of sleep:

> Trust not to moche in the fauour of youre foos,
> ffor þei be double in wirking, as þe worlde gos,
> Promysing feithfully obesisaunce to kepe,
> But perfite loue in þeire hertis is leyde for to slepe.[119]

Sleep, here, encapsulates the absence or fickleness of loyalties; it communicates a disillusioned cynicism, but it is also a means of expressing a desire to know the truth of what is in others' 'hertis'. Elsewhere, sleep offers a way of revealing, rather than a language of lamenting, truths about identity and integrity. Sleep bodies forth truths that cannot be concealed, as when the sleeping Havelok in the thirteenth-century romance *Havelok the Dane* inadvertently reveals his true nature while sleeping: while he is fast asleep, his royal nature shines forth from his mouth, a light 'swilk so the sunne-bem' that in turn leads to the discovery of the king-mark on his shoulder.[120] Sleep can reveal truths about the sleeping subject which s/he might be unable or unwilling to disclose through conscious will; sleep, here, does not deceive.[121]

Of course, sometimes 'sleep' is not actually sleep. Sleep and death have expressive symmetries in medieval and early modern literature. Those who are in fact merely sleeping can appear to be dead – as given expression most famously in Shakespeare's *Romeo and Juliet*, when the heroine drinks a potion that creates an unnatural sleep, tricking her beloved into thinking she has died. And in medieval representations, the appearance of natural sleep can connote sanctity. For instance, in the late fourteenth-century alliterative poem *St Erkenwald*, an unnamed saint, when disinterred, is said to look as though he has been only sleeping: he is 'als freshe hyn þe face [...] / As he in sounde sodanly were slippid opon slepe'.[122] The semblance of sleep, here, ennobles death; death that resembles sleep implies a spiritual purity that can preserve bodily integrity. On the one hand, the phrase 'dead sleep' often simply means sound sleep, as when Gower's Amans and Chaucer's Criseyde are, respectively, taken by 'the dede slep'.[123] On the other hand, sleep, as a signifier, can stand in for death, in a figure of speech common in Middle English and early modern literature: from the fourteenth-century *Prik of Conscience*'s 'In pouder sal slepe ilk man, / And wormes sal cover hym þan' and the fifteenth-century *Everyman*'s 'in to this cave must I crepe / And tourne to erth, and there to slepe', to *Hamlet*'s 'To die, to sleep. [...] For in that sleep of death what dreams may come / When we have shuffled off this mortal coil / Must give us pause'.[124] *The Tempest* offers another well-known example when Prospero says to Ferdinand, 'We are such stuff / As dreams are made on, and our little life / Is rounded with a sleep'.[125] A comparison between sleep and death is conventional, with biblical precedents including 1 Thess 4:12, 'And we will not have you ignorant brethren, concerning them that are asleep, that you be not sorrowful'.[126] Where saintly corpses can appear to be merely sleeping, to say that someone who has died is merely sleeping is elsewhere to open up the possibility of their return, as in the nationalistic legends that deceased heroes such as King Arthur or Owain Glyndŵr will return at the hour of their country's greatest need to bring succour. Just as when we say that something is 'dormant', we imply that its state of inactivity is temporary, sleep is a liminal state, 'the space in between',[127] which carries the potential for transformation, and connotes value.

The idea of sleep, then, can encode powerful desires for salvation in this life, as well as the next.

'of that I seigh slepynge': dreams and the medieval imagination

In medieval depictions, sleep also offers access to truth in the form of divine revelations or dream visions. While sleep is characterised by the inactivity of the rational faculty and a closing of the senses, including sight (due to the smokiness that blocks passageways in the brain during sleep),[128] sleep is nonetheless, as Langland's Will puts it, a state in which one might be able to perceive more than one could waking. Sleep frequently opens up channels of seeing in *Piers Plowman*: Will wishes he had 'yseighen moore' before waking, and when he falls asleep again he 'saugh [...] muche moore'.[129] When Will wakes due to the debate between Piers and a priest, he finds himself

> Metelees and moneiless on Malverne hulles,
> Musynge on this metels a myle wey ich yede.
> Many tyme this metels hath maked me to studie
> Of that I seigh slepynge – if it so be myghte.[130]

Here, Langland foregrounds the value of what one can 'see' while sleeping – while one's eyes are shut – and of the learning such seeing can provoke. This is, of course, a reference to the dreams that occur during Will's sleep, but, as this section shows, it is not insignificant that his focus is explicitly on what is enabled by sleep, rather than dreams.

While it is on one level a statement of the obvious to say that dreams take place during sleep, the ways in which it was obvious to late medieval people that dreams were shaped by sleep, through contemporary understandings of physiology and psychology, invite more attention. Dreams were understood to result from the same moist humours rising to the head that produce sleep; these moist humours block the external senses, meaning that the mind no longer receives external stimuli. In medieval psychology, mental processing occurs through the three 'inward wits', *phantasia*, *cogitatio* and *memoria*, or imagination, cognition and memory; the imagination, which while waking perceives external stimuli, in sleep instead can perceive the internal creations of dreams.[131] The imagination – including dreams – was understood as visual, formed of images stored in the mind and recombined or altered while asleep: as Trevisa puts it, 'in slepinge þe spirit seeþ þe ymage of þinges', and while asleep, the visionary Margery Kempe sees 'wyth hir gostly eye'.[132] Thus, sleep has an important role to play in the medieval 'imagination', understood as a cognitive faculty as well as a cultural horizon of expectation. Sleep, although in some ways a state marked by incapacity and irrationality, also enables vision and understanding.

Dreams offer access to different types of knowledge, including supernatural visions (whether divine or demonic) and revelations of external truths (such as prophecies), but also to a dreamer's past or embodied preoccupations. Two central approaches to interpreting dreams and their putative truth-value inherited by the later Middle Ages differ as to whether or not dreams resulting from the dreamer's own preoccupations are valued. Much attention has been given to medieval discussions of the origins of dreams thought to result from divine visions or prophetic encounters, following the theories of Macrobius in particular. However, as Steven Kruger has shown, in medieval mentalities, valuable dreams could also result from the preoccupations of body or mind, a view that drew especially on Aristotle's *Parva Naturalia*.[133] As I argue in Chapter 4, the late medieval reclamation of Aristotle's works, as part of a 'growing tendency to associate dreams with somatic and psychological process',[134] are particularly significant for an understanding of Chaucer's dream visions, which have primarily been read in relation to Macrobius's theories. Kruger's argument is an important precedent for my own, though he does not offer a reading either of Chaucer's dream visions or of sleep. In the theories that did accord significance to dreams arising from within the dreamer, sleep is especially important: not just as a platform allowing access to revelations, but as a process shaping (or we might even say 'cooking', via concoction) the dreamer's embodied experience into the dream.

Whereas after Freud and Jung, twenty-first century approaches prioritise the ways in which dreams give insight into psychological preoccupations and processes, in the Middle Ages, some of the dominant philosophies of dreams created hierarchies of their origins that disregarded those generated by the dreamer, in favour of privileging external, supernatural sources for dreams.[135] Late antique, neoplatonic writers such as Macrobius and Calcidius, and the patristic authorities Augustine and Gregory the Great, wrote hierarchical classifications of dreams known and respected in the later Middle Ages, and in which divine or spiritual visions were the most prized.[136] Macrobius's c.400 *Commentary on the Dream of Scipio* was not the first or only late antique classification of the types and causes of dreams as either true and reliable (of divine origin) or false or unknowable (of mundane origin), but his version of this theory was transmuted to the later Middle Ages. Macrobius's *Commentary* was known in England by the eleventh century at the latest,[137] and popularised (for modern critics as for late medieval readers) thanks to Chaucer's name-dropping of Macrobius in his dream poetry.[138] Macrobius classifies dreams into five types, and dismisses two of these:

> there is the enigmatic dream, in Greek *oneiros*, in Latin *somnium*; second, there is the prophetic vision, in Greek *horama*, in Latin *visio*; third, there is the oracular dream, in Greek *chrematismos*, in Latin *oraculum*; fourth, there is the nightmare, in Greek *enypnion*, in Latin *insomnium*; and last, the apparition, in Greek *phantasma*, which Cicero, when he has occasion to use the word, calls *visum*. The last two, the nightmare and the apparition, are not worth interpreting since they have no prophetic significance.[139]

Dreams in poems such as Chaucer's *Book of the Duchess* can fit within the purview of dreams that Macrobius deems 'worth interpreting', as an 'enigmatic' dream that

> conceals with strange shapes and veils with ambiguity the true meaning of the information being offered, and requires an interpretation for its understanding.[140]

However, where Macrobius was only interested in dreams with supernatural origins and prophetic significance, another view of dreams, valuing those of somatic origin, developed from Aristotle's thinking.

Aristotle's theory of dreams – recopied and developed in the later Middle Ages – connected the content of dreams to the dreamer's psychology and physiology, rather than derogating the value of embodied or mundane causes.[141] Aristotle was sceptical that dreams could have divine origins,[142] and his treatises also differ from our post-Freudian inclination to privilege dreams over sleep; instead, 'they ascribe the greatest significance to sleep', and 'regard dreams as something that can only be understood if sleep itself is understood'.[143] According to Aristotle, 'an appearance in sleep (whether it occurs simply or in some particular way) is what we call a dream – it is plain that dreaming is the work of the perceptual part, but belongs to this part in its imagining capacity', and 'what a dream is, and how it occurs, we may best study from the circumstances attending sleep'.[144] Dreams, that is, are the result of lingering (and potentially distorted) 'sense-impressions', received while waking and re-presented through the process of sleep. Aristotle's *Parva Naturalia* had been translated into Latin by the beginning of the thirteenth century, after which numerous other Latin versions and commentaries proliferated; works such as Bartholomaeus Anglicus's *De proprietatibus rerum*, and Trevisa's translation, incorporated Aristotelian views on dreams.[145] Connections between mind and body were also reinforced by other Greek and Arabic texts made available to the Latin West through translation in the twelfth century, including both Aristotle's *De anima* and Avicenna's Aristotelian psychology, in which – in contradistinction to Plato or the neoplatonic writers – the soul is viewed as closely linked to the body.[146] This linkage also informs Aquinas's view of bodily sleep as a remedy for sorrow in the soul, cited earlier; Aquinas similarly asserts that 'dreams have their causes in waking people's imagination'.[147]

While Aristotle was less interested in dreams themselves than in the physiological insights they could offer, thirteenth- and fourteenth-century thinkers incorporated his work on the embodied causes of dreams in a way that did ascribe value to these sorts of dreams. For Aristotle, dreams often give insight into illness, and can be used in medical diagnoses, as symptoms or warning signs; for Galen, dreams similarly demonstrate the condition of the dreamer's body, and register any disturbance in the balance of the humours.[148] Stephen Kruger notes that 'in twelfth-century dream theory, the new medicine and Aristotelian philosophy were indeed often invoked along with Neoplatonic material to explain the bodily involvement in the processes of sleep and dreaming. We perceive, during the twelfth century, a clear "somaticization" of certain aspects of dream theory', which thirteenth and fourteenth-century writers on dreams reinforced.[149] According to the thirteenth-century physician Arnoldus de Villa Nova, who translated medical texts by Galen and Avicenna, dreams arising from the humours and from 'distracting physical and mental experiences' are called natural dreams, as opposed to doctrinal dreams.[150] These theories formed part of the way in which, in the central and later Middle Ages, 'more attention was devoted to dreams deriving solely from the human being, his or her mind and body'.[151] As Pertelote knowingly observes in Chaucer's 'Nun's Priest's Tale',

> the humour of malencolie
> Causeth ful many a man in sleep to crie
> For feere of blake beres, or boles blake,
> Or elles blake develes wole hem take.
> Of othere humours koude I telle also
> That werken many a man sleep ful wo.[152]

While Pertelote speaks scornfully, this also reminds us that Chaucer could expect his readers to be familiar with theories of the somatic origins of dreams, including the way in which dreams caused by certain humours were thought to focus on particular themes or images.

Chaucer's contemporary, Trevisa, discusses the various embodied origins and causes of dreams in *De proprietatibus rerum* in ways that gives purchase to the theories of both Macrobius and Aristotle:

> somtyme such sweuenes comeþ of to moche replecioun oþir of to grete fastinge, and somtyme of grete ymaginacioun and þouȝt þat is toforehonde in wakynge. [...] Also diuers sweuenes comeþ of diuers causes, somtyme of complexioun, as he þat is *sanguineus* haþ glad and likinge sweuenes, *malancolius* metiþ of sorwe, *colericus* of fire and of firy þinges, and *flewmaticus* of reyne and snowe, and of watres and of watery þinges and of oþire such. And so eueriche man metiþ sweuenes acordinge to his complecioun, witt, and age. And somtyme sweuenes comeþ of appetite, affeccioun, and desire, as he þat is anhongred metiþ of mete, and a dronken man þat is aþurst metiþ of drinke [...]. Somtyme of gret study and þouȝt iset on a þing, as a coueitous man alwey metiþ of golde.[153]

Trevisa, that is, 'strongly emphasises the dream's involvement in corporeality', while also citing Augustine's views on the possibility of supernatural origins – whether divine or demonic – for dreams:[154]

> Somtyme sweuenes beþ trewe and somtyme fals, somtyme clere and playne and somtyme troubly. Sweuenes þat beþ trewe buþ somtyme

opun and playne and somtyme iwrappid in figuratif, mistik, and dim and derke tokenynges and bodinges.[155]

Trevisa, then, recognises the difficulty of both interpreting the meaning, and determining the truth-value, of dreams. Alongside these hermeneutic reflections – testifying to contemporary interest in, as well as recognition of the ambiguity of, dreams – most significant for my purposes is Trevisa's emphasis on the dreamer's individual humoral disposition and also any subject to which s/he might have devoted 'gret study and þouȝt' as causes of dreams. Though it has not been well recognised in criticism, Chaucer's dream visions – especially the *Book of the Duchess* and the *Parliament of Fowls* – engage with exactly these sorts of causes for dreams, exploring how the dreamer's lived experience can be transmuted into, and mediated by, the dream.

Moreover, while one of my aims here is to show that there are new insights to be gained about Middle English dream visions when we attend to the understudied role of sleep in that genre, it is not my intent to suggest that sleep matters only inasmuch as it enables and shapes dreams. At the beginning of Pars Secunda of Chaucer's 'Squire's Tale', when everyone falls asleep after a feast, the tale's focus on sleep – 'the norice of digestioun, the sleep' – might, in a different story, be the prelude to a dream vision.[156] However, Chaucer uses the 'Squire's Tale' to satirise the respect for that genre, just as he uses the 'Squire's Tale' to mock Arthurian literature and its 'olde' or 'deed' representatives, Gawain and Launcelot.[157] Here, when everyone falls asleep, the narrator comments:

> Hire dremes shul nat now been told for me;
> Ful were hire heddes of fumositee,
> That causeth dreem of which ther nys no charge.[158]

Dreams could be narrated, but will not be, because – here at least – they have 'no charge': no significance.[159] The product of wine fumes, these dreams are not to be fetishised. Rather than engendering a dream vision, this sleep goes on too long, producing an ethical commentary instead:

> They slepen til that it was pryme large,
> The mooste part, but it were Canacee.
> She was ful mesurable, as wommen be;

> For of hir fader hadde she take leve
> To goon to reste soone after it was eve.
> Hir liste nat appalled for to be,
> Ne on the morwe unfeestlich for to se,
> And slepte hire firste sleep, and thanne awook.[160]

This commentary about the length and timing of sleep marks Canacee out as more temperate than other members of her father's court, who have overindulged during a feast and in the slumber that follows it. When, and for how long, figures sleep in late medieval English society and literature are indices of ethical and spiritual (and emotional) well-being, as well as of physical health. Following this chapter's consideration of the medical, emotional and epistemic dimensions of sleep, the next two chapters consider, respectively, sleep's ethical dimensions and its spatial dimensions in more detail across a range of genres, before these strands are drawn together to address in full the implications of sleep in Chaucer's dream visions.

Notes

1 Chardri, *La Vie des Set Dormanz*, ed. Brian S. Merrilees (London: Anglo-Norman Text Society, 1977), ll. 615–20; *The Works of Chardri: The Little Debate, The Life of the Seven Sleepers, and The Life of St Josaphaz*, ed. and trans. Neil Cartlidge (Tempe, AR: Arizona Centre for Medieval and Renaissance Studies, 2015), p. 50.
2 See Carolyn Dinshaw, *How Soon Is Now? Medieval Texts, Amateur Readers, and the Queerness of Time* (London: Duke University Press, 2012), pp. 55–9.
3 'It sometimes happens that on account of sorrow and anxiety people find it easy to fall suddenly asleep': *Josaphaz*, ll. 1943–4; Cartlidge, *The Works of Chardri*, pp. 101–2.
4 England may have been at the forefront of Western Europe's acquisition of this learning. As Charles Burnett has shown, the twelfth-century English manuscripts in this medical tradition are contemporary with, or precede, manuscripts surviving from Italy and elsewhere, and 'works supposedly written by Salernitan masters include English words. One can only suppose that the contacts between England and South Italy were very close': Charles Burnett, *The Introduction of Arabic Learning into England* (London: British Library, 1997), p. 28; see also Shazia Jagot, '*Fin*' amors, Arabic Learning, and the Islamic World

in the Work of Geoffrey Chaucer' (PhD dissertation, University of Leicester, 2013), esp. p. 34.

5 Cartlidge, *The Works of Chardri*, p. 8.

6 For a late medieval English discussion of mental illness, see Hoccleve's reflections on 'the þouȝtful maladie', melancholia: Thomas Hoccleve, 'My compleinte', in *'My Compleinte' and Other Poems*, ed. Roger Ellis (Exeter: Exeter University Press, 2001), pp. 115–27, l. 21. Given the connections between mind, body and affect in medieval thought, Corinne Saunders has cautioned against applying the 'modern distinction between physical and mental illness' to the Middle Ages; medieval views of mental health instead considered an imbalance in the humours, a strong emotion, and illness as all, in some ways, synonymous or coterminous: Saunders, 'Bodily Narratives', p. 177, and 'Mind, Body and Affect', p. 32; see also Rawcliffe, 'The Concept of Health in Late Medieval Society'.

7 On science ('in the Aristotelian sense of a body of knowledge') and medicine as part of natural philosophy, see Siraisi, *Medieval and Early Renaissance Medicine*, pp. 23–4.

8 Chaucer, *Canterbury Tales*, I.416; Corinne Saunders, *Magic and the Supernatural in Medieval English Romance* (Cambridge: D. S. Brewer, 2010), p. 101.

9 *On the Properties of Things: John Trevisa's Translation of Bartholomæus Anglicus De Proprietatibus Rerum*, ed. M. C. Seymour et al., 2 vols (Oxford: Clarendon Press, 1975), I, 331.37.

10 *Middle English Dictionary*, 'kinde' as noun, 1(a), 2(a) and 3(a); also, as adjective, 5(a) and 6(a). The heightened lexical charge of 'kynde' as 'nature' is familiar from Langland's *Piers Plowman*; examples of 'kynde' as 'benevolent' include Chaucer's Wife of Bath's Prologue, 'After that day we hadden never debaat. / God helpe me so, I was to hym as kynde / As any wyf from Denmark unto Ynde, / And also trewe' (III.822–5), and Malory's 'Tale of Sir Gareth', when, after Gareth's and Gawain's duel ends with their discovery that they are brothers, 'eythir of them gaff other the pryse of the batayle, and there were many kynde wordys betwene them' (*Morte Darthur*, 282.31–2).

11 Medieval thought distinguished between healthful and unhealthful passions, or emotions: 'In terms of hygiene, there were healthful passions, such as joy, which had no contraindications. [...] There were other, unhealthful passions, chief among them sorrow and anxiety, two states of mind contrary to vital dynamism, which tended to chill and dry out the body and heart. [... another] unhealthful passion was wrath, characterized by a faster and centripetal movement of heat and spirits. [...] The attitudes of physicians towards wrath were varied.

Some felt that its effects were harmful to health and warned against it; others felt that in certain situations an outburst of wrath might be a good thing. To soothe a state of wrath, physicians recommended music, reading, and especially a sound and restorative sleep': Sotres, 'The Regimens of Health', pp. 313–14.
12 Gilbert Hay's *Buik of Alexander*, l. 16240; for discussion, see Aisling Byrne, *Otherworlds: Fantasy and History in Medieval Literature* (Oxford: Oxford University Press, 2016), p. 138.
13 *The Book of the Duchess*, 571.
14 Chaucer, *Canterbury Tales*, I.429–34; see Huling E. Ussery, *Chaucer's Physician: Medicine and Literature in Fourteenth-Century England* (New Orleans, LA: Tulane University, 1971), and Jagot, 'The Islamic World in the Work of Geoffrey Chaucer', esp. p. 20.
15 The *Gouernayle of Helthe*, the simplified version of the *Regimen Sanitatis Salernitanum* (a late medieval treatise on general hygiene), lists some medical authorities known in the Middle Ages, including 'Bernard Austyn Plato Tholome Sidrac Arystotell Auyven Galyen and Ypocras among oder diu[erse] acording to the same': p. 10 of the *Gouernayle*, in BL Sloane MS 989 (fifteenth century).
16 Through Byzantine compilers such as Paul of Aegina (625–90), Greek medical texts were absorbed into the Arabic world, and the combined Greek and Arabic medical tradition later entered the medieval west thanks to translation activities in the late eleventh century (in southern Italy) and the mid-twelfth century (in Spain). See Carol Falvo Heffernan, *The Melancholy Muse: Chaucer, Shakespeare and Early Medicine* (Pittsburgh, PA: Duquesne University Press, 1995), esp. pp. 13–19; William F. MacLehose, 'Fear, Fantasy and Sleep in Medieval Medicine', in Elena Carrera (ed.), *Emotions and Health, 1200–1700*, pp. 67–94; see also Siraisi, *Avicenna in Renaissance Italy*.
17 Sotres, 'The Regimens of Health', p. 294.
18 Western writers referred to the physician Ibn Sina (c.980–1037) as Avicenna, and Haly Abbas is 'the usual Latin rendering of the name of 'Ali ibn al-'Abbas al-Majusi, the court physician at Shiraz'; the latter wrote a medical book in the late 900s (*The Royal Book*), part of which was translated into Latin by Constantine the African (d. 1087), and a complete version of which was made by Stephen the Philosopher in 1127 and printed at Venice in 1492: E. Ruth Harvey, *The Inward Wits: Psychological Theory in the Middle Ages and the Renaissance* (London: Warburg Institute, 1975), p. 13.
19 MacLehose, 'Fear, Fantasy and Sleep in Medieval Medicine', pp. 74–5.
20 Sotres, 'The Regimens of Health', p. 294; Harvey, *The Inward Wits*, p. 18.

21 *Galen: Selected Works*, trans. P. N. Singer (Oxford: Oxford University Press, 1997); see also Dannenfeldt, 'Sleep: Theory and Practice in the Late Renaissance', pp. 415–16, and Siraisi, *Medieval and Early Renaissance Medicine*, p. 101.
22 Galen, *Selected Works*, pp. 375–6.
23 Blood was moist and hot; phlegm was moist and cold; black bile was dry and cold; and yellow bile was dry and moist. On the four humours themselves, see Walter Clyde Curry, *Chaucer and the Medieval Sciences*, 2nd edn (1926; Barnes & Noble, 1960), esp. pp. 10–14. Razes (as he was known to the West; or Abu Bakr Muhammad ibn Zakariyya al-Razi), a physician and medical writer of the early 900s, drawing upon Galen, 'reduces all of the diseases of temperament to their excess qualities: thus heat causes melancholy cogitation, and, with dryness, insomnia; because moisture always causes sleep. Cold and dryness causes sloth; cold and moisture, a profound lethargy': Harvey, *The Inward Wits*, p. 12.
24 Heffernan, *The Melancholy Muse*, p. 7.
25 Sotres, 'The Regimens of Health', pp. 296–302.
26 See Daniel Wakelin, *Humanism, Reading, and English Literature 1430–1530* (Oxford: Oxford University Press, 2007). Educated at Oxford, Kymer (d. 1463) had a career as chancellor of the university of Oxford (1431–4) and dean of Salisbury (from 1449); he was also a prominent physician, working to regulate and educate medical practicioners in London in the 1420s, serving Humphrey Duke of Gloucester and attending King Henry VI as a physician in 1455. See Faye Getz, 'Kymer, Gilbert (d. 1463)', in *Dictionary of National Biography*, online edition (Oxford, 2004), www.oxforddnb.com (accessed 17 April 2019).
27 As Heffernan observes, with specific reference to melancholy, late medieval and early modern literary writing about the emotions could be informed by medical knowledge without the authors necessarily having book learning of, or formal instruction in, medicine: *The Melancholy Muse*, pp. 3–4.
28 Heffernan, *The Melancholy Muse*, p. 27; see also Jagot, '*Fin' amors*, Arabic Learning, and the Islamic World in the Work of Geoffrey Chaucer'.
29 Chaucer, *Canterbury Tales*, I.419–21. The medical knowledge of Chaucer's Physician is discussed in Curry, *Chaucer and the Mediaeval Sciences*, pp. 3–37, and Ussery, *Chaucer's Physician*.
30 Saunders, 'Mind, Body and Affect', p. 46. On the popular reception and practice of medicine in later medieval England, see also Saunders, 'Bodily Narratives', pp. 178–9; and, on late medieval distinctions between university-educated physicians, non-university educated surgeons, and 'lesser' healers or 'leeches', see Ussery, *Chaucer's Physician*, pp. 5–31.

31 MacLehose, 'Fear, Fantasy and Sleep in Medieval Medicine', pp. 90–1.
32 Siraisi, *Medieval and Early Renaissance Medicine*, p. 106; Sotres, 'The Regimens of Health'; Curry, *Chaucer and the Medieval Sciences*, pp. 203–4.
33 On how the process of digestion transformed food into the four humours, see Rawcliffe, 'The Concept of Health in Late Medieval Society', esp. pp. 318–19.
34 Siraisi, *Medieval and Early Renaissance Medicine*, p. 106.
35 Chaucer, 'Squire's Tale', V.347.
36 MacLehose, 'Fear, Fantasy and Sleep in Medieval Medicine'; Sotres, 'The Regimens of Health'; Curry, *Chaucer and the Medieval Sciences*, pp. 203–4.
37 Trevisa, *De Proprietatibus Rerum*, 332.4–6.
38 On the circulation and reception of Aristotle's writings in England from the thirteenth century, see Dorothee Metlitzki, *The Matter of Araby in Medieval England* (London: Yale University Press, 1977), esp. pp. 47–9; see also *Aristotle on Sleep and Dreams*, trans. David Gallop (Warminster: Aris & Phillips, 1996).
39 Marcia Sà Cavalcante Schuback, 'The Hermeneutic Slumber: Aristotle's Reflections on Sleep', trans. David Payne, in Claudia Baracchi (ed.), *The Bloomsbury Companion to Aristotle* (London: Bloomsbury, 2014), pp. 128–43 (p. 129).
40 Schuback, 'Aristotle's Reflections on Sleep', p. 131.
41 Kemp, *Medieval Psychology*, p. 21; Harvey, *The Inward Wits*, p. 19. See, for instance, Arnold of Villanova's *Speculum medicinae*, as discussed by Sotres, 'The Regimens of Health', p. 310, and Thomas Aquinas's *Opera omnia*, as discussed by Curry, *Chaucer and the Medieval Sciences*, pp. 204–5.
42 Schuback, 'Aristotle's Reflections on Sleep', p. 134.
43 Sotres, 'The Regimens of Health', p. 310.
44 'As early as 1330, the English term "disease" referred to an internal imbalance of the four humoral fluids': Jennifer C. Vaught, 'Introduction: Rhetorics of Bodily Disease and Health in Medieval and Early Modern England', in *Rhetorics of Bodily Disease and Health*, pp. 1–22 (p. 4–5).
45 Thomas Aquinas, *Summa Theologiae*, Question 38, 'The remedies of sorrow or pain', Article 5.
46 For an overview of the textual history, see 'A Note on the Text', in Trevisa, *De Proprietatibus Rerum*, I, xi–xix.
47 Trevisa, *De Proprietatibus Rerum*, p. 331.20–1.
48 Trevisa, *De Proprietatibus Rerum*, p. 332.26–9.
49 Trevisa, *De Proprietatibus Rerum*, p. 331.32–7.

50 Trevisa, *De Proprietatibus Rerum*, p. 332.33–6.
51 Trevisa, *De Proprietatibus Rerum*, pp. 334.35–335.5.
52 Trevisa, *De Proprietatibus Rerum*, pp. 333.35–334.1.
53 Kymer, *Dietarium*, fol. 86v.
54 Kymer, *Dietarium*, fol. 86v.
55 'die naturali dormi*re* nonem horis et vigilaris quindecim c*omi*tatus est cenandu*m* magis *tam*en dormiendu*m* est vere et hyeme q*uam* estate vel autumpno et plus post multa*m* reple*cion*em q*uam* paucam . Et magis in regione frigida q*uam* calida . Et plus post labores q*uam* quietem' ('in the natural day [you should try] to sleep nine hours and to be awake fifteen accompanied by eating, yet [you should] sleep more in spring and winter than in summer or autumn, and more after a great meal than a small one, and more in a cold region than a hot one, and more after labours than after inactivity'): Kymer, *Dietarium*, fol. 87r.
56 Kymer, *Dietarium*, fol. 87r. There is a similar reference to golden sleep in an interpolated stanza in Lydgate's *Dietary*: 'All this processe concludith vp[on] tyme, / Temperat diet, kyndly digestioun, / The golden sleep braidyng vpon pryme.'
57 See Thomas Cogan, *The Haven of Health* (London, 1588), 232–3.
58 See Dannenfeldt, 'Sleep: Theory and Practice in the Late Renaissance', pp. 422–4, and Ekirch, *A History of Nighttime*, p. 263.
59 *Sir Gawain and the Green Knight*, ed. J. R. R. Tolkien and E. V. Gordon, rev. Norman Davis (1925; Oxford: Clarendon Press, 1967), ll. 1094–5.
60 Douay–Rheims Bible, Luke 22:45–6, as discussed in the Introduction.
61 *Ywain and Gawain*, in *Sir Perceval of Galles and Ywain and Gawain*, ed. Mary Flowers Braswell (Kalamazoo, MI: Medieval Institute Publications, 1995), ll. 1739–40. In Chrétien's *Yvain*, the maiden's comment is: 'an puet bien de duel forsener' ('one can certainly go mad with grief', 2924, p. 332); for discussion, see Saunders, 'Mind, Body and Affect', p. 38. The protagonist's sleep here takes place 'Als Ywaine sleped under a tre' (1709), in parallel with other romance sleepers (for instance, Malory's Launcelot and *Sir Orfeo*'s Heurodis) discussed in Chapter 2.
62 *The York Plays*, ed. Richard Beadle, EETS ss 23 and 24, 2 vols (Oxford: Oxford University Press, 2009–2013), vol. I, Pageant 13, 240–5.
63 *The Book of Margery Kempe*, ed. Barry Windeatt (Harlow: Longman, 2000), 7004–6. Although a fuller analysis of Margery's autobiography is beyond the remit of this study, the science of sleep might prove illuminating in relation to the emotional embodiment and spiritual visions of medieval mysticism.
64 Chaucer, *The Parliament of Fowls*, ll. 88–94.

65 See Piero Boitani, 'Old Books Brought to Life in Dreams: the *Book of the Duchess*, the *House of Fame*, the *Parliament of Fowls*', in Piero Boitani and Jill Mann (eds), *The Cambridge Companion to Chaucer*, 2nd edn (Cambridge: Cambridge University Press, 2003), pp. 58–77.
66 See *The Middle English Dictionary*, ed. Hans Kurath et al. (Ann Arbor, MI, 1952–2001), 'hevyness', senses 4a, 4b, 5a, and 5b.
67 See Jill Mann's seminal article, 'Troilus' Swoon', *The Chaucer Review*, 14 (1980), 319–35.
68 Judith Weiss, 'Modern and Medieval Views on Swooning: The Literary and Medical Contexts of Fainting in Romance', in Rhiannon Purdie and Michael Cichon (eds), *Medieval Romance, Medieval Contexts* (Cambridge: D. S. Brewer, 2011), pp. 121–34; Barry Windeatt, 'The Art of Swooning in Middle English', in Christopher Cannon and Maura Nolan (eds), *Medieval Latin and Middle English Literature: Essays in Honour of Jill Mann* (Cambridge: D. S. Brewer, 2011), pp. 211–30.
69 On other ways in which emotion is embodied in Middle English literature, specifically romance, see Barry Windeatt, 'Towards a Gestural Lexicon of Medieval English Romance', in Elizabeth Archibald, Megan G. Leitch and Corinne Saunders (eds), *Romance Rewritten: The Evolution of Middle English Romance* (Cambridge: D. S. Brewer, 2018), pp. 133–51.
70 *Patience*, in *Gawain*-poet, *The Poems of the Pearl Manuscript*, ed. Malcolm Andrew and Ronald Waldron (Berkeley, CA: University of California Press, 1979), l. 442. All references to *Patience*, *Cleanness* and *Pearl* are to this edition.
71 John Capgrave, *The Life of St Katherine*, ed. Karen A. Winstead (Kalamazoo, MI: Medieval Institute Publications, 1999), 3.649.
72 Trevisa, *De Proprietatibus Rerum*, vol. 1, Book 7, p. 378.
73 Malory, *Morte Darthur*, p. 633.16–23.
74 Malory, *Morte Darthur*, p. 936.24–31.
75 Windeatt, 'Swooning in Middle English', p. 223.
76 Malory, *Morte Darthur*, p. 917.32–3; compare *La Mort le roi Artu*, pp. 220–1, and the Alliterative *Morte Arthure*, in *King Arthur's Death*, ed. Larry D. Benson, rev. Edward E. Foster (Kalamazoo, MI: Medieval Institute Publications, 1994), l. 3969.
77 Windeatt, 'Swooning in Middle English', pp. 224 and 213; see also Megan G. Leitch, '"Suche Maner of Sorow-Makynge": Affect, Ethics and Unconsciousness in Malory's *Morte Darthur*', *Arthurian Literature*, 31 (2014), 83–99.
78 Malory, *Morte Darthur*, p. 794.21–2.
79 Windeatt, 'Swooning in Middle English', pp. 222–3.
80 Malory, *Morte Darthur*, pp. 693.14–15 and 693.19–31.

81 Malory, *Morte Darthur*, pp. 693.22–3 and 694.7–9.
82 Malory, *Morte Darthur*, pp. 694.17–18 and 694.19–20.
83 Perceval's sorrow similarly culminates in sleep during the Grail Quest (Malory, *Morte Darthur*, pp. 704.34–705.1); upon waking in the middle of the night, Percival sees a woman from whom he accepts a horse that turns out to be a fiend, emblematising his poor decision-making.
84 Malory, *Morte Darthur*, p. 491.17–18.
85 See Dannenfeldt, 'Sleep: Theory and Practice in the Late Renaissance', p. 425; *Sir Orfeo*, in *The Middle English Breton Lays*, ed. Anne Laskaya and Eve Salisbury (Kalamazoo, MI: Medieval Institute Publications, 1995), 63–82, and, for an overview of critical readings of the importance of the location of Heurodis's sleep, Corinne Saunders, *Rape and Ravishment in the Literature of Medieval England* (Cambridge: D. S. Brewer, 2001), pp. 228–33.
86 Malory, *Morte Darthur*, pp. 490.32–4 and 491.16–17.
87 Gilbert Kymer, *Dietarium de sanitatis custodia*, British Library MS Sloane 4, fol. 63r–104r (fol. 86v).
88 In another example of overwhelming emotion producing sleep, in *Guy of Warwick* (in both the Middle English and Anglo-Norman versions of this romance), Thierry, after telling Guy about his woes and losses, quite literally falls asleep on Guy: see Stanzaic *Guy of Warwick*, ed. Alison Wiggins (Kalamazoo, MI: Medieval Institute Publications, 2004), ll. 1897–1935.
89 Malory, *Morte Darthur*, p. 34.30–5.
90 Malory, *Morte Darthur*, p. 34.8–12.
91 Malory, *Morte Darthur*, p. 34.13.
92 Malory, *Morte Darthur*, p. 36.22–3.
93 Vinaver, *Commentary*, p. 1298.
94 See, for instance, Jill Mann, 'Malory: Knightly Combat in *Le Morte Darthur*', in Boris Ford (ed.), *The New Pelican Guide to English Literature*, 9 vols (Harmondsworth, 1982–8), I, Part I, 331–9; Andrew Lynch, *Malory's Book of Arms: The Narrative of Combat in 'Le Morte Darthur'* (Cambridge: D. S. Brewer, 1997).
95 William Langland, *The Vision of Piers Plowman: A Critical Edition of the B-Text Based on Trinity College Cambridge MS B.15.17*, ed. A. V. C. Schmidt, 2nd edn (1978; London: Dent, 1995), XI.1–5. Subsequent references to *Piers Plowman* are to this edition unless otherwise stated.
96 *Mum and the Sothsegger*, in *The Piers Plowman Tradition*, ed. Helen Barr (London: Dent, 1993), ll. 866–72.
97 Langland, *Piers Plowman*, B Prologue 14 and I.99.
98 Kymer, *Dietarium*, fol. 87r.
99 Ekirch, *At Day's Close*, p. 79.

100 Trevisa, *De Proprietatibus Rerum*, 335.20–31.
101 Trevisa, *De Proprietatibus Rerum*, 352.20–8.
102 This is according to Matt. 8:20 and Luke 9:58, where the statement is grouped with pre-Passion stories about the ministry of Christ.
103 MacLehose, 'Fear, Fantasy and Sleep in Medieval Medicine', pp. 90–1.
104 Harvey, *The Inward Wits*, p. 19. Sleepiness, meanwhile, is more unambiguously associated with a phlegmatic disposition: 'the fflewmatyk is sompnelent and slowe', in the words of the fifteenth-century poem from Harley MS 2251 edited as 'The Complexions, II', in *Secular Lyrics of the XIVth and XVth Centuries*, ed. Rossell Hope Robbins (Oxford: Clarendon Press, 1952), p. 73, l. 15. According to Galen: 'motion, emptiness, sleeplessness, evacuation, and all mental affectations dry the body, while their opposites moisten it': Galen, *Selected Works*, p. 377.
105 Chaucer, *Book of the Duchess*, ll. 16–23.
106 Shakespeare, *Henry IV Part II*, 3.i.5–6.
107 Shakespeare, *Henry IV Part II*, 3.i.31.
108 Indeed, Shakespeare name-checks Galen in *Henry IV Part II* (or has Falstaff do so), just as Chaucer has the Man in Black do in the *Book of the Duchess*. Here, Falstaff medicalises Hal's 'lethargy', describing his affliction as 'a kind of sleeping in the blood', and declaring that 'It hath its original from much grief, from study, and perturbation of the brain. I have read the cause of his effects in Galen; it is a kind of deafness' (*Henry IV Part II*, 1.ii.102 and 105–07). Falstaff seems to be extemporising freely, but his metaphor of sleepy blood as a lethargic disposition (if muddled) nonetheless gestures towards contemporary familiarity with Galenic medicine.
109 Cogan, *Haven of Health*.
110 Shakespeare, *Macbeth*, 5.i.8–9.
111 See MacLehose, 'Fear, Fantasy and Sleep in Medieval Medicine'.
112 Chaucer, *Canterbury Tales*, I.9–11.
113 Chaucer, *Canterbury Tales*, I.97–98.
114 Chaucer, 'Knight's Tale', I.1361–2.
115 Chaucer, 'Knight's Tale', I.1918–20.
116 This is a recurring theme in compline texts, which often opened with 1 Peter 5: 8–9: 'Be sober and watch: because your adversary the devil, as a roaring lion, goeth about seeking whom he may devour'. For a patristic precedent for the view that one needed to be vigilant (thinking of Christ) even while asleep (in contrast with the way that Gregory the Great opposes vigilance and sleep), see Prudentius (c.400), 'Hymnus Ante Somnium': Prudentius, *Liber Cathemerinon*, Loeb Classical Library: Prudentius, I, ed. J. J. Thomson (Cambridge, MA: Harvard University Press, 1949), p. 6.

117 Peter Idley, *Peter Idley's Instructions to his Son*, ed. Charlotte D'Evelyn (London: Oxford University Press, 1935), 574–6.
118 Richard Firth Green, *A Crisis of Truth: Literature and Law in Ricardian England* (Philadelphia, PA: University of Pennsylvania Press, 1999), p. 9.
119 'Take Good Heed', in Trinity College Dublin MS 432; edited as #87 in *Historical Poems of the XIVth and XVth Centuries*, ed. Rossell Hope Robbins (New York: Columbia University Press, 1959), pp. 206–7, ll. 13–16. Robbins observes that the poem was likely produced during or shortly before the Yorkist ascendency of the 1450s–1485.
120 *Havelok the Dane*, in *Four Romances of England: King Horn, Havelok the Dane, Bevis of Hampton, Athelston*, ed. Ronald B. Herzman, Graham Drake, and Eve Salisbury (Kalamazoo, MI: Medieval Institute Publications, 1999), 2108 and 2123.
121 Elsewhere, sleep and truth are connected in the twelfth-century 'recipe' entitled 'Vt mulier dormiens interroganti verum dicat de adulterio' ('How to question a sleeping woman so that she tells the truth about adultery'): 'Write the names [of the Seven Sleepers] (Aiohel, Deomedius, Eugenius, Probatus, Sabatus, Stephanus, Quiriacus) on clean paper; place between her breasts while she sleeps; [she will then] name all adulteries': MS Bern Codex 803, a twelfth-century gynecological manuscript quoted in Lucille B. Pinto, 'The Folk Practice of Gynecology and Obstetrics in the Middle Ages', *Bulletin of the History of Medicine*, 47.5 (1973), 513–23 (p. 523). Here, it is legendary, exemplary sleepers – the saintly Seven Sleepers of Ephesus – who are to be invoked to elicit the truth, as male anxieties about female fidelity are written onto a woman's body. See Kathleen Coyne Kelly, *Performing Virginity and Testing Chastity in the Middle Ages* (London: Routledge, 2000), p. 31.
122 *St Erkenwald*, ed. Ruth Morse (Cambridge: D. S. Brewer, 1975), ll. 89–92.
123 John Gower, *Confessio Amantis*, ed. Russell A. Peck, 3 vols (Kalamazoo, MI: Medieval Institute Publications, 2000–4), 4.2890; Chaucer, *Troilus and Criseyde*, 2.924.
124 James H. Morey (ed.), *Prik of Conscience* (Kalamazoo, MI: Medieval Institute Publications, 2012), ll. 878–9; *Everyman*, in Clifford Davidson, Martin W. Walsh, and Ton J. Broos (eds), *Everyman and its Dutch Original, Elckerlijc* (Kalamazoo, MI: Medieval Institute Publications, 2007), ll. 792–3; Shakespeare, *Hamlet*, 3.i.66–70. See also the c.1400 *Destruction of Troy*: 'He slode doun sleghly, & sleppit euer after' (*The 'Gest Hystoriale' of the Destruction of Troy*, ed. G. A. Panton and David Donaldson, EETS OS 39 and 56 (London: Trübner, 1869, 1874), l. 8225.

125 Shakespeare, *The Tempest*, 4.i.158.
126 Here, this is closely followed by another of sleep's polysemous implications, in the exhortation 'let us not sleep, as others do: but let us watch, and be sober' (1 Thess 5:6).
127 Jean-Luc Nancy, *The Fall of Sleep*, trans. Charlotte Mandell (New York: Fordham University Press, 2009), p. 31.
128 MacLehose, 'Fear, Fantasy and Sleep in Medieval Medicine', p. 83.
129 Langland, *Piers Plowman*, B. V.4 and V.9. This parallels the way in which sleep is figured as a state of alertness in the Song of Songs: 'I sleep, and my heart watcheth' (Canticles, 5:2).
130 Langland, *Piers Plowman*, B. VII.142–5.
131 Harvey, *The Inward Wits*, pp. 2 and 49. 'Sweuenynge is a certeyn disposicioun of sleping men and prentiþ in here inwit by imaginacioun schap and liknes of diuers þings': Trevisa, *De Proprietatibus Rerum*, p. 336.
132 Trevisa, *De Proprietatibus Rerum*, p. 337.6; Michelle Karnes, *Imagination, Meditation and Cognition in the Middle Ages* (Chicago, IL: University of Chicago Press, 2011); *The Book of Margery Kempe*, 7006.
133 Kruger, *Dreaming in the Middle Ages*, esp. pp. 3 and 84.
134 Kruger, *Dreaming in the Middle Ages*, p. 84.
135 Nicolette Zeeman, 'Medieval Dreams', in *A Concise Companion to Literary Criticism and Psychoanalysis*, ed. Laura Marcus and Ankhi Mukherjee (Oxford: Blackwell, 2014), pp. 137–50.
136 Kruger, *Dreaming in the Middle Ages*, pp. 4–5.
137 Kruger, *Dreaming in the Middle Ages*, pp. 20–1 and 58–61.
138 'Macrobeus / He that wrot al th'avysyoun / That he mette, kyng Scipioun, / The noble man, the Affrikan': *Book of the Duchess*, 284–7; see also *The Parliament of Fowls*, 111, 'Nun's Priest's Tale', VII.3123, and the narrator's (slightly bewildered) discussion of different Macrobian causes and categories of dreams in *The House of Fame*, esp. I.7–11.
139 Macrobius, *Commentary on the Dream of Scipio*, trans. William Harris Stahl (New York: Columbia University Press, 1952), p. 88.
140 Macrobius, *Commentary on the Dream of Scipio*, p. 90. Kruger characterises Chaucer's *Book of the Duchess* as a 'middle' dream vision – that is, one of 'sustained ambiguity' in terms of the status of the dream in relation to truth; such middle visions, Kruger writes, 'offered writers a chance to explore, in the ambiguities of dream experience, anxieties about the ambiguity of literary art' (*Dreaming in the Middle Ages*, p. 135).
141 Kruger, *Dreaming in the Middle Ages*, pp. 18–19.
142 A. J. Minnis, *Oxford Guides to Chaucer: The Shorter Poems*, ed. A. J. Minnis, with V. J. Scattergood and J. J. Smith (Oxford: Clarendon Press, 1995), p. 40.
143 Schuback, 'Aristotle's Reflections on Sleep', p. 130.

144 *Aristotle on Sleep and Dreams*, p. 89.
145 Kruger, *Dreaming in the Middle Ages*, pp. 84–92.
146 Kruger, *Dreaming in the Middle Ages*, p. 69.
147 Thomas Aquinas, *Scriptum super libros sententiarum Magistri Petri Lombardi episcopi Parisiensis*, lib. 4: d.9, q.1, a.4, q.1, conclusio; quoted in William F. MacLehose, 'Captivating thoughts: nocturnal pollution, imagination and the sleeping mind in the twelfth and thirteenth centuries', *Journal of Medieval History*, 46.1 (2020), 98–131, p. 107.
148 Gallop, in *Aristotle on Sleep and Dreams*, p. 30; Curry, *Chaucer and the Medieval Sciences*, p. 205.
149 Kruger, *Dreaming in the Middle Ages*, pp. 70 and 84. For other arguments in favour of reading medieval dream visions, including the *Roman de la Rose*, through Aristotelian, not Macrobian, dream theory, see C. H. L. Bodenham, 'The Nature of the Dream in Late Medieval French Literature', *Medium Aevum*, 54 (1985), 74–86, and Alison M. Peden, 'Macrobius and Medieval Dream Literature', *Medium Aevum*, 54 (1985), 59–73 (which, despite the title, downplays Macrobius's influence).
150 Curry, *Chaucer and the Medieval Sciences*, pp. 211–12.
151 Jean-Claude Schmitt, 'The Liminality and Centrality of Dreams in the Medieval West', in David Shulman and Guy G. Stroumsa (eds), *Dream Cultures: Explorations in Comparative History of Dreaming* (Oxford: Oxford University Press, 1999), pp. 274–87 (p. 278). On other types of dreams arising from waking preoccupations, see MacLehose, 'Captivating Thoughts'.
152 Chaucer, 'Nun's Priest's Tale', VII.2933–8. On the detailed knowledge of medicine and dream theory that Chaucer's Pertelote displays, see Pauline Aiken, 'Vincent of Beauvais and Dame Pertelote's Knowledge of Medicine', *Speculum* 10 (1935), 281–7.
153 Trevisa, *De Proprietatibus Rerum*, pp. 336.30–338.5; emphasis original.
154 Kruger, *Dreaming in the Middle Ages*, p. 91.
155 Trevisa, *De Proprietatibus Rerum*, p. 337.7–10.
156 Chaucer, 'Squire's Tale', V.347.
157 Chaucer, 'Squire's Tale', V.95 and 287.
158 Chaucer, 'Squire's Tale', V.357–9.
159 We are later told of Canacee that 'in hire sleep, right for impressioun / Of hire mirour, she hadde a visioun' (V.371–2); this 'visioun', however, is not narrated, but instead prompts an end to her dreaming and sleeping: 'Wherfore, er that the sonne gan up glyde, / She cleped on hir maistresse hire bisyde, / And seyd that hir liste for to ryse' (V.373–5).
160 Chaucer, 'Squire's Tale', V.360–7.

2

Ethics, appetite and the dangers of sleep

In the fifteenth-century morality play *Mankind*, the title character rejects labour and prayer by indulging in intemperate sleep. When he sinks into sinful sloth, Mankynde declares:

> 'Of labure and preyer, I am nere yrke of both;
> I wyll no more of yt, thow Mercy be wroth.
> My hede ys very hevy, I tell yow forsoth.
> I xall slepe full my bely and he wore my broþer.'[1]

Mankynde's rebellious declaration – that, although he knows it is wrong, he will satisfy his urge to sleep during the day rather than dutifully work and worship God – is explicitly figured as an appetite. This unrestrained appetite for sleep marks the moment of the devil's triumph in the play. Sleep, here, is something of which Mankynde, problematically, wants a belly-full; it is, like food, something to be consumed and by which to be satiated. It is also something that is, as conduct manuals emphasise, engendered by eating too much: by literally filling one's belly. While, on the one hand, medical texts that circulated and were translated in medieval and early modern England explain why sleep (or the urge to sleep) follows naturally after eating and supports both physical and mental health, on the other hand, premodern conduct manuals show how, and why, individuals should resist the desire to sleep too soon after a meal. These discourses are complementary, rather than contradictory; together, they encourage a careful, balanced performance of sleep. Temperance and timing are important: where medical tracts recommend the 'profite' of sleep (at night), dietaries and courtesy books admonish against improper indulgence, especially during the day. Homiletic literature also condemns daytime sleep, as epitomised by Chaucer's 'Parson's Tale':

> Thanne cometh sompnolence, that is sloggy slombrynge, which maketh a man be hevy and dul in body and in soule, and this synne comth of Slouth / And certes, the tyme that, by wey of resoun, men sholde nat slepe, that is by the morwe.[2]

In Middle English romances, fabliaux, dream visions and drama, untimely, daytime sleep is similarly frowned upon, and shown to be perilous for reputation and/or well-being. These genres share a pronounced interest in untimely sleep as a mode of admonition, but generic expectations also shape the consequences in distinctive ways. Across these genres, an appetite for sleep, especially when linked to other appetites – for food, for drinking to excess, for sex or sloth – variously marks a neglect of duties (ranging from chivalric endeavour to Christian labour and prayer), a lack of perception (of right conduct or religious truths) or a lack of vigilance (against attacks or abduction).

This chapter argues that literary sleep, both physical and metaphorical, often operates as an admonitory discourse that is characteristic of Middle English literature, mediating dangers both material and immaterial – especially when sleep occurs at a time or in a place that signals a failure of bodily decorum and/or of duty. Falling asleep usually requires a sense of security,[3] but to sleep is also to lose the ability to monitor one's surroundings. Sleep has a long history of signifying vulnerability. It is no accident that the Fall of Troy happens when the Trojans are asleep, thinking they are secure after the enemy fleet sails away; as Aeneas recalls in Book II of Virgil's *Aeneid*, sleep left them vulnerable to attack by the Greeks hidden in the horse.[4] However, there is a marked difference between such stratagems to take advantage of the normal night-time sleep of an opponent, and Middle English literature's frequent focus on the consequences of sleeping at the wrong time. It is not only Malory's Launcelot, alighting at midday on the edge of the forest and succumbing to both a lust for sleep and an enemy abduction, for whom an untimely appetite for sleep creates and underscores ethical problems and dangerous vulnerabilities. This chapter analyses sleep in the works of Chaucer, Langland, Gower, the *Gawain*-poet and Malory, and in a range of anonymous literary texts, alongside instructions about sleep in courtesy books, dietaries and homiletic writing. Here, sleep is deployed to evaluate the conduct and aspirations of characters and contemporary readers. Moments where characters sink into untimely sleep reflect on their identities and reputations and offer readers exempla of what not to do, emphasising the dangers of transgressing expectations.

One of the main contentions of this chapter is that the untimely, appetite-driven sleep of knights and kings, and that of ladies and queens, both constitute hitherto unrecognised but significant motifs of Middle English romance – motifs that are culturally specific, and that engage with gendered conceptions of honour.[5] English romances often depart from their sources to figure sleeping (at the wrong time or in the wrong place) as the antithesis of courtesy and ethical conduct. The ethical deployments of sleep in Middle English romances such as *Ywain and Gawain*, *Sir Gawain and the Green Knight*, *Sir Orfeo*, *Sir Degaré* and *Melusine*, in addition to Malory's *Morte Darthur*, are often unparalleled in existing sources or analogues. In these departures, representations of sleep both contribute to, and challenge, the ways in which Middle English romance has been seen to differ from earlier French romance. In addition, these medieval English memes for signifying through sleep persist in early modern English romance.

This chapter also demonstrates how widespread the English cultural grammar of sleep is by analysing other Middle English genres in which the politics of daytime sleep likewise make striking contributions to discourses of appetite and intemperance. The negative overtones of Mankynde's sleep are similar to the feast-time sleep of Arthur in *Ywain and Gawain*, and to other representations of mealtime sleep in, for instance, *Sir Gawain and the Green Knight* and *Cleanness*. Some characteristics of untimely sleep cross genres – but not all genres: in Chaucer's fabliaux, Langland's allegory, the York cycle plays and the non-romance works of the *Gawain*-poet, untimely sleep is also accompanied by a more churlish embodiment than that of romance protagonists, and more often induced by drunkenness. Frequent representations of snoring across all of these genres (apart from romance) resonate with medieval condemnations of snoring and drunken stupor as sinful, animal-like and subhuman.

To establish the nature of this English ethical discourse about sleep, the first section of this chapter considers the tenets of medieval and early modern conduct manuals and sermons. The second section analyses romance motifs of untimely sleep from the fourteenth through sixteenth centuries, and also considers the value of vigil and of figurative sleep in romance. Thirdly, this chapter shows how the ethical implications and politics of sleep are deployed in Middle English fabliaux, allegorical dream visions and drama. It concludes with a case study of the language of sleep in the alliterative tradition – encompassing chivalric romance, devotional literature and dream vision, and homing in on the ways in which sleep embodies concerns that distinguish, but also reach across, these genres. The poetics of sleep profoundly inflect the works of the *Gawain*-poet and William Langland, suggesting a new understanding of how these authors navigate questions of ethics, appetite and epistemology.

Reading for the ethics of sleep

As conduct manuals for aristocrats, gentry and the aspiring middle classes, late medieval and early modern courtesy books and dietaries prescribe behaviour for hospitality and mealtimes,[6] offering models that are negotiated in contemporary literary texts, as has been demonstrated by Jonathan Nicholls, Ad Putter and others.[7] That conduct manuals often accompany romances in medieval miscellanies further testifies to the readiness with which these genres were read alongside each other.[8] What has been less well recognised is courtesy books' and dietaries' related code of conduct regarding sleep, and the corresponding way in which sleep informs fiction. Just as self-control was fundamental to courteous speech, table manners and receiving or being a guest for readers wishing to perform courtly behaviour, so self-regulation was required with regard to sleep, particularly after a meal. Just as conduct manuals and romances encouraged regulating appetites for food,[9] that is, so these texts encouraged the regulation of other appetites, such as sleep, to which overindulgence in food could lead. Conduct manuals urged readers to be careful about where, when, how and why they slept. Medieval people were expected to ensure they slept both at the right time and in the right place; in the right postures; for the right intervals and overall duration. Individuals' performance of this premodern habitus of sleep – the where and when, in what postures and periods – contributed to (perceptions of) their virtue, social reputation and health; and this way of evaluating sleep, this hermeneutic of sleep, shaped Middle English literature.

Conduct literature's prescriptions (and proscriptions) do not, of course, confirm that practice always conformed to these tenets; indeed, injunctions such as those against midday or post-prandial naps are most likely evidence that people *did* indulge, despite knowing that they should not. An attempt to prevent such behaviour shapes Gilbert Kymer's instruction, in his early fifteenth-century dietary for Humphrey Duke of Gloucester, that 'ob quae fugere debetis de die sompnum meridianum [...], et non dormiatis in mediate post aliquam refectionem quin inter ipsam at soporem due hore ad minus intercipiantur' ('you ought to avoid sleeping in the day after noon, [...] and you should not sleep in the middle [of the day] after any meal or during one, until at least two hours have intervened').[10] That Kymer exhorts not only against sleeping *after* a meal, but also against sleeping *during* one, may at first glance seem superfluous; however, lavish medieval feasts were conducive to overindulging in a way that could induce slumber.[11] And, as this chapter demonstrates, sleep (both literal and metaphorical) during mealtimes or feasts shapes romances such as *Ywain and Gawain* and *Sir Gawain and the Green Knight*, and inflects devotional texts such as the *Gawain*-poet's *Cleanness* and drama such as Shakespeare's *Macbeth* as well as *Mankind*. In these parallels, such literary texts deploy the connotations of a regimenal discourse familiar to their audiences in order to probe the worthiness of their characters.

Instructions such as Kymer's, exhorting readers not to sleep during the middle of the day and/or after a meal, are similarly propounded in a variety of other regimens of health and courtesy books. These instructions aim to encourage both health and proper social conduct.[12] Kymer specifies that from nine in the morning until nine hours after noon, 'colera et melancolia regnant' ('choler [yellow bile] and melancholia rule'),[13] and that it is not the best time to sleep when these unhealthful humours are dominant. Similarly, the poem entitled *Regimen sanitatis Salernitanum*, a popular medical text surviving in many different versions and often dedicated 'to England's king', instructs all to 'rise after meat, sleep not at afternoon'.[14] The poem also admonishes its readers to 'Sleep not too long in mornings, early rise', and returns to a longer condemnation of the evils of afternoon sleep:

> Let little sleep or none at all suffice
> At afternoon, but waking keep thine eyes.
> Such sleep engenders fevers, headaches, rheums,
> Dullness of soul, and belcheth up ill fumes
> From forth thy stomach. All these harms ensue
> By sleep in afternoons: believe it true![15]

For effective digestion, sleep naturally follows eating, but it should not follow too closely upon the consumption of food – and particularly, should not take place during the day. As another such conduct manual, Andrew Borde's *Regyment of Helthe*, explains,

> Whole men of what age or complexion so euer they be of, shulde take theyr naturall rest and slepe in the nyght: and to eschewe merydyall sleep. But and nede shall compell a man to slepe after his meate: let hym make a pause, and than let hym stande & lene and slepe agaynst a cupborde, or els let hym sytte upryght in a chayre and slepe.[16]

The measures and postures prescribed here for unnatural but irresistible daytime or post-prandial sleep involve exerting – and visibly displaying – temperance. Moreover, even when sleeping *is* fully sanctioned – at night – correct procedures must be observed:

> To slepe grouellynge vpon the stomacke and bely is not good [...]. To slepe on the backe vpryght is vtterly to be abhorred: whan that you do slepe, let not your necke, nother your sholders, nother your hands, nor feete, nor no other place of your bodye, lye bare vndiscouered. Slepe not with an emptye stomacke, nor slepe not after that you haue eaten meate one howre or two after. In your bed lye with your head somwhat hyghe, leaste that the meate whiche is in your stomacke, thorowe eructuacions or some other cause, ascende to the oryfe of the stomacke.[17]

Sleep, then, was something that required a great deal of thought and care. Courtly persons needed to be conscientious about how they performed their loss of consciousness. Such principles are frequently expounded in late medieval and early modern courtesy books and dietaries.[18] Borde's sixteenth-century *Regiment of Helthe*, like other sixteenth-century courtesy books and dietaries, offer instructions on sleep that parallel those of medieval regimens of health such as Kymer's, and that continue the concerns of fourteenth- and fifteenth-century manuals.[19]

Such manuals imply that, and sometimes explain how, the consequences of failing to adhere to such standards of conduct were not merely bodily. To sleep sitting upright in a chair or nap while leaning against a cupboard is to perform an ability to at least temper one's bodily appetites, as a form of social capital: it enhances or sustains social reputation in a way that sprawling on the floor amongst the rushes and remnants of a feast would not. The social significance of regulating sleep is paralleled by the spiritual significance of such regulation, for instance in John Lydgate's early fifteenth-century version of these concerns in the *Dietary*:

> Suffer no surfytys in thy hous at nyght;
> Were of rere-sopers and of grete excese
> And be wele ware of candyll lyght,
> Of sleuth on morow and of idelnes,
> The whych of all vyces is chefe, as I gesse.
> [...]
> After mete bewere: make not long slepe;
> Hede, fete, and stomoke preserve from colde.[20]

Here, injunctions to avoid excess – in eating, drinking, etcetera – are conjoined to injunctions not to do that to which festive excess leads – namely, sleep too long – because it would be not only bad for one's health, but also bad for one's soul. That this was a very popular didactic tradition is attested not least by the fact that fifty-seven manuscripts of the *Dietary* survive.[21] In 1491, William Caxton also appended the *Dietary* to his printing of a longer, prose *Gouernayle of Helthe*,[22] a version of the regimens of health which circulated widely in England in Latin from the mid-fourteenth century, and in English from the early fifteenth century (at the latest).[23] In its discussion of sleep, the *Gouernayle* suggests that 'after mete', and before sleeping, one should walk, until the 'mete goo downe to the botom of thy stomak'. This practical advice is accompanied by some serious warnings about the dangers of not sleeping appropriately:

> sleepe is full helþy to the dygestyo[n] of thi metes but not anone after that thou hast eten / for thou myghtist be strangled / [...] and of one thing beware that to longe slepe or to shorte febleth a ma[n]nys body and breketh it.[24]

This text was reprinted by Wynkyn de Worde in the early sixteenth century, again in a quarto edition, and it is a precursor to later regimens such as Andrew Borde's.

Penitential manuals used by preachers to prepare sermons corroborate the conduct manuals' vexed associations between untimely sleep, sloth and ill health.[25] For instance, in Robert Mannyng's early fourteenth-century *Handlyng Synne*, the slothful are criticised for sleeping rather than attending mass:

> *how sey þese men þat are þus slogh,*
> *þat oute of mesure slepe a throwe?*
> whan he heryþ a bel ryng,
> To holy cherche men kallyng,
> þan may he nat hys bedde lete
> But þan behoueþ hym to lygge and swete,
> *And take þe mery mornyng slepe.*[26]

The italicised lines, focusing on sleep 'oute of mesure', are not in Mannyng's French source, William of Wadington's *Manuel des Pechiez*. The sinfulness of this sort of conduct is also underlined in a Middle English poem that laments late medieval churchgoers' inattentiveness, especially their sleeping, during sermons:

> Sum men at sarmones er to blame
> And war wele better be at hame:
> [...]
> Sum other unto sarmon cumes
> Bot in thaire brest no thing it blomes;
> ffor slepe thai may no tent take,
> (Bot at the taverne will thai wake.)
> fful light thai er, ill laykes to lere,
> And hevy sarmons for to here.
> His hevide than may he noght hald up,
> But wele he kepes the fendes cup.
> That the fendes cup, call I,
> That makes tham slepe and be hevy.[27]

To state that it is 'the fendes cup' that makes people sleep inappropriately here highlights connections between sleep, sin and intemperance. Monitoring sleeping habits, then, affected well-being on the three levels associated with courtesy and ethics: somatic, social and spiritual. We see these concerns combined in Lydgate's *Dietary*

Ethics, appetite and the dangers of sleep

(above) and in Hugh Rhodes' *Book of Nurture*, which instructs readers who wish to learn good manners and avoid vice to

> Ryse you earely in the morning,
> for it hath propertyes three:
> Holynes, health, and happy welth.[28]

Sleeping at an inappropriate time or place is viewed as unethical – or used to connote the unethical; it would, if observed, affect one's social reputation, and it would also denote sinful sloth.

Just as one was not supposed to sleep during the day, one was not supposed to sleep for too long at night, in order to avoid being slothful. The advice given by courtesy books and dietaries on the number of hours of sleep required per night varied, but recommendations were usually between six and eight or nine hours a night.[29] On the more generous end of the spectrum, Kymer encourages nine hours of sleep.[30] From this perspective, the advice offered by daun John to the wife in Chaucer's 'Shipman's Tale' seems rather restrictive: 'it oghte ynough suffise / Fyve houres for to slepe upon a nyght.'[31] Temperance was generally the aim, rather than sleep deprivation; sleeping too little was considered dangerous for one's health. As Caxton's *Gouernayle* puts it, 'they that slepe to lityel / [...] truly of suche it may be sayd But yf they leue of: they shall not asterte the stroke of deth.'[32] This stark warning that those who neglect sleep cannot avert death is the final word here, concluding the text of the *Gouernayle*; the dangers associated with sleep, then, are not restricted to overindulging, though the latter receives more textual attention.

To obtain the right amount of sleep, it was common – and, indeed, considered proper practice – to sleep in two segments or intervals, known as 'first sleep' and 'second sleep'. Not least because candles were very expensive, secular medieval people would generally go to bed when darkness fell, and to fill the long hours of darkness (especially long on winter nights), would often have a break from sleep of an hour or more, sometime after midnight, during which they might engage in contemplation, reading, conversation or sex before falling asleep again for another few hours. (In monasteries and nunneries, different sleeping patterns prevailed, since performing the divine offices (particularly Matins) entailed organising sleep according to the requirements of the liturgical hours rather than diurnal rhythms and worldly social conventions.)[33] Dietaries offer instructions on how to perform one's first sleep and second sleep, and temporal tags presuming the currency and normalisation of this bifurcated sleeping pattern are found in a variety of literary texts.[34] Middle English literary references to 'first sleep' often register the vulnerability associated with being asleep by depicting treachery and assaults during the first sleep, as villains use the expectations of relatively standard nocturnal sleeping patterns to their advantage. For instance, 'the false Greke Synoun / In Troie waker gan to take kepe / the hour whan men wern in her first slepe.'[35] There is a similar reference in Caxton's *The Game and Playe of the Chesse*, printed in Bruges in 1475 and reprinted at Westminster in 1482, and offered as reading material 'ful of holsom wysedom and requysyte unto every astate and degree'.[36] Here, in an excursus about the importance of chastity and 'shamefastnes' for women (figured by the queen-piece in chess), the rape of Lucretia takes place when Sextus, son of Tarquin, 'supposid and knewe that every body was in his first sleep', and therefore unlikely to be able to stop him.[37]

Sleeping postures were also important for health, and for reputation and social capital. Conduct literature encouraged readers to sleep on their sides, with the head somewhat higher than the rest of the body to aid digestion, and to change sides between the first sleep and second sleep. These recommendations were made by Avicenna and frequently cited by medieval physicians; other sleeping positions were thought to 'lead to various disorders'.[38] Caxton's *Gouernayle* illuminates the medical reason for these recommendations:

> Sleep first on the right side, for thy digestion shall be better, for then lieth thy liver under the stomach as fire under a cauldron, and after thy first sleep turn on thy left side that thy right side may be rested, and when thou hast lain thereon a good while and slept turn again on thy right side and sleep all night forth.[39]

In addition to the tilt of the body, one was also expected to think about the angle of one's legs:

> and loke þ[a]t thou lye not to streight ne to croked wyth thi legges but in a meane bytwene streight & croked. And in no wyse be not vpryght / for the[n] will the superfluytees abyde wythin the and turne to wyeked & greuous euylles contrarye to helthe.[40]

The conscious positioning of one's body for sleep, then, was a constant reminder of the nature of the body as a collection of fluids and vapours that needed to be properly managed in order to preserve well-being. Andrew Borde's *Regimen*, as cited earlier, offers a similar commentary on the disposition of body and limbs in order to regulate digestion and vapours during sleep.[41] These instructions show that attention to the performance of sleep was required through the night, not just at the moment of going to bed.

Given that sleeping was not often a private affair – since, for reasons of expense and warmth, multiple sleepers usually shared the same bed – the performance of night-time sleeping was, like midday naps, subject to surveillance as well as self-regulation. Some of the implications of contravening these instructions feature in Chaucer's 'Miller's Tale', where John the Carpenter, when asleep in his bathtub boat awaiting the fictional flood, 'routeth, for his heed myslay'.[42] John, a 'gnof' or churl, represents a social class that would presumably be unaware of the tenets of the courtly courtesy books; here, having his head in the wrong position causes uncouth sleep, and demarcates John's difference from literate audiences, as well as entailing a more genre-specific consequence by providing the cue for Nicholas and Alison to go about their furtive business. The bodily performance of sleep, then, can be a signifier of either courtly, or churlish, subjectivity.

Yet as conduct manuals proliferated in the fourteenth through sixteenth centuries, they were increasingly addressed not only to audiences which could, strictly speaking, be defined as 'courtly'; during this period, conduct literature was written for bourgeois readerships as well as aristocratic and gentry ones.[43] These manuals are often gendered, but despite their differences in other aspects of conduct, they convey similar condemnations of sloth and idleness for both male and female readerships. For instance, 'How the Wise Man Taught His Sonne' (which survives in six manuscripts copied between c.1430 and the early sixteenth century) instructs the intended youthful reader to 'geeve thee not to ydilnesse' and warns:

> Be waar of reste and ydilnesse,
> Whiche thingis norischen slouthe,
> And evere be bisi more or lesse,
> It is a ful good signe of trouthe.[44]

Here, sloth or lack of busy-ness is figured as the opposite of trouthe; to be idle is to show a lack of integrity.[45] The poem 'How the Good Wijf Taughte Hir Doughtir' (surviving in five manuscripts from c.1350 to 1500) shows how troth matters for women, too; here, sloth is similarly contrasted with honourable behaviour. Young women are instructed that they should be 'Trewe in worde and in dede, and in conscience good; / Kepe thee from synne, fro vilonye, and fro blame', and that they should avoid 'Pride, reste, and ydilnes'.[46] Such conduct texts are 'attempts at engineering gender', rather than straightforward reflections of social practice;[47] however, their discussions of valorised and unvalorised behaviour index contemporary judgements of actions and appetites. Conduct manuals for both male and female aristocratic readers also explicitly inveigh against indulging bodily appetites such as sleep and either fussy eating or overeating, as part of their condemnations of sloth. In Caxton's 1489 *Book of Fayttes of Armes and of Chivalry* (translated from Christine de Pisan's tract), the ideal knight or military commander should display temperance: he should be 'not slouthful, sluggyssh, ne slepy, ne curyous in metes & festes in lyf delycate'.[48] Similarly, in the *Book of the Knight of the Tower* (circulating in English from at least the mid-fifteenth century, and also printed by Caxton in 1484), ladies are instructed to 'custume youre self [...] in etinge and drinking' and to control their 'flesshely appetite' so that 'vertu and worship gouerne' them, instead of appetite.[49]

To read for the ethics of sleep, then, is to read in a way familiar to medieval and early modern readers; it is part of a culturally determined habitus, propounded across a range of conduct literature for readers aristocratic and bourgeois, female and male. The copying of conduct literature and romances alongside each other – as in MS Ashmole 61, which contains texts such as the *Dietary*, 'How the Wise Man Taught His Sonne', and 'How the Good Wijf Taughte Hir Doughtir' alongside *Sir Orfeo* – not only invites readers to connect these genres. It also underscores the overlapping ways in which England's conduct manuals and popular literary texts negotiate sleep's importance to bodily self-regulation and to social and spiritual expectations.

Untimely sleep and valiant vigil in romance

Middle English romances often depict untimely sleep and its consequences in ways that animate the admonitory instructions in conduct literature, and that depart from any sources in so doing, constructing a distinctively English emphasis on an ethical understanding of sleep. This book opened with an episode of Launcelot's sleep in Malory's *Noble Tale of Sir Launcelot du Lake*, where the *Morte* departs from its source. At this point in the thirteenth-century French Prose *Lancelot*, it is explained that due to weariness and heat it was considered 'expedient' or 'appropriate' for the knights to sleep until the heat of the day passed.[50] We can recall that in Malory's rewriting, by contrast, it is Launcelot's appetite for sleep, his 'great lust to sleep',[51] that is instead articulated, emphasising a lack of temperance. Here, yielding to this explicitly daytime sleep represents a lack of self-control that the courtesy books would find reprehensible, and this points up Launcelot's responsibility for the subsequent events, when he fails to protect both his nephew Lionel and himself from ambush and captivity. Daytime sleep, here, marks a failure of proper chivalric conduct. Such untimely sleep, I argue, is a motif developed and adapted by a range of Middle English romances from the fourteenth to sixteenth centuries. Sometimes, however, the knights do get it right, and resist the urge to sleep: romances figure this as a virtuous resistance, exemplified by those who successfully perform vigils. For ladies and queens in Middle English romance, as for knights and kings, untimely sleep emphasises the importance of bodily self-regulation, though not always in the same ways; for women, untimely sleep mediates a variety of dangers, both material and supernatural, and engages with the centrality of chastity to medieval conceptions of female honour.

In *Ywain and Gawain*, another Arthurian romance adapted (like Malory's *Noble Tale of Sir Launcelot du Lake*) from a French source, daytime sleep likewise carries an ethical charge, this time with a focus on food. At the beginning of *Ywain and Gawain*, unexpected and improper sleep features when King Arthur and Queen Guenevere fall asleep after a meal:

> After mete went the Kyng
> Into chamber to slepeing,
> And also went with him the Quene.
> That byheld thai al bydene,
> For *thai saw tham never so*
> *On high dayes to chamber go.*
> Bot sone, when thai war went to slepe,
> Knyghtes sat the dor to kepe.[52]

This is a sight the knights have never seen before; their surprise here registers the untoward nature of the monarchs' post-prandial sleep, reflecting the tenets of contemporary courtesy books and dietaries, which, as we have seen, offer injunctions against daytime naps, and which especially discourage sleeping after (or during) meals. Arthur, here, does not resist the feasting-induced desire to sleep; he does not go for a walk, or stand and lean against a cupboard, or sit upright in a chair to sleep, as the courtesy books would advise. Arthur and Guenevere transgress the norms of courtesy by retiring to sleep in the middle of the day during a feast, and this transgression produces a story about learning courtesy – since it is while they are asleep that, to pass the time, Colgrevance tells the tale that prompts Ywain's quest and the central narrative of the poem. This fourteenth-century text is based on Chrétien de Troyes' *Yvain* (c.1180); however, the causal connection between the royals' feasting and their sleeping is less strong in Chrétien's *Yvain*, where 'la reïne le detint' ('the queen detained') Arthur away from the feast for so long that he falls asleep, which has rather more erotic insinuations than the Middle English version's ethical ones.[53] In the Middle English poem, the queen is present as an 'and also'; the sexual implications may still be present, but as a paractactic accompaniment rather than a causal force. Here, the English writer has declined to emphasise Chrétien's sexual insinuation, instead favouring an ethical critique. This striking emphasis on the ethical significance of the when and how of falling sleep in *Ywain and Gawain* and the *Morte Darthur*, as a recognisable mode of exploring chivalric ethics, is replicated and refracted across a range of insular romances.

Malory's Palomydes makes clear the negative connotations of daytime sleep for the chivalric subject when he is travelling with King Mark:

> Than they alyght and sette them downe and reposed them a whyle. And anone wythall Kynge Marke fylle on slepe. So whan Sir Palomydes saw hym sounde on slepe he toke his horse and rode his way and seyde to them, 'I woll nat be in the company of a slepynge knyght.' And so he rode a grete pace.[54]

Like the ethical judgement framing Launcelot's midday sleep in the *Noble Tale of Sir Launcelot du Lake*, this diegetic commentary on sleep, censuring midday naps as conduct unbecoming a knight, is not in Malory's source for this episode (another thirteenth-century French romance, the Prose *Tristan*).[55] Palomydes' decision to ride 'a grete pace' emphasises the gulf between his chivalric virtue and Mark's, between the vigour of his active agency and Mark's unconsciousness. Here, Palomydes' pronouncement corroborates the way in which, in Middle English romance, knights' and kings' performance of unconsciousness often is – and is read as – an ethical act. Those who wish to 'doo after the good and leve the evyl',[56] should not be a 'slepynge knyght'. And as discussed in Chapter 1, when unhealthful emotions precipitate sleep in romance, such sleep can also mark an unethical state. This is clear in the sinful sleep that symbolises Launcelot's failure of spiritual perception in Malory's the 'Tale of the Sankgreal', when Launcelot's inability to perceive the Grail is embodied in his inability to wake up in its presence; and in Arthur's midday, outdoor sleep brought on by worry or thought, which testifies to his failings following the incestuous union that generates Mordred. In these instances, sleep supports and elucidates the ethical codes of the romance genre.

Similarly, though more figuratively, in the prose *Melusine*, translated into English from French in the late fifteenth century, sleep again has ethical implications. When the protagonist Raymond first encounters Melusine, and twice fails to answer her greetings, Melusine 'toke and pulled strongly hys hand, sayeng in this manere: "Sire vassal, ye slep." Thanne Raymondyn was astonyed and affrayed, as one is whan another awaketh hym fro slepe.'[57] These similes about sleep concern a lack of perception, but also more than that: since Raymond fails to greet Melusine as a courteous knight ought, this language of sleep registers a failure to behave according to ethical standards. Moreover, where the English Melusine says 'he semeth to be asleep', in the French source she concentrates on saying 'pensif' (thoughtful) instead of 'asleep'.[58] English romances, then, deploy an admonitory discourse of sleep at moments where their French sources do not. I am not claiming that this emphasis is never found in continental medieval literature; it is not that English is the only medieval vernacular to ever develop opportunities to deploy the ethical legibilities of sleep.[59] However, these instances of cultural translation – in *Ywain and Gawain*, Malory's *Morte* and the prose *Melusine* – are some of many examples of a trend in which

English adaptations of French narratives, and new English compositions such as *Sir Gawain and the Green Knight*, show an unprecedented degree of investment in the social capital (or lack thereof) signified by the performance of sleep.

Magical sleep, meanwhile, often has different implications to mundane sleep. While sleep sometimes permits access to (or for) the supernatural – as when a sleep contains a divine revelation, or a visit by an incubus – sleep can sometimes more directly *be* supernatural. For instance, early in Malory's *Morte Darthur*, when King Arthur is about to be decapitated by King Pellinor after losing a duel, Merlin resorts to magic to rescue Arthur: 'therewith Merlion caste an inchauntemente on the knyght, that he felle to the erthe in a grete slepe. Than Merlion toke up Kynge Arthure and rode forthe on the knyghtes horse.'[60] Here, enchanted sleep is a chivalric cheat, as Merlin goes on to stress after this scene in which Arthur, carried on the horse Merlin is riding, is rescued much as a damsel in distress might be. Pellinor would have slain Arthur if it had not been for Merlin's magical provision of sleep. Perhaps this is not only a chivalric cheat, but also a generic one: romance protagonists, it seems, can triumph – or at least survive – when vulnerable by having someone else render their opponent(s) even more vulnerable, through the incapacitation that sleep represents.

Soporific sorcery again has uncomfortable, if diegetically celebrated, implications in the late romance *Valentine and Orson*, translated by Henry Watson and printed by Wynkyn de Worde in the early 1500s. The dwarf magician Pacolet uses his magic to rescue the brothers Valentine and Orson from prison and helps the protagonists avoid being detected by any guards when he 'threwe so his charme that he made al them of the place to slepe so strongly that they knewe nothing of their comyng'.[61] In fact, Pacolet employs this strategy of putting enemies to sleep more than half a dozen times in the text, including during battles; as a result, antagonists are repeatedly slain in their sleep or circumvented while unconscious until Pacolet himself is killed.[62] Here, enchanted sleep is a weapon as well as a plot device, and it is a rather unchivalric, underhanded way of ensuring a martial victory. Having a sorcerer on one's side evidently helps to stack the odds in one's favour.

Significantly, the opponents slain in their sleep are Saracens, and Pacolet begins as a Saracen who switches allegiances to serve the protagonist Valentine. That this soporific sorcery is disassociated from its beneficiary and from the cultural identities of its intended readers – because it is performed by an underling rather than by the text's protagonist and characterised by both non-Christian agency and non-Christian victims – allows romance and protagonist to benefit from such supernatural suberfuge seemingly without tarnishing the chivalric reputation of the knight Valentine. As Pacolet explains when he is about to deploy a sleeping spell against a Saracen army,

> to the ende that none thynke that Valentyne hath wrought the treason I shall make hym to abyde in his tente, and shal make a great nombre of Sarazyns to goo vnto the watche, and [...] I shall caste my charme in suche maner that they shall all sleepe, soo harde that you maye passe them and enter in to the hoost surely in puttyng theym vnto death without any mercye.[63]

Here, that is, the non-chivalric dwarf sorcerer enables or supports his master's chivalric successes in the same way that other, non-magic-wielding dwarves do elsewhere in Middle English romance. When Gareth's dwarf reveals his master's noble identity against the latter's wishes in Malory's *Morte Darthur*, or when Lybeus's dwarf helps his master to win a fight by stealing his opponent's horse mid-duel – as when Pacolet assists Valentine by rendering his enemies unconscious – the dwarves of Middle English romance (beneath or outside the chivalric code) use unchivalric means to contribute to chivalric ends.[64]

On one occasion in *Valentine and Orson*, the Saracens who are overcome by supernatural sleep are accused of idleness and immorality, and put to death by their own commander: 'Ha false harlottes sayde Lucar I knowe wel how it goeth, you were al dronke and layde you downe to slepe. But [...] the wyne that you haue dronken shall bee derely bought.'[65] These sleep-spelled Saracens are accused of giving in to their appetites and failing in their duty to be vigilant, even though they have succumbed to a magical spell, rather than to intemperance (as their accuser does not know about the magic); and when they are hanged, we are told that 'Pacolet laughed'.[66] The magical sleep in this romance, then, while a plot device and a witness to the uncomfortable, nastily belligerent joy that romance sometimes takes in the downfall of those perceived as the enemies of medieval Christendom (as when, for instance, *Sir Isumbras* encourages its readers to rejoice in the slaughter of Saracens), also provides a diegetic corroboration of the condemnation expected for intemperate sleep.

The way in which fourteenth- and fifteenth-century English romances deploy sleep as an ethical language persists through the sixteenth century, though such continuities have not received much attention. When the early Tudor poet John Skelton writes that people should not be like 'sluggysh slovyns, that slepe day and nyght' (c.1495; revised and printed 1523),[67] or when Surrey writes c.1542 that 'In Prynces hartes Goddes scourge yprinted depe / Myght them awake out of their synfull slepe', invoking sleep remains a means of admonition about both sociopolitical and spiritual conduct.[68] In Sidney's *Old Arcadia* (1580), the vulgarity of daytime sleep is emblematised by the shepherd Dametas, who lies with 'his sleepy back upon a sunny bank [...], gaping as far as his jaws would suffer him', not long before we are told that the duke, Basilius, likewise 'lay at that time sleeping, as it was in the heat of the day'.[69] Basilius's incompetence and incontinence as a ruler are embodied in his later unhealthy enchanted sleep (with 'a dark yellowness dyeing his skin and a cold deadly sweat principally about his temples'), which is induced when he greedily consumes a magic potion intended for another because his 'belly had no ears'.[70] Here, Basilius is, as Garrett A. Sullivan observes, fittingly overcome by his own appetite, and it is only through restoration from this lack of temperance that he is able to become a just ruler.[71] Sullivan's reading of the ethics of sleep in the *Old Arcadia* locates Sidney's model in Plato,[72] but eschews any mention of medieval precedents or insular continuities.

Perhaps unsurprisingly, given Edmund Spenser's deliberate medievalism, we also find this medieval mode of signifying through sleep in Spenser's *Faerie Queene* (c.1590–6),[73] where seductresses such as Acrasia coax knights to sin by lulling them to sleep, effacing proper chivalric identity. When Acrasia dallies with Verdant, she 'had him now laid a slombering' and 'His warlike Armes, the ydle instruments / Of sleeping praise, were hong vpon a tree.'[74] Here, sleep is both the somatic mode of unethical activity, and the metaphorical language for discussing behaviour antithetical to proper self-fashioning. It is fitting, then, that it is Guyon who destroys the Bower of Bliss, Acrasia's domain, in this early modern continuation of a medieval English opposition,[75] since Guyon is Spenser's embodiment of temperance, the virtue that the courtesy books oppose to improper sleep. Shakespeare's indebtedness and contributions to this medieval way of thinking about sleep are addressed in more detail in the Coda.

The untimely sleep of ladies and queens in Middle English romance also registers danger and vulnerability; this motif, like the one featuring romance knights and kings, flags a reprehensible lack of temperance and vigilance, and accompanying dangers for reputation. For the ladies, however, there is often what we might see as either a disconnect, or an extremely problematic conflation, between being responsible for somatic (in)temperance, and the consequences to which the vulnerability of sleep makes them susceptible. Here, that is, representations of women's untimely sleep are informed by medieval conceptions of female honour embodied by a woman's 'degree of sexual continence', as the romance genre participates in a tradition of exempla 'inviting women to contemplate how shameful it would be to be judged unchaste', and encouraging them to be 'hypervigilant' to maintain their chastity and practice shamefastness in the face of ever-present risks of sexual violation.[76] Perhaps most famously, in the early fourteenth-century *Sir Orfeo*, the queen Heurodis, like Malory's Launcelot, falls asleep outside on a hot day:

> This ich quen, Dame Heurodis
> Tok to maidens of priis,
> [...]
> Thai sett hem doun al thre
> Under a fair ympe-tre,
> And wel sone this fair quene
> Fel on slepe opon the grene.
> The maidens durst hir nought awake,
> Bot lete hir ligge and rest take.
> So sche slepe til after none,
> That undertide was al y-done.
> Ac, as sone as sche gan awake,
> Sche crid, and lothli bere gan make;
> Sche froted hir honden and hir fete,
> And crached hir visage – it bled wete –
> Hir riche robe hye al to-rett
> And was reveyd out of hir wit.[77]

While readings of Heurodis's sleep have often focused on the enigmatic 'ympe'-tree under which she lies,[78] more important for my argument is that she sleeps at 'undertide', or during the middle of the day: a context that is distinctive to this medieval English romance retelling of the myth of Orpheus and Eurydice.

Sleeping during the middle of the day was viewed as dangerous in connection with the tradition of the 'noon-day demon', understood as *acedia* and also exegetically interpreted as Satan; John Friedman's connection of the noon-day demon tradition to Heurodis's sleep has been widely accepted.[79] However, while Friedman concludes that if 'the *Orfeo* poet did not know a mediaeval version of the story of Orpheus and Eurydice, or the convention of Satan's noon-day appearance, the "vndrentide" abduction of Heurodis remains inexplicable', the connotations of this daytime sleep also include the implication of unethical or intemperate behaviour widespread in conduct manuals and dietaries, according to which it cannot be said, as Friedman does, that 'the conduct of Heurodis is blameless'.[80] This meridial sleep, the result of Heurodis's lack of temperance, makes her vulnerable, as meridial sleep makes other romance figures vulnerable too: for Heurodis, it produces both mutilation and madness, as a symbolic rape; and it leads to her abduction by the fairies, which makes it a rape or *raptus* in the other medieval sense of the word too.[81] Here, since Heurodis does not practice 'hypervigilance',[82] one medieval discourse about the dangers of lack of bodily decorum seems to be blending into another such discourse. While I am certainly not arguing that we should see Heurodis as to blame for the raptus, we can recognise here and in *Sir Degaré* a way in which some Middle English romances deploy the conventional ascription of blame for failing to regulate an appetite for untimely sleep as a way of participating in a wider medieval tendency to blame women for their own rape or abduction. The representation of Heurodis also ties in with the way in which chastity as bodily self-regulation was redefined in the later Middle Ages to be relevant not only to virgins, nuns and martyrs, but also to wives.[83]

In the early fourteenth-century romance *Sir Degaré*,[84] which has no direct source, a form of otherworldly raptus is again the danger associated with maidens falling asleep outdoors under trees. In this case, however, it is not the sleeping maidens, but rather their thereby unattended mistress, who is subjected to the unwanted attentions of a fairy knight. The maidens are induced to sleep when

The weder was hot bifor the non;
Hii leien hem doun upon a grene,

> Under a chastein tre, ich wene,
> And fillen aslepe everichone.⁸⁵

As this midday, outdoor sleep beneath a chestnut tree overcomes those who should be guarding the princess, their lack of vigilance is marked in a way that parallels both Heurodis's sleep in *Sir Orfeo* and Launcelot's sleep at the beginning of Malory's *Noble Tale of Sir Launcelot du Lake* (which offers a verbal echo of *Sir Degaré*'s 'the weder was hot bifor the non').⁸⁶ While the maidens are asleep, the princess, their mistress, is accosted by a knight, described as a handsome, 'gentil, yong, and jolif man': he introduces himself as 'a fairi knyghte' who has loved her for 'mani a yer', and proceeds to force himself upon her, saying:

> 'Thou best mi lemman ar thou go,
> Wether the liketh wel or wo.'
> Tho nothing ne coude do she
> But wep and criede and wolde fle;
> And he anon gan hire at holde,
> And dide his wille, what he wolde.
> He biname hire here maidenhod.⁸⁷

In *Sir Degaré*, then, the dangers of rape are not transmuted into an abduction to a fairy kingdom; the text spells out the actualisation of this threat in unmistakable terms. Untimely romance sleep foregrounds the dangers women face from men, but also shows what seems to be a generic reticence to blame the perpetrators, focusing instead on the absence of vigilance or protection.⁸⁸

This focus on sleep as a lack of vigilance that endangers female chastity or safety is continued later in *Sir Degaré*, where the protagonist – himself the progeny of this act of rape – is denigrated for sleeping rather than protecting the ladies, when the mistress of the castle tells him:

> 'Thou art worth to suffri schame,
> That al night as a best sleptest,
> And non of mine maidenes ne keptest.'⁸⁹

Although Degaré sleeps at night here, and in a bed that has been prepared specially for him, the lady is able to call his immoderate sleep beast-like and shameful because of the unusual situation of this castle, where there are dwelling 'so fele wimman / Allone, withouten any man'.⁹⁰ That sleep registers the perils of lack of vigilance not once, but twice, in *Sir Degaré* seems especially significant alongside the way in which this romance is attuned to the dangers women can face from male violence. In this Middle English romance, sleep marks a lack of vigilance, for both women and men; and, also for both, it marks a failure in interpersonal ethics – here, especially a failure (by the maiden attendants in the forest, and by Degaré) to protect women from men. Because these are medieval romances, generically disposed towards happy endings, the violated women do not afterwards kill themselves as they might in classical exempla about women such as Lucrece – as per the list cited by Chaucer's Dorigen in the 'Franklin's Tale', when Dorigen contemplates how to maintain her honour as a married woman who has inadvertently promised to have sex with another man.

In addition to attacks from human men and fairy monarchs while sleeping, the women of romance also suffer visitations and assaults by incubi, whom men need not fear in the same way. Incubi are a direct, rather than indirect, danger of sleep, since incubi were thought to be able to possess women's bodies while they slept; in addition, incubi often appear at night, rather than during untimely daytime sleep. In the fourteenth-century *Sir Gowther*, however, an incubus, or 'felturd fende', who takes the form of the Duchess of Austria's husband ('As lyke hur lorde as he myght be'), assaults her during the day in her orchard, 'undur a tre', offering a spatial parallel to the women's encounters with menacing supernatural male figures in *Sir Orfeo* and *Sir Degaré*.[91] From this encounter with the incubus, the duchess conceives Gowther, the 'demonic child' who commits many evil deeds but who also demonstrates 'God's power to reassert order' by reclaiming and redeeming him.[92] In medical texts, incubi were sometimes pathologised as a perception of a crushing or suffocating sensation brought about by fear, mental confusion and loss of control of the body; however, they also featured in medieval scholastic debates about 'the possibilities of conception from these encounters with an incubus', paralleling romances' 'association of the incubus's attack with sexual intercourse'.[93] In the opening section of the c.1450 Prose *Merlin* (and its source, in the thirteenth-century Old French Vulgate Cycle), a holy man tells the woman who will become Merlin's mother to sleep with a light and to avoid the devil by crossing herself before she goes to bed. She neglects to perform these precautions on one occasion, and, although her door is locked,

> when the feende sye that she hadde foryete that the holy man hadde taught her, he thought that she stode owte of Goddes grace [...]. And this feende that hadde power to make woman conceyve was all redy and lay by hir while she was slepynge.[94]

Here, Merlin's mother 'was begiled in her slepe' in a way that resonates with cultural anxieties about the loss of control that accompanies sleep.[95] The judges who interview her, inclined to condemn her for having conceived a child out of wedlock, have to be persuaded that she did not in fact sleep with a mortal man. The consequences for female honour and bodily autonomy are similar, and similarly dire, but where faerie attacks on sleeping women in romance suggest a need for bodily temperance and hypervigilance, the attacks of incubi instead (or also) suggest a need for spiritual vigilance. Thus, while sleep's dangers are sometimes gendered, they are not definitively so;[96] elsewhere, as we have seen, Launcelot's midday sleep renders him vulnerable to both forms of raptus as well, since the four queens not only abduct him but also seek to make him their lover. Thus, for both knights and ladies in romance, inappropriate sleep can mark a lack of the vigilance necessary for protecting one's virtue, as a failure to the self; and for male protagonists in romance (and occasionally for ladies in waiting), giving in to an appetite for sleep often also marks a shortfall in duty, as a failure in interpersonal ethics.

Sometimes romance instead focuses on those who resist the urge to sleep. Where giving in to improper sleep, or sleeping where there is no security or protection, is dangerous – with unethical connotations or risks to reputation and well-being – the vigils of Middle English romance instead showcase ethical triumphs. Vigil, or wakefulness and watchfulness, was foundational to medieval chivalric identity, especially in the tradition of squires performing a vigil on the eve of their knighting ceremony. As expressed in Ramon Llull's thirteenth-century *Book of the Ordre of Chyvalry*, which circulated widely in the later Middle Ages in a variety of European languages (cited here in the English translation printed by William Caxton in 1484), on the night before his dubbing ceremony, a squire 'ouȝt to go to the chirche for to pray god. & ought to wake the nyȝt & be in his prayers'.[97] Such ritual vigils were intended to encourage the knights-to-be to focus on their duty to serve and protect others, in an emphasis on wakefulness as vigilance that parallels Gregory the

Great's glossing of Proverbs 6:4, 'give not sleep to your eyes', as an exhortation to those who have a pastoral duty to be vigilant.[98] A vigil to protect others is, of course, what Degaré fails to perform.

In the prose and verse *Melusine* romances, Melior (one of Melusine's two sisters), subject to her mother's curse, presides over a castle in which she keeps a sparrowhawk and must challenge high-born knights to perform a lengthy vigil watching the sparrowhawk. In this permutation of the custom of the castle motif (a narrative also related in *Mandeville's Travels*),[99] visiting knights must stay awake 'for thre dayes and thre nyghtes without slepe / the lady shuld appiere tofore them and gyue them suche worldly yeftes as they wold wysshe and were desyryng to haue, except only her self'.[100] Yet it is not only material wealth that those who succeed in this vigil – this challenge to manifest extreme temperance, if that is not a contradiction in terms – are able to obtain. Social capital, too, is their reward: in the verse version (the *Romance of Parthenay*), for instance, the narrator declares of the three knights who have succeeded in completing the vigil that

> Full uaillant and wurthy were thys men tho,
> Which noght ne went to sompnolent sleping,
> But myghtyly and pusantly were waking.[101]

Here, it is not only martial prowess that makes a knight 'uailliant' and 'wurthy'; regulating sleep is also a way of testing chivalric mettle.

The importance of temperance to knightly identity and endeavour is foregrounded especially by the way in which the prose *Melusine* connects one chivalric venturer's approach to resisting sleep to the need to resist other appetites. Here, a king who is trying his luck seems well aware of the science of how consuming food and drink leads to a desire to sleep, when he 'ete a lytel and drank of that lyked best & kept good dyete and made none exces, For wel he knewe that to moch meet & drynk causeth the body to be pesaunt & slepy'.[102] This explicit articulation that the king 'wel [...] knewe' the consequences of 'exces' in appetite suggests a familiarity with the tenets of the courtesy books regarding the need for a temperate diet. When he succeeds in his vigil, Melior appears and commends him, telling him he has 'wel & valyantly endeuoired'.[103] However, because he asks for too much – he wants Melior herself, and when she says no, he 'wold haue take the lady by manere of vyolens and by force' – he is beaten by an invisible foe and removed from the castle. His punishment conveys another message about the importance of bodily self-control (and respect for another's embodied autonomy).[104]

The consequence of attempting but failing this chivalric challenge, meanwhile, is perpetual imprisonment. In the *Romans of Parthenay*, any knight who attempts the challenge over which Melior presides, but who

> do slepe in tho nightes thre
> (Wher lytell or moche) in sampnolence there,
> Alway perpetuall there abide shall he
> In the paleis with melior the fre
> As prisonere in prison alway.[105]

That is, knights who cannot perform temperance, cannot keep themselves within performative bounds, are subject to physical bounds. Unlike the motif(s) of untimely sleep, this focus on the value of chivalric vigil is not particular to Middle English romances (we also find it, for example, in the French sources for both the prose and verse English Melusine romances: Jean d'Arras's *Mélusine*, and la Couldrette's versification of it). However, the genre's focus on the importance of vigil and vigilance is sharpened when it is juxtaposed with Middle English romance's distinctive emphasis on unethical sleep. As when the English prose *Melusine* emphasises that Raymond, failing in his chivalric duty, seems to be asleep (in a departure from the French source), Middle English romance pursues admonitory instruction through the connotations of sleep. As the c.1460 verse tract *Knyghthode and Bataile* would gloss such a failure of vigilance, 'whoso is taken sleping, hath a scorn'.[106]

Similarly, utterances about figurative sleep in chivalric literature, where sleep serves as a metaphor rather than a material reality, are often about urging ethical conduct, about the importance of being both vigilant and valiant. In *Blanchardyn and Eglantine*, translated and printed by William Caxton in 1488, sleep is invoked in a litotic description of a protagonist's valiant prowess in the middle of a battle: 'blanchardyn, whiche at that owre slept not, smot hym self emonge them [his enemies; and] he kutte and cloue them that nother helmet nor shelde coude help there / Soo that none was so hardy to approche hym'.[107] A similar, but more admonitory, language of sleep shapes the epilogue criticising contemporary knighthood that William Caxton penned and appended to his 1484 print of the *Book of the Ordre of Chyualry*. Caxton admonishes his readers: 'O ye knyghtes of Englond where is the custome and vsage of noble chyualry that was vsed in tho dayes [...] Allas what doo ye / but slepe & take ease / and ar al disordred from chyualry.'[108] This 'slepe', physical and figurative, implies sloth and a lack of commitment to knightly duties. To counteract this decline, Caxton prescribes reading romances of Launcelot and of Gawain – romances that offer ethical instruction. Here, in this manual for the aristocracy and gentry, sleep offers a warning about improper chivalric conduct; sleep is figured as the opposite of romance and its ethical aims. When figurative sleep occurs *in* romances, it has similar connotations. For instance, in Malory's *Morte*, which Caxton published the following year, the besieged Launcelot is compelled to answer his foes' taunts by an invocation of the honour-shame ethos that is explained through sleep:

> hys kynne and hys knyghtes [...] seyde at onys unto Sir Launcelot, 'Sir, now muste you deffende you lyke a knyght, othir ellis ye be shamed for ever, for now ye be called uppon treson, hit ys tyme for you to styrre! For *ye have slepte over longe*, and suffirde overmuche.'[109]

Here, sleep again reads as a comment about improper chivalric conduct, and is used to urge the opposite. Similarly, when the Red Knight (Lancelot) in the late fifteenth-century Scots romance *Lancelot of the Laik* lingers at a ford deep in thought (about his sorrowful love for Guinevere) before an impending battle, a herald accosts the knight, 'Saying, "Awalk! It is no tyme to slep. / Your worschip more expedient uare to kep."'[110] Sleep is a signifier for inactivity, idleness, passiveness, perhaps even cowardice; it is contrasted to worship, to chivalric honour and active endeavour.

Malory's *Morte* and the Epilogue to *The Book of the Order of Chivalry*, a romance and a conduct manual printed on the cusp of the Tudor dynasty – in the case of the *Morte* (31 July 1485), nearly on the eve of the Battle of Bosworth (22 August 1485) – both use sleep as a language of identity formation in a way that resonates in early modern, as well as in late medieval, England. The ethics of metaphorical sleep persist in early modern English texts, such as Baldassare Castiglione's popular early modern *The Book of the*

Courtier, published in Italian in 1528 and translated into English by Sir Thomas Hoby in 1561. Here, the activity, bravery and loyalty of the ideal courtier are articulated in opposition to sleep, to those who shun their martial duties 'where they suppose that without missing they may convey them selves from danger' in order to 'sleep in a whole skinne'.[111] This metaphorical implication of sleep is also deployed in Shakespeare's *Henry VI Part I*, where Richard Duke of York laments, 'thus we die while remiss traitors sleep'.[112] Here again, as in Middle English romance, untimely and/or inappropriate sleep signals problematic failures to self-regulate appetites, with consequences for reputation and safety.

Reading Middle English romances' deployments of sleep in relation to the genre's conventional foci and modes of adaptation challenges some of the value judgements that have been made about these texts. Within the broader genre of romance, criticism tends to approach Middle English romances, and more particularly Middle English popular romances, by opposing them to the earlier French romance tradition from which they are seen to be derived or differentiated. Middle English romances are often perceived as privileging action over interiority, and public ethics over private concerns or erotic encounters;[113] popular romances are frequently seen as focusing on plot or narrative drive at the expense of the sophisticated dilemmas and formal qualities that characterise courtly romances such as Chrétien de Troyes' *Le chevalier de la charrette* or Chaucer's 'Knight's Tale'. Correspondingly, Middle English romances have often been seen as directed towards an audience of a somewhat lower social standing than courtly French romances.[114] And yet, of course, as is now well recognised, these Middle English romances' 'popularity' encompasses not only their status as the opposite of 'high-culture' courtly romances, but also their avid consumption during the fourteenth and fifteenth centuries – by aristocratic, gentry and, increasingly, middle class readers.[115] The way in which *Ywain and Gawain* departs from its source to show a marked interest in the ethics of sleep aligns with other ways in which this Middle English romance is more interested in troth than love,[116] and this trend is also paralleled in other Middle English romances. Untimely sleep – for male romance protagonists, at least – is indeed often about public ethics. However, I would suggest that, counter to some conventional readings of the genre, Middle English romance's pronounced interest in ethics does not necessarily come at the expense of interest in emotions. As recent work by Marcel Elias has shown, the authors and adapters of other Middle English romances often use emotion words and emotional displays in order to refashion their sources, inviting audience response to or judgement of characters' motives and conduct.[117] While this chapter foregrounds characteristic movements such as *Ywain and Gawain*'s shift away from the sexual potential of monarchical sleep towards the ethical problems this sleep poses, we have also seen that sleep can embody and mediate strong emotions; and, as Chapter 3 shows, Middle English romances also develop a characteristic way of dwelling on and negotiating sexual possibilities by discussing the spaces of sleep. The multiplicity of ways in which English romances repeatedly turn to sleep, then, together showcase the genre's interests in ethics, emotions and sex.

Sloth and snoring in fabliau, allegory and drama

This strong focus on the ethics of sleep is shared with other Middle English genres, in which sleep likewise interrogates proper conduct, but with different signs and consequences. Strikingly, while the codes of conduct that sleep transgresses can vary, in fabliau, allegory and drama, unlike in romance, problematic sleep is often accompanied by snoring: a corporeal concomitant of sleep with churlish connotations. It is perhaps not surprising that the sleepers of fabliau, a genre in which scatological humour is expected, are much more likely to snore than the sleepers of romance;[118] however, we also find this sort of vulgar or visceral embodiment, and snoring in particular, for the untimely and improper sleepers of allegorical or admonitory dream visions and drama. These instances of sleeping and snoring offer ethical commentaries through their negation of ideals of courtesy, temperance and spiritual observance espoused in conduct literature and homiletic writing. Here, improper sleep signifies a failure, and sometimes a concerted renunciation, of right conduct, especially of Christian labour and prayer in English drama and in allegorical dream visions such as *Piers Plowman*.

Homiletic writing on sloth shows what reading for the ethics of snoring can add to our understanding of the ethics of sleep. As one of the Seven Deadly Sins, sloth encompasses much more than physical inactivity. Sloth, or *acedia*, was first and foremost a failure of spiritual activity – a neglect of prayer or active faith – but in the later Middle Ages, writers turned increasingly to 'sloth's external characteristics, rather than its psychology'.[119] From the time of desert monasticism in the third and fourth centuries, the Christian church condemned *acedia* as 'spiritual torpor, dislike for religious exercises, and a disheartening sorrow that kept the soul from any desire to serve God or even live'.[120] Idleness inheres to the later, more capacious (and increasingly secularised) sin of sloth, which, along with *acedia*, includes 'evil desire, infidelity, curiosity, dissoluteness';[121] idleness has three main branches, which, as articulated by a late medieval shepherds' calendar featuring medical advice and religious instruction, are:

> (a) Ceasing to do good. Namely, ceasing good thoughts, good words, and good works. (b) Seeking to do evil. Namely seeking concupiscence of the flesh, and concupiscence of the eyes. It is avarice, and the concupiscence of proud living. (c) Not resisting evil. For the love one has for evil. For the tedium one finds in good. For one's own self-negligence.[122]

To refuse to do work, to eschew active labour, is to cease to do good, or even to seek to do or not resist evil, if time is instead devoted to indulging appetites.

From the thirteenth century onwards, 'sloth increasingly relates to the body', and humorally, it suggests a phlegmatic or melancholic disposition.[123] Sloth also figures as the enemy of prosperity, as in a late medieval poem containing advice for 'ye that ar comons' (on a flyleaf of a copy of Lydgate's *Fall of Princes*): 'expell enve and slovth, moste chefe of all – / where slovth hath place, there welth es faynt and small'.[124] Moreover, physical idleness can also be the cause of *acedia* if, for instance, someone misses Sunday mass due to a lie-in or a hangover; 'somnolence [...] deadens the body and soul'.[125] As Peter Idley observes in his fifteenth-century *Instructions to His Son*, sleep is the enemy of attending, and attending to, church services:

> Slomer ne slepe not when the Belle ryngeth;
> Be redy at churche by the laste peele
> To hire eueri worde that the preist seith and syngeth
> And please God, thy maker, while thow hast heele.[126]

Because, as Chaucer's 'Parson's Tale' admonishes, 'synful men' 'been holden to laboure in preiynge to God for amendement of hire synnes', to neglect to pray is a deadly offence, and 'this foule synne Accidie is eek a ful greet enemy to the liflode of the body'.[127] As these various examples show, to choose sleep rather than labour or prayer in late medieval England has negative moral associations.

Representations of snoring make particular contributions to sleep's moral implications. Peter the Venerable, abbot of the Benedictine abbey of Cluny, wrote in 1147 that to 'snore in a drunken stupor' should be

> far from human minds, may it be absent from souls capable of reason and may it be remote from all those who know God. Reason does not support this and justice herself denies that man, who was placed before all irrational creatures by the Creator, should be compared to animals in all things and made similar to them.[128]

Although this exhortation is sparked by his diatribe against the Jews, Peter's condemnation of snoring as animal-like and subhuman is presented as a universal.[129] The impropriety represented by snoring is both physical (in its vulgarity) and figurative (as a sign of vice).

This interpretation of snoring resonated in Middle English literature. For instance, in Book 5 of the *Confessio Amantis* (on Avarice), John Gower embellishes his Ovidian source to write that some servants who ought to have been keeping watch, instead

> what of travail, what of wyn,
> The servantz lich to drunke swyn
> Begunne for to route faste.[130]

When they were supposed to be guarding their master and mistress (Hercules and his love Eolen), these servants instead 'route' (snore); that they do so like 'drunke swyn' underscores the animalistic connotations of snoring and drink-induced sleep. Their lack of vigilance allows an enemy intruder to enter. Although Russell Peck contends that 'to be drunk as a swine is a common saying that is more descriptive than pejorative',[131] in light of Peter the Venerable's damning condemnation of snoring in a drunken stupor as animal-like and subhuman, and given that Gower opts to include the swine metaphor where Ovid does not, this corporeal description of heedless servants neglecting their duty seems rather pointedly pejorative. Chaucer's writings also engage with contemporary condemnations of drinking to excess and the oblivious slumber to which such an appetite can yield, for instance when the 'Pardoner's Tale' presents Attila's death as an exempum against drinking:

> Looke, Attilla, the grete conquerour,
> Deyde in his sleep, with shame and dishonour,
> Bleeding ay at his nose in dronkenesse.
> A capitayn sholde lyvve in sobrenesse.[132]

Here, the Pardoner's hypocritical but highly effective moralising rhetoric deploys the connotations of drunken slumber as something shameful and dishonourable, in a tale in which the gluttony and avarice of the three central characters results in their deaths. Gower, meanwhile, does specify that Hercules' servants' slumber is caused not only by 'wyn', but also by 'travail': for those who must perform manual labour, sleep is sometimes presented as a more powerful urge; class complicates the politics of sleep. The tensional ways in which sleep relates to vigilance and labour are also negotiated in Chaucer's fabliaux, Langland's allegory, and the morality play *Mankind*.

Where Gower's servants sleep like drunken swine, one of Chaucer's (working-class) fabliau cuckolds, in the 'Reeve's Tale', snores like a horse, in an animalistic act that again carries uncouth connotations. Sleeping times and postures have clear ethical connotations in fabliau, even though ethical concerns are not, of course, paramount in the genre. In Chaucer's 'Miller's Tale', when John climbs into the tub suspended from the ceiling, he promptly falls asleep. Chaucer further specifies that John snores, giving Alison and Nicholas their cue to go about their furtive business:

> The dede sleep, for wery bisynesse,
> Fil on this carpenter right, as I gesse,
> Aboute corfew-tyme, or litel moore;
> For travaille of his goost he groneth soore,
> And eft he routeth, for his heed myslay.
> Doun of the laddre stalketh Nicholay,
> And Alisoun ful softe adoun she spedde;
> Withouten wordes mo they goon to bedde.[133]

Here, there is a physiological reason posed for John's snoring: Chaucer specifies that 'he routeth, for his heed myslay'. To state that John snores because he is not lying correctly suggests a connection with conduct manuals' instructions that sleepers should lie on their side and with the head higher than the rest of the body. Poor sleeping posture and concomitant snoring also feature as an ethical commentary in *Wynnere and Wastoure*, where Wastoure says that Wynnere and his ilk snore and sleep with their bums in the air: 'ye negardes appon nyghte ye nappen so harde, / Routten at your raxillyng, raysen your hurdes'.[134] While the likes of carpenters and millers would not likely have been familiar with the tenets of the conduct manuals, clerks such as the trickster figures in the 'Miller's Tale' and 'Reeve's Tale' belong to a class which did have access to the manuals. Snoring, then, contributes to fabliau class commentary, and the ethics of snoring form part of the comedy of the genre.

The working-class target figures of fabliaux are also more likely than the clerkly tricksters to succumb to deep sleep because of their hard labour, or their 'wery bisynesse'. The 'Reeve's Tale' extends its quiting of the 'Miller's Tale' to a parallel – yet expanded – commentary on drunken snoring, stating that Simkin's whole family snores before the two clerks start bed-hopping, but (again), this applies especially to the vindictive cuckold:

> This millere hath so wisely bibbed ale
> That as an hors he fnorteth in his sleep,
> Ne of his tayl bihynde he took no keep.
> His wyf bar hym a burdon, a ful strong;
> Men myghte hir rowtyng heere two furlong;
> The wenche rowteth eek, *par compaignye*.[135]

Like John the Carpenter's snoring in the 'Miller's Tale', Simkin the Miller's snoring in the 'Reeve's Tale' enables the plot, because it covers the other noises to follow and lets the tricksters know that the husband is asleep. Moreover, Chaucer links these scatological, explicitly animalistic descriptions of Symkin's sleep to his intemperate drinking, which both secular and spiritual writings would condemn: his uncouth sleeping and snoring registers both physical and moral blindness. The 'Reeve's Tale' and its clerks also mock the family's collective snoring by comparing it to song. The tale's description of the wife's snoring as a 'burdon' suggests the chorus of a carol, and the daughter also provides accompaniment; Aleyn then says to John 'Herdestow evere slyk a sang er now?', before they each 'sleep with' one of the two women.[136] Like Simkin the Miller, Shakespeare's Falstaff also snorts like a horse: at the end of Act 2 of *Henry IV Part I*, Falstaff is found, in Peto's words, 'Fast asleep / Behind the arras, and snorting like a horse',[137] an apt epithet for this bawdy descendant of fabliau.

Langland draws upon the same English cultural grammar of sleep and snoring to register vulgarity and explore its consequences. Early in the poem, in the description of the faults of humanity after Will enters his first dream vision, sleep features as part of the sins of 'bidderes and beggeres' who live in 'glotonye' and 'ribaudie', and 'sleep and sory sleuthe seweth hem evere'.[138] Here, sleep is personified as a rather active menace: condemned in the same breath as 'sory sleuthe' or wretched sloth, and pursuing or shadowing those who do not resist it.[139] Gluttony and Sloth are repeatedly linked in the poem in ways that foreground the sinfulness of excessive appetite, as in Passus II, when, in the charter False has created for his pending marriage with Meed, Gluttony is figured as making people eat and drink to excess all day until they are overcome by Sloth: 'And thanne to sitten and soupen til sleep hem assaille, / [...] Til Sleuthe and sleep sliken hise sydes'.[140] The beneficial connotations of food as nourishment are certainly central to Langland's allegory: emphasised, for instance, in the importance of the ploughing of the half-acre to provide necessary sustenance for society; in how this cultivation of food is also a way of serving Truth; and, of course, in the way in which, in the sacrament of the eucharist, 'God's grace enters the body through the physical act of eating and drinking.'[141] However, Langland also repeatedly foregrounds the problems caused by excess of appetite, by a superfluity of food and drink, and often does so by deploying the ethical connotations of sleep. In the B-text, the cloak of Hawkin the Active Man is stained with Gluttony when Hawkin has 'moore mete eet and dronk than kynde myghte defie'; and, recognising the 'dedlich synne' that his 'surfetes' constitute, he descends into 'wanhope' and 'sleuthe'.[142] Here, Hawkin's consumption is explicitly against nature: it is more than 'kynde' can digest or accommodate. From this perspective, a degree of hunger is useful, because it not ony signifies temperate self-control; it also motivates continued labour. It is, after all, when Hunger is put to sleep in Passus VI that Wastour and his followers neglect their duties and disrupt social order.[143]

In the anthropomorphic treatment of the Seven Sins in *Piers Plowman*, Glutton sleeps slothfully due to excess of appetite, while Sloth, like an uncouth version of an intemperate romance protagonist, snores during an inappropriate daytime sleep. The sleep and snoring of Sloth and Glutton, induced by overindulgence in food and drink, offer an ethical commentary about a problem both social and spiritual: a commentary in which the figures' waking moral state, their failures to labour on behalf of the community or to attend church and pray, are mapped onto when, how and why they sleep. During the confession of the Seven Deadly Sins in Passus V, Glutton, like Simkin in the 'Reeve's Tale', drinks a great deal; afterwards, he is carried home, where

> his wyf and his wenche
> Baren hym to his bed and broughte hym therinne;
> And aftur al this excesse he had an accidie,
> That he sleep Saterday and Sonday, til sonne yede to reste.[144]

Glutton's 'accidie', or fit of sloth, indicates that due to his excess of appetite, he is overcome by his neighbouring sin; and for this behaviour, his wife reproaches him for his wicked living. Langland follows this with the appearance of Sloth, who comes 'al bislabered, with two slymed eighen', belches, and begins to snore ('raxed and rored – and rutte at the laste').[145] Both Sloth and Glutton sleep during the daytime, which, again as per conduct literature and sermons, constitutes a lack of temperance and a form of idleness deplored on both social and spiritual grounds.

The daytime sleep of Sloth and Glutton is also paralleled by that of Chaucer's Cook, who drowses on his horse in the Manciple's Prologue. The Host criticises the Cook and mocks him for this behaviour:

> 'See how he nappeth! See how, for cokkes bones,
> That he wol falle fro his hors atones!
> [...]
> Awake, thou Cook', quod he, 'God yeve thee sorwe!
> What eyleth thee to slepe by the morwe?
> Hastow had fleen al nyght, or artow dronke?
> Or hastow with som quene al nyght yswonke,
> So that thow mayst nat holden up thyn heed?'[146]

Here, drunkenness is again posited as a reason for a churlish figure's untimely sleep. After being verbally excoriated, the Cook falls off his horse in anger, and due to his drunkenness, it is thought best that he not tell his tale now.[147] The sinfulness of this sort of conduct is underlined by the poem in MS Harley 4196 discussed in the first section of this chapter, which laments late medieval church-goers' inattentiveness and sleeping during sermons, stating that it is 'the fendes cup' that makes them sleep, connecting drinking and sleep to sin and lack of (spiritual) perception. The fact that the Cook's unethical sleep takes place as the pilgrims are nearing Canterbury underscores his need to confess his sins. Elsewhere, Langland's Sloth is sleeping at a time when Repentance tells him he ought to 'awake' and hasten 'to shryfte' to confess his sins, and Sloth admits that he 'ligge abedde in Lenten and my lemman in myne armes / Til matyns and masse be do'.[148] The inappropriate sleep of these personified vices highlights their failures in work and prayer.

The politics of sleep, snoring and drunkenness also shape late medieval (and early modern) English drama. In the late fifteenth-century morality play *Mankind*, as mentioned earlier, the title character also sleeps intemperately when he is no longer willing to 'eschew ydullness' by undertaking the 'labure and preyer' encouraged by Mercy.[149] Here, a 'full [...] bely' or excess of sleep signifies a renunciation of duty; Mercy has explictly instructed Mankynde to espouse temperance:

> 'Mesure ys tresure. Y forbyde yow not þe use.
> Mesure yowrsylf ever; be ware of excess.
> þe superfluouse gyse I wyll þat 3e refuse.
> When nature ys suffysyde, anon þat 3e sese.'[150]

Significantly, Mankynde's assertion that he will take his fill of daytime sleep despite Mercy's express wishes to the contrary is further pointed up by the devil Titivillus's address to the audience when Mankynde is sleeping onstage: '3e may here hym snore; he ys sade aslepe'.[151] Titivillus reads this performance of churlish sleep as a guarantee that he has 'don my game, / For I have brought Mankynde to myscheff and to schame'.[152] That is, by persuading Mankind to sleep, to be idle, instead of labouring, the devil has undone humanity. Here, sleep is a physical manifestation of the spiritual sin of sloth or *acedia* – just as it is for Langland's Sloth and Glutton, or for Marlowe's Dr Faustus, when he chooses to 'confound these passions with a quiet sleep': to sink into the sleep of spiritual apathy rather than to repent.[153] After Mankynde's snoring marks the transition to the nadir of his spiritual fortunes, the devil and the vices persuade Mankynde to assent to lechery, and to rob, steal and kill, before Mercy again convinces Mankynde to pray and regain the promise of eternal life – achieving a redemption denied to Faustus.

In the York cycle of mystery plays, in Pageant 30, Christ before Pilate I: The Dream of Pilate's Wife, drunken slumber marks the transgressions of both Pilatus and his wife, Dame Percula. Here, both Pilatus and Percula drink to excess, and then when Pilatus goes to bed, he himself articulates the connections between his problematic appetite and his sinful conduct, between his somatic and spiritual states:

> Pilatus: 'Yha, I haue wette me with wyne.
> Yhit helde doune and lappe me even here,
> For I will slelye slepe vnto synne.
> Loke þat no man nor no myron of myne
> With no noyse be neghand me nere.'[154]

In the same way that Mankynde and Dr Faustus choose to sink into sleep when they sink into – and as their way of sinking into – sin, Pontius Pilate is shown to embrace (drunken) sleep in a play concentrating on his reprehensible act of condemning Jesus. Here we also have an aural, alliterative aggregation of the possibilities of sinful sleep produced by drunkenness: his sleep is conjoined to the idea of acting 'slyly', surreptitiously or underhandedly; and, while it may be the result of a scribal preference for spelling 'syne' (meaning 'later') as 'synne', the phrase 'slelye slepe vnto synne' suggests sleeping unto or into sin, in a literalisation of the spiritual implications of his sleep and other proximate actions.[155] Pilatus's wife also has her foreboding dream this same night while in an unhealthy and unethical drunken stupor. After she, like her husband, has been drinking, she retires with her servants to 'a bedde arayed of þe beste'; a devil then appears, and she has a dream, about which she proclaims, 'A! I am drecchid with a dreme full dredfully to dowte.'[156] This dream, as she reports afterwards, was the devil, 'Diabolus', prophesying her and her husband's downfall for Pilatus's impending decision to condemn Jesus to death:

> 'All naked þis nyght as I napped,
> With tene and with traye was I trapped,
> With a sweuene þat swiftely me swapped,
> Of one Jesu, þe juste man þe Jewes will vndoo.'[157]

Because sleep deprivation seems to have been understood as one of the torments Christ endured during the Passion, the way in which this succession of bed scenes emphasises luxuriousness and indulgence foregrounds the sinfulness of Christ's adversaries all the more.[158]

While Pilatus and his wife sleep (intemperately) at night, elsewhere in the York cycle, in Pageant 13, 'Joseph's Trouble about Mary', Joseph sleeps during the day. Here, as discussed in Chapter 1, Joseph falls asleep because his 'hert so heuy it is', when his emotions and the weight of his cares prompts him to slumber.[159] It is during this sleep that he has an enlightening visitation from an angel; however, the fact that he sleeps during the day makes a significant departure from biblical precedent. Biblical dreams, including Joseph's, generally occur at night.[160] Thus, by having its Joseph sleep and dream during the daytime, while he is out for a walk, the York play aligns his sleep with depictions of untimely sleep elsewhere in Middle English literature. What is problematic about Joseph's sleep here is his need for it (and for the corrective vision it brings); his heart is heavy before he sleeps because he is not yet willing to accept God's will. The Angel even has to spend some time encouraging Joseph to stop sleeping so that he may attend to his interpersonal responsibilities:

> Angelus: Waken, Joseph, and take bettir kepe
>   To Marie, þat is þi felawe fest.
> Joseph: A, I am full werie, late me slepe,
>   Forwandered and walked in þis forest.
> Angelus: Rise vppe, and slepe na mare,
>   þou makist her herte full sare
>   þat loues þe alther best.[161]

Sleep, here, while offering spiritual enlightenment and a rebalancing of the emotions, also carries connotations of sloth and despair, and the negative implications are pointed up all the more strongly by the fact that Joseph sleeps at a time when he should not.[162]

Thus far, this chapter has sought both to establish the currency and longevity of this widespread interest in the ethics of sleep in premodern English literature, and to explore moments and motifs through which sleep shapes a variety of genres. Of course ethical concerns are not always equally paramount across all the texts I have been discussing, but they are predominant in works such as *Piers Plowman* and *Mankind*, as well as romances, and play a role even in Chaucer's fabliaux. This chapter concludes with case studies of the four works of the *Gawain*-poet, and of Langland's Will, in order to further demonstrate how reading for the ethics of sleep illuminates Middle English narrative genres, and how sleep particularly informs the poetry of the alliterative revival.

Envoy: the poetics of sleep in the alliterative tradition

Sleep, as both signifier and state, features in all four of the *Gawain*-poet's works – *Pearl*, *Patience*, *Cleanness* and *Sir Gawain and the Green Knight* – and all four of these late fourteenth-century poems approach sleep as an ethical act with implications for courtesy in particular. Courtesy is foregrounded in these poems as an outward manifestation of inward virtue; criticism of the *Gawain*-poet has focused especially on the nature of courtesy as an ideal of personal integrity and politeness to be performed in one's actions and speech towards others, both human and divine.[163] This envoy explores the way in which sleep, an understudied topic in these poems, is figured as the antithesis of courtesy and temperance; it marks problematic appetites, especially in *Cleanness* and *Sir Gawain and the Green Knight*, and problematic despair or failures of duty, especially in *Patience* and *Pearl*. While attention has been drawn to the ways in which the *Gawain*-poet draws upon biblical and courtly (French) material,[164] the poet's interrogation of proper spiritual and social conduct through the medium of sleep instead participates in the widespread interest in signifying through sleep in Middle English literature. Moreover, through rhetorical collocations for the ethical figuration of sleep that are not paralleled elsewhere, the *Gawain*-poet also offers a distinctive contribution to the English poetics and politics of sleep. Meanwhile, in *Piers Plowman*, Langland engages with the signifying potential of sleep not only in his representation of Sloth and Glutton; the poetics of sleep also illuminate the ethical and oneiric implications of the dreamer's sleep.

In *Patience*, when Jonah disobeys God's command to go to Nineveh and takes ship in a different direction, God summons a storm. Jonah, cowering in the storm-tossed ship in a vain attempt to escape both God's wrath and the sacrificial impulses of his fellow mariners, falls asleep in despair:

> He watz flowen for ferde of þe flode lotes
> Into þe boþem of þe bot, and on a brede lyggede,
> Onhelde by þe hurrok, for þe heuen wrache,
> Slypped vpon a sloumbe-selepe, and sloberande he routes.[165]

Here, Jonah, like Langland's Sloth and Glutton, and like Mankynde, snores at the moment that marks his renunciation of duty and his surrender to despair. Jonah's slobbering and snoring highlight correspondences between his somatic vulgarity and his spiritual and social misconduct. In medieval religious writings, as we have seen, sleep can signify moral blindness, and Jonah's sleep was interpreted as such by medieval commentators because it contravenes ascetic observance.[166] Jonah's sleep also emphasises human imperfection in contrast with the poem's demonstration of divine wakefulness, since God 'ay wakes'.[167] The poet, however, by specifying that Jonah slobbers and snores, gives his Jonah a sleep more uncouth than that of his Vulgate source,[168] perhaps because Jonah has behaved unethically not only towards God, but also towards his community, since the other seafarers are endangered solely on his behalf. The sailors' accusation of Jonah demonstrates that his sleep is as recognisably uncommendable to his fellow characters as it would be to the poet's society: 'Hatz þou, gome, no gouernour ne god on to calle, / þat þou þus slydes on slepe when þou slayn worþes?' (199–200). Jonah also 'slides into sleep' on another occasion, after he expresses his hubristic and inconsiderate wish that God had not spared the Ninevites:

> He slydez on a sloumbe-slep sloghe vnder leues,
> Whil God wayned a worme þat wrot vpe þe rote,
> And wyddered watz þe wodbynde bi þat þe wyȝe wakned.[169]

Here, Jonah's immoral state, at this moment in which God must teach him another lesson, is marked again by 'sliding' into 'sleep'. This lexical collocation of 'slide' or 'slip' with 'sleep' recurs in the *Gawain*-poet's other investigations of the relation between sleep and morally questionable behaviour.

The poet embellishes the description of the aftermath of Belshazzar's feast in *Cleanness* to include a depiction of sleep not found in his sources, thereby enriching the didactic (de)construction of the characters' ethical identity. The *Gawain*-poet's narrative of Belshazzar's downfall is an expanded version of the end of Daniel 5,[170] which does not mention sleep itself but simply states, 'eadem nocte interfectus est Balthasar rex Chaldeus' ['on that night Balshazzar, king of the Chaldeans, was killed'].[171] While earlier acts of mealtime hospitality in *Cleanness* – such as in the Parable of the Wedding Feast or God's visit to Abraham – are models of courtesy, this final mealtime exemplum instead showcases the debauchery and sacrilege of Belshazzar's court.[172] When Belshazzar and his retinue are to be divinely punished for their improper conduct during feasting, they are slain, appropriately, during the sleep that is produced by (and continues) their gluttonous excess, their lack of courteous self-control:

> Segges slepande were slayne er þay slyppe myȝt;
> Vche hous heyred watz withinne a hondewhyle.
> Baltazar in his bed watz beten to deþe.[173]

This mention of 'segges slepande' (and the associated 'slipping' or cowardly escape they would otherwise have sought) is the only instance of 'sleep' in *Cleanness*. Here, at the climax of the poem, marking an excess of appetite, sleep is deployed to typify the characters' moral state – their intertwined social and spiritual failures – in a way that resonates with the other poems in the manuscript.

In *Sir Gawain and the Green Knight*, sleep figures most famously in Gawain's bedside dalliances; however, the first instance of the word 'slepe' in the poem in fact relates to conduct during a feast. When Bertilak arrives at Arthur's court and asks for the governor, he is greeted initially by a 'swoghe sylence':

> As al were slypped vpon slepe so slaked hor lotez
>   In hyȝe –
> I deme hit not al for doute
> But sum for cortaysye.[174]

While Nicholls proposes that the court keeps quiet to comply with the etiquette of hierarchy,[175] this literal reading seems more generous than the text invites. The poet's comment that the courtiers are silent 'not al for doute / But sum for cortaysye' surely has ironic overtones; the poet may be indulgent towards their failure to respond with courteous speech, but nonetheless emphasises that this is to be interpreted as a failure, particularly by remarking that they all fall silent as though they had slipped into sleep. Sleep, as the antithesis of proper conduct in a mealtime setting such as this one, symbolises the behavioural ambiguities of this silence. Here as in *Ywain and Gawain*, sleep – whether physical or metaphorical – during a feast is an unexpected and unsuitable display of intemperance, especially striking in *Sir Gawain and the Green Knight*, a poem deeply concerned with decorum or seemly behaviour as well as truth. King Arthur's custom of waiting for a wonder or marvel before eating at a feast, widespread in Arthurian literature, usually demonstrates Arthur's court's self-control; it is a moment at which, and a motif in which, the court, 'embodying civilization, rationality, order, peace and the known, interior world is suddenly intruded on by the forces of wilderness, conflict, churlishness and the unknown, exterior world'.[176] In *Gawain*, however, at the moment of the arrival of the Green Knight – the marvel himself – Arthur and his knights and ladies instead display churlish behaviour themselves. This metaphorical sleep suggests either that the courtiers are not entirely courteous, or that courtesy alone is not always a sufficient code of conduct for a chivalric society – or, perhaps, both.

Elsewhere in *Gawain*, the poet again uses sleep to hint at ways in which courtesy risks sliding into uncourageous inactivity. When Lady Bertilak approaches Gawain's bed at Hautdesert, he is drowsing: 'in slomeryng he slode'.[177] Once Gawain perceives the lady, he pretends to be fully asleep: he 'let as he slepte'.[178] The poem focuses less on Gawain's recovery from his traveller's fatigue than on his deceitful pretence of being asleep because he does not know what else to do when confronted with the Lady. Ad Putter perceptively observes that this pretence demonstrates Gawain's 'awareness of the intricate realities of social interaction';[179] but Gawain, by initially choosing sleep-like inactivity, also allows the ensuing morally precarious situation to occur and sets a spatial and behavioural precedent for the subsequent mornings. *Seeming* to sleep, then, in hall and bedchamber, produces results which *seem* to resemble courtesy, reminding the reader that true courtesy is not merely an outward show of self-restraint: it ought to correspond to inward virtue rather than to abstention from action. Sleep defines a boundary between courtesy and passivity in *Gawain*, offering a meditation upon when, and by what, politeness ought to be tempered in chivalric subjects' pursuit of virtuous conduct.

In *Pearl*, sleep similarly delineates both physical and figurative boundaries. The dream narrator's sleep, as the vehicle for his vision of the maiden and the New Jerusalem, begins when he 'slode vpon a slepyng-slaȝte / On þat precios perle withouten spot'.[180] This is of course a different kind of sleep: a contemplative sleep with positive spiritual connotations. It produces a dream vision that is divinely inspired and leads to the dreamer's spiritual awakening;[181] however, this sleep also shows the need for the dreamer's spiritual enlightenment. In *Pearl*, that is, sleep is again used to illustrate improper conduct. When the narrator is punished for trying to cross the river, his hubris results in the end not just of his vision but also of his sleep:[182] in seeking to cross one boundary, he is instead redirected across another. As in the other three poems (though with different complexities), sleep in *Pearl* again reads as an ethical event. While Spearing notes the dreamer's failure to adequately 'respond to and understand his visionary experience' and his initial tendency towards 'treating a person as if she were a thing', he does not question the cause of the dream.[183]

The dream offers moral instruction, yet the dreamer's act of falling asleep is itself dubious, because his sleep-inducing excessive grieving represents a lack of both spiritual and social decorum. Significantly, the poet's description of the transition to the dream as 'sliding into sleep' marks the unstable ethical state of the narrator's doctrinally and socially inappropriate mourning in the same terms as those used to point up unethical sleep elsewhere in his poetic oeuvre. Reading the sleep in this dream vision alongside sleep in other genres – and particularly the sleep in the romance and devotional texts with which it circulated – illuminates the complex politics of sleep in Middle English dream poetry that focuses on corrective religious instruction. A not-dissimilar conjunction of the epistemological benefits of sleep and the ethical problems it marks is found in *Piers Plowman*, as discussed below. Moreover – as discussed in Chapter 1 – in both *Pearl* and *Piers Plowman*, unhealthful and/or despairing emotions both mark and cause the dream vision narrators' transitions to a sleep that is profitable both medically (as a balancing of the humours or emotions conducive to mental health) and oneirically (as a conduit to spiritual understanding).

In each of these moments in *Patience*, *Cleanness*, *Gawain* and *Pearl*, 'slide' or 'slip' is the verb that precipitates the characters' sleep. The rhetorical specificity of these entrances to sleep signals their ethical import within the context of the Cotton Nero A.x poems and alliterative poetry more broadly. For the *Gawain*-poet's society, the verbs 'slide' or 'slip', as synonyms for 'fall', could also mean 'to fall into sin or evil', or 'to fall into error'.[184] By using signifiers with contemporary semantic connotations of downward moral transitions, the poet further highlights sleep's symbolic potential. These are, of course, alliterative poems, but it would be difficult to argue that the *Gawain*-poet was too dull to think of a synonym for 'slide', or for 'sleep'. Appropriately, other descriptions of sleep in these four poems do not use this phrasing. When Jonah is in the belly of the whale, he sleeps 'As in the bulk of þe bote þer he byfore sleped':[185] despite this connection, this sleep has a more positive spiritual nature than the earlier, since Jonah has now acknowledged his failings, and the poet accordingly does not figure him as 'sliding' into sleep. Other sleep in *Gawain* does signify on more than the mundane level, but not with the same meanings as the 'sliding' instances. When Gawain is journeying through the wilderness, the poet's comment that 'Ner slayn wyth þe slete he sleped in his yrnes / Mo ny3tez þen innoghe' demonstrates Gawain's successful endurance of hardships; later, his troubled sleep the night before his journey to the Green Chapel communicates his trepidation about the coming ordeal, and perhaps also about his recent unethical acceptance of the girdle.[186]

By contrast, the collocation of 'slide' or 'slip' with 'sleep', when occurring in other poems, seems to have been employed primarily for its alliterative utility. For instance, in the frequently alliterating late fourteenth-century *Avowyng of Arthur*, Arthur exhausts himself fulfilling his vow to kill the boar, and 'Forwerre, slidus he on slepe: / No lengur myghte he wake.'[187] This romance's description of sleep, roughly contemporary with the works of the *Gawain*-poet, appears experiential rather than ethical; it offers a reminder that, of course, sometimes literary sleep is just sleep: a needed restorative, a marker of completed labours rather than shirked ones. *St Erkenwald*'s use of this phrasing does have an ethical import; however, unlike its formal parallels in the Cotton Nero poems, this is not a moral valence to which such a detail contributes. When the people of London look upon a saint-like figure in his reopened tomb, they see him 'als freshe hyn þe face [...] / As he in sounde sodanly were slippid opon slepe'.[188] Whether or not one gives credence to the possibility of shared authorship for *Erkenwald* and the Cotton Nero poems,[189] this partial resonance with the works of the *Gawain*-poet is not surprising, given the two writers' shared Cheshire milieu and alliterative form. *Erkenwald*'s figurative construction of sleep, as the poem's hagiographical affiliations would suggest, stands in a different corner of the term's semantic field: it was a common belief that a miraculously-preserved corpse (one that could, for instance, appear to be a person merely asleep) connoted sanctity.[190] *Erkenwald* therefore uses sleep to establish the pious figure's irreproachable ethical state, rather than to question it.

Middle English literary sleep, as this chapter has shown, is often concerned with the current ethical state of those who enter it, or are propelled out of it. Yet the *Gawain*-poet is distinctive, within the context of the alliterative revival, in deploying a rhetorically specific mode of exploring ethical ambiguities both marginal and central to behavioural ideals. Sleep in the *Gawain*-poet's texts does not always or only have negative values; its positive side, as a constructive ethical act, is available in *Pearl* – but precariously so. Balance is immanent in courtesy, and sleep, in the Cotton Nero poems, offers a distinctive way of marking certain (potential) deviations from measured conduct. The *Gawain*-poet's interest in the ways in which literary sleep can be read produces a motif of the ethical intertwined with the experiential, of transgressive boundary-crossing that itself shows the ability to cross genre boundaries in contributing to romance, dream vision and devotional literature – that is, to each of the Cotton Nero poems' fused spiritual and secular codes of conduct.

Other alliterative poems sometimes focus primarily on the authoritative generation of sleep as the vehicle for dream visions. Several of the shorter poems in the Plowman tradition alliterate on 's' in the line in which the narrator enters sleep, but they neither use 'slip' or 'slide', nor share the *Gawain*-poet's ethical concerns regarding sleepers themselves.[191] William Langland's *Piers Plowman* itself, roughly contemporaneous with the *Gawain*-poet's writings as the other major alliterative Ricardian poem, treats sleep in ways that certainly do carry moral implications, though without the *Gawain*-poet's rhetorical construction. David Johnson observes that, given exegetical and homiletic perspectives on how context and type of sleep determines whether it is slothful and sinful or virtuous, Will's sleep has positive moral qualities.[192] This view is particularly persuasive in light of the language used when Will enters sleep. The word 'sleep' in *Piers Plowman* is rarely part of the alliteration of the lines in which it occurs, and 'slide' or 'slip', with their connotations of self-generated but improper movement, are never used to describe the entrance to sleep.[193] Instead, Langland tends to place the emphasis on external agency in the causation of the narrator's sleep: for instance, 'I bablede on my bedes þei brouȝte me aslepe', and 'reson hadde ruþe on me and rokked me aslepe'.[194] Here, Langland highlights the heuristic nature of sleep as a religiously guided vehicle travelling towards the next vision. The break between the first and second dream – at the beginning of Passus V – is accompanied by Will's awareness of the visionary value of sleep: 'Thanne waked I of my wynkyng and wo was withalle / That I ne hadde slept sadder and yseighen moore.'[195] While Will is infrequently responsible for producing his own sleep, on one occasion his contumacious rebuke of Reason makes him, like the dreamer in *Pearl*, responsible for being propelled out of it.[196] Will laments losing his sleep, because 'slepyng hadde I grace / To wite what dowel is, ac wakyng neuere':[197] here, sleep is valued as a state of spiritual enlightenment, and perhaps less ambiguously so than in *Pearl*. For Langland's Will, then, sleep is an object of desire, just as it is in Chaucer's *Book of the Duchess*, though in Langland's case it is for spiritual rather than for secular reasons.[198] Problematically, however, Will also indulges in his desire for sleep while in a church during mass – a sleep with distinctive spatial connotations that are discussed in the next chapter.

Notes

1 *Mankind*, in *Medieval Drama: An Anthology*, ed. Greg Walker (Oxford: Blackwell, 2000), 586–9.
2 Chaucer, 'Parson's Tale', X.705–6.
3 Handley, *Sleep in Early Modern England*, pp. 6–7; see also Crary, 24/7, p. 28.
4 'One of the essential factors in the fall of Troy is the sleep of the Trojans on that fatal night': B. M. W. Knox, 'The Serpent and the Flame: The Imagery of the Second Book of the *Aeneid*,' *American Journal of Philology*, 71.4 (1950), 379–400 (p. 387).
5 My approach here follows Helen Cooper's influential treatment of a romance motif as a '"meme", an idea that behaves like a gene in its ability to replicate faithfully and abundantly, but also on occasion to

adapt, mutate, and therefore survive in different forms and cultures': see Cooper, *English Romance in Time*, pp. 3–4.

6 Readerships widened with social mobility in the late fourteenth and fifteenth centuries: see Green, *Poets and Princepleasers*, pp. 9–10; Krueger, 'Medieval Conduct Guides for Youths', p. xii; Amos, 'Bourdieu, de Certeau, and the Common Appropriation of Noble Manners in the *Book of Courtesy*', pp. 45–6; Dannenfeldt, 'Sleep: Theory and Practice in the Late Renaissance', p. 420.

7 Nicholls, *The Matter of Courtesy*; Putter, *'Sir Gawain and the Green Knight' and French Arthurian Romance*, esp. pp. 51–139; Aaron Hostetter, *Political Appetites: Food in Medieval English Romance* (Columbus, OH: Ohio State University Press, 2017), esp. pp. 133–66. See also Ashley and Clark, 'Medieval Conduct: Texts, Theories, Practices'. For an analysis of the prandial focus of one such conduct text, see Claire Sponsler, 'Eating Lessons: Lydgate's "Dietary" and Consumer Conduct', in Ashley and Clark (eds), *Medieval Conduct*, pp. 1–22.

8 For instance, the fifteenth-century miscellany Oxford, Bodleian Library, MS Ashmole 61 contains a variety of romances – including *Sir Orfeo* – alongside five conduct texts: 'How the Wise Man Taught His Son', 'How the Good Wife Taught Her Daughter', 'Stans Puer ad Mensam', 'Dame Courtesy' and the 'Dietary'. See *Codex Ashmole 61: A Compilation of Popular Middle English Verse*, ed. George Shuffleton (Kalamazoo, MI: Medieval Institute Publications, 2008) and Hostetter, *Political Appetites*, p. 138.

9 See Hostetter, *Political Appetites*, esp. Chapter 4, '*Sir Gowther*: Table Manners and Aristocratic Identity', pp. 133–66.

10 Kymer, *Dietarium*, fol. 86v.

11 See Derek Brewer, 'Feasts in England and English Literature in the Fourteenth Century', in Detlef Altenburg, Jörg Jarnut, and Hans-Hugo Steinhoff (eds), *Feste und Feiern im Mittelalter: Paderborner Symposion des Mediävistenverbandes* (Sigmaringen: J. Thorbecke, 1991), pp. 13–26.

12 Sotres, 'The Regimens of Health', pp. 310–11.

13 Kymer, *Dietarium*, fol. 86v.

14 *Salerno Regimen of Health*, in *Medieval Medicine: A Reader*, ed. Faith Wallis (Toronto: University of Toronto Press, 2010), pp. 487–92, ll. 1 and 5 (translated here from a Latin incunable). The earliest manuscript containing this poem dates from the thirteenth century, and it circulated widely in the later Middle Ages; an English version was printed by Thomas Paynell in 1528.

15 *Salerno Regimen of Health*, p. 488.

16 Andrew Borde, *Regyment of Helthe*, in *The Babees Book*, ed. Frederick J. Furnivall, EETS OS 32 (London: Trübner, 1868), p. 244.

Ethics, appetite and the dangers of sleep   137

17 Borde, *Regyment of Helthe*, p. 245.
18 For instance, see also: 'A Diatorie', ll. 27–9 and ll. 37–8, William Bulleyn, *Bulwarke of Defence againste all Sicknes, Sornes, and Woundes*, p. 245, and Hugh Rhodes, *The Boke of Nurture* (all in *The Babees Book*); John Lydgate, *Dietary*; William Caxton, *Gouernayle of Helthe*; Thomas Elyot, *Castel of Helth*; Levinus Lemnius, *Touchstone of Complexions*; Thomas Cogan, *Haven of Health*. While many of these manuals date from the fifteenth and sixteenth centuries, Nicholls demonstrates that they continue the concerns of the infrequently extant thirteenth- and fourteenth-century courtesy books (*Matter of Courtesy*, pp. 145–57).
19 For an overview of the early modern dietaries' discussion of sleep, see Dannenfeldt, 'Sleep: Theory and Practice in the Late Renaissance'.
20 John Lydgate, *Dietary*, in *Codex Ashmole 61: A Compilation of Popular Middle English Verse*, ed. George Shuffelton (Kalamazoo, MI: Medieval Institute Publications, 2008), ll. 49–58.
21 George Shuffelton, 'The Dietary: Introduction', in *Codex Ashmole 61*, p. 528.
22 George D. Painter, *William Caxton: A Quincentenary Biography of England's First Printer* (London: Chatto & Windus, 1976), pp. 180–1.
23 Five fifteenth-century manuscripts containing the English version of *The Gouernayle* are described by William Blades in the facsimile edition of Caxton's *Gouernayle*. The manuscripts range from illuminated vellum (British Library, MS Sloane 3215) to a hastily penned paper copy (British Library, MS Harleian 2390); most are in medical miscellanies (see also British Library, MS Sloane 989; Oxford, Ashmolean Museum MS 1481; and Oxford, Ashmolean Museum MS 1498), but are not bound with Lydgate's *Dietary*: William Blades, ed., *The Gouernayle of Helthe: With The Medecyne of the Stomacke* (London, 1858).
24 William Caxton, *The Gouernayle of Helthe*, f. Bvi v – Bvii r.
25 Siegfried Wenzel, *The Sin of Sloth: Acedia in Medieval Thought and Literature* (Durham, NC: University of North Carolina Press, 1960), p. 70.
26 *Robert of Brunne's 'Handlyng Synne'*, ed. Frederick J. Furnivall, EETS OS 119 (London: Paul, Trench, Trübner, 1901), ll. 4253–9.
27 British Library, MS Harley 4196, fol. 88b; edited by Gerald Robert Owst, *Preaching in Medieval England: An Introduction to Sermon Manuscripts of the Period c.1350–1450* (Cambridge: Cambridge University Press, 1926), p. 174.
28 Hugh Rhodes, *The Book of Nurture*, in *The Babees Book*, ll. 57–9.
29 Ekirch, *A History of Nighttime*, p. 265; Sotres, 'The Regimens of Health', p. 311.
30 'die naturali dormire nonem horis et vigilaris quindecim' ['in the natural day you should try to sleep nine hours and to be awake fifteen']: Kymer, *Dietarium*, fol. 87r.

31 Chaucer, 'Shipman's Tale', VII.100–1.
32 Caxton, *Gouernayle*, f. B viii r.
33 However, the problem of unsanctioned naps also appears to have vexed medieval monastic communities. For instance, John Cassian (the fifth-century monk whose writings on monastic organisation influenced the sixth-century Rule of St Benedict, which in turn shaped western monasticism throughout the Middle Ages) writes that monks should pray standing up, because the dangers of horizontal prayer include falling asleep on the job: 'For when you lie prostrate for any length of time upon the ground you are more open to an attack, they say, not only of wandering thoughts but also slumber. And would that we too did not know the truth of this by experience and daily practice – we who when prostrating ourselves on the ground too often wish for this attitude to be prolonged for some time, not for the sake of our prayer so much as for the sake of resting' (John Cassian, *The Institutes* (Mahwah, NJ: Paulist Press, 2000), Book II, Chapter VII). Elsewhere, the thirteenth-century Cistercian prior Caesarius of Heisterbach seems to at least partially exculpate monks who fall asleep in church when they should not, attributing the heaviness that weighs monks down and makes them nap to invisible intermediaries such as snakes and cats: see *Dialogus miraculorum*, ed. N. Nösges and H. Schneider (Turnhout: Brepols, 2009), Chapters XXXII and XXXIII.
34 An early English mention of this sleeping pattern is found in the *Peterborough Chronicle* in an 1131 entry 'On an Moneniht æt þe forme [i.e. first] slæp' (p. 52); in Chaucer's 'Squire's Tale', Canacee ' slepte hir firste sleep and awook' (V.367); and in the late fifteenth-century prose *Melusine*, 'they departed about the first slepe' (p. 186.3). Roger Ekirch has collated numerous other references to first sleep and second sleep pertaining to medieval and early modern Europe. For Ekirch, this biphasic sleeping pattern, which lasted 'until the close of the early modern era', represents a natural way of sleeping that has been disrupted by the industrial revolution and the invention of inexpensive, widespread artificial lighting, which has facilitated shift work, later nights and compressed sleeping schedules: Ekirch, *A History of Nighttime*, esp. p. 301. For an alternative view of the biphasic sleeping patterns of pre-modern Europe as culturally constructed rather than natural, see Walker, *Why We Sleep*, p. 70. Either way, through widespread references in a range of texts, and through the instructions of conduct manuals, these sleeping patterns were recognised and reinforced.
35 John Lydgate, *Troy Book: Selections*, ed. Robert R. Edwards (Kalamazoo, MI: Medieval Institute Publications, 1998), 4.6278–80.

36 William Caxton, *The Game and Playe of the Chesse*, ed. Jenny Adams (Kalamazoo, MI: Medieval Institute Publications, 2009), Prologue ll. 19–20. Caxton translated *The Game and Playe of the Chesse* from a mid-fourteenth-century French version of the Latin *Liber de Ludo Scaccorum*; the first edition was dedicated to Edward IV's brother George of Clarence, but after Clarence's execution for treason in 1478, the second edition was directed towards a much wider readership.
37 Caxton, *Chesse*, II.241 and II.207–14.
38 Sotres, 'The Regimens of Health', p. 311.
39 Caxton, *The Gouernayle of Helthe*, f. Bvi v – Bvii r.
40 Caxton, *The Gouernayle of Helthe*, f. Bvi v – Bvii r.
41 For other early modern parallels, see Thomas Elyot, *The Castel of Helthe* (London, 1539), f. 46; *This Tretyse that Is Cleped Governayle of Helthe* (New York, 1969); William Bullein, *Goveriment of Health*, 90.
42 Chaucer, 'Miller's Tale', I. 3647.
43 Amos, 'Bourdieu, De Certeau, and the Common Appropriation of Noble Manners in the Book of Courtesy', p. 25; see also *The Household of Edward IV: The 'Black Book' and the Ordinance of 1478*, ed. A. R. Myers (Manchester: Manchester University Press, 1959), and Felicity Riddy, 'Mother Knows Best: Reading Social Change in a Courtesy Text', *Speculum*, 71 (1996), 66–86 (p. 67).
44 'How the Wise Man Taught His Sonne', in *Medieval Conduct Literature: An Anthology of Vernacular Guides to Behaviour for Youths, with English Translations*, ed. Mark D. Johnston (Toronto: University of Toronto Press, 2009), pp. 298–304 (ll. 33 and 37–40).
45 Similarly, in Francis Seager's mid-sixteenth-century *School of Virtue*, the poem 'How to Order Thyself when Thou Risest and in Apparelling thy Body' urges young readers to: 'Fly ever sloth and overmuch sleep; / In health the body thereby thou shalt keep. / Much sleep engendereth diseases and pain, / It dulls the wit and hurteth the brain. / Early in the morning, thy bed then forsake, / Thy raiment put on, thysself ready make': in *The Babees Book: Medieval Manners for the Young*, ll. 1–6. These are the opening lines of the poem, giving pride of place to sleep's proper performance, including its importance for health and the need to avoid sinful sloth.
46 'How the Good Wijf Taughte Hir Doughtir', in *Medieval Conduct Literature: An Anthology*, 288–97 (ll. 46–7 and 154).
47 Kim Phillips, *Medieval Maidens: Young Women and Gender in England, 1270–1540* (Manchester: Manchester University Press, 1993), p. 92.
48 William Caxton, *The Book of Fayttes of Armes and of Chyualrye*, ed. Alfred T. B. Byles, EETS OS 189 (1932; London: Oxford University Press, 1937), pp. 23–4.

49 On how these exhortations contribute to late medieval expectations for female self-regulation more broadly, see Flannery, *Practising Shame*, esp. pp. 60–89. In addition to Caxton's version, an anonymous mid-fifteenth-century English translation of Geoffrey de la Tour Landry's c.1371–2 *Le livre du Chevalier de la Tour Landry* is also extant in London, British Library, Harley MS 1764. Geoffroy de La Tour-Landry, *Book of the Knight of La Tour-Landry: compiled for the instruction of his daughters: translated from the original French into English in the reign of Henry VI*, ed. Thomas Wright (London: Paul, Trench & Trübner, 1906), p. 116.
50 *Lancelot*, vol. 4, p. 166: 'si furent si las et si travillié qu'*il les couvint a reposer tant que li chauz fust trespassez*' ('they were so weary that *it befitted them* to rest until the heat passed').
51 Malory, *Morte Darthur*, p. 190.24–5.
52 *Ywain and Gawain*, ll. 47–54. The Middle English *Ywain and Gawain* is thought to have been composed in the early fourteenth century (perhaps 1325–50), and is extant only in one early fifteenth-century manuscript, British Library MS Cotton Galba E. ix.
53 Chrétien de Troyes, *Le Chevalier au Lion (Yvain)*, ed. Mario Roques (Paris, 1960); *The Knight with the Lion (Yvain)*, in *Arthurian Romances*, trans. W. W. Kibler (London, 2004), p. 295. Intriguingly, in the Old Norse *Ivens saga* – which was translated from French in the thirteenth century – Arthur's sleep is produced by a 'heaviness' unparalleled in Chrétien's version: 'there fell such heaviness upon the king that he had above all to go out to his quarters and sleep. And all the people wondered at this, because he had never before done this. The queen was with him in his quarters' (the translation is Rikhardsdottir's: *Medieval Translations and Cultural Discourse*, p. 90; from the early fifteenth-century A copy, Holm 6 4to, Royal Library, Stockholm). In Chrétien's version, there is a precedent for the court's surprise; however, where Chrétien's version focuses on sex, the Middle English and Old Norse versions focus on what we might today call a food coma, or what the Middle Ages similarly understood as the result of the need for digestion after eating. Rikhardsdottir observes that sudden onset sleep occurs in Icelandic sagas in ways that testify to 'a Nordic motif familiar from native folklore' (*Medieval Translations and Cultural Discourse*, p. 91). Although the implications are not necessarily the same (Middle English romances often focus on responsibility and vulnerability rather than the Norse premonitions Rikhardsdottir highlights), this 'Nordic motif' offers a striking parallel to the ways in which Middle English romances feature knights and kings sleeping at 'inappropriate moments'. However, Rikhardsdottir does not observe

that *Ywain and Gawain*, like *Ivens saga*, has also altered the implications of Arthur's sleep. *Ivens saga* was written earlier than *Ywain and Gawain*, but all the extant manuscripts of *Ivens saga* are later than the manuscript of *Ywain and Gawain*. Old Norse writers sometimes drew upon Middle English sources, but it is much less likely that later medieval English writers had first-hand familiarity with Norse texts. Perhaps a fifteenth-century Norse scribe familiar with *Ywain and Gawain* adapted a copy of *Ivens saga* to follow suit; or, perhaps, here in the literatures of the North Atlantic, far from the siesta cultures of the south and at a remove from the particular sensual interests of Old French courtly romance, we find evidence of parallel sleep-related adaptations.

54 Malory, *Morte Darthur*, p. 466.24–9.
55 Vinaver, *Commentary*, p. 1488: 'In F Palomides gives a different reason for parting company with Mark: *il ne m'est pas avis, au semblant que j'ay veü, que il ait gramment chevauchié*' (emphasis original).
56 William Caxton, Preface to *Morte Darthur*, in Sir Thomas Malory, *Le Morte Darthur*, ed. P. J. C. Field, 2 vols (Cambridge, 2013), II, 854–7 (p. 856).
57 *Melusine*, p. 29.
58 *Melusine*, 28.25–6; d'Arras, *Mélusine*, pp. 36–7.
59 For example, slothful sleep is depicted as unethical for a knight in Chrétien's *Erec and Enide*, though as with Arthur's sleep at the beginning of Chrétien's *Yvain*, there is a sexual element here: when Erec eschews tournaments for his wife Enide's company, 'his companions were grieved by this and often lamented among themselves, saying that he loved her far too much. Often it was past noon before he rose from her side': *Erec and Enide*, p. 67.
60 Malory, *Morte Darthur*, p. 42.23–6.
61 Henry Watson, *Valentine and Orson*, ed. Arthur Dickson, EETS OS 204 (London: Oxford University Press, 1937), p. 152.10–12.
62 Pacolet similarly overwhelms enemies with magical sleep at pp. 160.12–15; 178.18–19; 192.5–15; 197.16–20; 255.9–10 and 256.18–19; 263.8–9; 263.20–1; and 264.26–7. Finally, at p. 282.2–4, the Saracen King Lucar succumbs to one of Pacolet's sleeping spells, but when he awakes, he stabs Pacolet to death (p. 282.11–12).
63 *Valentine and Orson*, p. 255.6–12.
64 See Megan G. Leitch, 'The Servants of Chivalry? Dwarfs and Porters in Malory and the Middle English Gawain Romances', *Arthuriana*, 27.1 (2017), 3–27.
65 *Valentine and Orson*, p. 264.31–4.
66 *Valentine and Orson*, p. 264.35–6.

67 John Skelton, 'Garlande or Chapelet of Laurell', in *John Skelton: The Complete English Poems*, ed. John Scattergood (Harmondsworth: Penguin, 1983), 191.
68 Henry Howard, 'The great Macedon', in *Poems*, ed. Emrys Jones (Oxford: Clarendon Press, 1964), ll. 13–14.
69 Philip Sidney, *The Old Arcadia*, ed. Katherine Duncan-Jones (Oxford: Oxford University Press, 1985), pp. 27 and 30.
70 Sidney, *Old Arcadia*, pp. 242 and 241.
71 Sullivan, *Sleep, Romance and Human Embodiment*, pp. 55–63.
72 Sullivan, *Sleep, Romance and Human Embodiment*, esp. pp. 50–1.
73 Stephen Greenblatt, *Renaissance Self-Fashioning: From More to Shakespeare* (Chicago, IL: University of Chicago Press, 1980), pp. 182–3; Sullivan, *Sleep, Romance and Human Embodiment*, pp. 29–46.
74 Edmund Spenser, *The Faerie Qveene*, ed. A. C. Hamilton, rev. 2nd edn (London: Routledge, 2007), II.xii.72–80 (72.5; 80.1–2).
75 Sullivan suggests that it is because reason has no influence over sleep or the passions that 'immoderate sleep itself, along with sexuality, is meaningfully at issue' in early modern romance: *Sleep, Romance and Human Embodiment*, pp. 17–18. My aim here is to show that this way in which immoderate sleep is 'meaningfully at issue' in early modern romance also follows medieval romance.
76 Flannery, *Practising Shame*, pp. 33 and 23; the romance motif I am discussing here, I suggest, fits with the admonitory focus on female honour Flannery perceptively identifies in conduct literature and in courtly, classicising texts by Chaucer, Gower and Lydgate.
77 *Sir Orfeo*, ll. 63–82.
78 Sharon Ann Coolidge, 'The Grafted Tree in *Sir Orfeo*: A Study in the Iconography of Redemption', *Ball State University Forum*, 23 (1982), 62–8; A. E. Lasater, 'Under the Ympe-Tre or: Where the Action is in *Sir Orfeo*', *Southern Quarterly*, 12 (1974), 353–63; Constance Bullock-Davies, '"Ympe-tre" and "Nemeton"', *Notes and Queries*, n.s. 9 (1962), 6–9. For a list of analogues for falling asleep under an apple tree, see A. J. Bliss (ed.), *Sir Orfeo* (1954; Oxford: Clarendon Press, 1966), pp. liv–lvii. The Stith Thompson motif index lists various associations between apple trees and the power of fairies, from Old Norse as well as English. However, in *King Orphius*, the fifteenth-century Older Scots version of *Sir Orfeo*, the queen instead falls asleep under a laurel tree.
79 John Block Friedman, 'Eurydice, Heurodis, and the Noon-Day Demon', *Speculum*, 41.1 (1966), 22–9.
80 Friedman, 'Eurydice, Heurodis, and the Noon-Day Demon', pp. 29 and 26.

81 Saunders, *Rape and Ravishment*, pp. 228–33.
82 Flannery, *Practising Shame*, p. 62.
83 Burger, *Conduct Becoming*, p. 5.
84 Unless it is to be seen as derived from a lost Breton lai, *Lai d'Esgaré*: Anne Laskaya and Eve Salisbury, 'Sir *Degaré*: Introduction', in *The Middle English Breton Lays*, pp. 89–100 (p. 90).
85 *Sir Degaré*, in Anne Laskaya and Eve Salisbury (eds), *The Middle English Breton Lays*, ll. 72–5.
86 It has also been suggested that midday heat in Middle English literature sometimes stands as an inducement to sexual desire: Robert Allen Rouse, '"Some Like it Hot": The Medieval Eroticism of Heat', in Hopkins and Rushton (eds), *The Erotic in the Literature of Medieval Britain*, pp. 71–81.
87 *Sir Degaré*, ll. 90–1, 100, 105, and 107–13.
88 In the Middle English *Octavian*, sleep again highlights vulnerability and danger to a woman's well-being. Here, however, the danger is not abduction or rape, but rather, false accusations of adultery, and the possibility of punishment by death. That this is a well-earned sleep, resulting from fatigue after labour (and after the empress's fulfilment of her duty to provide an heir), fits with this episode's nature as an instance of the calumniated queen motif (familiar from other romances such as Chaucer's 'Man of Law's Tale' and its analogue *Emaré*), rather than as an exemplum about the dangers of a lapse in bodily self-regulation. This episode occurs in both the Southern and Northern versions: see, for instance, *Octavian*, ed. Frances McSparran, EETS OS 289 (London: Oxford University Press, 1986), ll. 127–32.
89 *Sir Degaré*, 853–5.
90 *Sir Degaré*, 866–7.
91 *Sir Gowther*, in *The Middle English Breton Lays*, ll. 74, 70, and 71.
92 Saunders, *Rape and Ravishment*, p. 233.
93 MacLehose, 'Fear, Fantasy and Sleep in Medieval Medicine', pp. 70–2.
94 *Prose Merlin*, ed. John Conlee (Kalamazoo, MI: Medieval Institute Publications, 1998), p. 23, ll. 116–17.
95 *Prose Merlin*, p. 30, l. 346.
96 Dronzek emphasises important differences in conduct manuals' instruction of male and female readers: 'the consequences for women's loss of honor took on concrete physical form, while those for men did not' ('Fifteenth-Century Conduct Books', p. 151). However, sleep suggests some overlaps in terms of ethical standards and regulation.
97 Caxton, *Book of the Ordre of Chyvalry*, p. 67.2–4.
98 Gregory the Great, *Pastoral Care*, iii.4.

99 In Mandeville's version, unlike in *Melusine*, there is no focus on *how* knights successfully perform the vigil, but the story does end with a warning to resist the urge to sleep: 'it es gude to him þat schalle wake þis hawke þat he be wele warre þat he slepe noȝt, for if he slepe he bese lost for euer and neuermare comme whare men er': John Mandeville, *The Egerton Version of Mandeville's Travels*, ed. M. C. Seymour, EETS OS 336 (Oxford: Oxford University Press, 2010), p. 82.22–4. *Mandeville's Travels* circulated in English prose from the late fourteenth century, and the Egerton MS is c.1400.

100 Prose *Melusine*, p. 362.27–30.

101 *The Romans of Partenay*, ed. Walter W. Skeat, EETS ES 22 (London: Paul, Trench, Trübner, 1899), 5507–9. In the *Romans of Partenay*'s French source, la Couldrette's version, these knights are described as 'vaillans' (valliant) and are said to wake 'puissamment' (resolutely): *A Bilingual Edition of Couldrette's Mélusine or Le Roman De Parthenay*, ed. Matthew W. Morris (Lewiston, NY: Edwin Mellen Press, 2003), ll. 5995 and 5997. However, Couldrette's version has no precedent for calling the vigilant knights 'worthy' – a chivalric epithet chosen by the English translator, in parallel with other English romances (it is, for example, similarly central to Malory's lexis of chivalric praise).

102 Prose *Melusine*, p. 364.15–18.

103 Prose *Melusine*, p. 365.31–2.

104 Prose *Melusine*, p. 367.16–17.

105 *Romans of Partenay*, 4615–19; cf *Couldrette's Mélusine*, 5009–13.

106 *Knyghthode and Bataile*, ed. R. Dyboski and Z. M. Arend, EETS OS 201 (London: Oxford University Press, 1935), 1383, III. Translated in 1460 by a Lancastrian clerk from Vegetius's late-fourth- century prose *De re militari*, *Knyghthode and Bataile* periodically diverges from its source in order to comment upon the current political situation.

107 William Caxton, *Blanchardyn and Eglantine*, ed. Leon Kellner, EETS ES 58 (London, 1890), p. 107.12–15.

108 Caxton, *Book of the Ordre of Chyvalry*, pp. 122.8–123.10.

109 Malory, *Morte Darthur*, p. 909.26–31.

110 *Lancelot of the Laik*, in *Lancelot of the Laik and Sir Tristrem*, ed. Alan Lupack (Kalamazoo, MI: Medieval Institute Publications, 1994), ll. 1049–50.

111 Baldassare Castiglione, *The Book of the Courtier*, trans. Sir Thomas Hoby, ed. J. H. Whitfield (London: Dent, 1974), p. 36.

112 William Shakespeare, *Henry VI Part I*, 4.iii.29.

113 Christine Chism, 'Romance', in *The Cambridge Companion to Medieval English Literature, 1100–1500*, ed. Larry Scanlon (Cambridge: Cambridge University Press, 2009), pp. 57–69 (pp. 58–9).

114 As discussed in Ad Putter and Jane Gilbert, 'Introduction', in Ad Putter and Jane Gilbert (eds), *The Spirit of Medieval English Popular Romance* (Harlow: Longman, 2000), pp. 1–38 (pp. 2–3 and 16–20).
115 Nicola McDonald, 'A Polemical Introduction', in Nicola McDonald (ed.), *Pulp Fictions of Medieval England: Essays in Popular Romance* (Manchester: Manchester University Press, 2004), pp. 1–21.
116 See J. A. Burrow, 'The Fourteenth-Century Arthur', in Elizabeth Archibald and Ad Putter (eds), *The Cambridge Companion to the Arthurian Legend* (Cambridge: Cambridge University Press, 2009), pp. 69–83 (pp. 74–5); Rikhardsdottir, *Medieval Translations and Cultural Discourse*, esp. p. 97; Tony Hunt, 'Beginnings, Middles and Ends: Some Interpretive Problems in Chrétien's *Yvain* and its Medieval Adaptations', in Leigh A. Arrathoon (ed.), *The Craft of Fiction* (Rochester, MI: Solaris Press, 1984), pp. 83–117, esp. pp. 90–2; and Gayle K. Hamilton, 'The Breaking of Troth in *Ywain and Gawain*', *Mediaevalia*, 2 (1976), 111–35.
117 Marcel Elias, 'Interfaith Empathy and the Formation of Romance', in Mary Flannery (ed.), *Emotion and Medieval Textual Media* (Turnhout: Brepols, 2018), 99–124. Elias's work focuses on crusading romances in particular; see also Windeatt, 'Towards a Gestural Lexicon of Medieval English Romance'.
118 The protagonist of at least one romance does snore, but as a strategic choice, not a somatic contingency: when Bevis wishes to avoid having to speak with Josiane, in both the Anglo-Norman and the Middle English *Bevis of Hampton*, he 'began to snore' to feign sleep (Judith Weiss, '"The Courteous Warrior": Epic, Romance, and Comedy in *Boeve de Haumtone*' in Neil Cartlidge (ed.), *Boundaries in Medieval Romance*, pp. 149–60 (p. 155)). In the early sixteenth-century prose romance *Huon of Burdeux* (translated from a mid-fifteenth-century French prose redaction of a chanson de geste), snoring, perhaps more typically for the romance genre, emanates from the uncouth, unchristian giant Galafre, whose slothful sleep (p. 99.20) demonstrates Huon's honour in not attacking the giant while he is asleep and 'without having made a defiance' (pp. 102.19 and 103.14–18): John Bourchier (Lord Berners), *Duke Huon of Burdeux*, ed. S. L. Lee, EETS ES 40, 41, 43, 50 (London: Trübner, 1882–7).
119 Langum, *Medicine and the Seven Deadly Sins*, pp. 145 and 149.
120 Delumeau, *Sin and Fear*, p. 229.
121 Delumeau, *Sin and Fear*, pp. 230–2.
122 *Compost et Kalendrier*, as synthesised by Delumeau, *Sin and Fear*, p. 230.
123 Langum, *Medicine and the Seven Deadly Sins*, p. 146; see also Heffernan, *The Melancholy Muse*, p. 10.

124 MS Sloane 4031, edited as #97, 'Advice to the Several Estates, II', in *Historical Poems of the XIVth and XVth Centuries*, pp. 233–5, ll. 6–7.
125 Delumeau, *Sin and Fear*, p. 230. On other ways in which idleness features in Middle English literature as the antithesis of valorised productivity, see Gregory M. Sadlek, '*Otium, Negotium*, and the Fear of *Acedia* in the Writings of England's Late Medieval Ricardian Poets', in *Idleness, Indolence and Leisure in English Literature*, ed. Monika Fludernik and Miriam Nandi (New York: Palgrave Macmillan, 2014), pp. 17–39.
126 Idley, *Instructions to his Son*, II.797–800; see also II.ll.869–1540. Idley gives sloth a larger share of textual attention than he does most of the deadly sins, deploying more exempla from his main source, Robert Mannyng's *Handlyng Synne*, on this subject than on others: see Charlotte D'Evelyn, *Instructions to his Son*, p. 45.
127 Chaucer, 'Parson's Tale', X.682–4.
128 *Petri Venerabilis adversus Iudeorum inveteratam duritiem*, ed. Y. Friedman, Corpus Christianorum Continuatio Medievalis, LVIII (Turnhout: Brepols, 1985), p. 63 [Adv. Iud., 3, ll. 757–72]; translation Abulafia's (see next note).
129 See Anna Sapir Abulafia, 'Bodies in the Jewish-Christian debate', in Sarah Kay and Miri Rubin (eds), *Framing Medieval Bodies* (Manchester: Manchester University Press, 1994), pp. 123–37 (pp. 125–7).
130 Gower, *Confessio Amantis*, vol. 3, 5.6893–5. Similarly, in Book 4 of the *Confessio Amantis* (on Sloth), Gower writes that Somnolence, Sloth's chamberlain, who is too lazy to win love, 'routeth with a slepi noise' (4.2731).
131 Russell Peck, *Confessio Amantis*, vol. 3, note to 5.6893–5; for other occurrences of this proverbial phrase, see Bartlett Jere Whiting and Helen Wescott Whiting (eds), *Proverbs, Sentences, and Proverbial Phrases: From English Writings Mainly before 1500* (Cambridge, MA: Belknap Press of Harvard University Press, 1968), S955, p. 571.
132 Chaucer, 'Pardoner's Tale', VI.579–82.
133 Chaucer, 'Miller's Tale', I.3643–50.
134 *Wynnere and Wastoure*, in *Wynnere and Wastoure and The Parlement of the Thre Ages*, ed. Warren Ginsberg (Kalamazoo, MI: Medieval Institute Publications, 1992), 435–6. Warren Ginsberg argues that Wynnere is being accused of sleeping too soundly and slothfully, in a way that is 'seconded by Wastoure's charge that Wynnere wastes time by putting off making needed repairs to his storehouses and by failing to organize his household to react to a small harvest, if the weather is bad, or a large one, if it is good' (in *Wynnere and Wastoure and The Parlement of the Thre Ages*, p. 41).

135 Chaucer, 'Reeve's Tale', I.4162–7.
136 Chaucer, 'Reeve's Tale', I.4170.
137 Shakespeare, *Henry IV Part I*, 2.v.482–3.
138 Langland, *Piers Plowman*, B Prologue, 40–5.
139 Sloth is even more menacing later, when he, as part of team Antichrist, does battle against Conscience and his troops: in Passus XX, 'Sleuthe with his slynge an hard saut he made' (XX.217), and Sloth and Pride 'comen with a kene wille Conscience to assaille' (XX.374–5).
140 Langland, *Piers Plowman*, B II.97–9.
141 Jill Mann, 'Eating and Drinking in *Piers Plowman*', in *Essays and Studies*, NS 32 (1979), 26–43 (esp. pp. 29 and 40).
142 Langland, *Piers Plowman*, B XIII.404–8.
143 Langland, *Piers Plowman*, B VI.300–01; Mann, 'Eating and Drinking in *Piers Plowman*', p. 30.
144 Langland, *Piers Plowman*, B V.358–61. Compare the (virtually identical) passage in the C-Text: *Piers Plowman: The C-text*, ed. Derek Pearsall (Exeter: University of Exeter Press, 1994), VI.415–18.
145 Langland, *Piers Plowman*, B V.386–92 (and C-Text, VII.1–7).
146 Chaucer, Manciple's Prologue, IX.9–19.
147 However, in the Canterbury frame as it is extant, he has 'already' told his tale, so this commentary is untimely in another sense as well.
148 Langland, *Piers Plowman*, B V.393 (cf C-Text, VII.8), and B V.411–12.
149 *Mankind*, 330 and 586.
150 *Mankind*, 237–40.
151 *Mankind*, 593.
152 *Mankind*, 606–7.
153 Marlowe, *Dr Faustus*, A-text 4.1.135 and B-text 4.4.25.
154 *The York Plays*, vol. I, Pageant 30, 135–9. Richard Beadle observes that this pageant was perhaps associated with the tapiters because, as weavers, they produced household goods such as bedspreads, and this play centres on beds, with both Pilate and Percula going to bed, separately (followed by the staging of Percula's dream): *York Plays*, II, 250.
155 Because 'synne' at 30.137 is supposed to rhyme with 'wyne' and 'myne', in the glossary to his edition of the York Plays, Richard Beadle observes that it signifies not 'sin' but 'syne', meaning 'later', and so the spelling can be seen as the result of a scribal aberration. It is still, I would argue, a suggestive wordplay.
156 Pageant 30, ll. 153 and 176.
157 Pageant 30, ll. 186–9; the messenger then repeats this to Pilatus almost verbatum at 285–8.
158 For sleep deprivation in Passion narratives, see Matthew 8:20 and Luke 9:58. As Richard Beadle observes, 'the idea that one of Jesus'

torments was to be deprived of sleep is occasionally mentioned in meditative accounts of the Passion, but it seems to have been of particular interest to the York dramatists, who contrast his situation with the luxurious and drunken sleep of Cayphas, Pilate, and Herod': *York Plays*, II, 249. On deliberate sleep deprivation in late medieval devotional and ascetic practice, see Sarah Macmillan, '"The Nyghtes Watchys": Sleep Deprivation in Medieval Devotional Culture', *Journal of Medieval Religious Cultures*, 39.1 (2013), pp. 23–42.

159 *York Plays*, Pageant 13, 245.
160 Jacob's famous dream of the ladder leading to heaven, for instance, occurs at night (Genesis 28:10–17).
161 *York Plays*, Pageant 13, 246–52.
162 While most people are supposed to sleep at night, shepherds often wake, and work, during the night. In the Second Shepherds' Play in the Wakefield cycle, three shepherds display a lack of vigilance and care when they all fall asleep rather than looking after their flock, and allow a disreputable thief, Mak, to camp with them. Mak casts a spell to ensure that the shepherds stay asleep while he steals one of their sheep. In this comic-didactic play, in which the sheep, or lamb, stands in for Christ, both the comedy and the didacticism are mediated through sleep. The sleep is essential to the plot, but its ready symbolism as a lack of vigilance is foregrounded here.
163 D. S. Brewer, 'Courtesy and the Gawain-poet', in John Lawlor (ed.) *Patterns of Love and Courtesy: Essays in Memory of C. S. Lewis* (London: Edward Arnold, 1966), pp. 54–85; Nicholls, *The Matter of Courtesy*; Putter, *'Sir Gawain and the Green Knight' and French Arthurian Romance*, esp. pp. 51–139.
164 Ad Putter, *An Introduction to the* Gawain-*Poet* (Harlow: Longman, 1996); Putter, *'Sir Gawain and the Green Knight' and French Arthurian Romance*.
165 *Patience*, ll. 183–6.
166 Andrew and Waldron, *The Poems of the Pearl Manuscript*, p. 193.
167 Putter, *An Introduction to the Gawain-Poet*, p. 139.
168 Lorraine Kochanske Stock, 'The 'Poynt' of *Patience*', in Robert J. Blanch, Miriam Youngerman Miller, and Julian N. Wasserman (eds), *Text and Matter: New Critical Perspectives of the* Pearl-*Poet* (Troy, NY: Whitston, 1991), pp. 163–75 (p. 169).
169 *Patience*, ll. 466–8.
170 A. C. Spearing, 'Poetic Identity', in Derek Brewer and Jonathan Gibson (eds), *A Companion to the Gawain-Poet* (Cambridge: D. S. Brewer, 2007), pp. 35–51 (p. 47).
171 *Biblia Sacra: Iuxta Vulgatum Versionem*, ed. Robert Weber, vol. II (Stuttgart, 1975), Daniel 5:30.

172 The structural contrasts of *Cleanness*'s five exempla and the distinctiveness of Belshazzar's feast – but not of the sleep that follows – are addressed by Nicholls, *The Matter of Courtesy*, p. 85, and Jane K. Lecklider, *Cleanness: Structure and Meaning* (Cambridge: D. S. Brewer, 1997), pp. 202–14.
173 *Cleanness*, ll. 1785–7.
174 *Sir Gawain and the Green Knight*, ll. 243 and 244–7.
175 Nicholls, *The Matter of Courtesy*, p. 123.
176 Aisling Byrne, 'The Intruder at the Feast: Negotiating Boundaries in Medieval Insular Romance', *Arthurian Literature*, 27 (2010), 33–57 (p. 34).
177 *Sir Gawain and the Green Knight*, l. 1182.
178 *Sir Gawain and the Green Knight*, l. 1190.
179 Putter, *'Sir Gawain and the Green Knight' and French Arthurian Romance*, p. 121.
180 *Pearl*, ll. 59–60.
181 Spearing, *Medieval Dream-Poetry*, pp. 116–18.
182 *Pearl*, ll. 1170–1.
183 Spearing, *Medieval Dream-Poetry*, pp. 119 and 121. Nicholls notes the causes and implications of the dreamer's ejection from his vision (*Matter of Courtesy*, p. 111), but again neglects the entrance to sleep.
184 *Middle English Dictionary*, 'sliden', senses 1 and 3; 'slippen', senses 1 and 2.
185 *Pearl*, l. 292.
186 *Sir Gawain and the Green Knight*, ll. 729–30, 1991 and 2007.
187 *The Avowyng of Arthur*, in *Sir Gawain: Eleven Romances and Tales*, ed. Thomas Hahn (Kalamazoo, MI: Medieval Institute Publications, 1995), ll. 271–2.
188 *St Erkenwald*, ll. 89–92.
189 As expressed recently by John M. Bowers, *An Introduction to the Gawain-Poet* (Gainsville: University Press of Florida, 2012), esp. pp. 87–8; for a more cautious view, see Malcolm Andrew, 'Theories of Authorship', in *A Companion to the Gawain-Poet*, pp. 23–33.
190 Ruth Morse, Introduction, *St Erkenwald*, p. 18.
191 See, for instance, *Mum and the Sothsegger*, ll. 869–70; also *Wynnere and Wastoure*, ll. 45–6, and *The Parlement of the Thre Ages*, ll. 100–3.
192 David F. Johnson, 'The Figurative Significance of Sleep in *Piers Plowman*', pp. 240–5.
193 Not even for Sloth, Langland's notorious immoral sleeper: see V.391 and 441 in the B-text, as discussed in the previous section. As in Langland's representations of the sleep of Glutton and Sloth, Langland's discussions of Will's sleep in the A and C texts are consistent with that

150   *Sleep and its spaces in Middle English literature*

of the B text: *Piers Plowman: A Parallel-Text Edition of the A, B, C and Z Versions*, ed. A. V. C. Schmidt (London: Longman, 1995).

194 Langland, *Piers Plowman*, B V.8 and XV.11; see also VIII.67. Among Will's other entrances to sleep, alliterative stress is on 'sleep' twice (Pro. 10; XIX.5); here, Langland foregoes opportunities to use 'slip' or 'slide'. Apart from XVI.19–20, Will's other entrances to sleep do likewise use the word 'sleep', but do not alliterate on its 's': see XI.5, XIII.21, XVIII.4–5, and XX.51.

195 Langland, *Piers Plowman*, B V.3–4.

196 Langland, *Piers Plowman*, B XI.403–5.

197 Langland, *Piers Plowman*, B XI.408–9.

198 For a detailed discussion of sleep in Chaucer's dream visions, see Chapter 4.

3

Sleeping spaces and the circumscription of desire

In the literature of medieval England, the spaces of sleep mediate a range of desires. As the opening *descriptio* topos of Britain in Geoffrey of Monmouth's twelfth-century *Historia Regum Britanniae* asserts, this 'best of islands' is characterised by pleasant meadows and streams which 'offer[…] the assurance of gentle sleep to those who lie by their banks' ('pignus suauis soporis in ripis accubantibus irritant').[1] Here, certain insular spaces are understood as intimately connected with, and inherently conducive to, sleep. This topos of a *locus amoenus* or pleasant place includes the prospect of sleep, presented as a natural good, both peaceful and restorative. Sleep is desirable, and so are the spaces, pleasant and secure, that promise sleep. Insular space is also conducive to sleep in Shakespeare's *The Tempest*, where Caliban explains that 'the isle is full of noises, / Sounds and sweet airs that give delight and hurt not', which, even 'if I then had waked after long sleep, / Will make me sleep again'.[2] Between Geoffrey's influential description of the island of Britain and Shakespeare's imagined island – in both of which insular milieux themselves exude expectations of sleep – late medieval insular milieux generated literature in which a variety of spaces similarly evoke expectations of sleep: sometimes, though certainly not always, with peaceful prospects. Whether indoors or out, in gardens or under trees, in beds or in churches, the spaces of sleep in English literature host desires for sleep itself, and also convene other desires: for knowledge, for consolation, for salvation, for sex. Though sleep does not always take place in the literary episodes analysed in this chapter, the very way in which certain spaces are associated with sleep shapes the expectations raised by, and possibilities negotiated in, these spaces.

This chapter argues that Middle English literature is distinctive in its deployment of the spaces of sleep to explore various desires, especially sexual desire. In conjunction with the spaces that accommodate sleep, desire in Middle English literature is often circumscribed: 'written around', enclosed, enabled or curtailed. Henri Lefebvre's concept of 'social space' as the product of political and economic power structures has been used by medievalists to illuminate the implications of (for instance) distinctive religious, urban and aristocratic spaces,[3] and it informs this chapter's analysis of the spaces associated with sleep in late medieval English literature and culture. While place and space are linked, recent work has also emphasised their differentiation: a place, 'through the boundary or limit that belongs to it, also opens up a space – place is thus tied to a boundary, [...] and space to the openness within the boundary'.[4] As Jeff Malpas has observed, place both enables certain possibilities, and imposes certain demands; this helps us to recognise the ways in which space and place are productive, as well as being produced.[5] Where a sleeping place might be a bedroom, a public hall, or the bank of a river, the spaces such places contain are shaped by the sociopolitical power and wealth of their owners and occupants as well as by their walls, furniture or vegetation; and, in turn, they shape the possibilities and expectations of the actions they host. Like sleep itself, the spaces of sleep serve an epistemological function, shaping the emotional and ethical connotations of sleep, as well as of other activities. The spaces of sleep in Middle English literature reveal desires for spiritual enlightenment, poetic inspiration and sexual fulfilment, as well as the restoration (or slothfulness) that sleep itself embodies.

The first two sections of this chapter, focusing on sleeping spaces beyond the bedroom, and on beds themselves, consider how the implications of a character's sleep are shaped by the spaces in which it is performed. Generic conventions inform the expectations raised when a character falls asleep in a given space – whether in pleasant green surroundings, a public structure or a bedroom. For instance, where drowsing in a verdant locale in a dream poem raises expectations of a vision, to do the same in a romance raises expectations of some form of assault. Such conventions are powerful signifiers, and are deployed and adapted in individual texts. Where a bed features, the expectations, unsurprisingly, often depend on the number of occupants as well as the genre. Characters in bed are often shown either participating in a charged encounter, or expressing their emotions (if not both). While two in a literary bed usually signals sexual possibilities, a solitary bed often offers a platform for voicing discontented thoughts. Enclosed spaces enable inwardness; literary texts turn to these sleeping spaces to offer expressions of interiority not often otherwise found in genres such as Middle English romance. Thus, while sleep is itself frequently considered 'remarkable' in Middle English literature, here the spaces of sleep are used to remark upon other intimate discourses.

The final two sections of this chapter address the ways in which the spaces of sleep receive distinctive attention *as* spaces where sleep is expected, but in ways that negotiate sexual possibilities. In a culture of scarce and only semi-private bedrooms, the possibilities and limitations of bowers impact upon sexual opportunities and their representation; upon how sexual desire is conceived, conducted and controlled. Fabliau, of course (in both its French and English iterations), is a genre in which readers expect spatial manipulations: tricks to gain access to bedrooms, and traffic through bedchamber windows, are the genre's stock-in-trade. Yet Middle English romance also (and often more so than French sources or analogues) focuses on bedroom-related spatial strategising. While the sexualised spatiality of fabliau is well recognised, that of Middle English popular romance has been less well studied. In the sexual economy of Middle English romance, the commodities that circulate, that are desired and regulated, include not only bodies, but also spaces – especially the spaces of sleep. From *King Horn* to Malory's *Morte Darthur*, and *Sir Gawain and the Green Knight* to the *Squire of Low Degree*, Middle English romances often focus on the spaces of sleep, rather than the bodies that inhabit them, as a way of concentrating on and communicating sexual desire. Recognising this helps to qualify perceptions of Middle English romance as relatively uninterested in dwelling on sexual encounters and emotional dilemmas, when compared to French romance. While Middle English literature, and especially romance, often eschews moments of sexual interest in French sources such as Chrétien's *Yvain*, as I argue here, in Middle English romance, diegetic and narratorial attention to sexual desire is often conveyed instead through discussing the spaces of sleep.

As spaces convening, and showing tensions between, public and private desires, bedrooms both reinforce and interrogate gender norms. As Sarah Rees Jones observes, the medieval bedchamber is 'the key space in which the different functions assigned to men and women were most affirmed'.[6] Both beds and outdoor sleeping spaces serve as contested liminal environments in which gendered roles can become destabilised. The final section of this chapter explores this instability in relation to a recurring motif in Malory's *Morte Darthur*, in which a wounded knight bleeds on his beloved's bed, signalling threats to the adulterous knight's social status and marking unusually well-developed representations of female desire. Here, the implications of the spaces of sleep are inherently epistemological: literary beds structure discourses regarding chivalric identity (de)construction, and their sheets offer the texts for this interrogation, to be read by audiences both internal and external.

Beyond the bedchamber

Middle English literary figures often fall asleep in spaces that would seem unconventional to contemporary readers. Sleeping outdoors, or in public spaces designed for very different purposes, contravenes medieval societal expectations, but conforms to some literary expectations. For instance, sleeping outside on the ground was considered unhealthy in Galenic medicine, as vapours rising from the earth could be harmful to the body.[7] This shows that attitudes towards sleeping in a garden or by a stream were not as straightforward as either the classical tradition of the *locus amoenus*,[8] or the modern view of the benefits of 'fresh air', would suggest (even though medieval medicine did prize pure air). And yet, sleepers are drawn to these spaces in dream visions and romances in particular, though the consequences of sleeping in green spaces differ markedly in these two genres. Whether in a well-groomed garden or on the edge of a forest, under a leafy tree or by the burbling banks of a stream, chosen outdoor sleeping spaces, as in Geoffrey of Monmouth's opening *descriptio* topos, seem desirable and conducive to peaceful and pleasant slumber. Such conventional spaces, or what Charlotte Reinbold, in relation to the spaces of dream visions in particular, has termed 'conventions of setting',[9] raise expectations

Sleeping spaces and the circumscription of desire 155

of the sorts of encounters or adventures they will convene. While other aspects of some of the episodes discussed here are analysed in other chapters, this chapter reads them together to explore how conventional spaces establish sleep-related expectations, and how those expectations are thwarted as well as fulfilled. In addition, when sleeping spaces that are decidedly unconventional for perhaps any genre other than a condemnatory sermon, such as churches during mass, are used for sleep in either romance or dream vision, they inspire censure that is shared across these genres.

Unlike other studies of dream vision settings,[10] this chapter is concerned specifically with the space in which a given dreamer falls asleep. What interests me here is not the *loci amoeni* that feature in dreamscapes themselves – for instance, the garden in the *Roman de la Rose*, or the verdant surroundings outside the bedchamber when Chaucer's narrator 'awakes' into the dream in the *Book of the Duchess* – but rather, those that play host to (dream-filled) sleep. Langland's narrator, for instance, falls asleep at the beginning of *Piers Plowman* in a localised English *locus amoenus*, with a sleep-inducing stream reminiscent of Geoffrey of Monmouth's characterisation of insular waterways:

> In a somer seson, whan softe was the sonne,
> [...]
> on a May morwenynge on Malverne Hilles
> Me bifel a ferly, of Fairy me thoghte.
> I was wery ofwandred and wente me to reste
> Under a brood bank by a bournes syde;
> And as I lay and lenede and loked on the watres,
> I slombred into a slepyng, it sweyed so murye.
> Thanne gan me to meten a merveillous swevene–
> That I was in a wildernesse, wiste I nevere where.[11]

It is here, while slumbering in the Malvern hills, that Will sees a 'tour on a toft' and a 'dongeon' or fortress in a 'deep dale' between which symbolic sites a 'fair feeld ful of folk' are 'werchynge and wandrynge as the world asketh'.[12] Slumbering in a pleasant place, then, brings the possibility of enlightenment in a dream poem.

Similarly, but with a twist, the *Pearl* dreamer's vision-filled sleep comes to him when he is in an 'erber grene', lulled to slumber by the sweet smell of 'floury flaȝt' ('flowery turf').[13] This conventional location again raises expectations of a vision of love or spritual enlightenment. Yet whereas Will's first vision happens 'on a May morwenynge', at the expected time of budding new growth, the *Pearl* dreamer's instead occurs rather late in the season, 'in Auguste in a hyȝ seysoun', not long before outdoor sleeping spaces would become cold and inhospitable.[14] The *Pearl* dreamer is too late to do anything but mourn for his lost beloved, and he realises too late that excessive grieving is not the correct response to his daughter's ascent to heaven. Meanwhile, in the *Prologue* to the *Legend of Good Women*, not one but two pleasant green sleeping spaces feature in another reworking of expectations: the first, the meadow in which the narrator lounges to admire the daisy (but resists the generic expectation of sleep), and the second, the *hortus conclusus* or private garden in the narrator's home to which he retreats to sleep at night, in a makeshift bed constructed by his servants and enhanced by plucked flowers. Chaucer's narrator conscientiously defers his sleep until night-time despite musing on the daisy outdoors during the day, and goes to sleep not in a *locus amoenus*, but instead in the home (if in a sort of domesticated green space rather than a regular bed). As I argue in Chapter 4, here the *Prologue* uses the unethical implications of daytime sleep (as per the courtesy books) as a commentary on Chaucer's need for self-regulation: he needs to regulate both his bodily habits, and his compositional habits (by writing more positively about women).

While outdoor sleep in dream visions is undisturbed and productive, outdoor sleep in romance is dangerous and potentially destructive. If Will, the *Pearl* dreamer, or the narrator of the *Prologue* to the *Legend of Good Women* were suddenly awoken from their visions by someone seeking to attack or abduct them, readers would be entitled to be shocked, not least because such disruptions are not what the genre leads us to expect. Yet tangible dangers seem as much an expectation of outdoor sleeping in romance as a dream is an expectation of sleep in a dream poem. When *Sir Orfeo*'s Heurodis or *Sir Degaré*'s maidens fall asleep outside in the heat of the day under their respective trees, although these spaces are described as pleasant and peaceful, readers are invited to be alert to the generic expectation of an assault. The recognisable signifier of the shady tree, and the absence both of bodily self-regulation and of protection (whether by walls or guards), prime the reader to expect peril. The same is the case in *Sir Gowther*, where Gowther's mother is assaulted by an incubus when she sleeps outside under a tree. It is particularly the space in which this unprotected, daytime sleep occurs – outdoors under the shade of a tree – that conveys this motif's expectation of an attack, especially for romance women. This spatialised expectation also shapes the Wife of Bath's accusation that predatory friars have replaced romance's (predatory) 'fayeryes' and elves when she says, 'In every bussh or *under every tree* / Ther is noon oother incubus but he.'[15] However, when Launcelot falls asleep under the shade of a tree on a warm day in the *Morte Darthur*, Malory, as we have seen, alters his source in order to emphasise the ways in which the episode conforms to the expectations of this motif that, elsewhere in Middle English romance, signals an impending *raptus* of a lady. By highlighting Launcelot's slothful desire for daytime sleep, his 'grete luste to slepe', Malory underscores Launcelot's lack of bodily self-regulation and connects it to well-established expectations in English romance.[16] The *Morte*, then, invites readers to understand this episode in relation to other raptus scenes with which they may be familiar. Here, it is a knight who is unexpectedly shown to be in danger of a *raptus* – a fate more often inflicted upon romance ladies. Unexpected in the gender of its subject, this scene employs expectations familiar in the English genre to which it belongs. Desire for sleep in these episodes, because of the setting (spatial and temporal) in which it takes place, is circumscribed with attendant dangers and admonitions.

This admonitory, opprobrious expectation is also distinctive to the connotations of outdoor sleep both in other late medieval English genres such as drama, and in early modern romance. While retelling biblical dreams often involves more constraints than rewriting a romance or penning a dream poem, the York Cycle's representation of Joseph falling asleep to receive a vision from an angel differs markedly from biblical precedent. Although biblical visions usually occur at night, in bed, this Joseph instead has his vision when he goes for a walk and falls asleep on a grassy slope.[17] In deploying this setting for Joseph's sleep – a daytime, outdoor, pleasant place – the fifteenth-century York Cycle avails itself of the negative connotations of daytime outdoor sleep, since the vision the angel offers him while he is asleep here is a corrective for his sadness and distress at the idea that his wife is having another man's child. This seems a particularly medieval English way of using the conditions of sleep to comment on Joseph's spiritually inappropriate sorrow, in contrast to the way in which biblical dreams (including Joseph's) were often understood to take place at night. Chaucer's choice, in the *Prologue* to the *Legend of Good Women*, to call attention to a shift from a possible spontaneous daytime *locus amoenus* for his dream narrator's sleep to an orderly night-time location when Chaucer represents himself as in need of an ethical correction for and self-regulation of his (other) actions, also seems a recognisably English move. Later, when Spenser rewrites medieval romance in his *Faerie Queene*, his representation of Acrasia's entrapment of passing knights in her outdoor Bower of Bliss redeploys the *locus amoenus* tradition with strong ethical overtones. Before the knight of Temperance destroys the Bower, Acrasia's companion is the young knight Verdant, whose sleepy dalliance in these verdant spaces is, as it would be in medieval English romance (were he either a Launcelot or a lady), his undoing.

Churches, designed for communion and contemplation rather than sleep, also carry an ethical charge as a sleeping space in both romance and dream vision. In the fourteenth-century Middle English romance *Robert of Cisyle*, Robert, King of Sicily, falls asleep not only at an inappropriate time – during the afternoon – but also in a highly inappropriate place: in church, during a service. As perhaps the most popular Middle English penitential romance,[18] *Robert* both features sinful sleep and centres on an admonitory dream intertext. These two sleep-related moments 'mark the two points at which his [Robert's] knowledge of God's will is mediated through the church', since Robert has a disagreement with a priest in the episode in which he falls asleep in church, and since the allusion to an admonitory dream occurs in a narration of church teachings, the exemplum of Nebuchadnezzar's fate.[19] Sleep, then, especially because of where it takes place, is instrumental in highlighting the ethical stakes of penitential romance, as well as of chivalric romance. Here, sleeping in church signals a moral failure (as it does in sermons); it marks a change in the king's status, which in turn helps him to learn to amend his ways.

Robert's sleep in church encapsulates his sins: we are told that, although attending evensong, he 'thoughte more in worldes honour, / Than in Crist, ur saveour'.[20] He arrogantly challenges the priest and thinks that he is invincible and above all other men, declaring:

> 'Al your song is fals and fable!
> What mon hath such pouwer,
> Me to bringe lowe in daunger?
> I am flour of chivalrye,
> Myn enemys I may distruye;
> No mon lyveth in no londe,
> That me may withstonde.
> Then is this a song of nouht!'
> This errour he hedde in thought.
> And in his thouht a sleep him tok
> In his pulput, as seith the bok.[21]

The fact that Robert falls asleep while in church, when he ought to be listening to the sermon and thinking on God, underscores his unethical state here. This sleep also enables supernatural intervention: while Robert is asleep, an angel arrives in his likeness and issues from the church as King of Sicily. Sleep is fundamental to the plot, in that it immobilises Robert so the angel can take his place. As Edward Foster observes, 'Robert's nap during vespers has consequences harsher than the ordinary experience of most drowsy worshippers because of his high position and because it is a metaphor for his indifference to the word of God.'[22] However, I would argue that it is not, as Foster suggests, that Robert is 'so bored as to fall asleep';[23] the poet does not suggest boredom, but rather foregrounds Robert's 'errour [...] in thought', suggesting he is in need of a correction (and perhaps also implying the 'heaviness' in thought which sometimes induces sleep), when 'a sleep him tok'.[24] The purpose of this sleep as a spiritual corrective, and the way in which it leads to a divine intervention so that Robert can begin his outward journey of penitence and his inward journey to recognise the error of his thinking, parallels some aspects of Middle English dream vision narrators' sleep, especially in *Piers Plowman* and *Pearl*.

In addition to Robert's untimely sleep as a plot point and ethical marker, intemperate sleep and an admonitory dream are also intertexts in this penitential romance. First, Robert is made the angel-king's fool and eats with the hounds for three years (during which time, appetite itself is a form of penance), and goes unrecognised and unassisted by his powerful brothers (one the pope, the other an emperor). Finally, his atonement for his superciliousness results in self-awareness about his sins when, at the mid-point of the narrative, he thinks about King Nebuchadnezzar:

> 'Allas, allas,' was al his song:
> His heer he tar, his hondes wrong,
> And evere he seide, 'Allas, Allas.'
> And thenne he thoughte on his trespas.
> He thoughte on Nabugodonosore,
> A noble kyng, was him bifore.[25]

Robert thinks of the exemplum of Nebuchadnezzar's fall to help him understand his own fall from power and divine favour. In Daniel 4:22, the prideful King Nebuchadnezzar has a dream of a tree which makes him afraid, and which is interpreted as prophesying his insanity for seven years as divine punishment; after these seven years, he is restored to prosperity because he now humbly recognises God's power above his.[26] When protagonists dream in Middle English romances, their visions are also often admonitory.[27] Robert, repentant like Nebuchadnezzar, is similarly (eventually) restored to prosperity. The story of Nebuchadnezzar is both intertext for, and generator of, Robert's repentance and restoration to prosperity. After his punishment, Robert, like Nebuchadnezzar,

> lovede God and holi churche,
> And evere he thoughte wel to worche.
> He regned after two yer and more
> And lovede God and his lore.[28]

The romance is usually 444 lines long, and the Nebuchadnezzar exemplum features in eight of the extant manuscript copies; the remaining two manuscripts contain shorter versions – 374 in CUL MS Ii.4.9, and only 79 in TCD MS 432 C – from which Nebuchadnezzar is omitted, but in which Robert still falls asleep in church. Thus, apart from when copied at the moment of an English king's insanity or when reduced to a 79-line outline,[29] this romance both foregrounds the sinfulness of the king, and highlights his need for atonement, through sleep.

Although sleep is a desirable state for Langland's Will because of the visions it brings – because of the imaginative and educational possibilities it enables – his desire for sleep itself is not always unproblematic. Most troubling is the moment in Passus XIX when Will falls asleep in church, during mass. It is striking that it is towards the end of the poem, after Will has learned many lessons from his various guides and corrective visions, that when he goes 'to chirche, / To here holly the masse and to be housled after', he nonetheless 'in myddes of the masse [...] / fel eftsoones aslepe'.[30] Critics often either pass over this moment or treat it as an enigmatic (but positive) passage rather than an ethical problem, given that the dream this sleep enables is, of course, valuable: in it, Will re-encounters Piers the Plowman as Jesus, and has Conscience as his interlocutor as soon as this dream begins. As Chapter 1 has shown, Will's sleep is often emotionally restorative, as well as spiritually enabling. And yet, given the prevalence of contemporary condemnations of falling asleep in church while one ought to be listening to mass, not least in the popular romance *Robert of Cisyle*, it certainly seems that medieval readers would have been invited to see the location in which Will falls asleep into his penultimate vision as a red flag.[31] This is also borne out by Langland's poetics: where the agency generating Will's earlier visions is often rhetorically attributed to positives such as 'reson' or his 'bedes', here, by contrast, the action is solely the dreamer's own: 'I fel eftsoones aslepe.'

The poem's startling revelation that Will, nearing the end of his journey of spiritual enlightenment, is still capable of flouting a basic tenet of Christian practice by indulging in his bodily appetite for sleep when he ought to be attending to religious instruction, is more explicable in light of Nicolette Zeeman's compelling reading of the psychology of Langland's work. Focusing on the middle visions of the B-text in particular, Zeeman argues that the poem repeatedly shows a 'renewal of spiritual desire' originating 'in desires that are culpable'.[32] Langland's interest in 'how one desire turns into another, how you might use one desire to inculcate another one',[33] also, I argue, shapes the way in which Will falls asleep in church in Passus XIX. When Will indulges in the natural, 'kyndeliche' human desire to sleep, but does so during the day, and more specifically, during a church service, his act of falling asleep is a culpable lack of temperance – although it also demonstrates his spiritual receptivity. Fittingly, it is during the vision he has while in this sleep that Will is instructed in the nature of the cardinal virtues, including Temperance:

> The seconde seed highte *Spiritus Temperancie*
> He that ete of that seed hadde swich a kynde,
> Sholde nevere mete ne meschief make hym to swelle;

> Ne sholde no scornere out of skile hym brynge;
> Ne wynnynge ne wele of worldliche richesse,
> Waste word of ydelnesse ne wikked speche moeve;
> Sholde no curious clooth comen on his rugge,
> Ne no mete in his mouthe that Maister Johan spicede.[34]

Temperance, that is, involves regulating one's desires and appetites; it requires avoiding gluttony, which, as Langland shows in the allegorical narrative of the Seven Deadly Sins in Passus V, can readily lead to sloth and intemperate sleep. Sin may be inevitable, but it can still lead to spiritual renewal. By falling asleep in church, Will, like Glutton and Sloth (who both sleep instead of attending mass), yields to a culpable desire; in his sleep, however, Will also accesses the imaginative and corrective potential of dreams – especially, here, in terms of the Aristotelian view of embodied dreams, rather than the Macrobian visionary paradigm. The way in which Will's intemperate desire for sleep leads to a dream about temperance foregrounds the importance of embodied experience in generating dreams, as per Aristotle-influenced, somatic theories of dreams well-known in the later Middle Ages.

Beds and their discontents

Embodied experience is likewise mediated in Middle English bed scenes in which neither sleep nor dreams (nor sex) occurs. Medieval beds were designed to bring contentment, both to their occupants (as places of rest) and to their owners (as objects of display), insofar as their wealth would permit. A good night's sleep was sought by constructing a sleeping space that was comfortable, warm and secure.[35] However, medieval English literary beds, when they are not introduced as the sites of sexual encounters (as discussed in the next section), often feature as sites of communication and especially of discontentment, as this section explores. In this way, beds support and enable explorations of emotion, as sleep itself does elsewhere.

In medieval England, bedchambers were used not only for sleep, but also for private devotion and for reading; they were spaces to be shared, to encourage intimacy (whether conversational or sexual). In addition, as Morgan observes, 'the chamber was a status symbol in late medieval England. The relative privacy afforded by a chamber physically separated those who could afford a chamber from those who could not.'[36] Beds were the conventional location for many of life's most significant experiences – birth, sex and death, as well as sleep.[37] Morgan's examination of inventories of chambers between 1350 and 1500 shows the value ascribed to both beds and associated textiles. In addition to wooden frames and mattresses, the beds of the aristocracy and the bourgeoisie would have sheets, blankets, coverlets, pillows and/or bolsters, and canopies or curtains.[38] As symbols of wealth, beds were put on display to signify status,[39] and privacy was often limited: 'as houses containing chambers only had one or two chambers and significantly more occupants, the chamber would often be at best an occasional thoroughfare and at worst more like a dormitory'.[40] This did not mean privacy was not desirable;[41] as attested by fabliau and romance machinations, the difficulty of obtaining privacy often intensified desires for it.

The beds and bedchambers featured in Middle English literature are usually those of the wealthy. The bed and accompanying textiles that the narrator in the *Book of the Duchess* imagines for his offering to Morpheus when he prays for sleep are famously rich and well-appointed. The kings and queens, knights and ladies of romance take their repose in sumptuous curtained beds (such as at Hautdesert in *Sir Gawain and the Green Knight*), while Chaucer's dream vision narrators have quiet, private bedrooms in which they can read peacefully as well as sleep. In a fabliau such as Chaucer's 'Miller's Tale', John the Carpenter is, not without reason, described as a 'riche gnof' (3188), since his house contains not just one private bedchamber, but also a guest room, in which Nicholas lodges.

From bugs to noisy bedfellows, mundane factors could, of course, interfere with a peaceful sleep. The expense of beds often meant that multiple people would share one bed – friends and fellows, as well as couples – and lords and ladies would expect to have attendants sleeping in the same room. On one occasion in Chaucer's *Troilus and Criseyde*, Pandarus sleeps 'on a paillet […]/ By Troilus he lay', and on another, Pandarus asks his bedfellow Troilus to 'ly stylle and lat me slepe'.[42] Yet premodern accounts of bedfellows often show the desirable fellowship and conversation such shared sleeping arrangements facilitated, since 'communal sleep afforded persons a trusted comrade in whom to confide on a level of intimacy rare for daytime relationships'.[43] The bedtime conversation between Cecile and her husband Valerian in Chaucer's 'Second Nun's Tale' bears witness to the expected nature of such 'pillow talk':

> The nyght cam, and to bedde moste she gon
> With hire housbonde, as ofte is the manere,
> And pryvely to hym she seyde anon,
> 'O sweete and wel biloved spouse deere,
> Ther is a conseil, and ye wolde it heere,
> Which that right fayn I wolde unto yow seye,
> So that ye swere ye shul it nat biwreye.'[44]

Here, the private space of the shared bed facilitates confidences. When insomnia strikes in dream visions and romances, communication is similarly foregrounded. Here, it is more often characters' emotions, rather than their surroundings, that are shown to keep them awake. Yet those surroundings – and the textual space created when characters lie awake in bed – are vital to the expression and exploration of those emotions. The spaces of sleep, that is, allow interiority to be externalised, communicating with the reader.

In literature as in life, beds and bedchambers are enabling spaces: as a facilitator of monologues and dialogues, they are spaces of emotion – just as beds and bedchambers are spaces of emotion when they play host to articulations and acts of sexual desire. Beds facilitate not only couplings, but also thoughts and conversations, that would not otherwise take place or be given textual space (or to which readers of literary texts would not otherwise be privy). Desires for privacy, for individuals seeking peaceful slumber or contemplation, shape the ways in which beds and bedchambers feature in Middle English literature. As Sarah Rees Jones has observed, public and private spheres, and movement between them, can be considered aspects of the 'spatial experience' of both men and women in the Middle Ages: 'Individual women and men moved not between two discrete categories of public and private space, but between different continuous modes of spatial experience (the intimate or personal, the private or domestic, and the public or political).'[45] Going to bed, retreating into the heart of the home to a space of relative privacy, enables literary characters to give voice to their innermost thoughts. Here, representations of inwardness (or interior-ity) occupy a conventional (interior) locus.

This spatial expectation shapes Chaucerian romance and dream vision. In *Troilus and Criseyde*, it is not just the lovers' trysts that occur in the bedchamber; Troilus's frequent bouts of lovesickness and longing also take place in his bedroom, a space to which he retreats in order to express his emotions.[46] Chaucer's dream visions, unlike *Piers Plowman* and *Pearl* (but like the *Roman de la Rose*), generally use a bed rather than an outdoor *locus amoenus* as the site for the narrator to fall asleep;[47] this is fitting for the sorts of emotion-inspired dreams with which Chaucer is (apart from in the *House of Fame*) generally concerned. The secluded bedchamber in which the dreamer's bed is housed in the *Book of the Duchess* and the *Parliament of Fowls* suits the bookishness of Chaucer's dream visions. Bedrooms, for Chaucer, furnish both reading material and the solitude in which to read, and the reading of books precedes his dream visions in both the *Duchess* and in the *Parliament*. Moreover, as discussed further in Chapter 4, the way in which Chaucer's dream vision narrators have dreams presented as inspired by their melancholy, as well as by their reading material, situates them within a wider literary tradition of beds as sites for the expression of sorrow. The narrators in the *Duchess* and in the *Parliament* both dwell discontentedly on their troubles while trying to sleep in their beds, and this resonates not only with French models, but also with conventions in other Middle English genres.

This resonance is clear in the ways that Chaucer also employs the bed as a site of emotional insight beyond his dream visions. In the 'Legend of Dido' in the *Legend of Good Women*, as Sheila Delany has observed, the bed is 'the key image and *locus dramatis*'.[48] More specifically, the bed repeatedly serves as the platform for expressions of interiority, both for Dido and for Aeneas. At night in her bed, Dido wants to sleep, but cannot:

> This noble queene unto hire reste wente.
> She siketh sore, and gan hyreself turmente;
> She waketh, walweth, maketh many a breyd,
> As don these lovers, as I have herd seyd.
> And at the laste, unto hire syster Anne
> She made hire mone, and ryght thus spak she thanne.[49]

Dido's 'mone' to her sister Anne about her love for Aeneas suggests that, as was common in late medieval royal and aristocratic households, Anne sleeps in the queen's bedchamber as an attendant and companion, and the space they share enables expressions of interiority. Later in the tale, it is Aeneas whose interiority is expressed – if, perhaps, with some duplicity: 'in hir bed he lyth a-nyght and syketh; / She axeth hym anon what hym myslyketh'.[50] Aeneas proceeds to bemoan, with what the narrator terms 'false teres', that his 'destine' will take him thence, to Italy.[51] Finally, Aeneas's betrayal of Dido, and the sorrow and pain he causes her, centres once again on the bed:

> on a nyght, slepynge he let hire lye,
> And stal awey unto his companye,
> And as a traytour forth he gan to sayle
> Toward the large contre of Ytayle.
> Thus he hath laft Dido in wo and pyne.[52]

These moments exemplify how, as a literary device, a bed heralds the occurrence of something out of the ordinary – whether a vision, a voicing of discontentment, or a visit from a lover.

The way in which beds facilitate emotional expression intersects with the way in which sleep restores balance to the emotions. When Malory's Launcelot reads King Mark's letter defaming himself and Guenevere for their affair, his anger leads him to fall asleep on his bed: sleep can restore his humours to equilibrium, and the bed space signals to the reader that this is the character's private, and genuine, expression of emotion. Here again, as when Dido confides in Anne, the bed is a space for the expression of discontentment – and, more specifically, discontentment about troubled desire. This is also the case for Malory's Guenevere. When Launcelot (inadvertently) sleeps with Elaine rather than his beloved Queen Guenevere, and Guenevere discovers it because the proximity of their sleeping spaces allows her to hear Launcelot 'clatir in his slepe',

> she was wrothe oute of mesure, and than she cowghed so lowde that Sir Launcelot awaked. And anone he knew her hemynge, and than he knew welle that he lay nat by the quene, and therewyth he lepte oute of hys bedde as he had bene a wood man.[53]

As Molly Martin observes, 'the audibility and familiarity of both Launcelot's clattering and Gwenyver's hemming speak to the innate problems of domestic spaces and the queen's attempt to control the territory'.[54] Guenevere does not articulate a lengthy monologue here, but, as Launcelot's response testifies, her vocal 'hemynge' is perhaps just as telling of her emotional state. As the next section shows, the results are rather different when Launcelot does actually manage to find his way to Guenevere's bed.

Bedroom strategies

Middle English romances were produced within a society whose expectations and opportunities were shaped by particularly contingent private space due to the scarcity and control of bedrooms and beds. This section focuses on moments where these spatial contingencies are especially manifest, in order to address a distinctive deployment of the spaces of sleep. While fabliaux such as Chaucer's 'Miller's Tale' and 'Reeve's Tale' are well known for their physical tricks and spatial manipulations, and while Pandarus famously engineers bedroom encounters in Chaucer's more courtly *Troilus and Criseyde*,[55] the ways in which popular romances deploy such modes of expression have not been well recognised. When we attune ourselves to the architecture of desire in Middle English romances, we see that the texts and their characters are often strongly attuned to these spaces. This section focuses on moments of conflict about the fulfilment or frustration of desire in which spaces receive more attention than bodies, or compete with bodies for textual attention, in romances such as *King Horn*, *Sir Gawain and the Green Knight*, Malory's *Morte Darthur*, *Melusine* and the *Squire of Low Degree*. This mode is not unique to English literature – as shown, not least, by Lancelot's breach of bedchamber window bars in order to sleep with Guinevere in Chrétien de Troyes's *Le Chevalier de la charrette* and in the scenes in the French *Lancelot* on which Malory drew, as discussed below. However, the way in which a number of English romances that employ this mode – *Sir Gawain and the Green Knight*, Malory's 'Tale of Sir Gareth' and the *Squire of Low Degree* – have no (extant) sources, and others – *King Horn* and *Horn Childe* – focus on spatial manipulations in relation to sexual possibilities more than their French sources or analogues do, demonstrates the independence and frequency with which English romances deploy this spatial approach to sexual culture. Mapping the makeshift, the shifting, the fractured and forbidden bowers of Middle English romance shows how these texts and their characters manage sexual encounters. Inevitably, power and pleasure are not easily disentangled. In tracing this spatial practice across a variety of English romances, this section argues that manipulations of space constitute a powerful language for both pursuing and preventing amatory situations, for articulating or restraining sexual desire.

In the late fifteenth-century *Squire of Low Degree*, when the protagonist woos the princess of Hungary, the envious steward's attempts to ruin the Squire by exposing his amorous inclinations are predictable enough. The results, however, have been seen as uncharacteristic of romance, since the king does not object to the Squire courting his daughter,[56] but rather instructs the steward:

> if the squiere come to-night,
> For to speke with that lady bryght,
> Let hym say whatsoever he wyll,
> [...]
> So he come not her chambre within,
> No bate on hym loke thou begyn;
> Though that he kysse that lady fre,
> [...]
> But yf he wyl her chamber breke,
> No worde to hym that thou do speke.[57]

As far as the king is concerned, the lowly Squire may speak with and even kiss the princess, provided that he does not seek to enter her chamber (for which attempt he would be imprisoned). This stipulation belies the Squire's otherwise surprising liberty. The king does not want the Squire to have sex with his daughter, but that is not what he says. He expresses patriarchal control over his daughter not by restricting access to her person, but by restricting access to her private space, and the possibilities that space signals. This section argues that this is a significant distinction, and one that is characteristic of Middle English romance.

The *Squire of Low Degree*'s interest in desire is repeatedly conveyed through a focus on the boundaries and possibilities of intimate spaces.[58] When the Squire prepares to leave court to prove himself abroad, it is again a focus on architecture that conveys both the sexual tension and the perils of the situation. Attacked by the steward's thugs as he approaches the princess's bedroom to say farewell, the Squire 'came her chambre to', crying:

> 'Your dore undo!
> Undo,' he sayde, 'nowe, fayre lady!

> I am beset with many a spy.
> [...]
> Undo thy dore, my frely floure,
> For ye are myne, and I am your.'
> That lady with those wordes awoke,
> A mantell of golde to her she toke;
> She sayde: 'Go away, thou wicked wyght,
> Thou shalt not come here this nyght;
> For I wyll not my dore undo
> For no man that cometh therto.
> There is but one in Christenté
> That ever made that forwarde with me.' (533–54)

The princess, understanding the stakes of allowing access to her bedchamber – especially if the Squire is not who he claims to be – is sensibly wary of complying with his repeated plea to 'undo your doore'. Indeed, recognising the crux of the text, both Wynkyn de Worde and William Copeland entitled their editions of the *Squire of Low Degree* as 'vndo your Dore', with Copeland adding '*otherwise* called the squyer of lowe degré'.[59]

While criticism is attuned to how power and desire can be negotiated between subjects or bodies in medieval texts,[60] as the *Squire of Low Degree* shows, the currencies of the medieval sexual economy – the commodities that circulate, that are desired and regulated – include not just bodies, but also spaces. Siting desire within or beyond social conventions, space is not merely a passive presence.[61] Medieval England offered its own obstacles for those in search of privacy for sexual encounters, difficulties less likely to trouble today's lovers, clandestine or otherwise. In England, separate bedrooms – 'bowers' (from Old English), or 'chambers' (a word first appearing in English c.1300) – only became more common in the early thirteenth century, and even then pertained primarily to the elite.[62] Thus, Middle English romances flourished in, and were coextensive with, a society in which private domestic spaces were comparatively scarce and protected. Moreover, to obtain complete privacy, one had to do more than simply close (and lock) the door, as is suggested by Neptanibus's attempts to seduce Olympia in the metrical *King Alisaunder*. Neptanibus sends Olympia's retinue away, so that in her chamber 'hym-self was kniȝth, and swayn, / And bouremayde, and chaumberlayn'.[63] Since bedrooms and beds were often occupied by many people, indoor privacy for a transgressive lovers' tryst required the transformation of a normally semi-public space into an exclusive one. Would-be romance lovers worry about how to obtain such privacy, while their fathers, husbands, hosts or guardians worry about how to prevent it. For each of these conflicting aims, space is manipulated, and made to speak.

King Horn, the first extant Middle English romance, produced in the early thirteenth century when aristocratic bedrooms were becoming more common, explores how the economic and political possibilities and limitations of the bower shape sexual opportunities. When the exiled prince Horn travels to Westernesse, King Aylmar invites him to stay and princess Rymenhild invites him to enter into both her bedroom and a betrothal. Complying with her request, 'Horn ferde into bure / To sen aventure.'[64] For the male romance protagonist, the bedchamber is like the forest: a space of adventure, offering opportunities for knightly prowess and advancement – or ruin.[65] Horn's envious subordinate Fikenhild fulfils the revelatory role (like the *Squire of Low Degree*'s steward), telling Aylmar of Horn's whereabouts and claiming that Horn's intentions are less than honourable. When he finds Horn embracing Rymenhild in her bedroom, Aylmar is enraged:

> 'Awey ut,' he sede, 'fule theof,
> Ne wurstu me nevremore leof!
> Wend ut of my bure
> With muchel messaventure.
> Wel sone bute thu flitte,
> With swerde ich thee anhitte.
> Wend ut of my londe,
> Other thu schalt have schonde.'[66]

In his doubled imperative ejection, 'wend ut of *my* bure [...] wend ut of *my* londe' – not paralleled in the Anglo-Norman version – Aylmar articulates possession not only of his kingdom but also of what Rymenhild elsewhere refers to as 'my bur'.[67] Private space is not concrete, but rather produced, delimited, or forestalled by negotiations of power: 'a space is not a thing but rather a set of relations between things (objects and products)'. Alongside Henri Lefebvre, we can ask, 'if space embodies social relationships, how and why does it do so? And what relationships are they?'[68] Here, the patriarchal domain and its feudal interests subsume the marginal space

Sleeping spaces and the circumscription of desire 171

and personal desires of the princess and the young protagonist. In romances such as *King Horn*, it is not only bodies, but also bowers, that are contested by competing jurisdictions. We can understand the relationship between kingdom and (royal daughter's) bower as that between a dominant and a peripheral space respectively:

> The dominant form of space, that of the centres of wealth and power, endeavours to mould the spaces it dominates (i.e. peripheral spaces), and it seeks, often by violent means, to reduce the obstacles and resistance it encounters there.[69]

Certain conduct is expected in certain spaces; according to the dominant interests of the kingdom, ruled by the king from the hall, the bedchamber ought to contribute to the goals of this wider sociopolitical sphere by producing and nurturing legitimate heirs and fostering chivalric alliances.[70] Thus, Aylmar's assertion of ownership of the bower registers his anger at the perceived threat that an adulterous sexual encounter would make to social order – that is, to the normative relationship between dominant and peripheral spaces. Barring the couple from any further 'pleie / Bitwex you selve tweie', Aylmar's authoritarian response testifies to the importance of space in how sexual opportunities were conceived, conducted and controlled.[71]

In the fourteenth-century English version of the Horn narrative, *Horn Childe and Maiden Rimnild*, breach of social boundaries is again figured through breach of spatial barriers, but seemingly with more strategic awareness on Rimnild's part. This princess invites both Horn and a chaperone into her bower, and

> Þe mirie maiden hir biþouȝt
> In what maner þat sche mouȝt
> Trewe loue for to ginne.
> Sche sett hir hem bitvene;
> Þe maiden was briȝt & schene
> & comen of kinges kinne.
> Anon hirselue hadde hem ledde
> To sitten opon her owhen bedde:
> Arlaund & Horn wiþ him.[72]

Here, Rimnild manipulates her space both to declare her desire and to seek to elicit a similar response. It is worth noting that while Rimnild's counterpart Rigmel in the Anglo-Norman analogue does lead Horn to her bed and sit with him there, Rigmel does not strategise inwardly about what she will do.[73] It is the English Rimnild who asks herself in what manner she will encourage love between herself and Horn. She determines that she will speak her intentions and further her chances of fulfilling them alike by availing herself of the bedroom and then – more intimately – of the bed. Here, that is, space is the operative language for articulating and soliciting desire. In romances, enclosure is, and suggests, the erotic;[74] this is the case, for instance, here in *Horn Childe*, in the *Squire of Low Degree* and, as discussed below, in *Sir Gawain and the Green Knight*. The contingencies of this enclosure are brought to the fore in *Horn Childe*. Rimnild's bower, and any other bower in her father's court, is shown to belong to the king with particular violence. Firstly,

> Houlac king ȝaf Horn leue
> In his bour forto chese
> Þe maidens þat were fre.[75]

This 'bour', populated by available females but possessed by the king, sounds almost synonymous with 'harem'; the Emir in *Floris and Blancheflour* similarly describes those from among whom he selects his brides as 'his maidens in his bour'.[76] However, it becomes clear that the king in *Horn Childe* did not mean to include his daughter in his generous offer of the ladies of his court. When he is treacherously deceived into thinking that Horn has slept with Rimnild, the king,

>   as he were wode,
> Into boure anon he ȝode
> & Maiden Rimnild he souȝt;
> He bete hir so þat sche gan blede;
> [...]
> Þei þat Horn was sore adrad,
> Into boure he was ladde
> Þe maiden forto se.
> He fond hir liggeand on hir bedde,
> Mouþe & nose al forbled.[77]

The king's bloody beating of his daughter reclaims her as his own in a way that is redolent of rape. Both the beating and Horn's witnessing of the effects are explicitly anchored to the bower; neither bower confrontation is in the Anglo-Norman analogue.[78] Although Rimnild has proceeded less far with her desires, the consequences

Sleeping spaces and the circumscription of desire 173

for the desiring woman are more severe in *Horn Childe* than in the earlier *King Horn*; however, in both English versions, the chamber is instrumental for both sensual pleasure and the patriarchal power that does not condone it.

In *Sir Gawain and the Green Knight*, neither fulfilment nor retribution take place in the bedchamber at Hautdesert, but both are mediated there, largely through Gawain's and the Lady's physical and rhetorical spatial manoeuvers. As has been observed, 'Gawain's secluded bedchamber is [a] necessary element in the story', not least in having 'a door which can be locked or bolted'.[79] The bedchamber also has internal demarcations, in addition to the boundaries of walls and doors. Aristocratic chambers sometimes had a low partition delineating a more intimate or privileged portion of the room, and Gawain's curtained bed offers another layer of privacy and intimacy: the poet specifies that Gawain 'in gay bed lygez, / [...] Vnder couertour ful clere, cortyned aboute'.[80] Gawain's and the Lady's manipulations of the bedchamber space (door, curtains, bed) communicate their desires and intentions: as Gawain is drowsing,

> sle3ly he herde
> A littel dyn at his dor and derfly vpon;
> And he heuez vp his hed out of þe cloþes,
> A corner of þe cortyn he ca3t vp a lyttel,
> And waytez warly þiderwarde quat hit be my3t.
> Hit watz þe ladi, loflyest to beholde,
> þat dro3 þe dor after hir ful dernly and stylle
> And bo3ed towarde þe bed; and þe burne schamed
> And layde hym doun lystyly and let as he slepte.
> And ho stepped stilly and stel to his bedde,
> Kest vp þe cortyn and creped withinne
> And set hir ful softly on þe bed-syde
> And lenged þere selly longe to loke quen he wakened.[81]

The Lady penetrates the bedroom, and makes it exclusive by shutting the door before she approaches the bed, lifts the curtains and slips inside – each movement a breach of another layer of the decorous distance that ought to exist between a bachelor knight and a married lady. Gawain, meanwhile, by initially choosing sleep-like inactivity, pretending a lack of awareness seemingly in hopes of lowering the stakes of having his host's wife in his bedchamber, in fact allows the ensuing sexually charged situation to occur and establishes a spatial and behavioural precedent for the subsequent mornings.[82] In this voiceless yet lucid interchange, Gawain and the Lady speak *through* their relationship to and deployment of space; they also speak *about* space, to pursue or prevent the same potentially sexual ends. Here, space provides a language of innuendo, a currency with which to press one's desires:

> 'God moroun, Sir Gawayn,' sayde þat gay lady,
> 'ȝe ar a sleper vnslyȝe, þat mon may slyde hider.
> Now ar ȝe tan astyt! Bot true vus may schape,
> I schal bynde yow in your bedde – þat be ȝe trayst.'[83]

Gawain's reply includes the same parameters; he responds to the Lady in kind, but with different intent:

> 'Bot wolde ȝe, lady louely, þen, leue me grante
> And deprece your prysoun and pray hym to ryse,
> I wolde boȝe of þis bed and busk me better;
> I schulde keuer þe more comfort to karp yow wyth.'
> 'Nay forsoþe, beau sir,' sayd þat swete,
> 'ȝe schal not rise of your bedde.'[84]

While the Lady seeks to bind Gawain to his bed, Gawain seeks to escape it; in so doing, in engaging in this rhetorical dance, each of them tries to configure their surroundings to shape the expectations of their encounter. This chamber and its curtained bed are ambiguous spaces – in one sense a sexually charged bedchamber, in another sense a prison; and underlying both, of course, the political and moral testing-ground of Gawain by Bertilak, who has sent his wife to tempt Gawain. Gawain cannot fulfil, or even acknowledge, such desires as those the Lady seeks to attribute to and provoke in him, without inviting Bertilak's revenge.

Thus, in the bedroom encounters in *Gawain*, as in *King Horn* and *Horn Childe*, the homosocial prevails over the heterosexual – but not, in this case, because Bertilak physically enforces his interests. In the episodes in the Horn romances, the bedroom – like the woman's body – can be seen as the meeting place not only between a dominant and a peripheral interest, but also between two dominant ones, that of the father and that of the lover. The bedroom, in this sense, is a borderland, a space of cultural contact where two chivalric or feudal agendas rub against each other. Perhaps there is less friction between these in *Gawain* than in the Horn romances partly because Gawain is aware that he is not acting only on his own behalf; his sexual union with Bertilak's wife would not advance Arthur's kingdom in the same way that Horn's union with Rymenhild would advance Horn's own regal interests. Alternatively, if, as Sheila Fisher suggests, it is not Bertilak, but Morgan, who is the prime mover in the poem – who not only sends Bertilak to Arthur's court to frighten Guinevere but is also in charge of Gawain's testing[85] – then the female use of sexual temptation in the bedroom manoeuvres would be an attempt to use pleasure to subvert not one, but two, 'dominant' spaces – that of Arthur/Gawain and that of Bertilak.

In Launcelot's nocturnal encounters with Elaine and Gareth's with Lyonnesse in the *Morte Darthur*, manipulations of sleeping spaces again influence sexual events or intentions, and more so than in Malory's extant sources.[86] Acting on king Pelles's behalf, the enchantress dame Brusen dupes Launcelot into thinking that a messenger brings a ring from his beloved Guenevere to requisition him for a rendezvous at a castle, whereas in reality the lady in question is Pelles's daughter Elaine. When transported to the unfamiliar castle, spatial contrivances – magical and yet also thoroughly mundane – enable the situationally-dependent sexual encounter in which Launcelot otherwise would never have participated:

> he was receyved worshypfully wyth suche people, to his semynge, as were aboute Quene Gwenyvere secrete. So whan Sir Launcelot was alyght he asked where the quene was. So Dame Brusen seyde she was in her bed. And than people were avoyded and Sir Launcelot was lad into her chaumbir. And than Dame Brusen brought Sir Launcelot a kuppe full of wyne, and anone as he had drunken that wyne he was so asoted and madde that he myght make no delay but wythoute ony let he wente to bedde. And so he wente that mayden Elayne had bene Quene Gwenyvere. And wyte you well that Sir Launcelot was glad, and so was that lady Eleyne […].
>
> And so they lay togydir untyll underne of the morne; and all the wyndowys and holys of that chambir were stopped that no maner of day myght be seyne. And anone Sir Launcelot remembryd hym and arose up and wente to the wyndow, and anone as he had unshutte the wyndow the enchauntemente was paste. Than he knew hymselff that he had done amysse.[87]

The 'kuppe of wyne' enhances Launcelot's desire, but it is not just this magical potion that causes him to mistake the identity of the lady in the bed and accordingly sleep with her. The ways in which Launcelot's perceptions of the space he occupies are manipulated, without any magic but rather through discursive misdirection and darkness, seem much more functionally significant: the enchantment cannot work without the familiar-seeming sleeping space. Launcelot expects to find Guenevere in the bedchamber because he has been told to expect her there. His desire, while perhaps aroused by the potion, can be enacted because of the darkened – and enclosed – bedchamber, and is dissipated as soon as he opens a window, breaching the hermeneutically sealed space to which he has been brought and thus breaking the 'spell' of his dis-placed desire.[88]

Launcelot's second inadvertent bedchamber meeting with Elaine likewise results from manipulations to arouse the desire that is connected to certain spaces – that is, for Launcelot, spaces which he associates with Guenevere. Here, Launcelot has a potent warning not available to his counterpart in Malory's French source, which does not contain anything comparable to Guenevere's 'other ellys' reminder that Launcelot is not to repeat his previous misdemeanour, when he mistakenly slept with the wrong lady. In the *Morte*, Launcelot's second transgression is known because Elaine's room is so close to Guenevere's that voices carry from one to the other.[89] Regardless of dame Brusen's magic, on both occasions on which Launcelot's desire for Guenevere is channelled toward Elaine, the operative factor lies in space, and particularly in the shifting relationships between spaces. If there is an enchantment, it is one that operates through the management and 'duplicity' of sleeping spaces. And when Launcelot is reprimanded by Guenevere for his betrayal, he gives way to sorrow and madness, mental states that also have spatial dimensions: 'he lepte oute at a bay wyndow into a gardyne, [...] and so he ranne furth he knew nat whothir, and was as wylde woode as ever was man'.[90] Here, Launcelot flees from bower to garden, and then beyond such a benign environment to the forest itself. From one space of adventure, his madness catapults him to another, its opposite.[91] And yet, the bedrooms and forests of medieval romance are in other ways so much alike: dark, obscure, unknowable places where danger and desire lurk, where the knight can be made or unmade.

Similarly, when Malory's Gareth meets Lyonesse, manipulations of sleeping space shape sexual intentions and events. For Gareth, spatial

Sleeping spaces and the circumscription of desire 177

shifts are not only the cause of arousal, but also at times its demonstrable symptom, or its mode of diagnosis. After reclaiming his stolen dwarf at Gryngamoure's gates, Gareth (like Launcelot in the prelude to his first night with Elaine) is brought into new surroundings:

> And so Sir Gryngamoure toke hym by the honde and ledde hym into the halle where his owne wyff was. And than com forth Dame Lyones arayde lyke a prynces, and there she made hym passyng good chere and he hir agayne, and they had goodly langage and lovely countenaunce togyder. [...] and evermore Sir Gareth behelde that lady. And the more he loked on her the more he loved hir, amd so he brenned in love that he passed hymself farre in his reson. [...] *for his love was so hoote that he wyst nat were he was.*[92]

The italicised phrase reads on a figurative level, and yet also on a very physical level. In romances such as this one – as shown by Launcelot's meetings with Elaine – such language about spatial confusions is not an unrealistic metaphor for desire, but an effective component of a character's affect. When Gareth looks upon Lyonnesse, how he feels is rhetorically and cognitively expressed through his sense, or confusion, of space. For one thing, Gareth is unaware that his new lady-love is the same lady he has attempted to woo elsewhere, at her own castle; perhaps (if we are to read charitably) we can view the comment that 'he wyst nat were he was' as a hint of Gareth remembering that he ought not to be feeling desire except when he is somewhere else. This is the only comment Malory's narrator offers on the way in which Gareth is, at least in intent, unfaithful in love, but it is the first of several desire-induced and/or desire-inducing spatial confusions in Gryngamoure's castle.

When Gareth and Lyonnesse seek to consummate their love, they do so not in a bedchamber, but in the middle of the hall:

> they brente bothe in hoote love that they were acorded to abate their lustys secretly. And there Dame Lyonesse counceyled Sir Gareth to slepe in none other place but in the halle, and there she promysed hym to com to his bed a lytyll afore mydnyght.[93]

Given this surprising manoeuver, it is again understandable that Gareth 'wyst nat were he was', since his 'hoote' love is something that he and his society associate with a bedchamber rather than with the overtly public space of the hall. However, Lyonesse's plan sees the creation of a bower space in the middle of the hall:

aftir souper was made a clene avoydaunce, that every lorde and lady sholde go unto his reste. But Sir Gareth seyde playnly he wolde go no farther than the halle, for in suche placis, he seyde, was convenyaunte for an arraunte knyght to take his reste in. And so there was ordayned grete cowchis and thereon fethir beddis, and there he leyde hym downe to slepe. And within a whyle came Dame Lyonesse wrapped in a mantell furred with ermyne, and leyde hir downe bysydys Sir Gareth. And therewithall he began to clyppe hir and to kysse hir.[94]

Lyonesse's and Gareth's attempts to sleep with each other involve appropriating the hall space for the activities of the boudoir. Although the would-be lovers are twice prevented from fulfilling their desires by the appearance of a magical knight set upon them by Lyonesse's sister Lynet, nonetheless Lyonesse's transmogrification of her brother's hall into a bower produces a very different relationship of dominant to peripheral spaces to those in the Horn romances, as she (almost) appropriates the former for the pleasures of the latter. Here, again, spatial confusions and shifts have sexual insinuations. Lyonesse and Gareth, who do not have access to a ready-made bower, seek to construct such a space for their ends, in a way that resonates with the spatial contrivances of fabliau. Perhaps Lyonnesse would not need such means if she were in her own castle rather than her brother's. For those who lacked independence or wealth, bowers might be jury-rigged or loaned; they were shifting commodities subject to intercession.[95]

Usually, such intercessory functions – constructing, offering, denying, withdrawing private space – were controlled by men. However, in romances such as *Sir Gawain and the Green Knight* and the 'Tale of Sir Gareth', women are sometimes able to exert power and express their desires through manipulations of bowers. Moreover, in the Melusine romances, a woman forbids access to her own bower: a woman who has made her own marriage, and whose power (unlike Lady Bertilak's, or Triamour's in *Sir Launfal*) is not derived from her husband or father.[96] Cursed by her mother to turn into a serpent from the waist down on Saturdays and to remain mortal only if her husband does not see her in that state, in the prose *Melusine* the eponymous fairy requires Raymond to promise her 'vpon all the sacrements & othes', that 'neuer [...] ye shal not peyne ne force your self for to see me on the Satirday'.[97] After some years of happy marriage, Raymond's brother visits Raymond on a Saturday and tells him, 'wete it that the commyn talking of the peple is, that Melusyne your wyf euery saterday in the yere is with another man in auoultyre'.[98] Raymond, provoked into jealous suspicion even more easily than Othello, punctures his wife's door with his sword and, peering through, sees his wife bathing: with a serpent's tail, but entirely chaste. Realising his error, Raymond stops up the hole with wax and says 'My swete loue, now haue I betrayed you, & haue falsed my couenaunt.'[99] This visual breach of the bedchamber is precisely what Melusine forbade her husband. Melusine used her erstwhile 'private' bedchamber for a non-sexual purpose; however, the men around her seem only able to imagine a woman wanting private space if it is for sexual transgression, betraying anxieties about the role of space in the sexual economy.[100]

The ways in which enclosed, owned sleeping spaces can be made to speak also shape Shakespeare's late play, *Cymbeline*. A central crux of this romance aptly hinges on a reading of the heroine Imogen's bedchamber. In order to convince Imogen's husband Posthumous that she has been unfaithful, the villain Iachimo hides in a chest so that he can sneak out at night and surreptitiously record the details of both her body and her bedchamber. Shakespeare derives this subplot from Boccaccio's *Decameron*, but the bedroom becomes much more of a focus in Shakespeare's version, where Iachimo goes so far as to write down the details of the bedchamber, inscribing his evidence to incriminate Imogen. Iachimo's description of Imogen and her bedchamber then become the subject of a lengthy dialogue in which Iachimo seeks to convince Posthumous that he has slept with Imogen. In this false report to Posthumous, the description of the bedchamber is expansive. The fact that a man's access to Imogen's bedchamber is readily deployed and read as evidence of a sexual encounter bears witness to a shared expectation of the possibilities such a space enables, and also – as in *Melusine* – to male fascination with a woman's private space.

Although knowledge of the mole under Imogen's breast is the clinching detail in Iachimo's report, Shakespeare gives the bedroom itself more attention than Boccaccio does, in both the initial scene and the report afterward. And whereas in Boccaccio's version, the villain bribes someone to have the chest in which he hides carried into the lady's bedroom, in Shakespeare, he asks Imogen if she will keep some rich gifts he claims to have in a trunk safe overnight, and she replies:

> pawn mine honour for their safety, since
> My lord hath interest in them. I will keep them
> In my bedchamber.[101]

When Imogen volunteers her bedchamber as the place of safekeeping, she articulates a claim to her bedroom as in fact her own space (subject to her own authority, and implying a sense of privacy), but in so doing, she opens herself up to attendant dangers. In this cultural imagination, the sexual connotations of 'sleeping with' someone (a phrase current in premodern England) were more than just a euphemism: the challenges of gaining access to a private space of sleep were often seen as synonymous with the challenges of managing to have sex with someone. Shakespeare's *Cymbeline*, like other premodern English romances, concentrates on sleeping spaces as sexual signifiers and as battlegrounds in gendered power politics.

The stained sheets of romance

Meanwhile, in Arthurian romance, particularly in Malory's *Morte Darthur*, beds – and especially bedsheets – become incriminating evidence of adulterous encounters, and again intervene in contemporary discourses about gender and power. These beds are sites of epistemological interest.[102] In a motif in which male blood repeatedly stains the sheets, bedroom textiles become texts that interrogate the limits of knightly identity. We recognise Malory's greatest secular knights by the feats of arms they perform; Launcelot, Tristram and Gareth all sustain and inflict bloodshed to win duels and tournaments. Yet Malory shows these three chivalric paragons bleeding profusely not only on the battlefield, but also in the bedroom. Each knight has a forbidden encounter with a lady when he is wounded – Tristram with the wife of Sir Segwarydes, Launcelot with Guenevere in 'The Knight of the Cart', and Gareth with Lyonesse – and all three episodes show male blood circulating to a very different effect than is ordinarily permitted or promoted in the genre. When these knights sleep with their lovers – or try to, in Gareth's case – the results are transgressive on more levels than that of adultery. This motif, foregrounded by textual attention to the material culture of sleep, inverts the usual gendered values of blood flow and signals threats to the knight's social status. This motif is further transgressive in its representations of female desire, which are unusually well-developed compared to the male-dominated norms of lust in medieval romance. While this motif is not unique to Malory, his text is distinctive in using it several times and in foregrounding connections between each of the motif's manifestations – connections not found in his French sources. The spaces of sleep illuminate cruxes in the gender politics and ethics of Malory's English Arthuriad.

The motif's appearances in continental *Tristan* and *Lancelot* narratives show the material Malory later exploited. One of the earliest extant versions is in Gottfried von Strassburg's *Tristan und Isolde*, where the motif is the result of a trap Mark sets to try to expose Tristan and Isolde. King Mark and his counsellors have orchestrated a group blood-letting and have left Isolde alone in her bed, surrounded by sprinkled flour. Tristan is warned of the stratagem by Brangane; however, he seemingly cannot restrain his lust: 'sin herze in sinem libe / daz wart nach dem wibe / volmüetic unde in trahte, / wie er dar komen mahte' ('His desire for the woman was at its height and his heart yearned in his body as to how he could get to her').[103] Tristan overexerts himself in his attempts to reach Isolde's bed without recording telltale footprints in the flour. He reopens the vein from which his blood had been let:

> bette unde bettelachen
> diu missevarte daz bluot,
> alse bluot von rehte tuot:
> ez verwete wa unde wa.[104]
> (His blood stained the bed and its linen, as is the way with blood, dyeing it here, there and everywhere.)

Tristan's bedchamber blood loss is both excessive and uncontrollable. He cannot staunch his blood flow and must retreat unsatisfied, in what is a rather disempowering moment.

Perhaps due to Chrétien de Troyes' familiarity with *Tristan* narratives, particularly the courtly tradition to which Gottfried's text belongs, a similar motif marks the love of Lancelot and Guinevere in Chrétien's *Le Chevalier de la charrette*. Here, a lustful Lancelot wounds his finger getting through a barred window to honour the lovers' tryst, and bloodies Guinevere's bedsheets when she is held captive in Meleagant's castle. While, unlike Tristan and Isolde, Lancelot and Guinevere spend the night in bliss, oblivious to the blood, the stained sheets nonetheless give rise to the same inferences and implications as in the Tristan episode. Upon Lancelot's departure at daybreak, 'de son cors tant i remaint / que li drap sont tachié et taint / del sanc qui cheï de ses doiz' ('he left behind enough of his body that the sheets were stained and spotted by the blood that dripped from his fingers').[105] In both of these amorous episodes, as in later Arthurian romances that drew upon them, the protagonist, desperate to reach his beloved's bed, saturates her sheets with his blood while he fulfills his desire or, alternatively, when he is frustrated in his attempts to do so; and the sheets become texts to be read by adversaries the morning after.

According to medieval views on the gendered significance of types of, and venues for, expenditures of blood, these moments of identity (de)construction are emasculating: that is, symbolically so, and frequently socially as well. Peggy McCracken has observed that the general pattern of representations of blood in medieval (French) romance valorises men's bloodshed as a sign of their moral, mental and physical strength, whereas women's blood is perceived as an indication of their inherent infirmity.[106] While 'men bleed prominently in medieval fiction to prove valor, to avenge unjust wrongs, and to impose justice', all female blood in medieval culture is conceptually aligned with menstrual blood, seen as 'a polluting blood, a blood that [caused] both symbolic and practical harm'.[107] The location for the bloodshed is likewise conventionally gendered, with men's blood linked to the battlefield and women's blood linked to the bedroom. This opposition defines male blood as publicly acceptable, and female blood as something private, shameful and requiring concealment – except during the traditional display of the marriage bedsheets the morning after the consummation of a marriage to confirm that the bride was a virgin.[108] Men were also seen as in control of their bounded bodies while women were incapable of controlling theirs. Bettina Bildhauer observes that 'the idea of an integral body was used to essentialize and back up ... [ideological] distinctions, such as that between fully embodied subjects and imperfect bodies like those of women'.[109] However, the non-integral bodies under consideration here are male, and their bleeding takes place in the bedroom. The ways in which these textual moments deviate from expected displays of gendered blood render them particularly conspicuous.

In narratives of Tristan and Isolde and of Lancelot and Guinevere, the moments when blood-related gender values do not hold, and are arguably most completely inverted, occur in bed. The bed is an ambiguously gendered space, as it belongs to the domestic, feminised sphere and contrasts with the public arena of male action, yet is nonetheless a forum in which masculine prowess can be demonstrated or questioned. In this contested liminal environment, gendered binaries and roles are destabilised, and the knight, stripped of his protective armour and the trappings of chivalric identity, risks becoming socially marginalised and losing his signifying place in his community. The morning-after inspections pervert the cultural practice of scrutinising and displaying the marriage-bed sheets after the wedding night. The bloodstain resulting from the breach of the hymen would have provided the ocular proof that the bride had been a virgin. Here, however, the telltale stained sheets and their possible interpretation instead signify adultery, inverting the topos. While McCracken views the blood as a successful profusion that heightens status in the same way as male blood that is manifested on the battlefield,[110] this blood also generates a threat of exile or death for the knights' transgression – a form of social emasculation. Yet the women do not fare better, for in these scenes, women's blood is not permitted to signify even in the bedchamber; Meleagant summarily dismisses Guinevere's assertion that the stains came from her purported nosebleed. Female blood is supposed to be absent from the chivalric text, and women's claims to authorship (of blood) are not valorised. [111]

Although these textual moments may enhance the knightly lover's sexual reputation, they do not offer valorisation or enhanced status in either their symbolic or their social implications. To begin with, these episodes associate bleeding men with menstruating women and violated virgins. While medieval scientific thought viewed semen as 'a pure form of blood that demonstrates the superiority of the hot, dry male body over the humid, cold female body that is incapable of giving form to its blood',[112] in the bed-space motif of profusely bleeding male lover and morning-after witnessing, the focus of internal and external audiences is insistently directed towards the unrefined (feminising) variety of male blood, as if textually substituting for the 'purified' form of masculine emissions regardless of the individual knight's sexual success or failure. Moreover, these moments often mark the unravelling of the knight's position within his sociopolitical community. While the ways in which these encounters shape the knight's identities vary, the manifestations of the motif share a set of risks. The twin breaches of bodily boundaries, sex and bloody wounds – with the sheets as witness to both – correspond to the transgressive breach of social boundaries in both the heterosexual and the homosocial relationships of the bleeding romance knights. The bride who bleeds on her wedding night inscribes the sheets with her social propriety, constructing her married reputation and thereby gaining status and a legally binding relationship; male blood on the bedsheets, on the other hand, even though it arises from a moment of sexual conjunction, foregrounds the social divide between the two individuals. Masculine blood on the bedsheets, rather than the affirmation of 'proper' order that its feminine counterpart would constitute, is a symptom of disorder, and it sometimes undoes the knight's social reputation.

The early Lancelot and Tristan narratives influenced later generations of French romances, including the French Prose *Tristan* and the Prose *Lancelot*, on which Malory drew; however, Malory expands the focus on stained sheets. Male blood, in its normative appearances, fuels the economy and ideology of the society of the *Morte*, where, as Andrew Lynch has argued, 'blood is the basic currency of fights and quests, their operative factor as much as their issue'.[113] The bloodstained bed episodes are all the more striking in their deviation from the values of 'goodness and nobility' that male blood normally signifies.[114] As in the continental romances, the *Morte*'s depictions of Tristram's, Launcelot's and Gareth's uncontrollable bloodshed in the bedroom are conceptually aligned with displays of female blood; however, Malory goes much further than his sources in his deployment of beds and bed-related textiles to explore the connotations and consequences of these encounters, and repeatedly uses this motif to represent threats to chivalric identity and non-standard depictions of gendered power and desire.

In Malory's 'Book of Sir Tristram de Lyones', when Tristram is en route to a tryst with one of his and Mark's shared love interests, the unnamed wife of Sir Segwarydes, he is beset by Mark and two knightly thugs, and before Tristram defeats all three, 'Kynge Marke hurt Sir Trystrames on the breste ryght sore.'[115] Tristram meets the lady despite his wound, and the narrator comments that they 'wente to bedde with grete joy and plesaunce. And so in hys ragynge he toke no kepe of his grene wounde that Kynge Marke had gyffyn hym.'[116] Malory adapted the episode of a wounded Tristram sleeping with another knight's wife from the French Prose *Tristan*; however, Malory's specification that Tristram's wound, when reopened, 'bebledde bothe the over-shete and the neyther-sheete, and the pylowes and the hede-shete', is not in his source.[117] Again, Tristram's copious bleeding resembles the blood of both menses and hymen. Moreover, Segwarydes, reading the meme from within the text, seems to know precisely how to interpret the bloodstained sheets: 'whan he founde hys bedde troubled and brokyn and wente nere and loked by candyll-lyght, than he sawe that there had leyne a wounded knyght. "A, false traytoures!" he seyde, "why haste thou betrayde me?"'[118] While Tristram easily defeats the pursuing husband, he incurs more severe consequences from Mark. This is a transition point for Tristram, since he loses his king's favour and his previously exalted place in the Cornish chivalric community. Just prior to Tristram's rendezvous with Segwarydes' wife, the narrator twice emphasises Tristram's high status in the eyes of Mark and his knights.[119] Yet once Tristram sleeps with the lady, he has instantly and permanently lost Mark's good will: 'as longe as Kynge Marke lyved, he loved never aftir Sir Trystramys. So aftir that, thoughe there were fayre speche, love was there none.'[120]

In Malory's 'The Knight of the Cart', Launcelot bleeds on Guenevere's bedsheets in Mellyagaunce's castle in a scene that can be traced back through Malory's source, the French Prose *Lancelot*, to Chrétien's *Le Chevalier de la charrette*. Malory's Launcelot cuts his hand getting through the barred window to Guenevere, and the ensuing blood-bathed sexual encounter is Malory's sole unambiguous mention of Launcelot and Guenevere consummating their love in the entire *Morte Darthur*. Thus, when the narrator explains that 'Sir Launcelot wente to bedde with the quene and toke no force of hys hurte honde, but toke hys pleasaunce and hys lykynge untyll hit was the dawnyng of the day; for wyte you well he slept nat, but wacched', the text's comparative lack of prudishness already makes the moment arresting.[121] The next morning, Mellyagaunce interprets the blood in Guenevere's bed as a sign of adultery in connection with the blood of her wounded bodyguards, as in Chrétien's version. Intriguingly, however, Malory adds the phrase that explicitly mentions blood on the bedsheets. In the *Prose Lancelot*, we are told that Meleagant sees 'lez dras qui estoient honni del sanc Lancelot' ('the sheets that were defiled by the blood of Lancelot').[122] Malory, by contrast, specifies that Mellyagaunce finds that 'all the hedesheete, pylow, and over-shyte was all bebled of the bloode of Sir Launcelot and of hys hurte honde'.[123] This closely resembles the wording in Malory's 'Tristram' section; the wording is not found in Malory's sources for either episode. In creating this clear and original parallel between the Tristram and Launcelot episodes, Malory expands both moments to emphasise the bedsheets as texts, and associates them with each other.

Despite the fact that Mark found out about Tristram's success with the lady by other means than the stained sheets (since Mark had a dwarf informant), the bloodstains nonetheless signal the turning point in Tristram's chivalric reputation as Malory's readers witness it. Likewise, for Launcelot, this moment is associated with imminent loss of his community and his king's favour, since Arthur will shortly force him into exile and declare war on him. The way that the text applies the same phrase to describe each knight's hæmorrhage on all available bed-related fabrics acts as a cue to the attentive reader, highlighting the connection between these critical moments in each knight's chivalric and sexual careers. Malory selectively rearranges Launcelot's biography to position the 'Knight of the Cart' episode just prior to his exclusion from his community.[124] Launcelot is not discovered here, because the blood is not identified as his diegetically; however, the devalued figuration of his blood is nonetheless a culturally resonant harbinger of his downfall. Malory's selection and placement of this episode in Launcelot's life heralds the fact that Launcelot's name is about to be stained much as his blood stains the sheets. Thus, the bloodstained sheets in the *Morte Darthur* seem intended to serve as a red flag to the audience as well as to the cuckold in question.

I have left the 'Tale of Sir Gareth of Orkney' to the last due to its lack of a known source and its rearrangement of the elements of this scenario, factors that make it perhaps the most interesting example of the motif.[125] Gareth is temporarily emasculated when he is repeatedly attacked by Lynet's magical knight while he attempts to sleep with Lyonesse. Gareth, lying in the hall in Lyonesse's castle on 'grete cowchis and [...] fethir beddis', is visited by his beloved as they have prearranged.[126] When Lyonesse arrives and Gareth embraces her, an armed knight instantly materialises to fight him. This knight 'smote hym [Gareth] with a foyne thorow the thycke of the thygh, that the wounde was a shafftemonde brode and had cutte a-too many vaynes and synewys'.[127] Although Gareth is powerful enough to decapitate the hostile knight, he cannot control his own bleeding from the wound in his thigh (a symbolic castration): 'And than he bled so faste that he myght not stonde, but so he leyde hym downe uppon his bedde and there he sowned and lay as he had bene dede'.[128] Notably, his excessive blood flow and swooning occurs on the bed (if without explicit mention of besmirched linens). Here, Gareth's debilitating blood loss renders him passive and impotent for the time being.

When Gareth has (nearly) healed, Lyonesse pays another nocturnal visit to his makeshift bed; however, the same magical knight reappears, and Gareth reopens his wound in his efforts to defeat and dismember the knight: 'Sir Gareth strayned hym so that his olde wounde braste ayen on-bledynge. But he was hote and corragyous and toke no kepe, but with his grete forse he strake downe the knyght and voyded hys helme and strake of his hede.'[129] For Gareth, unlike Tristram and Lancelot, the danger is not that his sexual desire and its fulfillment may be discovered afterwards by bloodstains on the sheets; the risk is rather of being prevented from such an undertaking. Gareth's excessive blood flow thwarts his desire again: we are told that by the time he was done disposing of the pieces of the knight into the moat, 'he was so faynte that unnethis he myght stonde for bledynge, and by than he was allmoste unarmed he felle in a dedly sowne in the floure'.[130] While Gareth does not make it to the bed for his second swoon, the debilitating implications are nonetheless clear. Unlike Tristram and Launcelot, Gareth does not get the chance to establish his sexual reputation – but he does not afterwards lose his *social* reputation. The post-bloodbath public relations job is easier for Gareth than it is for Tristram or Launcelot: helpfully, Gareth's beloved is not someone else's queen but rather his own betrothed. Yet while Gareth's chivalric identity does not come undone, his symbolic castration is a threat he must overcome.

The motif establishes a connection between female sexual desire and the male character's symbolic and/or social emasculation. Before Gareth's and Lyonesse's first meeting, Malory mentions that their desire is mutual: 'And so they brente bothe in hoote love that they were acorded to abate their lustys secretly.'[131] The narrator again insists on mentioning their reciprocal desire in their second attempt to satisfy it: 'Than agayne Sir Gareth and Dame Lyonesse were so hoote in brennynge love.'[132] In addition, Lyonesse initiates the lovers' plans, taking the dominant role and arranging their encounter: 'Dame Lyonesse counceyled Sir Gareth to slepe in none other place but in the halle, and there she promysed hym to com to his bed a lytyll afore mydnyght.'[133] There is a similar focus on Guenevere's desires and her role in bringing about the sexual encounter with Launcelot. In Malory's version, Guenevere's desire, and its role as the instigator of the ensuing action, becomes the subject of a corroboratory dialogue between the lovers:

> 'Wyte you well,' seyde the queen, 'I wolde as fayne as ye that ye myght com in to me.'
> 'Wolde ye so, madame,' seyde Sir Launcelot, 'wyth youre harte that I were with you?'
> 'Ye, truly,' seyde the quene.
> 'Than shall I prove my myght,' seyde Sir Launcelot, 'for youre love.'[134]

This motif, then, sees the bedsheets saturated with interrogative potential. That these knights are rendered vulnerable to symbolic and social enervation during their amorous bloodbaths resonates with the way in which emasculation was a punishment for some cases of adultery in the medieval period;[135] the motif seems to mediate related somatic and social anxieties.

The epistemic pursuit that preoccupies Meleagant, Mark and their analogues speaks to recurring cultural concerns regarding gendered identities and betrayal. By focusing not only on the knights' bleeding, but also (in ways his sources do not) on how Tristram's and Launcelot's blood stains the sheets, enabling authority figures to witness the evidence, the *Morte Darthur* increases emphasis on the dangers of these encounters. If identity is performative, what these bleeding knights perform in bed, undressed, exposes the relevant gender roles as arbitrary constructions at risk of being stripped of their ability to order society stably. Segwarydes' wife not only reciprocates Tristram's desire; she further removes the difference between the two of them when she takes off his armour: 'than she unarmed hym, and so they [...] wente to bedde with grete joy and plesaunce'.[136] To the extent that the bed is a chivalric battleground where the knight must struggle to assert and maintain his signifying masculinity, it is a battleground on which he must do so without his accustomed protective trappings, embracing his exposure and his exposer alike despite the danger of undoing his identity. This textual attention to stained sheets, like the attention to beds, bedrooms and *loci amoeni* elsewhere, shows how literary sleeping spaces invite interpretation (especially in relation to emotions and ethics) as insistently as sleep itself does.

Notes

1. Geoffrey of Monmouth, *The History of the Kings of Britain*, ed. Michael D. Reeve, trans. Neil Wright (Woodbridge: Boydell, 2007), pp. 6–7. This idea of Britain as a generator of peaceful, beneficial sleep follows classical descriptions of such pleasant places and also appears in Gildas's sixth-century *De excidio Britanniae* (a direct source for Geoffrey of Monmouth's description of Britain), which mentions Britain's 'shining rivers flowing with gentle murmur, extending to those who recline on their banks a pledge of sweet slumber': Gildas, *De Excidio Britanniae, or The Ruin of Britain*, ed. and trans. Hugh Williams (Lampeter: Llanerch Press, 2006), p. 17; see Neil Wright, 'Geoffrey of Monmouth and Gildas', *Arthurian Literature*, 2 (1982), 1–40 (pp. 5–7).
2. Shakespeare, *The Tempest*, 3.iii.128–33.
3. Lefebvre, *The Production of Space*. For recent work applying spatial theory to medieval literature and culture, see Martin, *Castles and Space*; Goldie, *Scribes of Space: Place in Middle English Literature and Late Medieval Science*; Shaw, *Space, Gender and Memory in Middle English Romance: Architectures of Wonder in Melusine*; and Megan Cassidy-Welch, 'Space and Place in Medieval Contexts', *Parergon*, 27.2 (2010), 1–12.
4. Jeff Malpas, 'Introduction – The Intelligence of Place', in Malpas (ed.), *The Intelligence of Place*, pp. 1–10 (p. 3). See also Michel de Certeau, for whom 'space is a practiced place': de Certeau, *The Practice of Everyday Life*, trans. Steven Rendall (Berkeley, CA: University of California Press, 1984), p. 117.

5 Malpas, 'Place and Singularity', p. 79; Malpas, 'The Intelligence of Place', p. 3.
6 Sarah Rees Jones, 'Public and Private Space and Gender in Medieval Europe', in Judith M. Bennett and Ruth Mazo Karras (eds), *The Oxford Handbook of Women and Gender in Medieval Europe* (Oxford: Oxford University Press, 2013), pp. 246–61 (p. 251).
7 Dannenfeldt, 'Sleep: Theory and Practice in the Late Renaissance', p. 425.
8 Ernst Robert Curtius, *European Literature and the Latin Middle Ages* (Princeton, NJ: Princeton University Press, 1952), pp. 195–200.
9 Charlotte Reinbold, 'Unstable Dream, According to the Place: Setting and Convention in Chaucerian Dream Poetry' (PhD dissertation, University of Cambridge, 2017), p. 14.
10 See, for instance, Boyda Johnstone, 'Vitreous Visions: Stained Glass and Affective Engagement in John Lydgate's *The Temple of Glass*', *New Medieval Literatures* 17 (2017), 175–200; Reinbold, 'Setting and Convention in Chaucerian Dream Poetry'; Ad Putter, *An Introduction to the* Gawain-*Poet*, pp. 151–61; and Sarah Stanbury, *Seeing the* Gawain-*Poet: Description and the Act of Perception* (Philadelphia, PA: University of Pennsylvania Press, 1991).
11 Langland, *Piers Plowman*, ll. 1–12.
12 Langland, *Piers Plowman*, ll. 14–19.
13 *Pearl*, ll. 38 and 57.
14 *Pearl*, l. 39.
15 Chaucer, 'Wife of Bath's Tale', ll. 872–80.
16 Malory, *Morte Darthur*, p. 190.24–5.
17 *The York Plays*, Pageant 13, 240–5.
18 *Robert* survives in ten manuscripts (more than any other Middle English penitential romance), dating from the late fourteenth to the late fifteenth centuries.
19 Raluca L. Radulescu, 'Reading *King Robert of Sicily*'s Text(s) and Manuscript Context(s)', in Nicholas Perkins (ed.), *Medieval Romance and Material Culture* (Cambridge: D. S. Brewer, 2015), pp. 165–82 (p. 174).
20 *Robert of Cisyle*, in *Amis and Amiloun, Robert of Cisyle, and Sir Amadace*, ed. Edward E. Foster (Kalamazoo, MI: Medieval Institute Publications, 2007), ll. 33–4.
21 *Robert of Cisyle*, 49–60.
22 Edward Foster, 'Introduction', *Robert of Cisyle*, in Foster (ed.), *Amis and Amiloun, Robert of Cisyle, and Sir Amadace*, pp. 89–95 (p. 91).
23 Foster, 'Introduction', *Robert of Cisyle*, p. 91.

Sleeping spaces and the circumscription of desire 191

24 Yet medieval minds were certainly attuned to how boredom could generate sleep: in Chaucer's Clerk's Prologue, the Host tells the Clerk to tell a merry tale, and not to preach, and then further qualifies this request by saying 'Ne that thy tale make us nat to slepe' (*Canterbury Tales*, IV.14).
25 *Robert of Cisyle*, ll. 305–10.
26 See Russell A. Peck, 'John Gower and the Book of Daniel', in R. F. Yeager (ed.), *John Gower: Recent Readings* (Kalamazoo, MI: Medieval Institute Publications, 1989), pp. 159–87, and Foster, in *Robert of Cisyle*, p. 110. Nebuchadnezzar's admonitory dream is related at the end of the Prologue to John Gower's *Confessio Amantis*.
27 Salient examples include Criseyde's violent dream of the eagle and Troilus's dream of the boar in *Troilus and Criseyde* (II.925–31 and V.1233–43 respectively); Arthur's foreboding dreams in the Alliterative *Morte Arthur* (of the dragon and the bear, and of Fortune's Wheel, at 759–806 and 3227–455 respectively) and in Malory's *Morte Darthur* (of griffins and serpents, after the conception of Mordred, and of Fortune's Wheel, at 34.6–12 and 920.15–31 respectively); and several dreams in the mid-fifteenth-century *Pseudo-Turpin Chronicle* – notably, when St James the Apostle appears to Charlemagne in his sleep at the beginning of the text and berates him for failing in his duty: *Turpines Story: A Middle English Translation of the 'Pseudo-Turpin Chronicle'*, ed. Stephen H. A. Shepherd, EETS OS 322 (Oxford: Oxford University Press, 2004), ll. 110–29.
28 *Robert of Cisyle*, 421–4.
29 The omission may result from these two manuscripts' political contexts: CUL MS Ii.4.9, for instance, dates from c.1450, when 'the association between Nebuchadnezzar's folly and Henry VI's mental incapacity may have been perceived by the scribe or commissioner as too sensitive a topic to be included': Raluca L. Radulescu, *Romance and its Contexts in Fifteenth-Century England: Politics, Piety and Penitence* (Cambridge: D. S. Brewer, 2013), p. 51.
30 Langland, *Piers Plowman*, B XIX.2–5.
31 Margery Kempe also repeatedly falls asleep in church into visions: for instance, she does so several times in Chapter 85 of her *Book*. Significantly, however, in contrast to Langland's Will, she falls asleep here during private prayer and contemplation, rather than during a service: *The Book of Margery Kempe*, ll. 6958–61 and 7004–6.
32 Nicolette Zeeman, *Piers Plowman and the Medieval Discourse of Desire* (Cambridge: Cambridge University Press, 2006), p. 11.
33 Zeeman, *Piers Plowman and the Medieval Discourse of Desire*, p. 10.
34 Langland, *Piers Plowman*, B XIX.283–90.

35 Handley, *Sleep in Early Modern England*, pp. 6–8.
36 Morgan, *Beds and Chambers in Late Medieval England*, p. 16.
37 Sarah Stanbury, 'The Place of the Bedchamber in Chaucer's *Book of the Duchess*', *Studies in the Age of Chaucer* 37 (2015), 133–61 (p. 143).
38 Morgan, *Beds and Chambers in Late Medieval England*, pp. 20–37; see also Ekirch, *At Day's Close*, p. 274.
39 Camille, 'Manuscript Illumination and the Art of Copulation', p. 62; Penelope Eames, 'Furniture in England, France and the Netherlands from the Twelfth to the Fifteenth Century', *Furniture History: The Journal of the Furniture History Society* 13 (1977), 1–303 (pp. 85–6).
40 Morgan, *Beds and Chambers in Late Medieval England*, p. 41; see also Perrot, *The Bedroom: An Intimate History*, p. 2.
41 As Ekirch notes, 'concern for privacy seems to have intensified during the late Middle Ages […]. First used in the 1400s, the words "privacy" and "private" became part of popular parlance by the time of Shakespeare': *At Day's Close*, p. 151.
42 Chaucer, *Troilus and Criseyde*, III.229–30 and II.953.
43 Ekirch, *At Day's Close*, p. 281.
44 Chaucer, 'Second Nun's Tale', ll. 141–7.
45 Jones, 'Public and Private Space and Gender in Medieval Europe', p. 248.
46 For an insightful discussion of Troilus's use of privacy, see Charlotte Knight, 'The Literature of the Bedchamber in Late Medieval England' (PhD dissertation, King's College London, 2019), pp. 23–50. As Knight observes, 'Troilus spends some 3529 lines identifiably in a bedchamber, out of a total of 8240 lines, representing 42% of the entire poem' ('The Literature of the Bedchamber, p. 31).
47 With the partial exception of the narrator of the Prologue to the *Legend of Good Women*, who has servants bring the outdoors into his home, to make a bed space in his private garden. The dreams of Chaucer's dream vision narrators also often begin with the narrator 'awakening' in the bed to encounter the dreamscape: see Charlotte Reinbold, 'Setting and Convention in Chaucerian Dream Poetry', esp. p. 74.
48 Sheila Delany, *Impolitic Bodies: Poetry, Saints and Society in Fifteenth-Century England: The Work of Osbern Bokenham* (Oxford: Oxford University Press, 1998), p. 40.
49 Chaucer, 'Legend of Dido', ll. 1164–9.
50 Chaucer, 'Legend of Dido', ll. 1292–3.
51 Chaucer, 'Legend of Dido', ll. 1301 and 1299.
52 Chaucer, 'Legend of Dido', ll. 1326–30.
53 Malory, *Morte Darthur*, p. 633.6–10.
54 Martin, *Castles and Space*, p. 171.

55 Chaucer, *Troilus and Criseyde*, II.1710–50 and III.946–1316; see further Webb, *Privacy and Solitude*, pp. 114–16, and John Hines, *The Fabliau in English* (Harlow: Longman, 1993).
56 Erik Kooper, 'Introduction', in *Sentimental and Humorous Romances*, p. 131. See also Glenn Wright, '"Other Wyse Then Must We Do": Parody and Popular Narrative in *The Squyr of Lowe Degre*', *Comitatus*, 27 (1996), 14–41.
57 *Squire of Low Degree*, in *Sentimental and Humorous Romances*, ed. Erik Kooper (Kalamazoo, MI: Medieval Institute Publications, 2006), ll. 425–43. The *Squire* is extant in two early sixteenth-century fragments of a de Worde print based on a late fifteenth-century manuscript version; Copland's closely related 1560 print, the base text for the edition cited here, survives complete. The c.1650 Percy Folio manuscript contains a condensed version.
58 There is, however, a necrophiliac moment that takes the fetishisation of courtly love to an extreme, when the princess, mistaking the corpse of the envious steward for her beloved, embalms it to kiss and keep; on this aspect of the text, see Nicola McDonald, 'Desire Out of Order and *Undo Your Door*', *Studies in the Age of Chaucer*, 34 (2012), 247–75.
59 *Sentimental and Humorous Romances*, pp. 134 and 159. See also Julia Boffey and A. S. G. Edwards, '*The Squire of Low Degree* and the Penumbra of Romance Narrative in the Early Sixteenth Century', in Elizabeth Archibald, Megan G. Leitch and Corinne Saunders (eds), *Romance Rewritten: The Evolution of Middle English Romance* (Cambridge: D. S. Brewer, 2018), pp. 229–40.
60 See, for instance, Karma Lochrie, Peggy McCracken, and James A. Schultz (eds), *Constructing Medieval Sexuality* (Minneapolis, MN: University of Minnesota Press, 1997), and Hopkins and Rushton (eds), *The Erotic in the Literature of Medieval Britain*.
61 See Diane Wolfthal, *In and Out of the Marital Bed: Seeing Sex in Renaissance Europe* (New Haven, CT: Yale University Press, 2010), which focuses on late medieval and early modern visual culture to consider the 'ways in which people learned to transform space [such as the bed and the bath] to suit their sexual desires' (p. 8).
62 Webb, *Privacy and Solitude in the Middle Ages*, p. 98; Thompson, *The Medieval Hall*, p. 117; Blair, 'Hall and Chamber: English Domestic Planning 1000–1250', p. 15.
63 *Kyng Alisaunder*, ed. G. V. Smithers, EETS 227 (London: Oxford University Press, 1952), pp. 377–8.
64 *King Horn*, in Herzman, Drake and Salisbury (eds), *Four Romances of England*, ll. 653–4.

65 See Saunders, *The Forest of Romance*.
66 *King Horn*, ll. 711–18.
67 *King Horn*, l. 329. Compare the king's more moderate statement to Horn in *The Romance of Horn*, ed. Mildred K. Pope, rev. by T. B. W. Reid, 2 vols (Oxford: Anglo-Norman Text Society, 1964), I, 1920–6.
68 Lefebvre, *The Production of Space*, pp. 83 and 27.
69 Lefebvre, *The Production of Space*, p. 49.
70 Ruth Mazo Karras, *Sexuality in Medieval Europe: Doing unto Others* (New York: Routledge, 2005), pp. 123–4.
71 *King Horn*, ll. 349–50.
72 *Horn Childe and Maiden Rimnild*, ed. Maldwyn Mills (Heidelberg: Carl Winter, 1988), lines 364–72. I have reproduced these lines in the order in which they occur in the Auchinleck manuscript, rather than as they appear in Mills' edition. Mills relocates the final three lines of this passage to the beginning of it because he believes it 'makes better sense' (p. 113); however, in respecting the authority of the sole extant version, we see, as discussed below, the emergence of another 'sense'.
73 Compare *Romance of Horn*, ll. 1094–1101.
74 On erotic enclosure (though without a consideration of the romance genre), see Cary Howie, *Claustrophilia: The Erotics of Enclosure in Medieval Literature* (New York: Palgrave, 2007). Howie glosses 'the erotics of enclosure' as a spatial manifestation of a 'desire to hold and be held' (p. 139).
75 *Horn Childe*, ll. 433–5.
76 *Middle English Verse Romances*, ed. Donald B. Sands (New York: Holt, Rinehart and Winston, 1966), p. 199.
77 *Horn Childe*, ll. 496–521.
78 Maldwyn Mills, 'Introduction', in *Horn Childe*, p. 51.
79 Webb, *Privacy and Solitude*, p. 99.
80 Karras, *Sexuality in Medieval Europe*, p. 81; *Gawain and the Green Knight*, ll. 1178–80.
81 *Gawain and the Green Knight*, ll. 1181–94.
82 As on the third morning of this testing, when, with Gawain once again still in bed, the Lady similarly 'comez withinne þe chambre dore, and closes hit hir after' (1742).
83 *Gawain and the Green Knight*, ll. 1208–11.
84 *Gawain and the Green Knight*, ll. 1218–23.
85 Sheila Fisher, 'Taken Men and Token Women in Sir Gawain and the Green Knight', in Sheila Fisher and Janet E. Halley (eds), *Seeking the Woman in Late Medieval and Renaissance Writings: Essays in Feminist Contextual Criticism* (Knoxville, TN: University of Tennessee Press, 1989), pp. 71–105 (pp. 78–9).

86 Malory's heightened focus on aristocratic bedchambers seems part of the way in which his text, as Martin observes, 'routinely directs attention more closely' to castles: *Castles and Space*, p. 2.
87 Malory, *Morte Darthur*, pp. 623.26–624.10. The darkened chamber and the morning revelation are paralleled in Malory's source, *Lancelot*, IV, 211.
88 On the role of the window here, see also Molly Martin, *Vision and Gender in Malory's 'Morte Darthur'* (Cambridge: D. S. Brewer, 2010), p. 159.
89 Malory, *Morte Darthur*, pp. 631.26–633.10; see further Megan G. Leitch, 'Enter the Bedroom: Managing Space for the Erotic in Middle English Romance', in Amanda Hopkins, Robert Allen Rouse and Cory James Rushton (eds), *Sexual Culture in Late Medieval Britain* (Cambridge: D. S. Brewer, 2014), pp. 39–53.
90 Malory, *Morte Darthur*, p. 633.19–23.
91 As Martin insightfully observes, 'the *Morte* continually disallows domestic peace and domestic place': Martin, *Castles and Space*, p. 188.
92 Malory, *Morte Darthur*, p. 259.8–20.
93 Malory, *Morte Darthur*, p. 260.27–30.
94 Malory, *Morte Darthur*, p. 261.5–13.
95 Verdon, *Night in the Middle Ages*, pp. 140–1.
96 Triamour's pavilion and its fancy bed offer a private space, but both Triamour and her privacy are framed by her father's power (if at a remove), as revealed when Launfal 'fond yn the pavyloun / The kynges doughter of Olyroun': *Sir Launfal*, ll. 277–8.
97 Prose *Melusine*, p. 32.10–15.
98 Prose *Melusine*, p. 296.1–3.
99 Prose *Melusine*, p. 297.10–11. See, similarly, the verse *Romans of Partenay*, ll. 2767–835.
100 For an extended analysis of late medieval aristocratic architecture as 'inhibit[ing] the spatial practices of women and the narrative identities they inscribed through such practices' in relation to *Melusine* in particular, see Shaw, *Space, Gender, and Memory in Middle English Romance*, pp. 129 and 91–127.
101 *Cymbeline*, 1.vi.193–5.
102 See also Christopher Clason, 'Deception in the Boudoir: Gottfried's *Tristan* and 'Lying' in Bed', *Journal of English and German Philology*, 103.3 (2004), 277–96 (p. 296), and Sarah M. White, 'Lancelot's Beds: Styles of Courtly Intimacy', in R. T. Pickens (ed.), *The Sower and His Seed: Essays on Chrétien de Troyes* (Lexington, KY: French Forum, 1983), pp. 116–26 (p. 117).

103 Gottfried von Strassburg, *Tristan*, ed. G. Weber (Darmstadt: Wissenschaftliche Buchgesellschaft, 1967), ll. 15161–4; *Tristan*, trans. A. T. Hatto (London: Penguin, 2004), p. 241.
104 Gottfried, *Tristan*, ll. 15194–7; *Tristan*, trans. Hatto, pp. 241–2.
105 Chrétien de Troyes, *Lancelot*, ll. 4699–701; 'The Knight of the Cart', p. 265.
106 Peggy McCracken, *The Curse of Eve, the Wound of the Hero: Blood, Gender, and Medieval Literature* (Philadelphia, PA: University of Pennsylvania Press, 2003), pp. ix–x.
107 McCracken, *The Curse of Eve*, pp. 10 and ix.
108 McCracken, *The Curse of Eve*, p. x.
109 Bettina Bildhauer, *Medieval Blood* (Cardiff: University of Wales Press, 2006), p. 21.
110 McCracken, *The Curse of Eve*, p. 12.
111 McCracken, *The Curse of Eve*, p. 12.
112 McCracken, *The Curse of Eve*, p. 4.
113 Lynch, *Malory's Book of Arms*, p. 60.
114 Lynch, *Malory's Book of Arms*, p. 60.
115 Malory, *Morte Darthur*, p. 310.30–1.
116 Malory, *Morte Darthur*, p. 311.5–7.
117 Malory, *Morte Darthur*, p. 311.8–9; Vinaver, *Works*, p. 1460.
118 Malory, *Morte Darthur*, p. 311.13–17.
119 Malory, *Morte Darthur*, pp. 309.25–6 and 309.32–310.2.
120 Malory, *Morte Darthur*, p. 312.18–20.
121 Malory, *Morte Darthur*, p. 852.21–4; see R. S. Sturges, 'Epistemology of the Bedchamber: Textuality, Knowledge, and the Representation of Adultery in Malory and the Prose Lancelot', *Arthuriana*, 7.4 (1997), 47–62 (p. 47).
122 *Lancelot*, II.76; translation mine.
123 Malory, *Morte Darthur*, p. 853.24.
124 In the French Prose *Lancelot*, the 'Knight of the Cart' episode occurs much earlier.
125 Vinaver's supposition of a lost French source for the Gareth section (*Commentary*, pp. 1427–34) has been superseded by arguments for an English source based on vocabulary and syntax: P. J. C. Field, 'The Source of Malory's *Tale of Gareth*', in Toshiyuki Takamiya and Derek Brewer (eds), *Aspects of Malory* (Cambridge, 1981), pp. 57–70; Ralph Norris, *Malory's Library: The Sources of the 'Morte Darthur'* (Cambridge: D. S. Brewer, 2008). Alternatively, Malory may have synthesised his own tale: see Megan G. Leitch and Cory James Rushton, 'Introduction', in Leitch and Rushton (eds), *A New Companion to Malory* (Cambridge: D. S. Brewer, 2019), pp. 1–10 (esp. p. 6).

126 Malory, *Morte Darthur*, p. 261.9–10.
127 Malory, *Morte Darthur*, p. 261.20–2.
128 Malory, *Morte Darthur*, p. 261.25–7. See Karen Cherewatuk, 'Malory's Thighs and Launcelot's Buttock: Ignoble Wounds and Moral Transgression in the *Morte Darthur*', *Arthurian Literature*, 31 (2014), 35–60.
129 Malory, *Morte Darthur*, pp. 262.34–263.2.
130 Malory, *Morte Darthur*, p. 263.6–8.
131 Malory, *Morte Darthur*, p. 260.27–8.
132 Malory, *Morte Darthur*, p. 262.23–5.
133 Malory, *Morte Darthur*, p. 260.28–30.
134 Malory, *Morte Darthur*, p. 852.7–13.
135 White, 'Lancelot's Beds', p. 120.
136 Malory, *Morte Darthur*, p. 311.4–6. On the way in which, without his armour, a knight's appearance could be ambiguously gendered, see E. Jane Burns, 'Refashioning Courtly Love: Lancelot as Ladies' Man or as Lady/Man', in Karma Lochrie, Peggy McCracken and James A. Schultz (eds), *Constructing Medieval Sexuality* (Minneapolis, MN: University of Minnesota Press, 1997), pp. 111–34.

4

The hermeneutics of sleep in Chaucer's dream poems

When Chaucer's narrator falls asleep to dream in the *Book of the Duchess*, he connects his desire to sleep to a desire to interpret, and to the challenge of interpretation:

> sodeynly, I nyste how,
> Such a lust anoon me took
> To slepe that ryght upon my book
> Y fil aslepe, and therewith even
> Me mette so ynly swete a sweven,
> So wonderful that never yit
> Y trowe no man had the wyt
> To konne wel my sweven rede.[1]

In the lengthy account that precedes the dream, for the insomniac, possibly lovelorn narrator, sleep is an appetite – 'a lust'; it both is, and stands in for, the object of desire. Here, sleep follows and furthers the narrator's encounter with an old book, in which, for Alcyone grieving the loss of her husband Ceyx, sleep similarly substitutes for the object of desire. Yet although this is the first instance of a medieval dream vision narrator seeking to cure his insomnia by reading,[2] the narrator's sleep is not necessarily caused by reading: he falls asleep 'ryght upon my book', unconsciously united with his reading material in a way that emphasises propinquity rather than causality. Indeed, Chaucer is either unwilling or unable to state how this sleep is caused; the narrator has made his vow to offer a rich reward to Morpheus or anyone who can help him sleep, but still he 'nyste how' he falls asleep. Here, Chaucer foregrounds the question – and the difficulty – of interpreting the cause of this sleep, just as, in the next few lines, he foregrounds the difficulty of interpreting the narrator's dream, which 'never yit / Y trowe no man had the wyt / To [...] rede'. Readers are invited to assess his sleep as well as his dream. What causes this sleep? What does it contribute to the dream, and to the poet seeking inspiration – seeking a cure for 'ydel thoght' and 'sorwful ymagynacioun'?[3] And how does sleep relate to the books that Chaucer famously invokes as inspiration for dreams and the poems to which they give shape, to his 'programmatic bookishness' in the *Book of the Duchess* and other dream visions?[4]

Like his representations of dreams and their origins, Chaucer's representations of sleep are self-conscious and subject to poetic scrutiny. Dreams are inherently about interpretation; in this, they are insistently akin to literature, demanding to be read, to be analysed.[5] While it is well recognised that Chaucer's dream vision narrators 'experience highly significant slumber', such slumber is generally seen to be significant only inasmuch as it enables the dream.[6] Sleep is, of course, the necessary precondition for dreams such as the one in which the Man in Black grieves for 'goode faire White';[7] however, here as elsewhere in Chaucer's dream poems, sleep is far more than simply the platform for visionary experience. Sleep, I suggest, contributes to the way in which the *Book of the Duchess* 'addresses interpretation as a serious theme in its own right'.[8] Although Lisa Kiser and Rebecca Davis have astutely observed the importance of sleep and insomnia to the thematic coherence and metafictional concerns of the *Book of the Duchess*, Chaucerian sleep – here and in the *Parliament of Fowls* and the *Prologue* to the *Legend of Good Women* – receives more textual attention than its slim share of critical attention would suggest.[9] In this chapter, I argue that Chaucer's dream poetry explores the hermeneutics of sleep as well as the hermeneutics of dreams; and that through sleep, as through dreams, Chaucer reflects on the nature of poetry and poetic inheritance.

Significantly, the medieval science of sleep with which Chaucer engages here, and the precedents and parallels for his interest in sleep elsewhere in Middle English literature, have not yet been recognised in print. That the subject of sleep is a recurring preoccupation in Chaucer's dream visions can be seen not least in the focus of the longer, pre-dream narratives and framing devices that distinguish Chaucer's poems from his sources in French dream poetry.[10] Without sleep, the narrator-poet would not be supplied with the narrative material that allows him to write again at the end of the poem, when he awakes and feels able 'to put this sweven in ryme / As I kan best'.[11] Particularly in the *Book of the Duchess*, but also in the *Parliament of Fowls* and the *Prologue* to the *Legend of Good Women*, Chaucer engages with sleep in ways that depart from his French sources and analogues, and that offer intriguing parallels to treatments of sleep in other Middle English genres. These connections illuminate how sleep shapes Chaucer's exploration of the possibilities of consolation in the *Book of the Duchess*, and how, across Chaucer's dream visions, sleep contributes to Chaucerian debates about the inspiration for new poetry.

Accordingly, this chapter concentrates first and foremost on the *Book of the Duchess*, and later extends its analysis to the *Parliament of Fowls* and the *Prologue* to the *Legend of Good Women*. (Of Chaucer's dream visions, the *House of Fame* is least concerned with the science of sleep – fittingly so, since the *House of Fame* is about what happens to poetry after it is no longer under the author's control, rather than about the inspiration for and generation of poetry.) Chaucer's *Book of the Duchess* foregrounds sleep – proper sleep – as a *desideratum* whose present absence embodies the sorrow not only of the narrator and Alcyone, the poem's first two pining lovers, but also, in an understudied section of the poem, of the Man in Black. Here, Chaucer characterises troubled relationships to sleep through medically informed explorations of the physiology of sleep that link the frame narratives with the dream narrative, and that register sleep's multifaceted contributions to the poem's concerns with consolation. In addition, Chaucer's concerted emphasis on sleep, in its insistence on the embodiment of the dreamer, highlights the embodiment of poetic inspiration. Sleep, that is, offers a term for the role of experience as inspiration for poetry, alongside Chaucer's more high-profile explorations of the role of old books as inspiration for poetry. And as an earthly, corporeal language for poetic inspiration, Chaucer's deployment of sleep, I suggest, also serves as a rumination upon his debts to English literary traditions, alongside his more well-recognised debts to French and classical models.

'Y fil aslepe': Englishing the *Book of the Duchess*

Although the *Book of the Duchess* as a dream vision may not be prevailingly English, the *Book of the Duchess* as a poem about sleep has more English credentials. In suggesting that Chaucer draws upon an English tradition to shape the *Book of the Duchess* and his later dream poems, this chapter complements critical awareness of Chaucer's widespread debts to French traditions by offering another perspective, from which we can further appreciate both Chaucer's innovations and his influences.[12] In this earliest of his sustained narrative poems (written c.1368–74), Chaucer, as is well known, shows his influences and erudition in drawing upon classical sources and French precedents; he engages with 'Aristotelian epistemology, Boethian philosophy, the dream theory of Macrobius, medical practice and physiology derived from Galen and Hippocrates, the Bible, and the rules of chess'.[13] By choosing the dream vision genre for his first sustained narrative poem, Chaucer follows recent French models.[14] The *Duchess* has rightly been called 'Chaucer's most visibly "French" piece of writing', and the one of all his narrative poems that is 'most fully steeped in the French tradition'.[15] Yet as Helen Phillips has recently re-emphasised, Chaucer is, of course, 'often at his most original when following literary models'.[16] Chaucer's originality is visible not least in the way that, for his first dream poem, he chooses – unlike his French models – to write a 300-line prefatory narrative that is largely about not dreams, but sleep. Moreover, as later sections of this chapter demonstrate, while Chaucer is well known for his citations of Macrobian dream theory, his dream poems also offer underappreciated engagements with Aristotelian dream theory that intervene in debates about the nature of dreams and of fiction. By focusing on sleep in his dream poems, as well as by engaging with a wider range of theories on the origins of dreams than is commonly recognised, Chaucer draws upon, and responds to, English literary traditions as well as continental ones.

An insomniac narrator is a familiar figure from the French *dits amoureux* by which Chaucer was influenced;[17] however, Chaucer develops this trope in new directions, reflecting a different set of concerns – concerns which have precedents in English literature. When Chaucer's narrator begins the poem by declaring 'I may nat slepe wel nygh noght', he laments his 'Defaute of slep and hevynesse' for forty-five lines before he 'bad oon reche me a book, / A romaunce' to pass the sleepless night-time hours.[18] Chaucer's fixation on 'slepe' here is shown not least by the fact that he mentions it thirty-four times in the first 300 lines of the *Book of the Duchess*. Two of these instances are in the passage which is extant in Thynne's 1532 edition but not in any of the three surviving manuscripts of the *Book of the Duchess*.[19] This passage (lines 31–96) hints at reasons for the narrator's sleeplessness and introduces his recourse to 'a book, / A romaunce' in which he begins to read the story of Ceyx and Alcyone. However, it is likely that these lines are authorial,[20] and in any case, sleep figures here in ways that parallel Chaucer's interrogative focus on sleep in the rest of the prologue. Thus, even before the onset of the dream – when, as mentioned, Chaucer foregrounds a hermeneutic question specifically about the causation of sleep – sleep's immanence to this poem about love, loss, dreams, books, sorrow, consolation and poetry itself is writ large.

By contrast, in French literary precedents to Chaucer's poem, sleep often seems an insignificant accessory to the dream. For instance, in the seminal thirteenth-century *Roman de la Rose*, the sleep is perfunctory. Guillaume de Lorris begins the work with some brief comments on Macrobius and dream theory (but not on sleep), and then writes that

>   couchiez estoie
> Une nuit, si cum je souloie,
> Et me dormoie moult forment,
> Si vi ung songe en mon dormant,
> Qui moult fut biax, et moult me plot.
>
> (I lay down one night, as usual, and fell fast asleep. As I slept, I had a most beautiful and pleasing dream.)[21]

Here, sleep is merely a necessary precondition for dreaming; a prerequisite, certainly, but an untroubled, unremarkable one. Similarly, Jean de Meun ends his continuation of the poem by briefly stating 'Ainsinc oi la Rose vermeille, / Atant fu jor, et ge m'esveille' ('And so I won my bright red rose. Then it was day and I awoke').[22] The fragmentary Chaucerian *The Romaunt of the Rose*, as a translation of the French version, follows the model of this swift and unproblematic entry to dream-filled sleep. In the way that the first third or so of the *Book of the Duchess* is devoted to what is often seen as 'material prefatory to the central narrative', the *Duchess* does parallel Guillaume de Lorris's *Roman de la Rose*;[23] significantly, however, while in the *Roman de la Rose* this 'introductory section' takes place within the dream itself, Chaucer instead gives us a substantial narrative preceding the dream: a narrative in which sleep is a central subject.

Moreover, the medieval French dream visions and *dits amoreux* upon which Chaucer drew, even when featuring insomniac narrators, do not generally concern themselves with the what, where, when, how, or why of their narrators' acts of falling asleep (or being unable to), or of waking up, nearly as much as the *Book of the Duchess* does.[24] The *Book of the Duchess* explores the epistemological implications of sleep by altering partial textual precedents in French *dits amoureux*: by adapting continental sources, but in ways that show striking resonances with precedents and parallels in the thematisation of sleep in English literary culture. Where Chaucer's debts to French traditions in the construction of his dream visions are clearly demonstrated by his use of direct sources, his debts to English traditions are often more diffuse (and thus perhaps less readily detected), but nonetheless pronounced. In his prologue to the dream in the *Duchess*, the models Chaucer follows from the genre of *dits amoreux* include, in particular, Jean Froissart's *Paradis d'amour* (for the narrator's insomnia) and Guillaume de Machaut's *Le dit de la fonteinne amoureuse* (for the story of Ceyx and Alcyone).[25] However, the idea of sleep is much more prominent and generative – emotionally, oneirically and poetically – in the *Duchess* than in these models. The opening fifteen lines of the *Duchess*, lamenting the narrator's insomnia and the lack of both health and fertile imagination it causes, follows the first twelve lines of Froissart's c.1361–62 *Paradis d'amour*,[26] yet Chaucer both alters the terms of this lament and expands on it to create his extended prologue.[27] Writing that his narrator has 'so many an ydel thoght / Purely for defaute of slep', Chaucer links this lack of sleep to a depleted or 'sorwful ymagynacioun', foregrounding the way in which productive thoughts or imagination depend upon sleep.[28] Where Froissart focuses on the state of waking ('en vellant', 'par vellier', 'tant je vel'),[29] Chaucer instead insistently dwells on sleep itself, from the initial 'I may nat slepe' and 'defaute of slep' through to the end of the 300-line prologue.[30] Moreover, while Guillaume de Machaut's c.1360 *Fonteinne amoureuse* provided Chaucer with a model for the story of an insomniac narrator who overhears a lover's complaint, and a parallel for the inclusion of Ovid's story of the drowned King Ceyx and his grieving wife Alcyone, Chaucer reshapes these elements.[31] In the *Fonteinne amoureuse*, Machaut's melancholy duke considers asking the God of Sleep to send Morpheus not to himself (though he is indeed suffering from insomnia), but rather to his lady, so that a dream message might be conveyed to her (as is sent to Alceone in the inset narrative). By contrast, Chaucer connects the God of Sleep to his own narrator's melancholic state, to his need for sleep and renewal.

This is one of the ways in which Chaucer distinctively (in contrast to French dream vision and *dit amoreux* precedents) and typically (in relation to English dream vision and romance parallels) foregrounds sleep's role in resetting the balance between the humours or emotions, and in transmuting lived experience into dreams. In the *Duchess*, Chaucer uses sleep to communicate and negotiate emotional states and their implications for mental health, dreams and the matter of poetry. To do so, as this book shows, he deploys the same approach to sleep as other English texts, including earlier ones such as Chardri's saints' lives and *Ywain and Gawain*; contemporary ones such as *Pearl* and *Piers Plowman*; and later ones such as Malory's *Morte Darthur* and the York cycle plays.

The *Duchess* negotiates sleep's contributions to two aspects of what we would call mental health but which medieval mentalities viewed as part of a mind–body continuum: emotional well-being (particularly in relation to melancholia), and the functioning of the inward wits (particularly in relation to the imagination necessary for creating poetry). As different sides of the same coin, sleeping and waking are conjoined yet distinct; their importance for physical and emotional health was emphasised in the medical treatises of Galen, the influential second-century Greek physician and writer cited by the Man in Black.[32] As discussed in more detail in Chapter 1, Galenic medicine entered western Europe c.1070–1300 via Arabic medicine and shaped the prevailing scientific world view through the sixteenth century. In this medical paradigm, sleep was one of the six 'non-natural' influences on the body, and was considered beneficial for both physical and mental health.[33] Waking and sleeping were both necessary, but in the right balance; 'defaute of slep' or insomnia was detrimental to well-being. Sleep was understood to enable the restorative transformation of food into the four humours by facilitating digestion. For Galenic medicine, that is, sleep is a way of pressing the 'reset' button for an imbalance in the humours or passions, such as the excess of 'sorwe' (21) or 'melancolye' (23) that troubles the narrator in the *Duchess*, or the grief of the bereaved Alcyone and Man in Black in the prologue's inset narrative and in the dream narrative respectively. Sleep, that is, constitutes a physiological form of consolation (a literal soothing of strong emotions), and contributes to the poem's concerns with the possibilities and difficulties of consolation for loss.

In addition to the scientific distinction between 'vellant' and 'defaute of slep',[34] then, there is also an important semantic one. When Chaucer transforms Froissart's phrases such as 'tant je vel' ('I wake [or watch] so much') (12) to 'I may nat slepe' (3), he not only chooses to emphasise the side of the medical pairing of sleeping and waking that is absent, and that represents or facilitates the inspiraton that his poet-narrator desires and lacks; he also does so in a recognisably English register. As Steve Guthrie has shown, the opening lines of the *Duchess*, in their 'monosyllabism and Germanic consonance', offer a pronounced contrast to Froissart's 'near monorhyme of vowels and semivowels'.[35] Although of course the *Duchess*'s end-rhyming octosyllabic form is French, and, in 'advertizing itself as English, it draws attention to its Frenchness as well', the poem is also launched with a concerted emphasis on auditory Englishness.[36] Chaucer's fashioning of this auditory Englishness includes repeatedly replacing Froissart's rhymes on various conjugations of 'vellier' with a metrically diffuse, but lexically distinctive and concentrated, use of the English word 'slepe' to spearhead his engagement with this non-natural that signifies poetic inspiration. This lexical choice to use an English word, for a poet writing in English, is in fact still a choice, not least since Chaucer's vocabulary is half French, and he often introduced French words into written English.[37] Despite Chaucer's undoubted debts to French dream visions and *dits amoureux*, then, from the very beginning the *Duchess* signals a different approach to, and more concerted engagement with, sleep.

By focusing on lack of sleep rather than Froissart's excess of waking, Chaucer begins his poem by dwelling on something that is an important concern in English romance, dream visions and drama – and does so in the same terms as his English forebears and contemporaries. In the *Duchess*, sleep is fundamental to health, narrative and inspiration – yet it is also (agonisingly) deferred. This deferral is not a common feature of Middle English literary engagements with sleep; however, Chaucer's deferral creates poetic space to explore the hermeneutics of sleep in ways that do resonate with its widespread treatment elsewhere in Middle English literature. By dwelling on, yet deferring, sleep, then, Chaucer is able to reflect both on the insomnia of the French *dits amoreux*, and on the sleep of English literature – constructing a distinctive duality that is, perhaps unsurprisingly, his own stamp on the matter.[38] In light of this science of sleep and these English literary precedents and parallels, the next two sections offer a new reading of the significance of sleep for the *Duchess*'s concerns with, respectively, emotions and illness, and dreams. The final section, meanwhile, explores the implications of sleep for Chaucer's reflections on poetic inspiration in the *Parliament of Fowls* and the *Prologue* to the *Legend of Good Women* as well as the *Book of the Duchess*.

Sleep as medicine: emotions and illness

The *Duchess* has been seen as a poem about illness in its concerns with melancholy and its debilitating effects, as well as, though in a partially occluded way, in its central concern with Blanche's death as a result of plague or another disease.[39] And as is well recognised, the dream in the *Book of the Duchess* explores ideas about consolation (whether or not the poem or the dream is in fact effective in providing consolation for melancholy). I argue here that the poem's engagements with sleep are also about emotions and medicine. Sleep, as a longed-for present absence that is a proxy for absent loved ones, offers an embodied register of, and a desired form of medicine for, melancholy. This is made strikingly clear when Chaucer chooses – unlike Ovid or Machaut – to adapt this story from the *Metamorphoses* by having Juno instruct Morpheus to 'take up Seys body the kyng, / That lyeth ful pale and nothyng rody' and actually 'crepe into the body' and speak to the sleeping Alcyone through the reanimated body of her dead husband,[40] rather than merely appearing in the likeness of Ceyx.[41] Here, Chaucer's God of Sleep literally 'em-bodies' a (short-lived) form of consolation, as it is while in her husband's body that he tells Alcyone, 'Let be your sorwful lyf.'[42] Although it has not been well recognised, sleep is central to the 'lack' – the melancholy – of the patron-knight as well as of the poet-narrator and the grieving widow. Just as Chaucer highlights the problem of sleep for the narrator and for Alcyone in the long sleep-obsessed prologue to the dream, he also highlights sleep as a problematised object of desire for the Man in Black (who complains that his sleep has turned to waking). In forming this structural parallel,[43] sleep also contributes to the thematic unity of the poem as a form of consolation desired and needed by all three figures: a consolation enacted in the therapeutic resetting of the balance between the humours that sleep enables, as foregrounded by the poem's explicit invocations of Galenic medicine.

The *Duchess* approaches the subject of the restoration sleep can offer interrogatively, with a complexity and nuance that parallels its treatment of the subject of dreams. Where the narrator's dream invites questions about both its origin and its meaning – invoking theories of the origins of dreams and widespread interest in interpreting dreams – these subjects are treated with a combination of respect and scepticism. Similarly, the poem treats the cause and effect of sleep and insomnia as epistemologically significant, in ways that seem to recognise that these are a focus of intense contemporary interpretive interest, but that also question the knowability of sleep's cause and effect in a similar way to the poem's questioning of the knowability of the origins and meaning of dreams. Chaucer is famous for both invoking interpretive desires, and (at least partially) resisting them, and that sleep is no exception here shows all the more the depth of his engagement with the subject.

In treating the relationship between the narrator's emotions and his insomnia and eventual sleep, Chaucer both invokes the question of causality, and refuses to provide (straightforward) answers. Unlike Froissart's *Paradys d'Amour*, the *Duchess* does not specify an explicit cause for the narrator's insomnia, but Chaucer's hint that the reason why he 'may not slepe' is due to 'a sicknesse / That I have suffred this eight yer' has nonetheless been presumed to be lovesickness, as it is in his source, due to his specification that he lacks a remedy, and that 'there is phisicien but oon / That may me hele'.[44] If the narrator, then, desires an absent or aloof beloved, this desire also engenders a lack of, and desire for, sleep. When Chaucer leaves the cause of this melancholic sleeplessness open to question just as he later leaves the cause of his sleep itself open to interrogation, he playfully foregrounds the subject: 'men myght axe me why soo / I may not slepe'.[45] Following this with 'who aske this / Leseth his asking trewely', he emphasises not that this is a question that should not be asked, but rather one that cannot be answered (or that he refuses to answer).[46] It parallels the way in which Chaucer later writes that 'sodeynly, I nyste how, / Such a lust anoon me took / To slepe', rather than either specifying the cause, or simply (as in the *Roman de la Rose*, for instance) writing that he fell asleep and dreamed.[47] It also parallels the way in which Chaucer asserts that 'Y trowe no man had the wyt / To konne wel my sweven rede.'[48]

Notwithstanding these deliberate ambiguities – which, indeed, serve to provoke interpretive interest rather than forestall it – Chaucer repeatedly explores ways in which sleep serves as an embodied mediator for the emotions, as a way of accessing consolation and/or knowledge. In the tale that the narrator reads, Alcyone's sorrow for her absent husband King Seys has led to her suffering, like the narrator, for lack of sleep: she is described as 'forwaked'.[49] She prays for sleep in hopes of diminishing her emotional distress, asking Juno to

> 'Send me grace to slepe and mete
> In my slep som certeyn sweven
> Wherthourgh that I may knowen even
> Whether my lord be quyk or ded.'[50]

When Juno 'made hir to slepe',[51] then, sleep represents both consolation (as rest and closure) and knowledge (the truth about her husband). Similarly, of course, reading the book represents the possibility of consolation for the narrator and knowledge (the inspiration for poetry), but this is not least because of the story the narrator reads foregrounds the restorative and epistemic possibilities of sleep. As we have seen, medieval science positions sleep as a form of consolation in itself: a resetting or rebalancing of the humours, or passions. Both the narrator's negotiation of insomnia and his subsequent melancholic sleep fit this paradigm: according to medieval medicine and psychology, melancholic 'patients might suffer either from sleeping too much or too little'.[52] Melancholy can cause both sleepiness and insomnia because of different stages in the effects of black bile on the brain: while sleeplessness occurred if the brain dried following clogging of its pathways by black bile, excessive sleepiness resulted from a direct effect of black bile on the brain.[53] Here, Chaucer uses sleep to foreground connections between body and mind;[54] as an embodied experience in itself, sleep also foregrounds a link to the narrator's waking experience, to the melancholy that shapes his dream as well as his sleep.

While Chaucer here engages with the medical understanding of sleep as beneficial to physical and mental health, he also, elsewhere in the *Duchess*, engages with the social understanding of improper sleep as detrimental to well-being and reputation. Chaucer's engagement with the ethical connotations of sleep important to many of his literary contemporaries is evident in the way in which, relative to his sources, he gives the description of Morpheus's cave and its sleepers more scope, and a more corporeal depiction. Chaucer's description of the cave of sleep accounts for a far larger proportion of his poem than of his Ovidian source (or of Machaut's version), and, where Ovid's Morpheus is a son of the god of sleep, Chaucer's is the God of Sleep himself.[55] When Chaucer writes that in the cave of the God of Sleep, Morpheus and his heir 'slep and dide noon other werk', Rebecca Davis has suggested that he may be articulating the way in which sleep itself is a form of work – as sleep is certainly a form of work for Chaucer the poet.[56] However, as medieval courtesy books and dietaries reminded readers, there are healthy and proper ways to sleep, but also ways and times of sleeping that are not considered propitious to health or to social or spiritual reputation, and Chaucer here foregrounds the latter.

The bodily description Chaucer gives of how Morpheus and his son perform their sleep explicitly includes a number of things medieval sleepers are instructed not to do. The sleepers in Morpheus's cave 'route, / To envye who myghte slepe best'.[57] Snoring was viewed as uncouth and animal-like. This sort of vulgar embodiment, and snoring in particular, features in the description of the untimely and improper sleepers of English fabliau and drama. The negative connotations of snoring are clear when we recall that in the 'Miller's Tale', snoring is something that John the Carpenter does because 'his head mislay'; and in the 'Reeve's Tale', Simkin and his whole family snore, especially the cuckold, who is described as snoring like a horse. Similarly, when the title character in *Mankind* sinks into an apathetic slumber, the devil observes 'ȝe may here hym snore; he ys sade aslepe', and Langland's Sloth snores when he sleeps during the daytime: he 'raxed and rored – and rutte at the laste').[58] Snoring, then, is associated with uncouth fabliau figures, sinful persons and personified sins; it is antithetical to temperate, courteous behaviour. In addition to their snoring, the sleeping positions of those in Morpheus's cave are described vividly:

> Somme henge her chyn upon hir brest
> And slept upryght, hir hed yhed,
> And somme lay naked in her bed
> And slepe whiles the dayes laste.[59]

In the *Fointeinne amoureuse*, Machaut's God of Sleep lies 'De tel maintien / Que ses mentons a sa poitrine touche' ['In such a posture / That his chin touches his chest'], but there is no snoring, and no other commentary on the physicality of the sleepers.[60] Medieval sleepers were instructed to lie on their sides (not 'upryght'), and they were decidedly discouraged from sleeping slothfully 'whiles the days laste'. In the *Duchess* Chaucer does show, as Lisa Kiser has argued, that sleep is a positive process with particular benefits for poets;[61] however, that positivity applies to the sleep of the dream vision narrator, rather than the sleep on display in Morpheus's cave.[62] While it is, of course, not surprising that the god of sleep is shown to sleep, Chaucer, in his description of the cave, concertedly engages with the English focus on the ethics of sleep. Morpheus and his companions are framed in relation to the ways in which sleep is admonitorily regulated in contemporary conduct manuals, and the ways in which untimely or uncouth sleep is distinctively negotiated in Middle English romance, allegorical dream visions and drama.

When the narrator imitates Alcyone's prayer for sleep, earthly materiality is emphasised again, but in a way that oscillates back to the profitability of sleep, once more connecting contemporary interest in sleep (and in this case, the spaces of sleep) to the possibility of consolation. He declares that he would have died 'thurgh defaute of slep, / Yif I ne had red and take kep / Of this tale' of Alcyone.[63] Reading can itself be 'therapeutic', or offer consolation for sorrow, as other critics have discussed.[64] More to the point here, reading this story, the narrator elaborates, inspires him to pursue sleep as a therapeutic cure for melancholy – and we can recall that medieval authorities such as Aquinas explicitly discussed sleep as a form of redress for unhealthful passions such as melancholy. Where Alcyone asks for the 'grace to slepe and mete / In my slep som certeyn sweven' so that she can know whether her husband is dead or alive, the

The hermeneutics of sleep in Chaucer's dream poems 211

narrator similarly wants to 'slepe and have som reste', and through his restorative sleep, he will also meet a certain dream – one that restores his ability to write poetry.[65]

Yet where Alcyone makes her prayer to Juno, the narrator instead takes something of a 'blanket' approach, in what has been seen as a recognisably English elaboration: he addresses his request to 'thilke Morpheus, / Or his goddesse, dame Juno, / Or som wight elles, I ne roghte who', and in return, he offers 'the alderbeste / Yifte', which consists of all the furnishings to make a comfortable and ostentatious sleeping chamber. Chaucer here details 'a fether-bed, / Rayed with gold and ryght wel cled', and lists a variety of bed textiles with great specificity, including 'fyn black satyn doutremer' and pillowcases 'of cloth of Reynes' in France.[66] Sarah Stanbury has argued that the details of this bedding, and the geographical marking of the textiles as hailing from overseas, from France, give the voicing of Chaucer's proffered gift an up-to-date fourteenth-century and English specificity. While the appeal to Morpheus for an end to insomnia is in some ways conventional,[67] and while the narrator takes his cue in this from Alcyone, Chaucer's imagined bedchamber objects, as Stanbury suggests, invoke an embodied locus for composition: 'through named objects tied to the body and to the act of writing, [the *Duchess*] sets the act of composition on English ground'.[68]

In addition to this localised materiality of the bedroom textiles and objects, I am suggesting that the poem's composition is also connected to English ground, and English concerns, by the materiality, medicalisation and literary invocation of symptomatic, sleepy bodies, across the narratives that the poem juxtaposes. While Chaucer lacks a precedent in (French) dream poetry for the length and specificity of his pre-dream poetic commentaries,[69] he has both precedents and parallels in other English genres and other English dream visions for the focus on sleep that his dream poems manifest, as discussed further at the end of this section. And when Chaucer's narrator eventually does fall asleep, it is his desire for sleep that is emphasised again – in the passage with which this chapter opens:

> sodeynly, I nyste how,
> Such a lust anoon me took
> To slepe that ryght upon my book
> Y fil aslepe.[70]

The vow to Morpheus may be sucessful, but Chaucer does not offer certainty; instead, he emphasises both the question of the cause of his sleep, and the strength of his appetite for sleep. Although some critics have adduced a parallel in Froissart's *Paradys* for this way in which Chaucer's narrator states that he does not know how he fell asleep,[71] what each poem's narrator does not know is in fact quite different. Froissart's poem focuses on logistics, when declaring that 'the noble God of Sleep'

> m'envoia parmi l'air
> L'un de ses fils, Enclinpostair.
> Sitost qu'en ma cambre entrés fu,
> Je ne sçai le peruis par u,
> Je m'endormi en tels pensees
> Que chi vous seront recensees.[72]

> [sent through the air one of his sons, Enclimpostair. As soon as he entered my bedroom – and how he came in I do not know – I fell asleep and had such reflections as will be related to you.]

'Enclympasteyr' does appear in Chaucer's poem, as Morpheus's heir in the cave. However, Chaucer does not specify a visit from either God or heir; what his narrator does not know is *not* how his bedchamber was breached by a supernatural being, but rather, how he was overcome with 'such a lust [...] / To slepe'. The interpretive, epistemological stakes here are rather different. And in avoiding specifying whether or not the narrator's vow to Morpheus is succesful, Chaucer not only dodges the un-Christian implications of voicing faith in pagan deities; he also invites the reader to think about the cause of this sleep.

Where restful sleep is desired by and – eventually – available to the narrator, and where prayed-for sleep provides Alcyone with a vision in which her husband's body seeks to comfort her, restful sleep is also desired by the Man in Black; however, it is, seemingly, unobtainable for him, at least within the bounds of the narrative. Perhaps this speaks to the way in which the poem is about consolation for the grieving Man in Black, but does not necessarily contain it.[73] The dream narrative, of course, foregrounds one possible mode of consolation when the narrator's questions (whether bumblingly obtuse, or strategically solicitous) give the Man in Black an opportunity to talk about, and thus perhaps talk through, his grief: conversation can be consoling.[74] Narrative itself, then, is one shared form of consolation here – writing narrative, for the dreamer-poet, and voicing narrative, for the Man in Black. As A. J. Minnis has argued, Chaucer eschews models of Christian consolation in the *Book of the Duchess*, avoiding reference to the afterlife and focusing instead on the 'consolation of experience',[75] a term that is apt for both the way in which balanced sleep signifies unobtainable consolation for the patron-knight and the way in which experience of sleep also serves as restoration for the imaginative barrenness of the poet-narrator.

Chaucer's deployment of the science of sleep in this poem is explicitly articulated in the Man in Black's lament, and here again – as in the narrative that precedes the dream – Chaucer engages with sleep in ways that are not paralleled in his continental sources. From the poem's opening lack – the narrator's 'defaute of slep' – the poem builds to the Man in Black's lack: the loss of his 'fers', and his explanation to the narrator that he has 'lost more than thow wenest'.[76] This personal loss has in turn led to the loss of the natural oppositions that had structured the Man in Black's life, as he tells the dreamer:

> In travayle ys myn ydelnesse
> And eke my reste; my wele is woo,
> My good ys harm, and evermoo
> In wrathe is turned my pleynge
> And my delyt into sorwynge.
> Myn hele ys turned into seknesse,
> In drede ys al my sykernesse;
> To derke ys turned al my lyght,
> My wyt ys foly, my day ys nyght,
> My love ys hate, *my slep wakynge*,
> My myrthe and meles ys fastynge.[77]

There are various partial precedents for this list, but unlike the Man in Black's lament, they do not include sleep and waking among the collapsed or inverted oppositions.[78]

By contrast with the Man in Black's list, the short catalogues in various continental dream visions and *dits amoreux* that constitute sources or analogues for the *Book of the Duchess* concentrate primarily on the emotions. For instance, Alanus de Insulis's twelfth-century dream poem 'De planctu Naturae' on the proper order of things begins with: 'In lacrymas risus, in fletum gaudia verto; / In planctum plausus, in lacrymosa jocos' ['I turn my laughter into tears, my joy into weeping; / my applause into complaint, my jokes into grieving'].[79]

Similarly, in Jean de Meun's *Roman de la Rose*, Reason describes Love as a list of oxymorons, such as

> C'est faus delit de tristor lie,
> C'est leesce la corroucie;
> Dous maus, douceur malicieuse.[80]

> (a false delight, a joyful sorrow and an unhappy joy, a sweet torment and an unkind sweetness)

Here, Love is also

>   langor tretoute saintive,
> C'est santé toute maladive;
> C'est fain saoule en abondance,
> C'est convoiteuse soffisance;
> C'est la soif qui tous jors est yvre,
> Ivresce qui soëf enyvre.[81]

> [a most healthful sickness and a most sickly health; a hunger abundantly satisfied and a covetous affluence, a thirst that is always drunk, an intoxication drunk with thirst.]

Significantly, however, there is no mention of sleep in this list in the *Roman de la Rose*. Nor is there any mention of sleep in an otherwise similar list of happy emotions turned to unhappy ones in Guillaume de Machaut's c.1346 *Jugement du roy de Behaigne* (here voiced by a bereaved lady and overheard by the narrator):

> Lasse, dolente! Or est bien a rebours.
> Car mes douceurs sont dolereus labours,
> Et mes joies sont ameres dolours,
> Et mi penser,
> En qui mes cuers se soloit deliter
> Et doucement de tous maus conforter,
> Sont et seront dolent, triste, et amer.
> En obscurté
> Seront mi jour, plein de maleürté,
> Et mi espoir sans nulle seürté,
> Et ma douceur sera dure durté.[82]

> [Alas! What sorrow! Now the opposite is true.
> For my sweetness now is painful suffering.
> My joys are bitter hurt,
> And my thoughts,
> In which my heart used to delight

And find sweet solace for every hurt,
Are, and will remain, painful, bitter, sad.
My days
Will be dark and filled with misfortune,
My hope will lack all certainty,
And my pleasure will become enduring sorrow.]

Unlike these Latin and French precedents, Chaucer's list, by contrast, focuses more on the body, and on the embodiment of the emotions.

The Man in Black's lament, while certainly including the emotions, also features most of the other states that Galenic medicine understood as the six non-natural influences on health and well-being, including sleep. Air, the most important and universal of the non-naturals, is not explicitly mentioned, though it shapes the way in which 'hele ys turned into seknesse', but the others are: food and drink, and also inanition and repletion ('My [...] meles ys fastynge'); motion and rest ('In travayle ys myn ydelnesse / And eke my reste'); the emotions or passions ('my delyt into sorwynge' and 'My love ys hate'); and sleeping and waking ('my slep wakynge'). Chaucer, then, articulates an expanded, and more fully embodied, version of the science of lovesickness and grief; and he does so in part by foregrounding the importance of sleep – proper sleep – within the Galenic medical paradigm, in a way that his continental sources and analogues do not. Here, that is, as in the prologue, Chaucer foregrounds sleep as a process that interacts with the emotions and that is important for well-being, both physical and mental.

Moreover, shortly before this medically informed passage about the Man in Black's collapsed opposites, the grieving lover also bemoans the fact that 'Ne hele me may noo physicien, / Noght Ypocras ne Galyen.'[83] This parallels a reference in Jean de Meun's *Roman de la Rose* in which Nature says that Death catches victims despite physicians such as the great doctors of the classical world, Hippocrates and Galen.[84] Yet in the *Duchess*, when Chaucer signposts Galenic medicine with this reference, he does so – unlike the *Roman* – just before an emphasis on a Galenic understanding of health, and on the proper balance of the binary pairs that the six non-naturals, including sleep and waking, constitute. Chaucer, then, forges a different link, and it is one that highlights the interpretive and emotional significance of sleep, especially in relation to consolation. As I hope I have shown thus far, the *Duchess*'s interest in sleep cannot be reduced to just an unthinking or insignificant subsidiary of the dream; like dreams, the representations of sleep – and the narrator's and characters' relationships to sleep – are self-conscious and self-consciously hermeneutic, contributing to the experience and explication of loss and consolation.

Chaucer's representations of sleep in the *Duchess*, especially in how the narrator falls asleep, are paralleled in both earlier and later Middle English works, including romance and dream visions. While Chaucer's description of his narrator's entrance to sleep as the result of 'a lust [...] / To slepe' is not modelled on the Froissart poem that is a partial source here, it does find a parallel in the early fourteenth-century *Ywain and Gawain*, where the lust becomes for sleep itself, rather than – as in Chrétien's earlier French version – sexual desire; and another parallel, in Malory's late fifteenth-century *Morte Darthur*, when Launcelot succumbs to a literal 'grete luste to slepe' in the midday heat under a tree (in a turn of phrase again not found in the respective French source). Moreover, in *Pearl*, as in the *Duchess*, the dreamer falls asleep after a period of mournful melancholy: when he has a 'deuely dele' or desolating sorrow in his 'hert', he lies down and 'slode vpon a slepyng-slaȝte' – a sudden-onset sleep that responds to his unbalanced humoral state.[85] In romances such as *Ywain and Gawain* and Malory's *Morte Darthur*, as well as elsewhere (for instance, in Chardri's saints' lives, the Piers Plowman tradition, and the York cycle play), protagonists' sleep is similarly generated by – and read by characters and narrators as a sign of – humoral imbalance in need of redress. Malory's Launcelot becomes 'so wrothe that he layde hym downe on his bed to slepe', while Arthur is 'in a grete thought, and therewith he felle on slepe'; Langland's Will, when rebuked by Scripture, 'wepte I for wo and wraþe of hir speche / And in a wynkynge worþ til I was aslepe'.[86] In such texts of medieval England, and often in contradistinction to their sources where applicable, unhealthful emotions such as sorrow, anxiety and anger precipitate sleep. Sleep, here, is a recognisable cultural grammar, and it is striking in the extent to which it is employed in the literary culture of medieval England in particular. For Chaucer as for his fellow English writers, sleep offers a language for the relief of melancholy and for addressing mental health. Of course, in the *Duchess*, Chaucer's melancholy results in insomnia before it results in sleep, a deferral which does not follow other

Middle English literary treatments of sorrow-induced sleep; however, since Chaucer uses his creative deferral to dwell on another narrative of sleep and dreaming in the story of Ceyx and Alcyone, and reworks his sources here to dwell more on the embodiment of sleep, this seems a very Chaucerian way of engaging with the insomnia of French *dits amoreux* and the language and possibilities of the sleep of English romance together.

When the narrator of the *Duchess* has recourse to 'a book, / A romaunce', his reading material signifies a genre (even though it seems to narrow to the specificity of Ovid's *Metamorphoses* once the tale of Seys and Alcyone is mentioned, elevating that particular collection of stories as inspiration and consolation).[87] Deanne Williams has argued that the 'romaunce' Chaucer's narrator is reading is, because this term 'was used frequently in the Middle Ages to refer to the French language', 'a text that is identified with the French literary tradition'.[88] Minnis, meanwhile, has argued that Chaucer means a copy of the *Ovide moralisé*, and James Wimsatt posited that Chaucer meant a book containing court poetry, especially *dits amoreux*.[89] However, the term 'romaunce' could also refer to an English tradition.[90] Here again, as with the origins of his dream and his sleep, Chaucer raises a question (what is the provenance of his reading material?) that he does not fully answer. Perhaps it is English 'romance' more broadly that is invoked to offer the model of literary sleep: a model which Chaucer's narrator does, indeed, pursue after reading. While the following section demonstrates sleep's implications for dream theory, the final section of this chapter returns to the ways in which Chaucer engages with an English literary tradition in the *Book of the Duchess*.

Sleep as mediation: engendering and interpreting dreams

In the *Book of the Duchess*, sleep not only embodies concerns with melancholy and consolation; sleep also, as this section argues, generates the dream in more profound sense than the simple fact that one must be asleep in order to dream. While dreams and their causes meant something to medieval writers and readers, this book demonstrates that sleep and its causes also meant something, and in an interrelated way. We can see this all the more clearly when we recognise the influence of not only Macrobius's, but also Aristotle's, theories of dreams and sleep. As discussed in more detail in Chapter 1, where Macrobius privileged dreams that suggested divine visions or prophetic encounters and derogated those that resulted from within the dreamer him or herself, Aristotle instead focused on dreams that resulted from the preoccupations of body and mind, and later medieval writers reclaimed Aristotle's views as part of a growing emphasis on somatic and psychological causes for dreams. While Macrobius's *Commentary on the Dream of Scipio* and Aristotle's *Parva Naturalia* were both well known in the later Middle Ages, criticism has, with few exceptions, not recognised that Aristotle's work, as well as Macrobius's, exerted profound influence on the writers of late medieval dream visions;[91] there has been no sustained analysis of Chaucer's dream visions in relation to either somatic dream theory or the science of sleep. Yet as Kruger has observed, 'the dreamer has a body that plays an important part in determining the content and form of his or her dreams'.[92] This section argues that Chaucer's dream visions – especially the *Book of the Duchess*, but also the *Parliament of Fowls* and the *Prologue* to the *Legend of Good Women* – engage with bodily causes for dreams, exploring the implications of how the dreamer's lived experience is transmuted into, and mediated by, the dream.

While Chaucer's discussions of dream theory in the *House of Fame* and the *Parliament of Fowls* have pointed critical attention toward Macrobius, this does not mean Macrobius's classification is the only theory of dreams by which Chaucer was influenced. In the Proem to the *House of Fame* (c.1374–86), Chaucer offers his most sustained, explicit engagement with dream theory. In the *House of Fame*, Chaucer's focus shifts away from the inspiration for poetry to consider the fate of poetry: how poets (among others) receive reputations and name. In this poem about books, learning, fame and reputation – as Minnis has termed it, the 'most bookish of Chaucer's books'[93] – it is fitting that Chaucer offers less of a focus on the somatic side of poetic inspiration, since it is a poem about the arbitrary operations of Fame, rather than about anything innately connected to the poet. At the opening of the *House of Fame*, Chaucer writes that 'hyt is wonder […] / what causeth swevenes', demonstrating his knowledge of medieval dream theory even as he claims an inability to tell:

> Why that is an avision
> And why this a revelacion,
> Why this a drem, why that a sweven,
> And noght to every man lyche even;
> Why this a fantome, why these oracles,
> I not.[94]

Here, Chaucer refers to the interpretive traditions inspired by Macrobius. Chaucer's dream poems include dreams that can correspond to the three types that Macrobius considered to be 'worth interpreting' – the enigmatic, the prophetic and the oracular. The dream in the *Duchess* is enigmatic; that is, as Macrobius would put it, this dream

> conceals with strange shapes and veils with ambiguity the true meaning of the information being offered, and requires an interpretation for its understanding.[95]

When Chaucer's narrator claims in the *House of Fame* not to know 'why this more then that cause is', he speaks to an understanding of dreams as enigmatic, and also to the strong contemporary interest in interpreting dreams.[96] Yet he also cautions that dreams are not easily explained ('hyt is warned to derkly – / But why the cause is, noght wot I'), and cites a variety of possible causes for dreams, including humoral dispositions, anxiety or preoccupation, forlorn love, sorrow or other strong emotions, without explicitly endorsing any of them.[97]

Chaucer's discussion of the interpretation of dreams in the *Parliament of Fowls* (c.1380–2) has similarly been seen to prioritise Macrobius's hierarchising paradigm. Here, Chaucer's narrator pores over a copy of Cicero's *Somnium Scipionis*, the Dream of Scipio, in which the Roman general Scipio the Younger has an admonitory vision of his grandfather Scipio Africanus, and around which vision Macrobius wrote his lengthy treatise on dreams. When Chaucer's narrator himself falls asleep and dreams of Scipio Africanus, the latter announces:

> 'Thow hast the so wel born
> In lokynge of myn olde bok tortorn
> Of which Macrobye roughte nat a lyte,
> That sumdel of thy labour wolde I quyte.'[98]

This litotic name-dropping has been seen as a sign that Chaucer favours Macrobius's system of classifying dreams. However, Macrobius's theory was certainly not seen as the only way to approach dreams by Chaucer's contemporaries; Chaucer's engagements with other dream theories involve not high-profile name-dropping, but rather sustained exploration of the dreamer's embodied preoccupations and how these lead to dream-bearing sleep.

I am not suggesting that we should jettison Macrobian paradigms in favour of Aristotelian ones, but rather, that criticism of Middle English dream visions can be enriched by recognising the extent to which an author such as Chaucer navigates both. In Kruger's words, 'the assumption that one ancient or medieval conception of the dream (usually Macrobius's) provides a key for reading dream poetry often leads to interpretive distortions, to a narrowing of attention that may oversimplify poetic complexities'.[99] Alison Peden similarly cautions against overemphasising Macrobius's influence on dream poetry, focusing on Chaucer in particular.[100] A recent article by Michael Raby considers the transmutation of waking life into dream according to Aristotelian theories of the senses and of sleep and dreams in treatises translated into Latin in the early thirteenth century, and – in relation to Pandarus's dream of the Procne-Philomela myth in *Troilus and Criseyde* – has convincingly shown that Chaucer, like other central and late medieval poets, showed an interest in dreams from lived experience.[101]

In the *Book of the Duchess*, the *Parliament of Fowls* and the *Prologue* to the *Legend of Good Women*, a sustained focus on the physiological causes of sleep and of dreams alike suggests an interest not only in dreams that come from outside the subject, but also in dreams from within. In the 'Nun's Priest's Tale', Pertelote explains Chantecleer's dreams by stating that they are due to an imbalance in the humours, in a way that has often been assumed to indicate not just a spousal disparagement of humoral dreams, but also an authorial one:

> Swevenes engendren of repleccious, And ofte of fume and of complecciouns, Whan humours been to habundant in a wight.[102]

Dismissive of Chantecleer's concerns though Pertelote's words may be, they also speak to Chaucer's (and his readers') familiarity with the way in which dreams can be generated by embodied conditions. A similar understanding of dreams as the result of experience and humoral disposition informs the mid-fifteenth-century romance

King Ponthus and the Fair Sidone, in which King Brodas dreams that the protagonist, whom he has just wronged, has 'become a lion and devouryd me and hurte me in suche wyse that I dyed. So I haue be sore affrayd in my slepe.'[103] This dream results from Brodas's preoccupation with having condemned Ponthus and his companions to death, and the knight to whom Brodas relates this interprets the dream as the product of 'malyncoly', bespeaking an understanding of humoral, embodied dreams similar to the one on display in the 'Nun's Priest's Tale'.[104] Elsewhere in Chaucer's oeuvre, just because the 'Tale of Sir Thopas' parodies the preoccupations of chivalric romance, we do not presume either that Chaucer could not take chivalric romance seriously (as he does in the 'Knight's Tale') or that Chaucer's contemporaries were not interested in narratives of knights and quests, giants and fairy mistresses. Similarly, while some characters or commentaries dismiss humoral dreams as insignificant (particularly in a parody-infused text such as the 'Nun's Priest's Tale'), we should not conclude that this means that humoral dreams cannot form the premise for more serious narratives of dreams.

Dream poems involve boundary-crossing: to enter a dream is to cross a threshold.[105] To sleep is also to cross a threshold, from one state to another, and sleep foregrounds embodied inspirations for dreams. The way in which Chaucer's dream visions focus on sleep and its pathology – to, as I have demonstrated, a much greater extent than the French dream vision tradition – grounds this threshold-crossing, this liminality, much more firmly in the body, and in connections between body and mind. In the *Duchess*, when the narrator 'fil aslepe, and therewith even /[...] mette so ynly swete a sweven',[106] sleep is the embodied mediator of dreams not only in the sense that sleep is a necessary precondition for dreams, but also in the sense that sleep foregrounds the interpretive value of certain types of dreams, including those linked to the dominance of different humours, and the role of the dreamer's lived experience in generating dreams. This is despite Chaucerian narrators' characteristic claims to a lack of experience, which often mean lack of success in love, rather than lack of feelings (such as melancholy). Chaucer's extended emphasis on the narrator's own emotional turmoil in the prologue to the dream, that is, offers a reminder that dreams – significant dreams – can be the result of mental or bodily preoccupations, as well as resulting from divine visions or prophetic encounters.

Here and in the *Parliament of Fowls* (as discussed below), we see the idea that 'gret study and þouȝt'[107] can produce both sleep and dream alike – just as great study or heaviness of thought produces sleep elsewhere in Middle English literature.

Chaucer equates sleeplessness with lack of productive thoughts when the narrator of the *Duchess* claims that he has 'so many an ydel thoght / purely for defaute of slep'.[108] In medieval psychology, imagination, as the first of the three inward wits (followed by cognition and memory), is essential for making sense of one's lived experience and forming thoughts.[109] When Chaucer's narrator observes that 'purely for defaute of slep' he can 'take no kep / Of nothing, how hyt cometh or gooth', his inability to notice anything shows that his lack of sleep is 'expressly linked […] to a functional breakdown of his imaginative capacity to process *sensibilia*'; moreover, when he acknowledges that 'Ne me nys nothyng leef nor looth. / Al is ylyche good to me', it seems he is also 'unable to distinguish good from bad'.[110] These lapses of the ability to process and judge are evidently problematic for the would-be poet. He requires functioning inward wits in order to process experience and form images; sleep helps to restore the imagination, as well as to restore balance to the emotions. Sleep generates its own images in the form of dreams – since it is the way in which sleep blocks perception of external stimuli that allows the imagination to dwell on dream images. Sleep, then, is fundamental to the embodied ways in which experience can both be transformed into a dream, and transmuted into poetry. Thus, sleep contributes to the poem's key concerns with consolation and poetic inspiration, and, significantly, shows how lived experience (alongside old books) contributes to the generation of poetry.

Sleep and the matter of poetry

In writing this dream, Chaucer asserts that writing *is* the dream. Dreams are the material, and the metonymic substitute, for poetry, and writing poetry is what he desires to do. At the end of the poem, when Chaucer's narrator declares that he will 'put this sweven in ryme' (1332), the dreamer morphs into the poet who will compose the poem the reader has just finished.[111] This metafictional link (or loop) between dreaming and poetry is grounded in sleep and the renewed feeling or imagination it brings. Sleep is shown to be necessary not only for emotional health and for dreams, but also for the functioning of poetic imagination. Sleep, that is, signifies the possibility of a type of restoration and renewal for the poet, as well as for the bereaved, melancholic lovers about whom he writes. The way in which Chaucer's dream visions consider the matter of poetry is informed by their engagements with science – and this 'science' includes not only the science of dreams, but also the science of sleep. While Chaucer famously ruminates, across his dream visions, on how old books can inspire new poetry, also significant, though less well recognised, are his explorations of how lived experience can inspire the writing of literature. Chaucerian narrators' habitual performance of naïveté (in the *Duchess* and elsewhere) and professions of inexperience in love (most famously in *Troilus and Criseyde*) have perhaps contributed to the way in which Chaucerian reflections on non-bookish origins of poetry have been overlooked. Yet the texture of Chaucer's dream visions do suggest other inspirations for both poetry and dreams, and for the ways in which the latter two intersect.

In the Middle Ages, the process of composition was often understood as a sleep-like state,[112] and sleep itself, as Kiser and Davis have rightly foregrounded, is central to the *Duchess*'s concerns with poetry. Kiser oberves that

> If, as many critics have suggested, dreams are metaphors for the activities and results of the poetic imagination in medieval courtly works, then Chaucer's sleeplessness in the first lines of the poem represents not only his failure to dream, but also his inability to write. For a poet, whose business is to create well and create often, sleeplessness results in a poetically barren state of mind, a period of disturbingly unproductive idleness.[113]

Sleep, then, contributes to the generation of poetry. In addition, Davis has recently argued that, in the *Duchess*, Chaucer explores sleep's 'potential to facilitate creative output'; he 'not only represents sleep as "work" but understands it to *do* a certain kind of epistemological and imaginative work that underwrites the craft of poetry-making'.[114] For Kiser and Davis, sleep is a metaphorical 'vehicle for crossing from the realm of physical phenomena into the realm of the mind and back again'. However, when we also consider how the poem foregrounds the role of sleep in Galenic medicine and humoral balance, and the role of sleep in the generation of dreams from humoral imbalance (as per Aristotelian, rather than Macrobian, theories of dreams), we can recognise the striking way in which sleep informs Chaucerian reflections on how both lived experience, and English literary traditions, shape his dream poetry.

In both the *Book of the Duchess* and the *Parliament of Fowls*, sleep offers a term for the role of experience as inspiration for literature. Where the dream is the subject matter for poetry, sleep is the vital embodiment of the poet's craft and *matière*, offering the ability to restore and access the imagination – and also, to transmute lived experience into poetry. Lack of sleep is explicitly linked to lack of fertile imagination in the opening of the *Duchess*; and, awakening at the end of the poem from this restorative sleep, the narrator expresses more confidence about being able to create poetry again by putting his 'sweven in ryme'.[115] As David Lawton has argued, the narrator's 'psychological state and growth is vital to the meaning of' the *Book of the Duchess*.[116] I would add that the *physiological* state of the narrator – and the extent to which the narrator's physiological state and psychological state are intertwined – are also important to the poem's meaning. While Lawton suggests that at the beginning of the poem, the narrator suffers from an 'extreme frigidity of emotion' due to his insomnia,[117] we might see this as not a frigidity, but rather an extreme imbalance, of emotion, since the narrator's overwhelming melancholia, itself a strong emotion, inhibits other feeling(s): 'I take no kep / Of nothing, how hyt cometh or gooth, / Ne me nys nothyng leef nor looth' and 'I have felynge in nothyng'.[118] That the narrator is able to feel and express compassion before the end of the poem ('By God, hyt is routhe') is also the result of the way in which sleep (in the Galenic medical paradigm explicitly invoked in the poem) resets the balance between humours and passions.[119] That is, the narrator is once again able to feel other things, not just melancholy; the physiology of sleep itself (as well as the dream it contains) is a form of restorative 'consolation' for the narrator.

The way in which sleep features in the *Duchess* as a medicalised medium for exploring the inspiration for poetry, and the embodiment and consolatory potential of poetry, is paralleled by how the

Parliament engages with the science of sleep. In both the *Duchess* and the *Parliament*, how the narrator's emotional state before falling asleep to dream is foregrounded suggests that his lived experiences – his waking preoccupations – contribute to the sort of dream he has, and thus to the sort of poetry that might be written. Meanwhile, the *Prologue* to the *Legend of Good Women* focuses on the ethics of sleep in ways that deepen the poem's concerns with the ethics of writing: with the ethics of representing bad women as opposed to good (for instance), the choices Chaucer makes as an author, and how he (self-)regulates his poetic output.

The *Parliament of Fowls*, even more explicitly than the *Duchess*, is about the inspiration for new poetry. Chaucer's reflections on (named) dream theorists and old books in the openings of his later dream visions have underpinned critical perceptions not only of how Chaucer engages with theories of the origins and significance of dreams, but also of how he investigates dreams and books as the source and subject of poetry.[120] While Chaucer's dream vision narrators are notorious for presenting themselves as inexperienced in life or love, they are knowledgeable about what can be made anew from old books.[121] As Chaucer puts it in the opening to the *Parliament*,

> For out of olde feldes, as men seyth,
> Cometh al this newe corn from yer to yere,
> And out of olde bokes, in good feyth,
> Cometh al this newe science that men lere.[122]

This agricultural metaphor suggests that old books are the fertile ground out of which new books can grow. However, as in the *Duchess*, in the *Parliament* Chaucer uses the prologue to the dream to focus not only on dreams and books, but also sleep itself, in ways that suggest other seeds for poetic fruits. The *Parliament* also features a narrator who describes the state in which he falls asleep as the result of preoccupation and sorrow, when he puts down his

> bok for lak of lyght,
> And to my bed I gan me for to dresse,
> Fulfyld of thought and busy hevynesse;
> For both I hadde thyng which that I nolde,
> And ek I ne hadde that thyng that I wolde.[123]

Here, by specifying that the *Parliament* narrator falls asleep not only after reading (as is also the case in the *Duchess*), but, moreover, when he is also 'Fulfyld of thought and busy hevynesse' because of what he has and does not have, Chaucer suggests that the narrator is more preoccupied with his own experiences than with his reading material. 'Hevyness' can of course mean simply 'drowsiness' or 'weight', but 'thought and busy hevynesse' suggests the word's more affective implications of sorrow, anxiety, or annoyance.[124]

In this passage of the *Parliament* that concerns the narrator's act of falling sleep, Chaucer relies on, yet significantly transforms, two continental sources in ways that make the passage resonate with English treatments of sleep, and that shape a stronger emphasis on the ways in which emotions and embodied experience contribute to the dream that follows. Chaucer's focus on 'hevynesse' has been seen to follow the opening of Oton de Grandson's *Le Songe Saint Valentin*, which reflects that

> Quant ungs homs est pesans ou las
> Et il veult prandre son repoux,
> Il puit panser sur tel propoux
> Qu'en son propoux s'endormira.
> Et, en dormant, il songera
> Aucune chose merveilleuse,
> Bonne pour lui ou dangereuse.

> [when a man is heavyhearted or weary, and wishes to take his rest, he may think on such thoughts and plans that he will fall asleep with those thoughts. And while sleeping he will dream something wonderful or trying for him.][125]

By engaging with this idea, Chaucer's poem signals a focus on dreams emerging from the dreamer's waking preoccupations. There is also a Boethian resonance in the *Parliament* passage, given that it is from Boethius's *Consolation of Philosophy* that Chaucer adapted the lines 'For both I hadde thyng which that I nolde / And ek I ne hadde that thyng that I wolde.'[126] Chaucer, however, reshapes the meaning of both sources by the way he weaves them together: by connecting his narrator's heaviness of thought to the object of desire and to lack (as he does in the *Duchess*), and by choosing to highlight the narrator's affective state – as a result of what his experience has and has not gained him – Chaucer shows how his narrator's 'slepe' itself (as well as the subject of his dream) is generated by his emotions. This again resonates with the Galenic understanding of how the humours produce sleep, and with the ways in which sleep features in English romances, drama and saints' lives. Indeed, while de Grandson is commonly seen as the source for Chaucer's specification of sleep-inducing heaviness, one might also cite a number of insular parallels, from Chardri's Anglo-Norman saints succumbing to sleep due to the 'pesance de lur penser' ('weight of their worries'), to the York Cycle's Joseph's declaration that 'myn hert so heuy it is' when he too sleeps.[127] Not all of these insular parallels precede, or could be direct sources for, Chaucer, of course, but some of them fall into that category, and they all suggest that Chaucer is participating in a more widespread (and English) tradition in connecting sleep to the emotions.

Here, Chaucer again – as when borrowing and adapting material from French poetry to foreground the importance of Galenic medicine and the role of sleep in the Man in Black's lament – forges a different link. Chaucer is making something out of old books, but what he makes from these old books is a passage that emphasises the role of experience in producing a dream, and (thus) in producing new poetry. Thus, alongside his more high-profile reflections on old books as authorities – in this poem that features a debate about the roles of nature versus culture, or experience versus authority – Chaucer foregrounds sleep as a term for embodied experience, just as he does in the *Duchess*. Where books are a term for culture/authority (invoking continental literary precedents), and sleep is a term for nature/experience (evoking English literary precedents in which sleep is likewise accentuated), both are needed to create new literature.

In the *Prologue* to the *Legend of Good Women*, Chaucer again valorises books as a source of truth and imagination, yet he also shows how, in the month of May, books give way to experience: to an embodied engagement with life and its imaginative potential that is underpinned by his treatment of sleep. In spring, when the narrator lingers outdoors amongst the flowers rather than poring over a book indoors, he is inspired by 'the dayesie', which he desires to look at all day long. Yet in a perhaps surprising display of temperance, although he lies down in a *locus amoenus* to admire his flower of choice during the day, he does not fall asleep – not there and then. Sleep is instead deferred until night-time, and takes place within the home, where the narrator has a bed constructed as though it were a *hortus conclusus*. In this last of Chaucer's dream visions, the English preoccupation with sleep, and particularly with the ethics of sleep, is pressed into service to comment on the ethics of writing. Here, Chaucer's reflections on the gender politics of his poetic undertakings are shaped by the connotations of sleep, and of the spaces in which it takes place.

In both the F and G texts of the *Prologue* to the *Legend of Good Women*, there is a twofold delay or deferral in the onset of sleep,[128] and the ethics of sleep and its temperate deferral contribute to Chaucer's construction of a rebuke and a fresh start following his poetic persona's failure to have written positively about women. Firstly, as mentioned, the narrator resists falling asleep in a conventional locus for dream vision narrators to succumb to sleep, that is, during the day and out of doors – where he has been spending his time lounging in a meadow,

> lenynge on myn elbowe and my syde,
> [...]
> For nothing elles, and I shal nat lye,
> But for to loke upon the dayesie.[129]

While lying down and reflecting on an object of desire in a pleasant green space invokes generic expectations of sleep, Chaucer chooses to thwart these expectations. Instead, the narrator waits for nightfall – the proper time for sleep, according to dietaries and conduct manuals – when

> Hom to myn hous ful swiftly I me spedde
> To goon to reste, and erly for to ryse,
> To seen this flour to sprede, as I devyse.
> And in a litel herber that I have,
> That benched was on turves fressh ygrave,
> I bad men sholde me my couche make;
> For deyntee of the newe someres sake,
> I bad hem strawen floures on my bed.[130]

Moreover, the narrator's sleep is further deferred, for it takes him quite some time to fall asleep: 'Whan I was leyd and had myn eyen hed, / I fel on slepe within an houre or twoo.'[131] Although the narrator does eventually go to sleep in a 'litel herber' or garden, a *hortus conclusus*,[132] the heavy-handed construction of this sleeping space foregrounds Chaucer's reworking of generic conventions. That is, while, as Helen Phillips has observed, by invoking the idea of sleeping outside Chaucer summons 'an image of Golden Age innocence from Boethius',[133] I would emphasise that this is very much the *idea* of sleeping outside, rather than its usual practice. Here, the idea of sleeping outside is circumscribed by being re-constructed at night, within the home, and in a bed. The narrator has resisted daytime sleep and instead retires at the proper time; moreover, flowers (which, in the form of the daisy, are shown to be inspiration for dreams and poetry) are artificially added to this bed made by servants, rather than naturally accompanying an outdoor resting place. Thus, when he does eventually fall asleep to dream of the God of Love and Queen Alceste, this deliberate citing, yet also re-siting, of the connotations of a Golden Age and of the expectations of love narrative and dream vision emphasises temperance.

The narrator's eager desire (the fascination with the daisy) is in need of a check and redirection, in the same way that Chaucer's subject matter (his inspiration for poetry) is in need of a corrective and a redirection from Alceste, who instructs him to focus on the stories of virtuous or wronged women, rather than (as in *Troilus and Criseyde*) women in the wrong. Perhaps this focus on the narrator's and poet's somatic ethics is especially apt in the Prologue to a series of narratives about good women, inasumuch as virtue or ethics for late medieval women was often articulated as a matter of self-regulating bodily behaviour and appetites.[134] Chaucer accentuates a need to regulate his corporeal habits while discussing his need to regulate his compositional habits. In this deferral of sleep, the *Prologue* to the *Legend of Good Women*, in parallel with the *Duchess*, creates space to explore problems in the nature of poetic inspiration, though here ethically more than emotionally. For the *Prologue* poet, the ethics of regulating sleeping habits resonates with the ethics of regulating writing habits. This ethical turn in Chaucer's engagement with sleep in his last dream vision also parallels an approach to sleep prominent in other Middle English dream visions such as *Piers Plowman* and *Pearl*, as well as in English romances.

* * *

Sleep, in the *Book of the Duchess*, the *Parliament of Fowls* and the *Prologue* to the *Legend of Good Women*, offers a language for exploring how emotions, ethics, dreams and the matter of poetry are all embodied, interconnected practices. Mediated through the language of sleep, Chaucer's explorations of the role of experience in shaping dreams and poetry are also explorations of what he can gain from English literary traditions. Chaucer's borrowings from French poetry about dreams and *demandes-d'amour*, and his evocations and reworkings of English traditions concerned with sleep, cooperate to consider the possibilities of consolation and the sources of poetic inspiration. By both dwelling on sleep and foregrounding the ways in which sleep is important for poetic inspiration, Chaucer shows that his English literary heritage – in its concerns, in its imaginative potential – is fundamental to the embodied endeavour of the poet.

We have come a long way from Charles Muscatine's declaration, in 1957, that Middle English literary culture 'tells us very little about Chaucer, and Chaucer himself has very little good to say of it', or Ian Robinson's, in 1972, that English culture before Chaucer was 'pre-literary'.[135] However, Chaucer's French debts, and his Italian ones,[136] have still received the lion's share of more recent attention. The *Duchess*'s concerns with sleep and insomnia have also been seen as signs of an English poet writing in an unfamiliar French tradition: registering a sense of 'cultural alienation', and serving as 'an index of the narrator-poet's discomfort with the headily French genre of dream-vision'.[137] The *Duchess*, from this perspective, shows Chaucer as 'a poet working without the benefit of national models'.[138] However, I would argue that Chaucer *does* have national models here, in the ways that he draws upon English models for writing about sleep to shape his contributions to the French genre of dream vision.

It seems apt that Chaucer 'embeds' his debts to homegrown English habits of writing in the bodily, earthly, side of the poet's craft, and most strongly in his first sustained narrative poem. Where Chaucer's debts to French and Italian traditions are courtly, his debts to English ones are often popular.[139] This may be as true of Chaucer's dream visions as it is of his romances; indeed, perhaps the *Book of the Duchess* is in some ways the dream vision equivalent of the 'Tale of Sir Thopas' in this. Like 'Sir Thopas', the *Duchess* features recognisable (if transmuted) deployments of English literary conventions. The *Duchess* – again like 'Sir Thopas' – also features a principal character who seems to have little understanding of how to fulfil the expectations of the genre in which he finds himself. Where Sir Thopas has at best a superficial understanding of the behaviour that becomes a chivalric protagonist, riding around in the forest in search of adventure and spending his time ticking the boxes of the arming of the hero topos rather than actually fighting the giant he encounters, the narrator of the *Book of the Duchess* has been seen to demonstrate, in his infamous obtuseness about the nature of the Man in Black's grief, a lack of 'genuine understanding of French courtly codes and literary culture'.[140] Yet where the Man in Black voices the conventions of French literary precedents, the narrator, Alcyone, and the Man in Black also invoke and negotiate the conventions of English literary concerns with sleep and its spaces. Since negotiating the epistemological implications of sleep is an established mode across a range of insular genres, this aspect of Chaucer's corporeal, English poetics seems to result from a concern to show awareness of existing patterns and to engage with insular models. Chaucer, of course, engages with these insular models in distinctive ways, just as he does with his continental models.

In adumbrating a parallel between the *Book of the Duchess* and 'Sir Thopas', I am not suggesting that the former is a parody; rather, that Chaucer's first dream vision marks not only Chaucer's self-awareness as a poet writing in English, but also his understanding, and deployment, of an English literary inheritance. Moreover, Chaucer's gently parodic 'Tale of Sir Thopas' shows all the more his understanding of the significance of sleep in Middle English genres such as romance. For whereas in other English romances, chivalric protagonists often fall asleep (outside, in the middle of the day) in a way that signifies a failure of chivalric ethics, in 'Sir Thopas' it is not only the protagonist, but also his horse, who becomes overtired just from 'prikyng on the softe gras' in the forest of romance. Chaucer specifies that 'doun he leyde him in that plas' for an untimely sleep, as both knight and 'his steede [seek] som solas' by resting during the middle of the day when Thopas fails to perform the conduct expected of a knight.[141] One of the surest signs of a generic convention's familiarity is, after all, its readiness for parody. Here in this knowing reworking, as elsewhere, signifying through sleep is itself a lucid expectation of a medieval English tradition.

Notes

1 Chaucer, *The Book of the Duchess*, ll. 272–9.
2 Marshall W. Stearns, 'Chaucer Mentions a Book', *Modern Language Notes*, 57.1 (1942), 28–31.
3 Chaucer, *Duchess*, ll. 4 and 14.
4 Jamie C. Fumo, *Making Chaucer's* Book of the Duchess: *Textuality and Reception* (Cardiff: University of Wales Press, 2015), p. 40; see especially Boitani, 'Old Books Brought to Life in Dreams'.
5 Zeeman, 'Medieval Dreams', pp. 137–50.
6 Minnis, *Oxford Guides to Chaucer: The Shorter Poems*, p. 36.
7 Chaucer, *Duchess*, l. 948.
8 Fumo, *Making Chaucer's* Book of the Duchess, p. 53.
9 Kiser, 'Sleep, Dreams, and Poetry in Chaucer's *Book of the Duchess*'; Davis, '"Noon Other Werke": The Work of Sleep in Chaucer's *Book of the Duchess*'. There has also been some promising consideration of the transition between waking and sleeping as a significant threshold in dream poems: see Brown, 'On the Borders of Middle English Dream Visions'.
10 Spearing, *Medieval Dream Poetry*; Helen Phillips, 'Frames and Narratives in Chaucerian Poetry', in Helen Cooper and Sally Mapstone (eds), *The Long Fifteenth Century: Essays for Douglas Gray* (Oxford: Clarendon Press, 1997), pp. 71–97.
11 Chaucer, *Duchess*, ll. 1332–3.
12 D. Vance Smith persuasively argues that 'Chaucer uses English texts with the same kind of intelligent creativity with which he uses texts in other languages': 'Chaucer as an English Writer', in Seth Lerer (ed.), *The Yale Companion to Chaucer* (London: Yale University Press, 2006), pp. 87–119 (p. 89); see also Larry D. Benson, 'The Beginnings of Chaucer's English Style', in Stephen A. Barney and Theodore M. Andersson (eds), *Contradictions: From* Beowulf *to* Chaucer (New York: Routledge, 1995), pp. 243–65. On links between Chaucer's dream visions and a different insular tradition, see Jessica Jane Lockhart, 'Everyday Wonders and Enigmatic Structures: Riddles from Symphosius to Chaucer' (University of Toronto, PhD dissertation, 2017), esp. Chapter 3. At a time when there is increasing interest in the 'global Middle Ages' and when scholarship is rightly continuing to emphasise Chaucer's European connections (see, for instance, Turner, *Chaucer: A European Life*), seeking to better understand Chaucer's often devalued Englishness is not to counter this interest in literary and cultural connections, but rather to foreground further connections.
13 Kathryn L. Lynch (ed.), Geoffrey Chaucer, *Dream Visions and Other Poems* (London: Norton, 2007), p. 4. Boethius's sixth-century *De*

Consolatione Philosophiae has often been studied for its influence on later medieval dream visions: see, for instance, Michael H. Means, *The Consolatio Genre in Medieval English Literature* (Gainesville, FL: University of Florida Press, 1972), and Michael D. Cherniss, *Boethian Apocalypse: Studies in Middle English Vision Poetry* (Norman, OK: Pilgrim Books, 1987).

14 While some would see medieval dream vision as a mode rather than a genre, generic definitions for this rather capacious category of writing have emphasised the structure provided by 'the external form of the dream or vision' (Kathryn L. Lynch, *The High Medieval Dream Vision*, p. 7); have posited that 'to be a dream vision […], a poem must *both* contain certain motifs *and* be the product of a poet's intention to follow a tradition or imitate a generic model' in a way that makes meaning through 'the interdependence of form and content' (Russell, *The English Dream Vision*, p. 2); and have focused on 'the deployment of dream vision self-consciously to explore the nature of fiction', of authority, and/or of earthly knowledge (Stephen F. Kruger, 'Dialogue, Debate, and Dream Vision', in Larry Scanlon (ed.), *The Cambridge Companion to Medieval English Literature 1100–1500* (Cambridge: Cambridge University Press, 2009), pp. 71–82 (p. 73); see also Kruger, *Dreaming in the Middle Ages*).

15 Ardis Butterfield, 'Chaucer's French Inheritance', in Boitani and Mann (eds), *The Cambridge Companion to Chaucer*, pp. 20–35 (p. 26); Fumo, *Making Chaucer's* Book of the Duchess, p. 8. For recent work on the *Duchess*'s debts to French models, see, for instance, Phillip Knox, '"Hyt Am I": Voicing Selves in the *Book of the Duchess*, the *Roman de la Rose*, and the *Fonteinne Amoureuse*', in Jamie C. Fumo (ed.), *Chaucer's* Book of the Duchess*: Contexts and Interpretations* (Cambridge: D. S. Brewer, 2018), pp. 135–56, and Butterfield, *The Familiar Enemy*.

16 Helen Phillips, 'Chaucer: Dream Visions', in Siân Echard and Robert Rouse (eds), *The Encyclopedia of Medieval Literature in Britain* (Oxford: Wiley Blackwell, 2017), pp. 442–8 (p. 442). See also Helen Cooper, 'Chaucerian Poetics', in Robert G. Benson and Susan J. Ridyard (eds), *New Readings of Chaucer's Poetry* (Cambridge: D. S. Brewer, 2003), pp. 31–50, and Minnis, *Chaucer: The Shorter Poems*, p. 111.

17 Helen Phillips, 'The *Book of the Duchess*: Introduction', in Helen Phillips and Nick Havely (eds), *Chaucer's Dream Poetry* (London: Longman, 1997), pp. 29–49. See also Steven Davis, 'Guillaume de Machaut, Chaucer's *Book of the Duchess*, and the Chaucer Tradition', *The Chaucer Review*, 36.4 (2002), 391–405, and James Wimsatt, *Chaucer and the French Love Poets: The Literary Background of the* Book of the Duchess (Chapel Hill, NC: University of North Carolina Press, 1968).

18 Chaucer, *Duchess*, ll. 3, 25, 47–8.
19 Oxford, Bodleian Library: Fairfax 16, Bodley 638, and Tanner 346.
20 Helen Phillips, 'The Book of the Duchess, Lines 31–96: Are They A Forgery?', *English Studies*, 67.2 (1986), 113–21; see also Minnis, *Chaucer: The Shorter Poems*, p. 79. On the early transmission of the *Book of the Duchess*, see Fumo, *Making Chaucer's* Book of the Duchess, pp. 79–130.
21 *Le Roman de la Rose par Guillaume de Lorris et Jean de Meung*, ed. Pierre Marteau, 4 vols (Paris, 1878), I, 25–29; Guillaume de Lorris and Jean de Meun, *The Romance of the Rose*, trans. Frances Horgan (Oxford: Oxford University Press, 1994), p. 3.
22 *Le Roman de la Rose*, IV, 22579–80; *The Romance of the Rose*, p. 335.
23 Wimsatt, *Chaucer and the French Love Poets*, pp. 10–11.
24 Indeed, the French *dits* poets have sometimes been seen as more interested in inset lyrics than in anything to do with the dream frame: William Anthony Davenport, *Chaucer: Complaint and Narrative* (Cambridge: D. S. Brewer, 1988), p. 61; James Wimsatt, *Chaucer and His French Contemporaries: Natural Music in the Fourteenth Century* (Toronto: University of Toronto Press, 1991), pp. 55–8.
25 On Chaucer's debts to French models, see further *Chaucer's Dream Poetry: Sources and Analogues*, ed. and trans. B. A. Windeatt (Woodbridge: D. S. Brewer, 1982).
26 *Riverside* Explanatory Notes, p. 966; Ardis Butterfield, 'Lyric and Elegy in *The Book of the Duchess*', *Medium Aevum*, 60 (1991), 33–60.
27 Derek Brewer has similarly emphasised (other) differences between Chaucer's opening lines and Froissart's: 'The Relationship of Chaucer to the English and European Traditions', in Derek Brewer (ed.), *Chaucer and Chaucerians: Critical Studies in Middle English Literature* (London: Nelson, 1966), pp. 1–38 (pp. 2–3).
28 Chaucer, *Duchess*, ll. 4–5 and 14. On Chaucer's deployment here of the late medieval connotations of 'ydel' as empty, worthless, unoccupied or unproductive, see B. S. W. Barootes, 'Idleness, Chess, and Tables: Recuperating Fables in Chaucer's *Book of the Duchess*', in *Chaucer's* Book of the Duchess: *Contexts and Interpretations*, pp. 29–50 (esp. p. 30).
29 Jean Froissart, *Le paradis d'amour*, in *Le paradis d'amour; L'orloge amoureus*, ed. Peter F. Dembowski (Genève: Librarie Droz, 1986), ll. 1–12.
30 Chaucer, *Duchess*, ll. 3 and 5.
31 *Le dit de la fonteinne amoureuse*, in *Chaucer's Dream Poetry: Sources and Analogues*, pp. 26–40.
32 Chaucer, *Duchess*, l. 572.
33 The others are food and drink, inanition and repletion, air, exercise, and the passions or emotions: Dannenfeldt, 'Sleep: Theory and Practice

in the Late Renaissance', pp. 415–16; Siraisi, *Medieval and Early Renaissance Medicine*, p. 101.
34 Chaucer, *Duchess*, ll. 5 and 25.
35 Steve Guthrie, 'Dialogics and Prosody in Chaucer', in Thomas J. Farrell (ed.), *Bakhtin and Medieval Voices* (Gainesville, FL: University Press of Florida, 1995), pp. 94–108 (p. 103). More broadly, on the 'traditional' nature of Chaucer's English, see Christopher Cannon, *The Making of Chaucer's English* (Cambridge: Cambridge University Press, 1998), esp. p. 4.
36 Guthrie, 'Dialogics and Prosody in Chaucer', p. 103.
37 'Chaucer's total vocabulary is about 8,000 words, of which about 4,000 are French, and of these he introduced between 1,100 and 1,200 into written English': Guthrie, 'Dialogics and Prosody in Chaucer', p. 98. On Chaucer's concertedly English lexical choices elsewhere in his oeuvre, see Cooper, 'Chaucerian Poetics', esp. pp. 33–8.
38 Pre-dream insomnia becomes a recognisable feature of Chaucerian dream visions, figuring in *The Cuckoo and the Nightingale* (written by Sir John Clanvowe during Chaucer's lifetime) and recurring in fifteenth-century poems such as Lydgate's *Temple of Glass* and *Complaint of the Black Knight*, and the *Kingis Quair* attributed to King James I of Scotland. The *Kingis Quair*'s concerted emulation of Chaucer's dream visions includes its representation of sorrow precipitating the narrator's sleep and the dream it contains: 'Ovrset so sorow had bothe hert and mynd, / That to the cold stone my hede on wrye / I laid, and lent amaisit verily, / Half sleping and half suoun in suich a wise; / And quhat I met I will you now devise' (in *The Kingis Quair and Other Poems*, ed. Linne R. Mooney and Mary-Jo Arn (Kalamazoo, MI: Medieval Institute Publications, 2005), ll. 507–11). Like the narrator of the *Duchess*, the narrator of the *Kingis Quair* has resorted to a book in hopes of being able to 'borrow a slepe' (30), and, while sleeping and dreaming, the narrator discovers 'confort and hele' (518). Chaucer's interest in the science of sleep and the consolation it brings, then, was recognised and redeployed by this fifteenth-century Chaucerian poet.
39 Fumo, p. 69; Heffernan, *The Melancholy Muse*, esp. p. 41; Steven Kruger, 'Medical and Moral Authority in the Late Medieval Dream', in Peter Brown (ed.), *Reading Dreams*, pp. 51–83 (p. 69).
40 Chaucer, *Duchess*, ll. 142–4.
41 See Davis, 'The Work of Sleep', p. 55, and Julie Orlemanski, 'Prosopopoeial Heaviness in Chaucer's *Book of the Duchess*', in Thomas A. Prendergast and Jessica Rosenfeld (eds), *Chaucer and the Subversion of Form* (Cambridge: Cambridge University Press, 2018), pp. 125–45;

compare Machaut's *Livre de la fonteinne amoureuse*, in which Morpheus instead 'Prist la fourme que Ceïs avoit nus' ['Assumed the form of a naked Ceyx']: Guillaume de Machaut, *The Fountain of Love (La Fonteinne Amoureuse) and Two Other Love Vision Poems*, ed. and trans. R. Barton Palmer (New York: Garland, 1993), l. 659.

42 Chaucer, *Duchess*, l. 202.
43 On Chaucer's 'structuring by juxtaposition' throughout the *Duchess*, in contrast to his sources, see Windeatt, *Chaucer's Dream Poetry: Sources and Analogues*, p. xiii.
44 Chaucer, *Duchess*, ll. 31–40. It has also been suggested that the narrator is afflicted not by lovesickness, but rather by a psychological 'head melancholy', the result of dryness of the brain which can be cured by sleep and the resulting recovery of the ability to create: John M. Hill, 'The *Book of the Duchess*, Melancholy, and That Eight-Year Sickness', *Chaucer Review*, 9.1 (1974), 35–50 (p. 39).
45 Chaucer, *Duchess*, ll. 30–1.
46 Chaucer, *Duchess*, ll. 32–3.
47 Chaucer, *Duchess*, ll. 272–4.
48 Chaucer, *Duchess*, ll. 278–9.
49 Chaucer, *Duchess*, l. 126.
50 Chaucer, *Duchess*, ll. 118–21.
51 Chaucer, *Duchess*, l. 130.
52 Kemp, *Medieval Psychology*, p. 117.
53 Kemp, *Medieval Psychology*, p. 118.
54 Davis, 'The Work of Sleep', pp. 52–3.
55 Minnis, *Chaucer: The Shorter Poems*, p. 93.
56 Chaucer, *Duchess*, l. 169; Davis, 'The Work of Sleep', p. 55.
57 Chaucer, *Duchess*, ll. 172–3.
58 *Mankind*, 593; Langland, *Piers Plowman*, B V.386–92 (and C-Text, VII.1–7).
59 Chaucer, *Duchess*, ll. 174–7.
60 Machaut, *Fonteinne Amoureuse*, ll. 606–7.
61 Kiser, 'Sleep, Dreams, and Poetry', p. 4.
62 While it has been suggested that 'Finally giving in to the brute demands of the body rather than the aspirations of love, Chaucer's narrator succumbs to the kind of sleep identified [...] as slothful (rather than restorative or love-bringing – its depressive content being perhaps deserved)' (Fumo, *Making Chaucer's Book of the Duchess*, pp. 137–8), I would argue that Chaucer's narrator's sleep *is* restorative, both physically and mentally, and that, significantly, physical and emotional well-being are linked in sleep.
63 Chaucer, *Duchess*, ll. 223–5.

64 Heffernan, *The Melancholy Muse*, p. 49; Robert B. Burlin, *Chaucerian Fiction* (Princeton, NJ: Princeton University Press, 1977), p. 59.
65 Chaucer, *Duchess*, ll. 118–19 and 245.
66 Chaucer, *Duchess*, ll. 242–55.
67 Spearing, *Medieval Dream-Poetry*, p. 43.
68 Stanbury, 'The Place of the Bedchamber in Chaucer's *Book of the Duchess*', p. 161.
69 Spearing, *Medieval Dream-Poetry*, pp. 25 and 53.
70 Chaucer, *Duchess*, ll. 273–6.
71 Wimsatt, *Chaucer and the French Love Poets*, p. 157; see also *The Riverside Chaucer*, p. 968.
72 Froissart, *Le Paradis D'amour*, ll. 27–32. Trans. by Windeatt, in *Chaucer's Dream Poetry: Sources and Analogues*, pp. 41–57 (p. 42).
73 For an overview of criticism on the idea of consolation in the *Book of the Duchess* – and an argument that the potential for consolation for the Black Knight lies in the parallels with the stories of Alycone, the narrator, and the hunt – see Helen Phillips, 'Structure and Consolation in the *Book of the Duchess*', *Chaucer Review*, 16.2 (1981), 107–18; see also Fumo, *Making Chaucer's* Book of the Duchess, pp. 55–60. As Phillips has suggested, some form of consolation may be available at least to readers, the patron John of Gaunt grieving for the death of his wife Blanche (perhaps) included.
74 John Lawlor, 'The Pattern of Consolation in *The Book of the Duchess*', *Speculum*, 31.4 (1956), 626–48; G. L. Kittredge, *Chaucer and His Poetry* (Cambridge, MA: Harvard University Press, 1915).
75 Minnis, *Chaucer: The Shorter Poems*, p. 145.
76 Chaucer, *Duchess*, ll. 654 and 744.
77 Chaucer, *Duchess*, ll. 602–12; emphasis mine.
78 Charles d'Orleans, however, follows Chaucer's precedent and includes sleeping and waking in his own list of such inversions in the first suite of lyrics in his mid-fifteenth-century mourning ballades.
79 See *Riverside* Explanatory Notes, p. 971.
80 *Le Roman de la Rose*, ed. Daniel Poirion (Paris: Garnier-Flammarion, 1974), 4311–13; *The Romance of the Rose*, pp. 65–6.
81 *Le Roman de la Rose*, 4305–10; *The Romance of the Rose*, pp. 65–6.
82 Guillaume de Machaut, 'Le Jougement dou Roy de Behaingne', in *Guillaume de Machaut: The Complete Poetry and Music, Volume 1: The Debate Series*, ed. R. Barton Palmer and Yolanda Plumley (Kalamazoo, MI: Medieval Institute Publications, 2016), ll. 177–87.
83 Chaucer, *Duchess*, ll. 570–1.
84 *Le Roman de la Rose*, ll. 15927–30.
85 *Pearl*, ll. 51 and 59.

86 Malory, *Morte Darthur*, pp. 491.17–18 and 34.30–2; Langland, *Piers Plowman*, XI.1–5.
87 Chaucer, *Duchess*, ll. 47–8.
88 Deanne Williams, *French Fetish from Chaucer to Shakespeare* (Cambridge: Cambridge University Press, 2004), p. 23.
89 A. J. Minnis, 'Chaucer and the *Ovide moralisé*', *Medium Aevum*, 48 (1979), 254–7, and James I. Wimsatt, 'The Sources of Chaucer's "Seys and Alcyone"', *Medium Aevum*, 36 (1967), 231–41.
90 While the term 'romanz' did first designate a Latin-derived vernacular language, it also, of course, later identified a type of narrative more commonly generated in vernaculars – including English – than in the higher-status language of Latin. See especially Paul Strohm, 'Storie, Spelle, Geste, Romaunce, Tragedie: Generic Distinctions in the Middle English Troy Narratives', *Speculum*, 46 (1971), 348–59, and Strohm, 'The Origin and Meaning of Middle English Romance', *Genre*, 10 (1977), 1–28.
91 Most notably, Steven Kruger has sought to give the bodily causes of medieval dream visions their due, observing that 'Recognizing the somatic possibilities of the dream may move us away from the simple allegorizing and spiritualizing tendencies of much dream-vision criticism': Kruger, 'Medical and Moral Authority', p. 62. A productive middle way has been articulated by Helen Cooper, who suggests seeing the dream as 'a release into the superconscious, a realm of experience rooted in but going beyond the private concerns of the dreamer': 'Chaucerian Poetics', p. 40. For a recent study that seeks to foreground the body's connections to dreams in Chaucer's poetry, see Lenz, *Dreams, Medicine, and Literary Practice*.
92 Kruger, 'Medical and Moral Authority', p. 62.
93 Minnis, *Chaucer: The Shorter Poems*, p. 183.
94 Chaucer, *House of Fame*, ll. 2–3 and 7–12.
95 Macrobius, *Commentary on the Dream of Scipio*, p. 90.
96 Chaucer, *House of Fame*, 20.
97 Chaucer, *House of Fame*, ll. 51–2 and 21–30.
98 Chaucer, *Parliament*, ll. 109–12.
99 Kruger, *Dreaming in the Middle Ages*, pp. 63–7.
100 Peden, 'Macrobius and Medieval Dream Literature'.
101 Raby, 'Sleep and the Transformation of Sense'. Raby does not address Chaucer's dream visions.
102 Chaucer, 'Nun's Priest's Tale', VII.2923–5.
103 *King Ponthus and the Fair Sidone*, ed. Frank Jewett Mather (Baltimore, MD: Modern Language Association of America, 1897), p. 6.23–5.
104 *King Ponthus and the Fair Sidone*, p. 6.26.

105 Peter Brown has addressed the moment when, in Middle English dream visions, 'the narrator falls asleep to enter a dream', focusing on the specifics of the landscapes in which the narrator falls asleep, and noting the inwardness or anxiety that often precedes the dreams. As Brown argues, dream visions explore 'the experience of betweenness', or liminality, along the lines of the anthropological theory developed by Victor and Edith Turner: Brown, 'On the Borders of Middle English Dream Visions', p. 25; Edith Turner, 'The Literary Roots of Victor Turner's Anthropology', in K. M. Ashley (ed.), *Victor Turner and the Construction of Cultural Criticism: Between Literature and Anthropology* (Bloomington, IN: Indiana University Press, 1990), pp. 163–9.
106 Chaucer, *Duchess*, ll. 272–3.
107 Trevisa, *De Proprietatibus Rerum*, p. 338.5.
108 Chaucer, *Duchess*, 4–5.
109 Harvey, *The Inward Wits: Psychological Theory in the Middle Ages and the Renaissance*, p. 2.
110 Chaucer, *Book of the Duchess*, ll. 5–9; Frank G. Hoffman, 'The Dream and the Book: Chaucer's Dream-Poetry, Faculty Psychology, and the Poetics of Recombination' (PhD dissertation, University of Pennsylvania, 2004), p. 85.
111 David Lawton, *Chaucer's Narrators* (Cambridge: D. S. Brewer, 1985), p. 54.
112 See Carruthers, 'Mnemotechnique and Vision in Chaucer's *Book of the Duchess*'.
113 Kiser, 'Sleep, Dreams, and Poetry', p. 4.
114 Davis, 'The Work of Sleep', p. 52.
115 Chaucer, *Duchess*, l. 1332.
116 Lawton, *Chaucer's Narrators*, p. 53.
117 Lawton, *Chaucer's Narrators*, p. 53.
118 Chaucer, *Duchess*, ll. 6–8 and 11.
119 Chaucer, *Duchess*, l. 1310.
120 'In Chaucer, [...] the dream is developed as a means of pondering on the uncertain status of imaginative fiction': Spearing, *Medieval Dream-Poetry*, p. 183.
121 See Boitani, 'Old Books Brought to Life in Dreams'.
122 Chaucer, *Parliament*, ll. 22–5.
123 Chaucer, *Parliament*, ll. 88–91.
124 *Middle English Dictionary*, 'hevyness', senses 4a, 4b, 5a, and 5b; for other literary examples, see Chapter 1.
125 Oton de Granson, *Le Songe Saint Valentin*, in Joan Grenier-Winther (ed.), *Poésies* (Paris: Honoré Champion, 2010), ll. 14–20; trans. by Windeatt, *Chaucer's Dream Poetry: Sources and Analogues*, p. 120.

Though not all scholars agree, James Wimsatt argues that the influence goes the other way around, in that Oton de Granson's *Valentin* follows and borrows from the *Duchess*: Wimsatt, *Chaucer and His French Contemporaries*, pp. 220–34. Either way – whether Chaucer developed and repurposed these lines from a source, or whether Chaucer's invention of them was so striking that they were emulated by another poet – we can recognise Chaucer's concerted emphasis on how sleep mediates emotions.

126 See Boethius, *Consolation of Philosophy*, Book 3, prose 3, 33–6. In Chaucer's translation, *Boece*, the narrator claims that 'it ne remembreth me nat that evere I was so fre of my thought that I ne was alwey in angwyse of somwhat', and Lady Philosophy suggests in return (to the narrator's agreement): '"And was nat that [thought-induced anguish]," quod sche, "for that the lakkide somwhat that thow noldest nat han lakkid, or elles thou haddest that thow noldest nat han had?"' (Chaucer, *Boece*, Book III, Prosa 3, 29–36. On the way in which these lines in the Duchess are also 'evocative of late medieval riddles dealing with desire, lack, and frustration', see Lockhart, 'Everyday Wonders and Enigmatic Structures', esp. p. 170.

127 Chardri, *La Vie des Set Dormanz*, ll. 615–20, and *The Works of Chardri*, p. 50; *The York Plays*, Pageant 13, 240–5. See Chapter 1 for further examples.

128 Of the two extant versions of the *Prologue* to the *Legend of Good Women*, F is generally viewed as the first (composed c.1386 or later), and G as a revision but not necessarily a refinement. I cite F here because it praises the daisy more highly, and contains some passages not extant in G, but it is worth noting that the *Prologue*'s sleep discourse figures in G as well.

129 Chaucer, *Prologue* to the *Legend of Good Women*, F 179–82.

130 Chaucer, *Prologue* to the *Legend of Good Women*, F 200–7.

131 Chaucer, *Prologue* to the *Legend of Good Women*, F 208–9.

132 On the enclosed garden in medieval literature, see Derek Pearsall and Elizabeth Salter, *Landscapes and Seasons of the Medieval World* (Toronto: University of Toronto Press, 1973), pp. 76–118.

133 Phillips, *Chaucer's Dream Poetry*, p. 286. Phillips also notes that Chaucer's short poem 'Former Age' describes people sleeping outdoors: 'Slepten this blissed folk withoute walles / On gras or leves in parfit quiete […] / Hir hertes were al oon withoute galle; / Everich of hem his feith to other kepte' (43–8). This outdoors sleep testifies to innocence and the strength of social bonds in a bygone Golden Age (Phillips, *Chaucer's Dream Poetry*, p. 299).

134 Flannery, *Practising Shame*.

135 Charles Muscatine, *Chaucer and the French Tradition: A Study in Style and Meaning* (Berkeley, CA: University of California Press, 1957), p. 6; Ian Robinson, *Chaucer and the English Tradition* (Cambridge: Cambridge University Press, 1972), pp. 284–5. Robinson's argument, in D. Vance Smith's words, is not so much about Chaucer drawing upon an English tradition as it is about Chaucer 'as a poet who invented a tradition out of disparate modes and haphazard occasions': Smith, 'Chaucer as an English Writer', p. 99. See also Brewer, 'The Relationship of Chaucer to the English and European Traditions', who refers to the 'English taproot of Chaucer's poetry' (esp. pp. 15 and 17).
136 K. P. Clarke, *Chaucer and Italian Textuality* (Oxford: Oxford University Press, 2011).
137 Deanne Williams, 'The Dream Visions', in Seth Lerer (ed.), *The Yale Companion to Chaucer*, pp. 147–78 (pp. 150–1); Fumo, *Making Chaucer's* Book of the Duchess, p. 65.
138 Fumo, *Making Chaucer's* Book of the Duchess, p. 65.
139 Barry Windeatt, '"Troilus" and the Disenchantment of Romance', in Derek Brewer (ed.), *Studies in Medieval English Romances: Some New Approaches* (Cambridge: D. S. Brewer, 1988), pp. 129–47.
140 Williams, *French Fetish from Chaucer to Shakespeare*, p. 28.
141 Chaucer, 'Sir Thopas', VII.779–82.

Coda: 'all good letters were layde a slepe': medieval sleep and early modern heirs

In drawing attention to medieval and early modern continuities across its comparative chapters, this book has invoked a *longue durée* from the twelfth century to the early seventeenth: from Geoffrey of Monmouth's view of the pleasant spaces of the island of Britain as conducive to sleep, to both Caliban's insistence that the island in *The Tempest* similarly tenders slumber, and Macbeth's perception that he has murdered sleep in a way that causes the forest to rise up against him. The ambivalences of premodern literary sleep are not contradictory, but rather consistent with and informed by the social, spiritual and scientific understandings of sleep that prevailed from the twelfth century to the early seventeenth. As the preceding chapters have shown, sleep's medical, emotional and ethical connotations in late medieval English culture often depend on spatial considerations such as time, place and posture. Across this span of five centuries, the insular literary landscape bears witness to the importance of a language of sleep in the premodern cultural imagination.

Sir Brian Tuke's preface to William Thynne's 1532 edition of Chaucer states that, Chaucer apart, in medieval England 'all good letters were layde a slepe'.[1] This damning judgement of medieval English literature, repeated by Robert Braham in 1555,[2] deploys sleep to register value and thus to articulate the early 'modern' present in opposition to a constucted 'medieval' past. Yet the early modern language of sleep continues medieval discursive habits, and even the very terms of this value judgement – by deploying sleep as a metaphor for a neglect of duties – betray unacknowledged debts to medieval predecessors. I am arguing for a greater recognition of similarities between the likes of the works of the *Gawain*-poet and Shakespeare's plays, not to claim that Shakespeare must have read a text such as *Sir Gawain and the Green Knight* – though he is rather more likely to have come across Chaucer's dream visions, and was certainly familiar with both Chaucer's 'Knight's Tale' and other medieval romances[3] – but rather to foreground continuities within a shared habit of signifying through sleep. Remarks about sleep found in Middle English and early modern literature often centre on how it is performed and how it should be interpreted, and Shakespeare's use of the rich implications of sleep participates in this long-lived insular tradition.

When Shakespeare's Bottom, infamous for his habit of spouting malapropisms that turn words and ideas on their heads, is overcome by a desire to sleep under the trees, he announces that he has 'an exposition of sleep come upon' him.[4] Although he presumably wishes to say that he has a disposition to sleep, his inept turn of phrase here is, in fact, rather apt. With Lysander, Demetrius, Helena and Hermia all already asleep onstage and on the forest floor, and Bottom about to be lulled to sleep on Titania's bed of flowers beside the fairy queen herself, this moment is saturated with cultural expectations of sleep. Bottom's comment invokes the premodern expository, interpretive approach to sleep, and it exposes other desires as well. His sleep embodies, if in comically transmuted form, the same sylvan impulse to sleep that results in trouble with fairies or powerful queens in Middle English romances such as *Sir Orfeo*, *Sir Degaré* and the *Morte Darthur*. Bottom is at Titania's mercy, and she, for the magical origins of her desire, is at Oberon's – just as Heurodis is at the mercy of the fairy king when she sleeps under a tree, and as Launcelot is at the mercy of Morgan when he sleeps in the shade at the edge of the forest. As they sleep together on Titania's 'flowery bed',[5] a *locus amoenus* and constructed bower space in one, Titania's and Bottom's convergence is suggestively sexual. Shakespeare's sleeping labourer is transgressive in yet another way, too – reminiscent of medieval forebears who sleep slothfully when they ought to be working, such as the title character in *Mankind*, who slumbers onstage as a marker of his sinful idleness.

Some of Shakespeare's contemporaries criticised going to the theatre as a form of idleness conducive to sin: in Gosson's 1579 *The Schoole of Abuse*, theatres are condemned for leading people 'from pyping to playing, from play to pleasure, from pleasure to slouth, from slouth to sleepe, from sleepe to sinne'.[6] Here, theatre-going is explicitly connected to slothful sleep in a slippery-slope argument reminiscent of the causal links Chaucer's 'Parson's Tale' traces from one reprehensible act to another, including slothful sleep:

> Thanne cometh sompnolence, that is sloggy slombrynge, which maketh a man be hevy and dul in body and in soule, and this synne comth of Slouth / And certes, the tyme that, by wey of resoun, men sholde nat slepe, that is by the morwe.[7]

And yet, as one of two workers who sleep onstage in Shakespeare's plays (alongside Sly in *Taming of the Shrew*), Bottom is figured as 'a direct source of artistic creativity and theatrical enterprise' in a way that repositions idleness and theatre as creative and generative.[8] It is not only as a worker, but also as an actor and a would-be playwright, that Bottom's sleeping form occupies the stage. In offering his exposition of sleep, then, Shakespeare's Bottom not only reminds us of the outdoor, daytime sleepers of medieval romance and drama; he also foregrounds connections between sleep and literary production in a way that follows Chaucer's rearticulation, in the *Book of the Duchess*, of the poet's sleep not as sloth, but rather as creative work.[9]

To adduce these parallels, to compare medieval and early modern literary treatments of sleep, is to recall that Shakespeare read and drew upon both popular medieval romance and Chaucer's poems.[10] Bottom offers one example of how Shakespeare, like his contemporaries such as Spenser and Marlowe, deploy sleep in ways that follow the precedents of medieval English literature. While studies of sleep in Shakespeare are rather more numerous than those of sleep in medieval literature,[11] the ways in which early modern engagements with sleep are indebted to medieval conventions have not been addressed. Simon Estok posits that 'sleep in Shakespeare is bafflingly mercurial in early modern thinking' because early modern sleep has varied implications;[12] however, as with medieval representations of sleep, early modern ones are consistent in their inconsistency. The logic underlying the complex cultural grammar of sleep in Shakespeare's works is clearer when viewed in the context of the medieval literary and medical traditions that he inherited. From this transhistorical perspective, Shakespearean sleep emerges not as 'baffling', but rather as shaped by medieval habits of using sleep to explore affective and ethical predicaments.

Coda: 'all good letters were layde a slepe' 245

As William Sherman aptly observes, 'Shakespeare's entire corpus testifies to a deep and enduring preoccupation with sleep and dreams.'[13] How sleep figures in Shakespeare's plays varies by genre, with daytime, outdoor sleep more of a feature of comedies and romances; the tragedies, by contrast, are more likely to feature nocturnal disturbances of sleep, as when the Macbeths plot to kill Duncan in his bed. However, across his main dramatic genres, Shakespeare's representations of sleep also follow medieval ones. For Macbeth, sleep is what 'knits up the ravelled sleave of care'; it is

> The death of each day's life, sore labour's bath,
> Balm of hurt minds, great nature's second course,
> Chief nourisher in life's feast.[14]

This resonates with medieval comments on the beneficial nature of sleep, from Chardri to Chaucer and John Trevisa, as well as with Shakespeare's near-contemporary Sidney's *Astrophil and Stella* (1580s):

> sleepe, ô sleepe, the certaine knot of peace,
> The baiting place of wit, the balme of woe,
> The poore man's wealth, the prisoner's release,
> Th'indifferent Judge betweene the high and low.[15]

Moreover, in *Macbeth*, as in *Sir Gawain and the Green Knight* and *Cleanness*, sleep is again connected to feasting, and to what comes after feasting; it is the 'second course', associated with 'life's feast', though – as in the earlier representations – sleep's valences are also problematic. *Macbeth* famously anthropomorphises sleep as though it can be murdered just as Duncan and his heirs are:

> Methought I heard a voice cry 'Sleep no more,
> Macbeth does murder sleep' – the innocent sleep.[16]

In Shakespeare's *Macbeth* and *Richard III*, sleep is slippery: not, as in the *Gawain*-poet's works, due to the semantics of sleep's onset, but rather, as in Chaucer's *Book of the Duchess*, due to sleep's elusiveness. Yet there are close parallels between the implications of sleep in the literary oeuvres of the likes of the *Gawain*-poet and of Shakespeare, despite the two centuries that separate their composition.

With some recent auspicious exceptions, Shakespeare's broader debts to medieval forebears remain underappreciated.[17] Where sleep is concerned, critics have attended to the frequency and variety of its representations in Shakespeare's plays, from *The Tempest* and

A Midsummer Night's Dream to the tragedies and histories,[18] and have recognised how 'diurnal sleep is seen and represented in Shakespeare as disturbing humanity's place in nature's order'.[19] Garrett A. Sullivan has addressed the way in which immoderate sleep, as a state of being 'over which reason has no restraining influence', features in early modern literature, especially romance. Sullivan observes that 'readers of early modern literature [...] are repeatedly called upon to determine whether the slumbers of a given character are either a bodily requirement or a moral or ethical failure (if not both)'.[20] Ronald Hall and David Bevington provide valuable surveys of aspects of sleep in early modern drama, but the transhistorical comparisons in their articles are focused on contrasts rather than continuities between medieval literature and Shakespeare.[21] Their view that there is no medieval precedent for Shakespearean representations of sleep may be partly due to the selection of medieval genres for comparison: in making distinctions between medieval literature and Shakespeare, Hall only mentions medieval dream visions; Bevington, meanwhile, only mentions medieval drama, thus contrasting spiritual medieval texts with secular early modern ones. Yet as suggested by Bottom's example, medieval drama and dream visions do in fact offer precedents that Shakespeare followed where sleep is concerned. Moreover, comparing secular with secular reveals deeper sleep debts: medieval romance maps out even more clearly the territory that Shakespeare subsequently explores.

In relation to chivalric endeavour, metaphorical sleep carries the same connotations in Shakespearean drama as in Middle English romance. When Malory's Launcelot is told 'now ye be called uppon treson, hit ys tyme for you to styrre! For ye have slepte over longe', sleep is a form of inaction that borders upon cowardice.[22] Similarly, in Shakespeare's *Troilus and Cressida*, sleep is again opposed to honourable, martial action, when Troilus urges war during the Trojan council:

> Nay, if we talk of reason,
> Let's shut our gates and sleep. Manhood and honor
> Should have hare hearts, would they but fat their thoughts
> With this crammed reason. Reason and respect
> Make livers pale and lustihood deject.[23]

Sleep, here, is again associated with 'livers pale', or cowardice. In both cases, the language of sleep is deployed as an excoriation and exhortation to pursue a more vigourous, warlike course of action.

The ethical and behavioural dimensions of sleep similarly frame moments in which Shakespearean characters sleep onstage during the day. Falling asleep onstage – during the day – is slothful here, as in medieval representations: in *Henry IV Part I*, Hal berates Falstaff for being 'so fat-witted with drinking of old sack, / and unbuttoning thee after supper, and sleeping upon benches / after noon, that thou hast forgotten to demand that truly which / thou wouldst truly know'.[24] Falstaff's slothful and immoderate habits have made him forget to act as he ought. In *Henry IV Part II*, it is Hal who, according to Falstaff's whimsy, has 'a kind of sleeping in the blood' that accounts for the heir to the throne's disorderly behaviour.[25] Sleep is also, again, a dangerous form of vulnerability, as Nim wryly observes in *Henry V*: 'Men may sleep, / and they may have their throats about them at that time, and / some say knives have edges.'[26] Sloth and vulnerability are similarly among the hallmarks of sleep in Macbeth, where Lady Macbeth plans to induce 'swinish sleep' among Duncan's guards, in order to be able to murder the latter in his own sleep.[27] And it is when Old Hamlet is 'sleeping within my orchard' in the 'afternoon' that he is poisoned, echoing the danger of sleeping outdoors under trees for medieval figures such as Malory's Launcelot and *Sir Orfeo*'s Heurodis, and perhaps raising ethical questions about Old Hamlet's kingship in the process.[28]

Elsewhere in Shakespeare's tragedies, murdered heirs haunt sleep in ways that reveal early modern literary representations of sleep as themselves the heirs of medieval sleep. A quarter of all action in Shakespeare's tragedies, the highest proportion of any of his genres, takes place at night[29] – and while of course not all nocturnal activity is sleep, much of it involves either what is inflicted upon those who are sleeping, or the afflictions of those who cannot sleep. Sherman claims that in Shakespearean drama, sleep is not therapeutic, not a positive force. However, Shakespeare's troubled insomniacs in *Macbeth* and *Richard III* suggest that, on the contrary, sleep does have positive connotations in these plays, but ones that are difficult to obtain or are out of reach. In these plays, that sleep is desired by but unavailable to the guiltily transgressive only strengthens the idea that sleep *is* to be understood as therapeutic and positive.

As we have seen, in Galenic medicine, sleep was understood to enable the restorative transformation of food into the four humours[30] – and it is that restoration to a healthy equilibrium that is unavailable to Shakespeare's machiavels after their transgressions.

This scientific understanding of sleep – proper sleep – is a positive one, and its implications surface in Shakespeare's *Macbeth*, where not only does the title character famously murder sleep, as addressed above, but his wife also negotiates her troubled conscience through unnatural sleepwalking. By referring to Lady Macbeth's sleepwalking as 'A great perturbation in nature, to receive at once the benefit of sleep and do the effects of watching', the Doctor figures restful sleep as the natural, normative state that is ruptured by the transgressive actions of the Macbeths.[31] Macbeth's own nights are repeatedly afflicted by 'wicked' or 'terrible' dreams; like his wife's, Macbeth's sleep is also in disorder.[32] The disorder represented by all this irregular sleep is both somatic and societal; for the upside-down world the Macbeths create, absent sleep represents absent order and peace. Sleep, a '*non*-natural' influence, is ironically an object of desire that represents the natural.

As in *Macbeth*, in *Richard III* disturbed sleep is a marker of a troubled soul, of one who has put the world out of joint; Richard too longs for the 'sweet sleep' that ghosts, or guilt, disturb. Richard refers to his nephews, whom he terms the 'bastards in the Tower', as 'Foes to my rest, and my sweet sleep's disturbers':[33] his guilt, anxiety, and fear obstruct his sleep. Indeed, 'disturbed' and 'perturbed' are the perennial characteristics of Richard's sleep. Early in the play, Queen Margaret wishes that Richard will have 'no sleep' except 'while some tormenting dream / Affrights thee with a hell of ugly devils'.[34] Anne's speech about Richard's disturbed sleep troubling her own shows that Margaret has got her wish:

> never yet one hour in his bed
> Did I enjoy the golden dew of sleep,
> But with his timorous dreams was still awaked.[35]

Moreover, when Richard attempts to sleep the night before the Battle of Bosworth, in which he loses his life, ghosts appear to reproach and curse him. Anne's ghost tells Richard, 'thy wife, / That never slept a quiet hour with thee, / Now fills thy sleep with perturbations', articulating the ethical disorder of Richard's sleep in the same terms that the Doctor applies to Lady Macbeth's.[36] The shades of the Lancastrian King Harry and his son, Richard's brother Clarence, and his two little nephews, among others, all command Richard to 'despair and die' while inviting his opponent to 'Sleep, Richmond, sleep in peace and wake in joy.'[37] Registering sleep's restorative nature as well speaking to would-be sleepers' ethical states, these murdered heirs give voice to the literary tradition of signifying through sleep that Shakespeare and his contemporaries inherited from their medieval forebears. Here, sleep is invoked in ways that are insistently about subjects' conscience, embodied emotions and society, all together.

Whereas the *Gawain*-poet's characters are often shown to be unethical by excess of deep sleep, Shakespearean machiavels are shown to be unethical by their inability to sleep deeply. However, after Gawain fails to confess his deception in retaining the girdle, he has quite a lot of trouble sleeping, in what may be a sign of troubled conscience.[38] More significantly, however, the representations of sleep in the *Gawain*-poet's writings and in Shakespeare's *Macbeth* and *Richard III*, like others in between, share a focus on ruptured or improper sleep, on sleep out of order. Whether too much or too little, sleeping at the wrong time or being unable to sleep at the right time, both forms of imbalance offer ethical commentaries. While there is some differentiation between the two, there is also a more profound continuity in the ways in which sleep is remarked upon, and employed to interpret important textual moments.

For both the *Gawain*-poet and Shakespeare, sleep implicates and explores conscience. At the risk of oversimplifying, the way in which the *Gawain*-poet uses sleep supports a collective ethic in which figures demonstrate guilt according to a universal understanding of conscience. Here, everyone is supposed to aspire to the same ideal behaviour and to feel guilty for transgression, as Jonah and Gawain and the *Pearl*-narrator do (at least eventually). Shakespeare's *Macbeth* and *Richard III* both preserve and diverge from this medieval use of sleep. On the one hand the murderers' reprehensibility and guilt is again performed in a universalised way through their relationship to sleep; but on the other hand, Shakespeare's use of sleep in these plays is also employed as a way of delving further into the murderers' individual subjectivity. *Patience*'s Jonah, *Cleanness*'s immoral sleepers and the Arthurian court's metaphorical sleep are immoral *because of* the manner and context of their sleep; the wrongness of Shakespeare's insomniacs is rooted in the same understanding of the moral, medical and social implications of unbalanced sleep, yet they further reveal their guilt *through* their inability to sleep.

However, the fact that Shakespeare's Macbeths and Richard III cannot control or disguise what their sleep reveals about their conscience *is* like the medieval representations: here as in the *Gawain*-poet's works and romances such as *Melusine* and Malory's *Morte Darthur*, sleep, or lack thereof, does not lie with respect to the figure's ethical state and emotions. Critics often focus on the increasing self-awareness and performativity of identity in early modern literature and drama. Of course we need look no further than Chaucer's Pardoner for a medieval example of deceptive self-performance,[39] but Katharine Eisamann Maus has convincingly argued that 'in late sixteenth- and early seventeenth-century England the sense of discrepancy between "inward disposition" and "outward appearance" seems' especially 'urgent and consequential', and for more people.[40] In Maus's seminal reading, machiavels such as Shakespeare's Richard III deploy the gap between inward self and outward self for personal gain – to manipulate others and pursue political power:

> By recognising, or constructing, a boundary isolating himself from other people, the machiavel enables himself to organize his behavior on the basis of the difference between what he knows about himself and what others can learn of him. In relation to other characters, he exploits the invisibility of his own interior.[41]

Yet this difference between the inward truth and intentions, and the outward seeming or performance of self, is precisely what is confounded by the machiavels' relationship to sleep: like a dramatic soliloquy, the troubled sleep of Shakespearean murderers tells the audience what the character really thinks or means. More so than a soliloquy, however, such sleep serves as an ethical commentary, and it does not have to break the dramatic frame in order to confound deceptive performance; it is simultaneously the outward performance of self and the inward self. Thus, for Shakespeare's *Macbeth* as for *Sir Gawain*, unconsciousness, whether achieved or attempted, bodies forth an ethical truth. And desired restful, restorative sleep – unavailable to murderous machiavels, but, in the c.1593 *Richard III*, proffered to Elizabethan England's dynastic progenitor, Henry Tudor – speaks to continued awareness of the benefits of sleep for emotional balance and mental health.

* * *

In this transhistorical view of sleep, we can also see how sleep is intimately involved in perceptions of time. Medieval and early modern mentalities distinguished between timely and untimely sleep: sleeping at night, for the length of time required for good health, is timely; sleeping too long, or sleeping during the day – as Chaucer's Cook does in the Canterbury frame, or as a host of medieval romance protagonists and allegorical figures do in drama and dream visions – is untimely. Unnecessary or slothful sleep, in other words, is construed as a 'waste of time'; time, and its allocation to sleep, carries ethical significance. By contrast, saintly or divinely ordained sleep confers positive moral status that only increases with the duration of the sleep, as in the Life of the Seven Sleepers of Ephesus, a hagiographical narrative in which 'God intervenes in time' and that was used to explain the doctrine of the resurrection.[42] More broadly, sleep marks time – in a sense, sleep creates time, structuring diurnal rhythms and demarcating days. Yet sleep is also a marker of being outside of time, in that, for the sleeper, time seems to jump from the moment of falling asleep to the moment of waking. As Schuback remarks, 'The phenomenon of sleep announces itself with the same paradoxical structure as the past: it is only when we no longer possess it that it appears as such.'[43] In dreams, sleep can offer connections to different times, and reading sleep is also insistently about reading the past and future of sleeping subjects – about the causes and consequences of their sleep.

While this analysis of sleep is 'timely' in addressing a topic of serious concern to our sleep-starved modern society, it also follows the lead of premodern characters and contemporary audiences in reading for the significance of sleep. The medieval and early modern English investment in the epistemic qualities of sleep is especially clear in light of this study's cross-genre approach. Setting romances, fabliaux, drama and dream visions in dialogue with each other, and alongside conduct literature and medical tracts, this book has taken a comparative approach that illuminates continuities across these different types of texts, as well as sleep's distinctive contributions to genre-specific treatments of emotions, ethics and dreams. Sleep itself is a process that connects mind and body, revealing concerns about supporting and sustaining what we would now call mental health as well as physical health, and offering a fertile bed for cross-disciplinary approaches to the history of the emotions and the medical humanities. The distinctive English focus on signifying through sleep (often in contrast to continental sources) that this book has uncovered both contributes to recognition of transformative engagements with texts and ideas from the continent (in classical, Arabic and other medieval European cultures), and sheds light on other, understudied, insular connections, including ones that situate Chaucer more clearly in relation to his English predecessors and contemporaries. Through this cross-genre perspective, as well as by drawing more attention to Aristotelian, Galenic causes of dreams, this book has also offered a new, more embodied way of understanding Middle English dream visions by Chaucer, Langland and others. Middle English dream poetry's self-conscious interest in interpretation is not confined to dreams themselves, but also extends to the sleep that enables and contains these dreams. In its multifaceted epistemic implications, sleep is itself an object of desire and a mediator of both desire and morality, exposing and testing the intersections of imagination and practice.

Notes

1 James E. Blodgett, 'William Thynne (d. 1546)', in Paul G. Ruggiers (ed.), *Editing Chaucer: The Great Tradition* (Norman, OK: Pilgrim, 1984), pp. 35–52 (p. 35).
2 Robert Braham, 'The Pistle to the Reader', in *Lydgate's Troy Book*, ed. Henry Bergen, 4 vols, EETS ES 97, 103, 106, and 156 (London: Paul, Trench, Trübner, 1906–1935), IV, pp. 62–5 (p. 63).
3 Kathryn L. Lynch, 'Baring Bottom: Shakespeare and the Chaucerian Dream Vision'; Helen Cooper, *Shakespeare and the Medieval World*.
4 Shakespeare, *A Midsummer Night's Dream*, 4.i.36–7.
5 Shakespeare, *A Midsummer Night's Dream*, 4.i.1.
6 Gosson, *The Schoole of Abuse*, quoted in Michelle M. Dowd, 'Shakespeare's Sleeping Workers', *Shakespeare Studies*, 41 (2013), 148–76 (p. 150).
7 Chaucer, 'Parson's Tale', X.705–6.
8 Dowd, 'Shakespeare's Sleeping Workers', p. 150.
9 Kathryn L. Lynch argues that Shakespeare draws on medieval dream visions, especially Chaucer's, to shape *A Midsummer Night's Dream*'s focus on 'the imagination and the proper relationship of that faculty to reason' (though she does not consider sleep itself here): see 'Baring

Bottom: Shakespeare and the Chaucerian Dream Vision', in Brown (ed), *Reading Dreams*, pp. 99–124 (p. 103).
10 Michael L. Hays, *Shakespearean Tragedy as Chivalric Romance: Rethinking Macbeth, Hamlet, Othello, and King Lear* (Cambridge: D. S. Brewer, 2003), p. 57; Cooper, *Shakespeare and the Medieval World*.
11 Claude Fretz, '"Full of Ugly Sights, of Ghastly Dreams": Dreams and Tragedy in Shakespeare's *Richard III*', *Cahiers Elizabethiens*, 92.1 (2017), 32–49, and '"Either His Notion Weakens, or His Discernings | Are Lethargied": Sleeplessness and Waking Dreams as Tragedy in *Julius Caesar* and *King Lear*', *Etudes Episteme*, 30 (2017); Estok, *Ecocriticism and Shakespeare*; Totaro, 'Securing Sleep in Hamlet'; see further notes 18–21 below.
12 Estok, *Ecocriticism and Shakespeare*, p. 111.
13 Sherman, 'Shakespearean Somniloquy: Sleep and Transformation in *The Tempest*'.
14 Shakespeare, *Macbeth*, 2.ii.35–8.
15 Philip Sidney, *Astrophil and Stella*, in *The Poems of Sir Philip Sidney*, ed. W. A. Ringler, Jr (Oxford: Clarendon Press, 1962), 39.1–4.
16 William Shakespeare, *Macbeth*, 2.ii.33–4.
17 Martha W. Driver and Sid Ray (eds), *Shakespeare and the Middle Ages: Essays on the Performance and Adaptation of the Plays with Medieval Sources or Settings* (Jefferson, NC: McFarland, 2009); Cooper, *Shakespeare and the Medieval World*; Ruth Morse, Helen Cooper and Peter Holland (eds), *Medieval Shakespeare: Pasts and Presents* (Cambridge: Cambridge University Press, 2013).
18 Sullivan, *Sleep, Romance and Human Embodiment*, pp. 72–96.
19 Estok, *Ecocriticism and Shakespeare*, p. 111. Estok offers a useful survey of sleep in Shakespeare's plays, for instance: sleep as bestiality when Hamlet asks, 'What is a man / If his chief good and market of his time / Be but to sleep and feed? A beast, no more' (*Hamlet*, 4.iv.33–5), and sleep as vulnerability when Ariel warns, 'If of life, you keep a care, / Shake off slumber, and beware. / Awake, awake!' (*The Tempest*, 2.i.303–5).
20 Sullivan, *Sleep, Romance and Human Embodiment*, pp. 17–18.
21 Hall, 'Sleeping through Shakespeare'; Bevington, 'Asleep Onstage'.
22 Malory, *Morte Darthur*, p. 909.26–31.
23 Shakespeare, *Troilus and Cressida*, 2.ii.45–9.
24 Shakespeare, *1 Henry IV*, 1.ii.1–5.
25 Shakespeare, *2 Henry IV*, 1.ii.102.
26 Shakespeare, *Henry V*, 2.i.18–20.
27 Shakespeare, *Macbeth*, 1.vii.67.
28 Shakespeare, *Hamlet*, 1.v.59–60.

29 Jean-Marie Maguin, 'Rise and Fall of the King of Darkness', in Jean-Marie Maguin and Michele Willems (eds), *French Essays on Shakespeare and His Contemporaries: 'What Would France with Us?'* (Newark, DE: University of Delaware Press, 1995), pp. 247–70 (p. 248).
30 Early modern writers on the humours connected emotions and sleep in the same ways medieval writers did. See, for instance, Sir Thomas Elyot's *The Castell of Health* (1534), a vernacular medical handbook, or *A Treatise of Melancholie* (1586), as discussed by Heffernan, *The Melancholy Muse*, pp. 21–3.
31 Shakespeare, *Macbeth*, 5.i.8–9.
32 Shakespeare, *Macbeth*, 2.ii.50–1 and 3.ii.19–21.
33 Shakespeare, *Richard III*, 4.ii.74–6.
34 Shakespeare, *Richard III*, 1.iii.222–4.
35 Shakespeare, *Richard III*, 4.i.82–4.
36 Shakespeare, *Richard III*, 5.v.113–15.
37 Shakespeare, *Richard III*, 5.v.89, 94, 103 and 104.
38 *Sir Gawain and the Green Knight*, ll. 1991 and 2007. In parallel with the guilty Gawain's insomnia, and the initial melancholic insomnia of Chaucer's narrator in the *Book of the Duchess*, in *Romeo and Juliet* Shakespeare writes that 'where care lodges, sleep will never lie' (2.iii.36). This speaks to the medical understanding of melancholy as able to cause insomnia through dryness, alongside melancholy's ability to cause (and be ameliorated by) sleep through a direct effect of black bile on the brain.
39 Chaucer, 'Pardoner's Prologue and Tale'; see esp. ll. 398–406.
40 Katharine Eisaman Maus, *Inwardness and Theater in the English Renaissance* (Chicago, IL: University of Chicago Press, 1995), p. 13.
41 Maus, *Inwardness and Theater*, p. 49.
42 Dinshaw, *How Soon Is Now?*, p. 58.
43 Schuback, 'The Hermeneutic Slumber: Aristotle's Reflections on Sleep', p. 129; see also Matthew Fuller, *How to Sleep: The Art, Biology, and Culture of Unconsciousness* (London: Bloomsbury, 2018), pp. 1–3.

Bibliography

Manuscripts

Cambridge, Cambridge University Library MS Ff.2.38
Lincoln, Dean and Chapter Library MS 91
London, British Library, MS Cotton Galba E. ix
London, British Library, MS Cotton Nero A.x
London, British Library, MS Cotton Nero C.IV (Winchester Psalter)
London, British Library, MS Harleian 2390
London, British Library, MS Harley 1764
London, British Library, MS Harley 4196
London, British Library, MS Sloane 4, fol. 63r–104r (Kymer, Gilbert, *Dietarium de sanitatis custodia*)
London, British Library, MS Sloane 989 (*Gouernayle of Helthe*)
London, British Library, MS Sloane 3215
Oxford, Ashmolean Museum, MS 1481
Oxford, Ashmolean Museum, MS 1498
Oxford, Bodleian Library, MS Bodley 638
Oxford, Bodleian Library, MS Fairfax 16
Oxford, Bodleian Library, MS Tanner 346

Other primary sources

Alliterative *Morte Arthure*, in *King Arthur's Death*, ed. Larry D. Benson, rev. Edward E. Foster (Kalamazoo, MI: Medieval Institute Publications, 1994)

Aquinas, Thomas, *Commentary on the Letter of St Paul to the Romans*, ed. John Mortensen (Lander, WY: Aquinas Institute for the Study of Sacred Doctrine, 2012)

Aristotle, *Aristotle on Sleep and Dreams*, trans. David Gallop (Warminster: Aris & Phillips, 1996)
d'Arras, Jean, *Mélusine*, ed. M. C. Brunet (Paris: Jannet, 1854)
The Babees Book, ed. Frederick J. Furnivall, EETS OS 32 (London: Trübner, 1868)
Beowulf: A Dual-Language Edition, ed. and trans Howell D. Chickering (New York: Random House, 2006)
Bernard of Clairvaux, *On the Song of Songs*, trans. Kilian Walsh, 4 vols (Kalamazoo, MI: Cistercian Institute Publications, 1983)
Béroul, *The Romance of Tristan*, ed. and trans. N. J. Lacy (New York: Garland, 1989)
Biblia Sacra: Iuxta Vulgatum Versionem, ed. Robert Weber, vol. II (Stuttgart, 1975)
Boccaccio, Giovanni, *The Fates of Illustrius Men*, trans. Louis Brewer Hall (New York: Frederick Ungar, 1965)
Borde, Andrew, *Regyment of Helthe*, in *The Babees Book*, ed. Frederick J. Furnivall, EETS OS 32 (London: Trübner, 1868)
Bourchier, John, *Duke Huon of Burdeux*, ed. S. L. Lee, EETS ES 40, 41, 43, 50 (London: Trübner, 1882–7)
Braham, Robert, 'The Pistle to the Reader', in *Lydgate's Troy Book*, ed. Henry Bergen, 4 vols, EETS ES 97, 103, 106 and 156 (London: Paul, Trench, Trübner, 1906–1935), IV, pp. 62–5
Brunne, Robert of, *Robert of Brunne's 'Handlyng Synne'*, ed. Frederick J. Furnivall, EETS OS 119 (London: Paul, Trench, Trübner, 1901)
Capgrave, John, *The Life of St Katherine*, ed. Karen A. Winstead (Kalamazoo, MI: Medieval Institute Publications, 1999)
Cassian, John, *The Institutes* (Mahwah, NJ: Paulist Press, 2000)
Castiglione, Baldassare, *The Book of the Courtier*, trans. Sir Thomas Hoby, ed. J. H. Whitfield (London: Dent, 1974)
Caxton, William, *Blanchardyn and Eglantine*, ed. Leon Kellner, EETS ES 58 (London, 1890)
Caxton, William, *The Book of Fayttes of Armes and of Chyualrye*, ed. Alfred T. B. Byles, EETS OS 189 (1932; London: Oxford University Press, 1937)
Caxton, William, *The Book of the Ordre of Chyvalry*, ed. Alfred T. P. Byles, EETS OS 168 (London: Oxford University Press, 1926)
Caxton, William, *The Game and Playe of the Chesse*, ed. Jenny Adams (Kalamazoo, MI: Medieval Institute Publications, 2009)
Caxton, William, *Paris and Vienne*, ed. MacEdward Leach, EETS OS 234 (London: Oxford University Press, 1957)
Chardri, *La Vie des Set Dormanz*, ed. Brian S. Merrilees (London: Anglo-Norman Text Society, 1977)

Chardri, *The Works of Chardri: The Little Debate, The Life of the Seven Sleepers, and The Life of St Josaphaz*, ed. and trans. Neil Cartlidge (Tempe, AR: Arizona Centre for Medieval and Renaissance Studies, 2015)

Chaucer's Dream Poetry: Sources and Analogues, ed. and trans. B. A. Windeatt (Woodbridge: D. S. Brewer, 1982)

Chaucer, Geoffrey, *Chaucer's Dream Poetry*, ed. Helen Phillips and Nick Havely (London: Longman, 1997)

Chaucer, Geoffrey, *Dream Visions and Other Poems*, ed. Kathryn L. Lynch (London: Norton, 2007)

Chaucer, Geoffrey, *The Riverside Chaucer*, ed. Larry D. Benson, 3rd edn (Boston, MA: Houghton Mifflin, 1987)

Codex Ashmole 61: A Compilation of Popular Middle English Verse, ed. George Shuffleton (Kalamazoo, MI: Medieval Institute Publications, 2008)

Cogan, Thomas, *The Haven of Health* (London)

Couldrette, *A Bilingual Edition of Couldrette's Mélusine or Le Roman De Parthenay*, ed. Matthew W. Morris (Lewiston, NY: Edwin Mellen Press, 2003)

Everyman and its Dutch Original, Elckerlijc, ed. Clifford Davidson, Martin W. Walsh, and Ton J. Broos (Kalamazoo, MI: Medieval Institute Publications, 2007)

Four Romances of England: King Horn, Havelok the Dane, Bevis of Hampton, Athelston, ed. Ronald B. Herzman, Graham Drake, and Eve Salisbury (Kalamazoo, MI: Medieval Institute Publications, 1999)

Fourteenth Century Verse and Prose, ed. Kenneth Sisam (Oxford: Clarendon Press, 1925)

Froissart, Jean, *Le Paradis D'amour*, in *Le paradis d'amour; L'orloge amoureus*, ed. Peter F. Dembowski (Genève: Librarie Droz, 1986)

Galen, *Galen: Selected Works*, trans. P. N Singer (Oxford: Oxford University Press, 1997)

Gawain-poet, *The Poems of the Pearl Manuscript*, ed. Malcolm Andrew and Ronald Waldron (Berkeley, CA: University of California Press, 1979)

The 'Gest Hystoriale' of the Destruction of Troy, ed. G. A. Panton and David Donaldson, EETS OS 39 and 56 (London: Trübner, 1869, 1874)

Gildas, *De Excidio Britanniae, or The Ruin of Britain*, ed. and trans. Hugh Williams (Lampeter: Llanerch Press, 2006)

The Gouernayle of Helthe: With The Medecyne of the Stomacke, ed. William Blades (London, 1858)

Gower, John, *Confessio Amantis*, ed. Russell A. Peck, 3 vols (Kalamazoo, MI: Medieval Institute Publications, 2000–4)

Granson, Oton de, *Le Songe Saint Valentin*, in Joan Grenier-Winther (ed.), *Poésies* (Paris: Honoré Champion, 2010)

Gregory the Great, *Pastoral Care*, ed. and trans. Henry Davis (Westminster, MD: Newman Press, 1950)

Heisterbach, Caesarius of, *Dialogus miraculorum*, ed. N. Nösges and H. Schneider (Turnhout: Brepols, 2009)

Higden, Ranulph, *Liber Ultimus: Polychronicon Ranulphi Higden monachi Cestrensis, together with the English translations of John Trevisa and of an unknown writer of the fifteenth-century*, 9 vols, ed. Joseph Rawson Lumby, Rolls Series, 41 (London: Stationer's Office, 1882; repr. New York: Kraus, 1964)

Historical Poems of the XIVth and XVth Centuries, ed. Rossell Hope Robbins (New York: Columbia University Press, 1959)

Hoccleve, Thomas, *'My Compleinte' and Other Poems*, ed. Roger Ellis (Exeter: Exeter University Press, 2001)

Horn Childe and Maiden Rimnild, ed. Maldwyn Mills (Heidelberg: Carl Winter, 1988)

Howard, Henry, 'The great Macedon', in *Poems*, ed. Emrys Jones (Oxford: Clarendon Press, 1964)

The Household of Edward IV: The 'Black Book' and the Ordinance of 1478, ed. A. R. Myers (Manchester: Manchester University Press, 1959)

Idley, Peter, *Peter Idley's Instructions to his Son*, ed. Charlotte D'Evelyn (London: Oxford University Press, 1935)

John Trevisa's Translation of the Polychronicon of Ranulph Higden, Book VI, ed. and trans. Ronald Waldron (Heidelberg: Universitätsverlag Winter, 2004)

Kempe, Margery, *The Book of Margery Kempe*, ed. Barry Windeatt (Harlow: Longman, 2000), 7004–6

The Kingis Quair and Other Poems, ed. Linne R. Mooney and Mary-Jo Arn (Kalamazoo, MI: Medieval Institute Publications, 2005)

King Ponthus and the Fair Sidone, ed. Frank Jewett Mather (Baltimore, MD: Modern Language Association of America, 1897)

Knyghthode and Bataile, ed. R. Dyboski and Z. M. Arend, EETS OS 201 (London: Oxford University Press, 1935)

Kyng Alisaunder, ed. G. V. Smithers, EETS 227 (London: Oxford University Press, 1952)

Lancelot of the Laik, in *Lancelot of the Laik and Sir Tristrem*, ed. Alan Lupack (Kalamazoo, MI: Medieval Institute Publications, 1994)

Lancelot: Roman en prose du XIIIe siècle, ed. Alexandre Micha, 9 vols (Genève: Droz, 1978–83)

Langland, William, *Piers Plowman: A Parallel-Text Edition of the A, B, C and Z Versions*, ed. A. V. C. Schmidt (London: Longman, 1995)

Langland, William, *Piers Plowman: The C-text*, ed. Derek Pearsall (Exeter: University of Exeter Press, 1994)

Langland, William, *The Vision of Piers Plowman: A Critical Edition of the B-Text Based on Trinity College Cambridge MS B.15.17*, ed. A. V. C. Schmidt, 2nd edn (1978; London: Dent, 1995)

Le Livre de Lancelot del Lac, Part II, vol. IV, ed. H. O. Sommer (Washington, DC, 1911)

Liebermann, Felix, *Die Gesetze der Angelsachsen* (Halle: M. Niemeyer, 1898–1912; Aalen: Scientia, 1960)

Lorris, Guillaume de and Jean de Meun, *The Romance of the Rose*, trans. Frances Horgan (Oxford: Oxford University Press, 1994)

Lorris, Guillaume de and Jean de Meun, *Le Roman de la Rose*, ed. Daniel Poirion (Paris: Garnier-Flammarion, 1974)

Lorris, Guillaume de and Jean de Meun, *Le Roman de la Rose par Guillame de Lorris et Jean de Meung*, ed. Pierre Marteau, 4 vols (Paris, 1878)

Lydgate, John, *Dietary*, in *Codex Ashmole 61: A Compilation of Popular Middle English Verse*, ed. George Shuffelton (Kalamazoo, MI: Medieval Institute Publications, 2008)

Lydgate, John, *Troy Book: Selections*, ed. Robert R. Edwards (Kalamazoo, MI: Medieval Institute Publications, 1998)

Machaut, Guillaume de, *The Complete Poetry and Music, Volume 1: The Debate Series*, ed. R. Barton Palmer and Yolanda Plumley (Kalamazoo, MI: Medieval Institute Publications, 2016)

Machaut, Guillaume de, *The Fountain of Love (La Fonteinne Amoureuse) and Two Other Love Vision Poems*, ed. and trans. R. Barton Palmer (New York: Garland, 1993)

Macrobius, *Commentary on the Dream of Scipio*, trans. William Harris Stahl (New York: Columbia University Press, 1952)

Malory, Thomas, *Le Morte Darthur*, ed. P. J. C. Field, 2 vols (Cambridge: D. S. Brewer, 2013)

Malory, Thomas, *The Works of Sir Thomas Malory*, ed. Eugène Vinaver, 3rd edn, rev. by P. J. C. Field, 3 vols (Oxford: Clarendon Press, 1990)

Mandeville, John, *The Egerton Version of Mandeville's Travels*, ed. M. C. Seymour, EETS OS 336 (Oxford: Oxford University Press, 2010)

Mankind, in *Medieval Drama: An Anthology*, ed. Greg Walker (Oxford: Blackwell, 2000)

Marlowe, Christopher, *Dr Faustus*, ed. David Scott Kastan (New York: Norton, 2005)

Medieval Conduct Literature: An Anthology of Vernacular Guides to Behaviour for Youths, with English Translations, ed. Mark D. Johnston (Toronto: University of Toronto Press, 2009)

Melusine, ed. A. K. Donald, EETS ES 68 (London: Paul, Trench, Trübner, 1895)

The Middle English Breton Lays, ed. Anne Laskaya and Eve Salisbury (Kalamazoo, MI: Medieval Institute Publications, 1995)

Middle English Verse Romances, ed. Donald B. Sands (New York: Holt, Rinehart and Winston, 1966)

Mirk, John, *Instructions for Parish Priests*, ed. Edward Peacock, OS 31 (London: Early English Text Society, 1868)

Monmouth, Geoffrey of, *The History of the Kings of Britain*, ed. Michael D. Reeve, trans. Neil Wright (Woodbridge: Boydell, 2007)

La Mort le roi Artu, ed. Jean Frappier, 3rd edn (Genève: Droz, 1964)

Mum and the Sothsegger, in *The Piers Plowman Tradition*, ed. Helen Barr (London: Dent, 1993)

Octavian, ed. Frances McSparran, EETS OS 289 (London: Oxford University Press, 1986)

Owst, Gerald Robert, *Preaching in Medieval England: An Introduction to Sermon Manuscripts of the Period c.1350–1450* (Cambridge: Cambridge University Press, 1926)

The Peterborough Chronicle, 1070–1154, ed. Cecily Clark (Oxford: Clarendon Press, 1970)

Prik of Conscience, ed. James H. Morey (Kalamazoo, MI: Medieval Institute Publications, 2012)

Prose Merlin, ed. John Conlee (Kalamazoo, MI: Medieval Institute Publications, 1998),

Proverbs, Sentences, and Proverbial Phrases: From English Writings Mainly before 1500, ed. Bartlett Jere Whiting and Helen Wescott Whiting (Cambridge, MA: Belknap Press of Harvard University Press, 1968)

Prudentius, *Liber Cathemerinon*, Loeb Classical Library: Prudentius, I, ed. J. J. Thomson (Cambridge, MA: Harvard University Press, 1949)

Robert of Cisyle, in *Amis and Amiloun, Robert of Cisyle, and Sir Amadace*, ed. Edward E. Foster (Kalamazoo, MI: Medieval Institute Publications, 2007)

The Romance of Horn, ed. Mildred K. Pope, rev. by T. B. W. Reid, 2 vols (Oxford: Anglo-Norman Text Society, 1964)

The Romans of Partenay, ed. Walter W. Skeat, EETS ES 22 (London: Paul, Trench, Trübner, 1899)

Salerno Regimen of Health, in *Medieval Medicine: A Reader*, ed. Faith Wallis (Toronto: University of Toronto Press, 2010), pp. 487–92

Secular Lyrics of the XIVth and XVth Centuries, ed. Rossell Hope Robbins (Oxford: Clarendon Press, 1952)

A Selection of English Carols, ed. Richard Greene (Oxford: Clarendon Press, 1962)

Sentimental and Humorous Romances, ed. Erik Kooper (Kalamazoo, MI: Medieval Institute Publications, 2006)

Shakespeare, William, *The Tragedy of King Richard the Third*, in *The Norton Shakespeare*, ed. Stephen Greenblatt et al., 2nd edn (London: Norton, 2008)

Sidney, Philip, *Astrophil and Stella*, in *The Poems of Sir Philip Sidney*, ed. W. A. Ringler, Jr (Oxford: Clarendon Press, 1962)
Sidney, Philip, *The Old Arcadia*, ed. Katherine Duncan-Jones (Oxford: Oxford University Press, 1985)
Sir Gawain and the Green Knight, ed. J. R. R. Tolkien and E. V. Gordon, rev. Norman Davis (1925; Oxford: Clarendon Press, 1967)
Sir Gawain: Eleven Romances and Tales, ed. Thomas Hahn (Kalamazoo, MI: Medieval Institute Publications, 1995)
Sir Orfeo, ed. A. J. Bliss (1954; Oxford: Clarendon Press, 1966)
Sir Perceval of Galles and Ywain and Gawain, ed. Mary Flowers Braswell (Kalamazoo, MI: Medieval Institute Publications, 1995)
Skelton, John, *The Complete English Poems*, ed. John Scattergood (Harmondsworth: Penguin, 1983)
Spenser, Edmund, *The Faerie Qveene*, ed. A. C. Hamilton, rev. 2nd edn (London: Routledge, 2007)
Stanzaic *Guy of Warwick*, ed. Alison Wiggins (Kalamazoo, MI: Medieval Institute Publications, 2004)
St Erkenwald, ed. Ruth Morse (Cambridge: D. S. Brewer, 1975)
Strassburg, Gottfried von, *Tristan*, ed. G. Weber (Darmstadt: Wissenschaftliche Buchgesellschaft, 1967)
Strassburg, Gottfried von, *Tristan*, trans. A. T. Hatto (London: Penguin, 2004)
Tour-Landry, Geoffroy de La, *Book of the Knight of La Tour-Landry: compiled for the instruction of his daughters: translated from the original French into English in the reign of Henry VI*, ed. Thomas Wright (London: Paul, Trench & Trübner, 1906)
Trevisa, John, *On the Properties of Things: John Trevisa's translation of Bartholomæus Anglicus De Proprietatibus Rerum*, ed. M. C. Seymour et al., 2 vols (Oxford: Clarendon Press, 1975)
Troyes, Chrétien de, *Arthurian Romances*, trans. W. W. Kibler (London, 2004)
Troyes, Chrétien de, *Le Chevalier au Lion (Yvain)*, ed. Mario Roques (Paris, 1960)
Troyes, Chrétien de, *Lancelot, ou le chevalier de la charrette*, ed. Jean-Claude Aubailly (Paris, 1991)
Turpines Story: A Middle English Translation of the 'Pseudo-Turpin Chronicle', ed. Stephen H. A. Shepherd, EETS OS 322 (Oxford: Oxford University Press, 2004)
The Vulgate Bible: Douay–Rheims Translation, ed. Swift Edgar and Angela M. Kinney (Cambridge, MA: Harvard University Press, 2010)
Watson, Henry, *Valentine and Orson*, ed. Arthur Dickson, EETS OS 204 (London: Oxford University Press, 1937)
Wynnere and Wastoure and The Parlement of the Thre Ages, ed. Warren Ginsberg (Kalamazoo, MI: Medieval Institute Publications, 1992)

The York Plays, ed. Richard Beadle, EETS ss 23 and 24, 2 vols (Oxford: Oxford University Press, 2009–2013)

Ywain and Gawain, ed. Albert B. Friedman and Norman T. Harrington, EETS 254 (London: Oxford University Press, 1964)

Secondary sources

Abulafia, Anna Sapir, 'Bodies in the Jewish-Christian debate', in Sarah Kay and Miri Rubin (eds), *Framing Medieval Bodies* (Manchester: Manchester University Press, 1994), pp. 123–37

Aiken, Pauline, 'Vincent of Beauvais and Dame Pertelote's Knowledge of Medicine', *Speculum*, 10 (1935), 281–7

Alvaro, P. K., R. M Roberts, and J. K. Harris, 'A Systematic Review Assessing Bidirectionality between Sleep Disturbances, Anxiety, and Depression', *Sleep*, 36 (2013), 1059–68

Amos, Mark Addison, '"For Manners Make Man": Bourdieu, de Certeau, and the Common Appropriation of Noble Manners in the *Book of Courtesy*', in Kathleen Ashley and Robert A. Clark (eds), *Medieval Conduct* (Minneapolis, MN: University of Minnesota Press, 2001), pp. 23–48

Andrew, Malcolm, 'Theories of Authorship', in Derek Brewer and Jonathan Gibson (eds), *A Companion to the Gawain-Poet* (Cambridge: D. S. Brewer, 2007), pp. 23–33

Ashe, Laura, *The Oxford English Literary History, Volume I, 1000–1350: Conquest and Transformation* (Oxford: Oxford University Press, 2017)

Ashley, Kathleen, and Robert L. A. Clark, 'Medieval Conduct: Texts, Theories, Practices', in Kathleen Ashley and Robert L. A. Clark (eds), *Medieval Conduct* (Minneapolis, MN: University of Minnesota Press, 2001), pp. viii–xx

Bachelard, Gaston, *The Poetics of Space*, trans. Maria Jolas (Boston, MA: Beacon Press, 1994; first published in English 1964)

Barnett, K., and N. Cooper, 'The Effects of a Poor Night's Sleep on Mood, Cognitive, Autonomic and Electrophysiological Measures', *Journal of Integrative Neuroscience*, 7 (2008), 405–20

Barootes, B. S. W., 'Idleness, Chess, and Tables: Recuperating Fables in Chaucer's *Book of the Duchess*', in Jamie C. Fumo (ed.), *Chaucer's* Book of the Duchess: *Contexts and Interpretations* (Cambridge: D. S. Brewer, 2018), pp. 29–50

Battles, Paul, 'Dying for a Drink: "Sleeping after the Feast" Scenes in *Beowulf*, *Andreas*, and the Old English Poetic Tradition', *Modern Philology*, 112.3 (2015), 435–57

Bellis, Joanna, *The Hundred Years War in Literature: 1337–1600* (Cambridge: D. S. Brewer, 2016)

Benson, Larry D., 'The Beginnings of Chaucer's English Style', in Stephen A. Barney and Theodore M. Andersson (eds), *Contradictions: From Beowulf to Chaucer* (New York: Routledge, 1995), pp. 243–65

Bevington, David, 'Asleep Onstage', in John A. Alford (ed.), *From Page to Performance: Essays in Early English Drama* (East Lansing, MI: Michigan State University Press, 1995), pp. 51–83

Bildhauer, Bettina, *Medieval Blood* (Cardiff: University of Wales Press, 2006)

Blair, John, 'Hall and Chamber: English Domestic Planning 1000–1250', in Gwyn Meirion-Jones and Michael Jones (eds), *Manorial Domestic Buildings in England and Northern France* (London: Society of Antiquaries of London, 1991), pp. 1–21

Blamires, Alcuin, *Chaucer, Ethics, and Gender* (Oxford: Oxford University Press, 2006)

Blodgett, James E., 'William Thynne (d. 1546)', in Paul G. Ruggiers (ed.), *Editing Chaucer: The Great Tradition* (Norman, OK: Pilgrim, 1984), pp. 35–52

Bodenham, C. H. L., 'The Nature of the Dream in Late Medieval French Literature', *Medium Aevum*, 54 (1985), 74–86

Boffey, Julia, and A. S. G. Edwards, '*The Squire of Low Degree* and the Penumbra of Romance Narrative in the Early Sixteenth Century', in Elizabeth Archibald, Megan G. Leitch and Corinne Saunders (eds), *Romance Rewritten: The Evolution of Middle English Romance* (Cambridge: D. S. Brewer, 2018), pp. 229–40

Boitani, Piero, 'Old Books Brought to Life in Dreams: The *Book of the Duchess*, the *House of Fame*, the *Parliament of Fowls*', in Piero Boitani and Jill Mann (eds), *The Cambridge Companion to Chaucer*, 2nd edn (Cambridge: Cambridge University Press, 2003), pp. 58–77

Boquet, Damien, and Piroska Nagy, *Medieval Sensibilities: A History of Emotions in the Middle Ages*, trans. Robert Shaw (Cambridge: Polity Press, 2018)

Bourdieu, Pierre, *Outline of a Theory of Practice*, trans. Richard Nice (Cambridge: Cambridge University Press, 1977)

Bowers, John M., *An Introduction to the Gawain-Poet* (Gainsville: University Press of Florida, 2012)

Breen, Katharine, *Imagining an English Reading Public, 1150–1400* (Cambridge: Cambridge University Press, 2010)

Brewer, D. S., 'Courtesy and the Gawain-poet', in John Lawlor (ed.) *Patterns of Love and Courtesy: Essays in Memory of C. S. Lewis* (London: Edward Arnold, 1966), pp. 54–85

Brewer, Derek, 'Feasts in England and English Literature in the Fourteenth Century', in Detlef Altenburg, Jörg Jarnut, and Hans-Hugo Steinhoff (eds), *Feste und Feiern im Mittelalter: Paderborner Symposion des Mediävistenverbandes* (Sigmaringen: J. Thorbecke, 1991), pp. 13–26

Brewer, Derek, 'The Relationship of Chaucer to the English and European Traditions', in Derek Brewer (ed.), *Chaucer and Chaucerians: Critical Studies in Middle English Literature* (London: Nelson, 1966), pp. 1–38

Bridges, Venetia, *Medieval Narratives of Alexander the Great: Transnational Texts in England and France* (Cambridge: D. S. Brewer, 2018)

Brown, Peter, 'On the Borders of Middle English Dream Visions', in Peter Brown (ed.), *Reading Dreams: The Interpretation of Dreams from Chaucer to Shakespeare* (Oxford: Oxford University Press, 1999), pp. 22–50

Bullock-Davies, Constance, '"Ympe-tre" and "Nemeton"', *Notes and Queries*, n.s. 9 (1962), 6–9

Burger, Glenn D., *Conduct Becoming: Good Wives and Husbands in the Later Middle Ages* (Philadelphia, PA: University of Pennsylvania Press, 2018)

Burlin, Robert B., *Chaucerian Fiction* (Princeton, NJ: Princeton University Press, 1977)

Burnett, Charles, The *Introduction of Arabic Learning into England* (London: British Library, 1997)

Burns, E. Jane, 'Refashioning Courtly Love: Lancelot as Ladies' Man or as Lady/Man', in Karma Lochrie, Peggy McCracken and James A. Schultz (eds), *Constructing Medieval Sexuality* (Minneapolis, MN: University of Minnesota Press, 1997), pp. 111–34

Burrow, J. A., 'The Fourteenth-Century Arthur', in Elizabeth Archibald and Ad Putter (eds), *The Cambridge Companion to the Arthurian Legend* (Cambridge: Cambridge University Press, 2009), pp. 69–83

Butterfield, Ardis, 'Chaucer's French Inheritance', in Piero Boitani and Jill Mann (eds), *The Cambridge Companion to Chaucer*, 2nd edn (Cambridge: Cambridge University Press, 2003), pp. 20–35

Butterfield, Ardis, *The Familiar Enemy: Chaucer, Language, and Nation in the Hundred Years War* (Oxford: Oxford University Press, 2009)

Butterfield, Ardis, 'Lyric and Elegy in *The Book of the Duchess*', *Medium Aevum*, 60 (1991), 33–60

Byrne, Aisling, 'The Intruder at the Feast: Negotiating Boundaries in Medieval Insular Romance', *Arthurian Literature*, 27 (2010), 33–57

Byrne, Aisling, *Otherworlds: Fantasy and History in Medieval Literature* (Oxford: Oxford University Press, 2016)

Calin, William, *The French Tradition and the Literature of Medieval England* (Toronto: University of Toronto Press, 1994)

Camille, Michael, 'Manuscript Illumination and the Art of Copulation', in Karma Lochrie, Peggy McCracken, and James A. Schultz (eds), *Constructing Medieval Sexuality* (Minneapolis, MN: University of Minnesota Press, 1997), pp. 58–90

Cannon, Christopher, *The Making of Chaucer's English* (Cambridge: Cambridge University Press, 1998)

Carrera, Elena (ed.), *Emotions and Health, 1200–1700* (Leiden: Brill, 2013)
Carruthers, Mary, '"The Mystery of the Bed Chamber": Mnemotechnique and Vision in Chaucer's *Book of the Duchess*', in John M. Hill and Deborah M. Sinnreich-Levi (eds), *The Rhetorical Poetics of the Middle Ages: Reconstructive Polyphony: Essays in Honor of Robert O. Payne* (Madison, NJ: Fairleigh Dickinson University Press, 2000), pp. 67–87
Cassidy-Welch, Megan, 'Space and Place in Medieval Contexts', *Parergon*, 27.2 (2010), 1–12
Certeau, Michel de, *The Practice of Everyday Life*, trans. Steven Rendall (Berkeley, CA: University of California Press, 1984)
Chartier, Roger, 'Histoire des mentalités', in Lawrence D. Kritzman (ed.), *The Columbia History of Twentieth-Century French Thought* (New York: Columbia University Press, 2006), pp. 54–8
Cherewatuk, Karen, 'Malory's Thighs and Launcelot's Buttock: Ignoble Wounds and Moral Transgression in the *Morte Darthur*', *Arthurian Literature*, 31 (2014), 35–60
Cherniss, Michael D., *Boethian Apocalypse: Studies in Middle English Vision Poetry* (Norman, OK: Pilgrim Books, 1987)
Chism, Christine, 'Romance', in *The Cambridge Companion to Medieval English Literature, 1100–1500*, ed. Larry Scanlon (Cambridge: Cambridge University Press, 2009), pp. 57–69
Clarke, K. P., *Chaucer and Italian Textuality* (Oxford: Oxford University Press, 2011)
Clason, C., 'Deception in the Boudoir: Gottfried's *Tristan* and 'Lying' in Bed', *Journal of English and German Philology*, 103.3 (2004), 277–96
Classen, Albrecht (ed.), *Mental Health, Spirituality, and Religion in the Middle Ages and Early Modern Age* (Berlin: De Gruyter, 2014)
Coolidge, Sharon Ann, 'The Grafted Tree in *Sir Orfeo*: A Study in the Iconography of Redemption', *Ball State University Forum*, 23 (1982), 62–8
Cooper, Helen, 'Chaucerian Poetics', in Robert G. Benson and Susan J. Ridyard (eds), *New Readings of Chaucer's Poetry* (Cambridge: D. S. Brewer, 2003), pp. 31–50
Cooper, Helen, *The English Romance in Time: Transforming Motifs from Geoffrey of Monmouth to the Death of Shakespeare* (Oxford: Oxford University Press, 2004)
Cooper, Helen, *Shakespeare and the Medieval World* (London: Methuen Drama, 2010)
Crary, Jonathan, *24/7: Late Capitalism and the Ends of Sleep* (London: Verso, 2013)
Crocker, Holly A., *The Matter of Virtue: Women's Ethical Action from Chaucer to Shakespeare* (Philadelphia, PA: University of Pennsylvania Press, 2019)

Crocker, Holly A. and Glenn Burger (eds), *Medieval Affect, Feeling, and Emotion* (Cambridge: Cambridge University Press, 2019)

Culpin, Vicki, *The Business of Sleep: How Sleeping Better Can Transform Your Career* (London: Bloomsbury, 2018)

Cummings, Brian, and James Simpson, 'Introduction', in Cummings and Simpson (eds), *Cultural Reformations: Medieval and Renaissance in Literary History* (Oxford: Oxford University Press, 2010)

Curry, Walter Clyde, *Chaucer and the Medieval Sciences*, 2nd edn (1926; Barnes & Noble, 1960)

Curtius, Ernst Robert, *European Literature and the Latin Middle Ages* (Princeton, NJ: Princeton University Press, 1952)

Damasio, Antonio, *Looking for Spinoza: Joy, Sorrow and the Feeling Brain* (London: Harcourt, 2003)

Dannenfeldt, Karl H., 'Sleep: Theory and Practice in the Late Renaissance', *Journal of the History of Medicine and Allied Sciences*, 41 (1986), 415–41

Davenport, William Anthony, *Chaucer: Complaint and Narrative* (Cambridge: D. S. Brewer, 1988)

Davis, Alex, *Chivalry and Romance in the English Renaissance* (Cambridge: D. S. Brewer, 2003)

Davis, Rebecca, '"Noon Other Werke": The Work of Sleep in Chaucer's *Book of the Duchess*', in Jamie C. Fumo (ed.), *Chaucer's* Book of the Duchess: *Contexts and Interpretations* (Cambridge: D. S. Brewer, 2018), pp. 51–69

Davis, Steven, 'Guillaume de Machaut, Chaucer's *Book of the Duchess*, and the Chaucer Tradition', *The Chaucer Review*, 36.4 (2002), 391–405

Delany, Sheila, *Impolitic Bodies: Poetry, Saints and Society in Fifteenth-Century England: The Work of Osbern Bokenham* (Oxford: Oxford University Press, 1998)

Delumeau, Jean, *Sin and Fear: The Emergence of a Western Guilt Culture, 13th–18th Centuries*, trans. Eric Nicholson (1983; New York: St Martin's Press, 1990)

Diamond, Arlyn, 'Meeting Grounds: Gardens in Middle English Romance', in Laura Ashe, Ivana Djordjevic and Judith Weiss (eds), *The Exploitations of Medieval Romance* (Cambridge: D. S Brewer, 2010), pp. 125–38

Dinshaw, Carolyn, *Getting Medieval: Sexualities and Communities, Pre- and Postmodern* (London: Duke University Press, 1999)

Dinshaw, Carolyn, *How Soon Is Now? Medieval Texts, Amateur Readers, and the Queerness of Time* (London: Duke University Press, 2012)

Dixon, Thomas, *From Passions to Emotions: The Creation of a Secular Psychological Category* (Cambridge: Cambridge University Press, 2003)

Dowd, Michelle M., 'Shakespeare's Sleeping Workers', *Shakespeare Studies*, 41 (2013), 148–76

Driver, Martha W., and Sid Ray (eds), *Shakespeare and the Middle Ages: Essays on the Performance and Adaptation of the Plays with Medieval Sources or Settings* (Jefferson, NC: McFarland, 2009)
Dronzek, Anna, 'Gendered Theories of Education in Fifteenth-Century Conduct Books', in Ashley and Clark (eds), *Medieval Conduct*, pp. 135–59
Eames, Penelope, 'Furniture in England, France and the Netherlands from the Twelfth to the Fifteenth Century', *Furniture History: The Journal of the Furniture History Society*, 13 (1977), 1–303
Ekirch, A. Roger, *At Day's Close: A History of Nighttime* (London: Weidenfeld & Nicolson, 2005)
Elias, Marcel, 'Interfaith Empathy and the Formation of Romance', in Mary Flannery (ed.), *Emotion and Medieval Textual Media* (Turnhout: Brepols, 2018), 99–124
Elias, Norbert, *The Civilizing Process* (Oxford: Blackwell, 2000)
Estok, Simon C., *Ecocriticism and Shakespeare: Reading Ecophobia* (New York: Palgrave Macmillan, 2011)
Field, P. J. C., *Malory: Texts and Sources* (Cambridge: D. S. Brewer, 1998)
Field, P. J. C., 'The Source of Malory's *Tale of Gareth*', in Toshiyuki Takamiya and Derek Brewer (eds), *Aspects of Malory* (Cambridge: D. S. Brewer, 1981), pp. 57–70
Field, Rosalind, 'Patterns of Availability and Demand in Middle English Translations *de romanz*', in Laura Ashe, Ivana Djordjevic and Judith Weiss (eds), *Exploitations of Medieval Romance* (Cambridge: D. S. Brewer, 2010), pp. 73–89
Fisher, Sheila, 'Taken Men and Token Women in Sir Gawain and the Green Knight', in Sheila Fisher and Janet E. Halley (eds), *Seeking the Woman in Late Medieval and Renaissance Writings: Essays in Feminist Contextual Criticism* (Knoxville, TN: University of Tennessee Press, 1989), pp. 71–105
Flannery, Mary C., 'Personification and Embodied Emotional Practice in Middle English Literature', *Literature Compass*, 13 (2016), 351–61
Flannery, Mary C., *Practising Shame: Female Honour in Later Medieval England* (Manchester: Manchester University Press, 2019)
Foucault, Michel, *Discipline and Punish: The Birth of the Prison*, trans. Alan Sheridan (New York: Pantheon, 1977)
Fowler, Alastair, *Kinds of Literature: An Introduction to the Theory of Genres and Modes* (Oxford: Clarendon Press 1982)
Freeman, D., B. Sheaves, G. M. Goodwin et al., 'The Effects of Improving Sleep on Mental Health (OASIS): A Randomised Controlled Trial with Mediation Analysis', *Lancet Psychiatry*, 4 (2017), 749–58
Fretz, Claude, '"Either His Notion Weakens, or His Discernings | Are Lethargied": Sleeplessness and Waking Dreams as Tragedy in *Julius Caesar* and *King Lear*', *Etudes Episteme*, 30 (2017)

Fretz, Claude, '"Full of Ugly Sights, of Ghastly Dreams": Dreams and Tragedy in Shakespeare's *Richard III*', *Cahiers Elizabethiens*, 92.1 (2017), 32–49

Friedman, John Block, 'Eurydice, Heurodis, and the Noon-Day Demon', *Speculum*, 41.1 (1966), 22–9

Fuller, Matthew, *How to Sleep: The Art, Biology, and Culture of Unconsciousness* (London: Bloomsbury, 2018)

Fumo, Jamie C., *Making Chaucer's* Book of the Duchess: *Textuality and Reception* (Cardiff: University of Wales Press, 2015)

Goldie, Matthew Boyd, *Scribes of Space: Place in Middle English Literature and Late Medieval Science* (Ithaca, NY: Cornell University Press, 2019)

Gray, Douglas, *Themes and Images in Medieval English Religious Lyric* (London: Routledge, 1972)

Green, Richard Firth, *A Crisis of Truth: Literature and Law in Ricardian England* (Philadelphia, PA: University of Pennsylvania Press, 1999)

Green, Richard Firth, *Poets and Princepleasers: Literature and the English Court in the Late Middle Ages* (Toronto: University of Toronto Press, 1980)

Greenblatt, Stephen, *Renaissance Self-Fashioning: From More to Shakespeare* (Chicago, IL: University of Chicago Press, 1980)

Gregg, Melissa, and Gregory J. Seigworth (eds), *The Affect Theory Reader* (Durham, NC: Duke University Press, 2010)

Gregory, Alice, *Nodding Off: The Science of Sleep from Cradle to Grave* (London: Bloomsbury, 2018)

Guthrie, Steve, 'Dialogics and Prosody in Chaucer', in Thomas J. Farrell (ed.), *Bakhtin and Medieval Voices* (Gainesville, FL: University Press of Florida, 1995), pp. 94–108

Hall, Ronald, 'Sleeping through Shakespeare', *Shakespeare in Southern Africa*, 12 (2000), 24–32

Hamilton, Gayle K., 'The Breaking of Troth in *Ywain and Gawain*', *Mediaevalia*, 2 (1976), 111–35

Handley, Sasha, *Sleep in Early Modern England* (London: Yale University Press, 2016)

Harré, Rom (ed.), *The Social Construction of Emotion* (Oxford: Blackwell, 1988)

Harré, Rom, and W. Gerrod Parrott (eds), *The Emotions: Social, Cultural and Biological Dimensions* (London: Sage Publications, 1996)

Harvey, E. Ruth, *The Inward Wits: Psychological Theory in the Middle Ages and the Renaissance* (London: Warburg Institute, 1975)

Hays, Michael L., *Shakespearean Tragedy as Chivalric Romance: Rethinking Macbeth, Hamlet, Othello, and King Lear* (Cambridge: D. S. Brewer, 2003)

Heffernan, Carol Falvo, *The Melancholy Muse: Chaucer, Shakespeare and Early Medicine* (Pittsburgh, PA: Duquesne University Press, 1995)

Hill, John M., 'The *Book of the Duchess*, Melancholy, and That Eight-Year Sickness', *Chaucer Review*, 9.1 (1974), 35–50

Hines, John, *The Fabliau in English* (Harlow: Longman, 1993)

Hoffman, Frank G., 'The Dream and the Book: Chaucer's Dream-Poetry, Faculty Psychology, and the Poetics of Recombination' (PhD dissertation, University of Pennsylvania, 2004)

Holland, Peter, '"The Interpretation of Dreams" in the Renaissance', in Peter Brown (ed.), *Reading Dreams: The Interpretation of Dreams from Chaucer to Shakespeare* (Oxford: Oxford University Press, 1999), pp. 125–46

Holsinger, Bruce, *The Premodern Condition: Medievalism and the Making of Theory* (Chicago, IL: University of Chicago Press, 2005)

Hostetter, Aaron, *Political Appetites: Food in Medieval English Romance* (Columbus, OH: Ohio State University Press, 2017)

Howie, Cary, *Claustrophilia: The Erotics of Enclosure in Medieval Literature* (New York: Palgrave, 2007)

Hsy, Jonathan, *Trading Tongues: Merchants, Multilingualism, and Medieval Literature* (Columbus, OH: Ohio State University Press, 2013)

Hughes, Andrew, *Medieval Manuscripts for Mass and Office: A Guide to Their Organization and Terminology* (Toronto: University of Toronto Press, 1995)

Huizinga, Johan, *The Autumn of the Middle Ages*, trans. R. J. Payton and U. Mammitzch (Chicago, IL: University of Chicago Press, 1997)

Hunt, Tony, 'Beginnings, Middles and Ends: Some Interpretive Problems in Chrétien's *Yvain* and its Medieval Adaptations', in Leigh A. Arrathoon (ed.), *The Craft of Fiction* (Rochester, MI: Solaris Press, 1984), pp. 83–117

Jagot, Shazia, '*'Fin' amors*, Arabic Learning, and the Islamic World in the Work of Geoffrey Chaucer' (PhD dissertation, University of Leicester, 2013)

Jauss, Hans Robert, *Toward an Aesthetic of Reception*, trans. Timothy Bahti (Minneapolis, MN: University of Minnesota Press, 1982)

Johnson, David F., '*In Somnium, In Visionem*: The Figurative Significance of Sleep in *Piers Plowman*', in L. A. J. R. Houwen and A. A. MacDonald (eds), *Loyal Letters: Studies on Mediaeval Alliterative Poetry & Prose* (Groningen: Egbert Forsten, 1994), pp. 240–5

Johnstone, Boyda, 'Vitreous Visions: Stained Glass and Affective Engagement in John Lydgate's *The Temple of Glass*', *New Medieval Literatures*, 17 (2017), 175–200

Jones, Sarah Rees, 'Public and Private Space and Gender in Medieval Europe', in Judith M. Bennett and Ruth Mazo Karras (eds), *The Oxford*

Handbook of Women and Gender in Medieval Europe (Oxford: Oxford University Press, 2013), pp. 246–61

Karnes, Michelle, *Imagination, Meditation and Cognition in the Middle Ages* (Chicago, IL: University of Chicago Press, 2011)

Karras, Ruth Mazo, *Sexuality in Medieval Europe: Doing unto Others* (New York: Routledge, 2005)

Kelly, Kathleen Coyne, *Performing Virginity and Testing Chastity in the Middle Ages* (London: Routledge, 2000)

Kemp, Simon, *Medieval Psychology* (New York: Greenwood Press, 1990)

King, Andrew, *The Faerie Queene and Middle English Romance: The Matter of Just Memory* (Oxford: Clarendon Press, 2000)

Kiser, Lisa J., 'Sleep, Dreams, and Poetry in Chaucer's *Book of the Duchess*', *Papers on Language & Literature*, 19 (1983), 3–12

Kittredge, G. L., *Chaucer and His Poetry* (Cambridge, MA: Harvard University Press, 1915)

Kittredge, G. L., 'Guillaume de Machaut and *The Book of the Duchess*', *Modern Language Association*, 30.1 (1915), 1–24

Knight, Charlotte, 'The Literature of the Bedchamber in Late Medieval England' (PhD dissertation, King's College London, 2019)

Knox, B. M. W., 'The Serpent and the Flame: The Imagery of the Second Book of the *Aeneid*', *American Journal of Philology*, 71.4 (1950), 379–400

Knox, Phillip, '"Hyt Am I": Voicing Selves in the *Book of the Duchess*, the *Roman de la Rose*, and the *Fonteinne Amoureuse*', in Jamie C. Fumo (ed.), *Chaucer's* Book of the Duchess: *Contexts and Interpretations* (Cambridge: D. S. Brewer, 2018), pp. 135–56

Krueger, Roberta L., 'Introduction: Teach Your Children Well: Medieval Conduct Guides for Youths', in Mark D. Johnston (ed.), *Medieval Conduct Literature: An Anthology of Vernacular Guides to Behaviour for Youths, with English Translations* (Toronto: University of Toronto Press, 2009), pp. ix–xxxiii

Kruger, Stephen F., 'Dialogue, Debate, and Dream Vision', in Larry Scanlon (ed.), *The Cambridge Companion to Medieval English Literature 1100–1500* (Cambridge: Cambridge University Press, 2009), pp. 71–82

Kruger, Stephen F., *Dreaming in the Middle Ages* (Cambridge: Cambridge University Press, 1992)

Kruger, Steven, 'Medical and Moral Authority in the Late Medieval Dream', in Peter Brown (ed.), *Reading Dreams: The Interpretation of Dreams from Chaucer to Shakespeare* (Oxford: Oxford University Press, 1999), pp. 51–83

Kurath, Hans, et al. (eds), *The Middle English Dictionary* (Ann Arbor, MI, 1952–2001)

Langum, Virginia, *Medicine and the Seven Deadly Sins in Late Medieval Literature and Culture* (New York: Palgrave Macmillan, 2016)

Lasater, A. E., 'Under the Ympe-Tre or: Where the Action is in *Sir Orfeo*', *Southern Quarterly*, 12 (1974), 353–63

Lawlor, John, 'The Pattern of Consolation in *The Book of the Duchess*', *Speculum*, 31.4 (1956)

Lawrence, C. H., *Medieval Monasticism: Forms of Religious Life in Western Europe in the Middle Ages* (London: Longman, 1984)

Lawton, David, *Chaucer's Narrators* (Cambridge: D. S. Brewer, 1985)

Lecklider, Jane K., *Cleanness: Structure and Meaning* (Cambridge: D. S. Brewer, 1997)

Lefebvre, Henri, *The Production of Space*, trans. Donald Nicholson-Smith (Oxford: Blackwell, 1991)

Leitch, Megan G., 'Enter the Bedroom: Managing Space for the Erotic in Middle English Romance', in Amanda Hopkins, Robert Allen Rouse and Cory James Rushton (eds), *Sexual Culture in Late Medieval Britain* (Cambridge: D. S. Brewer, 2014), pp. 39–53

Leitch, Megan G., 'The Servants of Chivalry? Dwarfs and Porters in Malory and the Middle English Gawain Romances', *Arthuriana*, 27.1 (2017), 3–27

Leitch, Megan G., '"Suche Maner of Sorow-Makynge": Affect, Ethics and Unconsciousness in Malory's *Morte Darthur*', *Arthurian Literature*, 31 (2014), 83–99

Leitch, Megan G. and Cory James Rushton, 'Introduction', in Leitch and Rushton (eds), *A New Companion to Malory* (Cambridge: D. S. Brewer, 2019), pp. 1–10

Lenz, Tanya S., *Dreams, Medicine, and Literary Practice: Exploring the Western Literary Tradition through Chaucer* (Turnhout: Brepols, 2014)

Liu, Yin, 'Middle English Romance as Prototype Genre', *The Chaucer Review*, 40.4 (2006), 335–53

Lochrie, Karma, Peggy McCracken, and James A. Schultz (eds), *Constructing Medieval Sexuality* (Minneapolis, MN: University of Minnesota Press, 1997)

Lockhart, Jessica Jane, 'Everyday Wonders and Enigmatic Structures: Riddles from Symphosius to Chaucer' (University of Toronto, PhD dissertation, 2017)

Lynch, Andrew, *Malory's Book of Arms: The Narrative of Combat in 'Le Morte Darthur'* (Cambridge: D. S. Brewer, 1997)

Lynch, Andrew, 'Malory and Emotion', in Megan G. Leitch and Cory James Rushton (eds), *A New Companion to Malory* (Cambridge: D. S. Brewer, 2019), pp. 177–90

Lynch, Andrew, 'Positive Emotions in Arthurian Romance: Introduction', *Journal of the International Arthurian Society*, 4.1 (2016), 53–7

Lynch, Kathryn L., 'Baring Bottom: Shakespeare and the Chaucerian Dream Vision', in Peter Brown (ed.), *Reading Dreams: The Interpretation of*

Dreams from Chaucer to Shakespeare (Oxford: Oxford University Press, 1999), pp. 99–124

Lynch, Kathryn L., *The High Medieval Dream Vision: Poetry, Philosophy, and Literary Form* (Stanford, CA: Stanford University Press, 1988)

MacLehose, William F., 'Captivating thoughts: nocturnal pollution, imagination and the sleeping mind in the twelfth and thirteenth centuries', *Journal of Medieval History*, 46.1 (2020), 98–131

MacLehose, William F., 'Fear, Fantasy and Sleep in Medieval Medicine', in Elena Carrera (ed.), *Emotions and Health, 1200–1700* (Leiden: Brill, 2013), pp. 67–94

Macmillan, Sarah, '"The Nyghtes Watchys": Sleep Deprivation in Medieval Devotional Culture', *Journal of Medieval Religious Cultures*, 39.1 (2013), 23–42

Maguin, Jean-Marie, 'Rise and Fall of the King of Darkness', in Jean-Marie Maguin and Michele Willems (eds), *French Essays on Shakespeare and His Contemporaries: 'What Would France with Us?'* (Newark, DE: University of Delaware Press, 1995), pp. 247–70

Malpas, Jeff (ed.), *The Intelligence of Place: Topographies and Poetics* (London: Bloomsbury, 2015)

Mann, Jill, 'Eating and Drinking in *Piers Plowman*', in *Essays and Studies*, NS 32 (1979), 26–43

Mann, Jill, 'Malory: Knightly Combat in *Le Morte Darthur*', in Boris Ford (ed.), *The New Pelican Guide to English Literature*, 9 vols (Harmondsworth, 1982–88), I, Part I, 331–9

Mann, Jill, 'Troilus' Swoon', *The Chaucer Review*, 14 (1980), 319–35

Martin, Molly, *Castles and Space in Malory's 'Morte Darthur'* (Cambridge: D. S. Brewer, 2019)

Martin, Molly, *Vision and Gender in Malory's 'Morte Darthur'* (Cambridge: D. S. Brewer, 2010)

Maus, Katharine Eisaman, *Inwardness and Theater in the English Renaissance* (Chicago, IL: University of Chicago Press, 1995)

McAlpine, Thomas H., *Sleep, Divine and Human, in the Old Testament* (Sheffield: Sheffield Academic Press, 1987)

McCracken, Peggy, *The Curse of Eve, the Wound of the Hero: Blood, Gender, and Medieval Literature* (Philadelphia, PA: University of Pennsylvania Press, 2003)

McDonald, Nicola, 'A Polemical Introduction', in Nicola MacDonald (ed.), *Pulp Fictions of Medieval England: Essays in Popular Romance* (Manchester: Manchester University Press, 2004), pp. 1–21

McDonald, Nicola, 'Desire Out of Order and *Undo Your Door*', *Studies in the Age of Chaucer*, 34 (2012), 247–75

McNamer, Sarah, *Affective Meditation and the Invention of Medieval Compassion* (Philadelphia, PA: University of Pennsylvania Press, 2010)

Means, Michael H., *The Consolatio Genre in Medieval English Literature* (Gainesville, FL: University of Florida Press, 1972)

Metlitzki, Dorothee, *The Matter of Araby in Medieval England* (London: Yale University Press, 1977)

Minnis, A. J., 'Chaucer and the *Ovide moralisé*', *Medium Aevum*, 48 (1979), 254–7

Minnis, A. J., V. J. Scattergood and J. J. Smith, *Oxford Guides to Chaucer: The Shorter Poems* (Oxford: Clarendon Press, 1995)

Mitchell, J. Allan, *Ethics and Exemplary Narrative in Chaucer and Gower* (Cambridge: D. S. Brewer, 2004)

Morgan, Hollie L. S., *Beds and Chambers in Late Medieval England: Readings, Representations and Realities* (Woodbridge: York Medieval Press, 2017)

Morse, Ruth, Helen Cooper and Peter Holland (eds), *Medieval Shakespeare: Pasts and Presents* (Cambridge: Cambridge University Press, 2013)

Muscatine, Charles, *Chaucer and the French Tradition: A Study in Style and Meaning* (Berkeley, CA: University of California Press, 1957)

Nancy, Jean-Luc, *The Fall of Sleep*, trans. Charlotte Mandell (New York: Fordham University Press, 2009)

Nicholls, Jonathan W., *The Matter of Courtesy: A Study of Medieval Courtesy Books and the Gawain-Poet* (Cambridge: D. S. Brewer, 1985)

Nolan, Barbara, 'The Tale of Sir Gareth and the Tale of Sir Lancelot', in Elizabeth Archibald and A. S. G. Edwards (eds), *A Companion to Malory* (Cambridge: D. S. Brewer, 1996), pp. 153–81

Norris, Ralph, *Malory's Library: The Sources of the 'Morte Darthur'* (Cambridge: D. S. Brewer, 2008)

Norris, Ralph, 'Malory and His Sources', in Megan G. Leitch and Cory James Rushton (eds), *A New Companion to Malory* (Cambridge: D. S. Brewer, 2019), pp. 32–52

Orlemanski, Julie, 'Prosopopoeial Heaviness in Chaucer's *Book of the Duchess*', in Thomas A. Prendergast and Jessica Rosenfeld (eds), *Chaucer and the Subversion of Form* (Cambridge: Cambridge University Press, 2018), pp. 125–45

Orlemanski, Julie, *Symptomatic Subjects: Bodies, Medicine, and Causation in the Literature of Late Medieval England* (Philadelphia, PA: University of Pennsylvania Press, 2019)

Painter, George D., *William Caxton: A Quincentenary Biography of England's First Printer* (London: Chatto & Windus, 1976)

Paster, Gail Kern, *Humoring the Body: Emotions and the Shakespearean Stage* (Chicago, IL: University of Chicago Press, 2004)

Pearsall, Derek, and Elizabeth Salter, *Landscapes and Seasons of the Medieval World* (Toronto: University of Toronto Press, 1973)

Peck, Russell A., 'John Gower and the Book of Daniel', in R. F. Yeager (ed.), *John Gower: Recent Readings* (Kalamazoo, MI: Medieval Institute Publications, 1989), pp. 159–87

Peden, Alison M., 'Macrobius and Medieval Dream Literature', *Medium Aevum*, 54 (1985), 59–73

Pender, Stephen, 'Subventing Disease: Anger, Passions, and the Non-Naturals', in *Rhetorics of Bodily Disease and Health in Medieval and Early Modern England*, pp. 193–218

Perrot, Michelle, *The Bedroom: An Intimate History*, trans. Lauren Elkin (New Haven, CT: Yale University Press, 2018)

Petri Venerabilis adversus Iudeorum inveteratam duritiem, ed. Y. Friedman, Corpus Christianorum Continuatio Medievalis, LVIII (Turnhout: Brepols, 1985)

Phillips, Helen, 'The Book of the Duchess, Lines 31–96: Are They A Forgery?', *English Studies*, 67.2 (1986), 113–21

Phillips, Helen, 'Chaucer: Dream Visions', in Siân Echard and Robert Rouse (eds), *The Encyclopedia of Medieval Literature in Britain* (Oxford: Wiley Blackwell, 2017), pp. 442–8

Phillips, Helen, 'Frames and Narratives in Chaucerian Poetry', in Helen Cooper and Sally Mapstone (eds), *The Long Fifteenth Century: Essays for Douglas Gray* (Oxford: Clarendon Press, 1997), pp. 71–97

Phillips, Helen, 'Structure and Consolation in the *Book of the Duchess*', *The Chaucer Review*, 16.2 (1981), 107–18

Phillips, Kim, *Medieval Maidens: Young Women and Gender in England, 1270–1540* (Manchester: Manchester University Press, 1993)

Pilcher, J., and A. Huffcut, 'Effects of Sleep Deprivation on Performance: A Meta-Analysis', *Sleep*, 19 (1996), 318–26

Pinto, Lucille B., 'The Folk Practice of Gynecology and Obstetrics in the Middle Ages', *Bulletin of the History of Medicine*, 47.5 (1973), 513–23

Plazzi, Giuseppe, 'Dante's Description of Narcolepsy', *Sleep Medicine*, 14.11 (2013), 1221–3

Putter, Ad, *An Introduction to the Gawain-Poet* (Harlow: Longman, 1996)

Putter, Ad, *'Sir Gawain and the Green Knight' and French Arthurian Romance* (Oxford: Clarendon Press, 1995)

Putter, Ad, and Jane Gilbert, 'Introduction', in Ad Putter and Jane Gilbert (eds), *The Spirit of Medieval English Popular Romance* (Harlow: Longman, 2000), pp. 1–38

Raby, Michael, 'Sleep and the Transformation of Sense in Late Medieval Literature', *Studies in the Age of Chaucer*, 39 (2017), 191–224

Radulescu, Raluca L., *Romance and its Contexts in Fifteenth-Century England: Politics, Piety and Penitence* (Cambridge: D. S. Brewer, 2013)

Radulescu, Raluca L., 'Reading *King Robert of Sicily*'s Text(s) and Manuscript Context(s)', in Nicholas Perkins (ed.), *Medieval Romance and Material Culture* (Cambridge: D. S. Brewer, 2015), pp. 165–82

Rawcliffe, Carole, 'The Concept of Health in Late Medieval Society', in *Le interazioni fra economia e ambiente biologico nell'Europa preindustriale secc. XIII–XVIII* (Firenze: Firenza University Press, 2010), pp. 317–34

Reinbold, Charlotte, 'Unstable Dream, According to the Place: Setting and Convention in Chaucerian Dream Poetry' (PhD dissertation, 2017)

Riddy, Felicity, 'Mother Knows Best: Reading Social Change in a Courtesy Text', *Speculum*, 71 (1996), 66–86

Rikhardsdottir, Sif, *Emotion in Old Norse Literature: Translations, Voices, Contexts* (Cambridge: Boydell and Brewer, 2017)

Rikhardsdottir, Sif, *Medieval Translations and Cultural Discourse: The Movement of Texts in England, France and Scandinavia* (Cambridge: D. S. Brewer, 2012)

Roberts, David, 'Sleeping Beauties: Shakespeare, Sleep and the Stage', *The Cambridge Quarterly*, 35.3 (2006), 231–54

Robinson, Ian, *Chaucer and the English Tradition* (Cambridge: Cambridge University Press, 1972)

Robson, Margaret, 'Sex and the Adolescent Girl in *Sir Degarré*', in Amanda Hopkins and Cory James Rushton (eds), *The Erotic in the Literature of Medieval Britain* (Cambridge: D. S. Brewer, 2007), pp. 82–93

Rosenwein, Barbara, *Anger's Past: The Social Uses of an Emotion in the Middle Ages* (Ithaca, NY: Cornell University Press, 1998)

Rosenwein, Barbara, *Emotional Communities in the Early Middle Ages* (Ithaca, NY: Cornell University Press, 2006)

Rouse, Robert Allen, '"Some Like it Hot": The Medieval Eroticism of Heat', in Amanda Hopkins and Cory James Rushton (eds), *The Erotic in the Literature of Medieval Britain* (Cambridge: D. S. Brewer, 2007), pp. 71–81

Russell, J. Stephen, *The English Dream Vision: Anatomy of a Form* (Columbus, OH: Ohio State University Press, 1988)

Ryrie, Alec, 'Sleeping, Waking and Dreaming in Protestant Piety', in Jessica Martin and Alec Ryrie (eds), *Private and Domestic Devotion in Early Modern Britain* (Farnham: Ashgate, 2012), pp. 73–92

Sadlek, Gregory M., '*Otium, Negotium*, and the Fear of *Acedia* in the Writings of England's Late Medieval Ricardian Poets', in *Idleness, Indolence and Leisure in English Literature*, ed. Monika Fludernik and Miriam Nandi (New York: Palgrave Macmillan, 2014), pp. 17–39

Salter, Elizabeth, 'Chaucer and Internationalism', *Studies in the Age of Chaucer*, 2 (1980), 71–9

Saunders, Corinne, 'Bodily Narratives: Illness, Medicine and Healing in Medieval Romance', in Neil Cartlidge (ed.), *Boundaries in Medieval Romance* (Cambridge: D. S. Brewer, 2008), pp. 175–90

Saunders, Corinne, *The Forest of Romance: Avernus, Broceliande, Arden* (Cambridge: D. S. Brewer, 1993)

Saunders, Corinne, *Magic and the Supernatural in Medieval English Romance* (Cambridge: D. S. Brewer, 2010)

Saunders, Corinne, 'Mind, Body and Affect in Medieval English Arthurian Romance', in Frank Brandsma, Carolyne Larrington, and Corinne Saunders (eds), *Emotions in Medieval Arthurian Literature: Body, Mind, Voice* (Cambridge: D. S. Brewer, 2015), pp. 31–46

Saunders, Corinne, *Rape and Ravishment in the Literature of Medieval England* (Cambridge: D. S. Brewer, 2001)

Scheer, Monique, 'Are Emotions a Kind of Practice (and Is That What Makes Them Have a History)? A Bourdieuian Approach to Understanding Emotion', *History and Theory*, 51.2 (2012), 193–230

Schmitt, Jean-Claude, 'The Liminality and Centrality of Dreams in the Medieval West', in David Shulman and Guy G. Stroumsa (eds), *Dream Cultures: Explorations in Comparative History of Dreaming* (Oxford: Oxford University Press, 1999), pp. 274–87

Schoenfeldt, Michael C., *Bodies and Selves in Early Modern England: Physiology and Inwardness in Spenser, Shakespeare, Herbert, and Milton* (Cambridge: Cambridge University Press, 1999)

Schuback, Marcia Sà Cavalcante, 'The Hermeneutic Slumber: Aristotle's Reflections on Sleep', trans. David Payne, in Claudia Baracchi (ed.), *The Bloomsbury Companion to Aristotle* (London: Bloomsbury, 2014), pp. 128–43

Shaw, Jan, *Space, Gender and Memory in Middle English Romance: Architectures of Wonder in Melusine* (New York: Palgrave Macmillan, 2016)

Sherman, William H., 'Shakespearean Somniloquy: Sleep and Transformation in The Tempest', in Margaret Healy and Thomas Healy (eds), *Renaissance Transformations: The Making of English Writing (1500–1650)* (Edinburgh: Edinburgh University Press, 2009), pp. 177–91

Simpson, James, *Piers Plowman: An Introduction to the B-text* (London: Longman, 1990)

Simpson, James, *Reform and Cultural Revolution: 1350–1547* (Oxford: Oxford University Press, 2002)

Siraisi, Nancy G., *Avicenna in Renaissance Italy: The* Canon *and Medical Teaching in Italian Universities after 1500* (Princeton, NJ: Princeton University Press, 1987)

Siraisi, Nancy G., *Medieval and Early Renaissance Medicine: An Introduction to Knowledge and Practice* (Chicago, IL: University of Chicago Press, 1990)

Smith, D. Vance, 'Chaucer as an English Writer', in Seth Lerer (ed.), *The Yale Companion to Chaucer* (London: Yale University Press, 2006), pp. 87–119

Sotres, Pedro Gil, 'The Regimens of Health', in Mirko D. Grmek (ed.), *Western Medical Thought from Antiquity to the Middle Ages* (Cambridge, MA: Harvard University Press, 1998), pp. 291–318

Spearing, A. C., *Medieval Dream Poetry* (Cambridge: Cambridge University Press, 1976)

Spearing, A. C., 'Poetic Identity', in Derek Brewer and Jonathan Gibson (eds), *A Companion to the Gawain-Poet* (Cambridge: D. S. Brewer, 2007), pp. 35–51

Sponsler, Claire, *Drama and Resistance: Bodies, Goods, and Theatricality in Late Medieval England* (Minneapolis, MN: University of Minnesota Press, 1997)

Sponsler, Claire, 'Eating Lessons: Lydgate's "Dietary" and Consumer Conduct', in Ashley and Clark (eds), *Medieval Conduct*, pp. 1–22

Stanbury, Sarah, 'The Place of the Bedchamber in Chaucer's *Book of the Duchess*', *Studies in the Age of Chaucer*, 37 (2015), 133–61

Stanbury, Sarah, *Seeing the* Gawain-*Poet: Description and the Act of Perception* (Philadelphia, PA: University of Pennsylvania Press, 1991)

Steptoe, A., K. O'Donnell, M. Marmot and J. Wardle, 'Positive Affect, Psychological Well-Being and Good Sleep', *Journal of Psychosomatic Research*, 64 (2008), 409–15

Stearns, Marshall W., 'Chaucer Mentions a Book', *Modern Language Notes*, 57.1 (1942), 28–31

Stock, Lorraine Kochanske, 'The 'Poynt' of *Patience*', in Robert J. Blanch, Miriam Youngerman Miller, and Julian N. Wasserman (eds), *Text and Matter: New Critical Perspectives of the* Pearl-*Poet* (Troy, NY: Whitston, 1991), pp. 163–75

Strohm, Paul, 'The Origin and Meaning of Middle English Romance', *Genre*, 10 (1977), 1–28

Strohm, Paul, 'Storie, Spelle, Geste, Romaunce, Tragedie: Generic Distinctions in the Middle English Troy Narratives', *Speculum*, 46 (1971), 348–59

Sturges, R. S., 'Epistemology of the Bedchamber: Textuality, Knowledge, and the Representation of Adultery in Malory and the Prose Lancelot', *Arthuriana*, 7.4 (1997), 47–62

Sturken, Marita, and Lisa Cartwright, *Practices of Looking: An Introduction to Visual Culture* (Oxford: Oxford University Press, 2012)

Sullivan, Garrett A., *Sleep, Romance and Human Embodiment: Vitality from Spenser to Milton* (Cambridge: Cambridge University Press, 2012)

Temkin, Owsei, *Galenism: Rise and Decline of a Medical Philosophy* (Ithaca, NY: Cornell University Press, 1973)

Tempesta, D., A. Couyoumdjian, G. Curcio, F. Moroni, C. Marzano, L. De Gennaro, and M. Ferrara, 'Lack of Sleep Affects the Evaluation of Emotional Stimuli', *Brain Research Bulletin*, 82 (2010), 194–208

Thompson, Michael, *The Medieval Hall: The Basis of Secular Domestic Life, 600–1600 AD* (Aldershot: Scolar Press, 1995)

Tomkin, Sylvan, 'Script Theory: Differential Magnification of Affects', in Herbert E. Howe and Richard A. Dienstbier (eds), *Nebraska Symposium on Motivation 1978*, vol. 26 (Lincoln, NE: University of Nebraska Press, 1979), pp. 201–36

Totaro, Rebecca, 'Securing Sleep in Hamlet', *Studies in English Literature, 1500–1900*, 50.2 (2010), 407–26

Trigg, Stephanie, 'Introduction: Emotional Histories – Beyond the Personalization of the Past and the Abstraction of Affect Theory', *Exemplaria*, 26 (2014), 3–15

Turner, Edith, 'The Literary Roots of Victor Turner's Anthropology', in K. M. Ashley (ed.), *Victor Turner and the Construction of Cultural Criticism: Between Literature and Anthropology* (Bloomington, IN: Indiana University Press, 1990), pp. 163–9

Turner, Marion, *Chaucer: A European Life* (Princeton, NJ: Princeton University Press, 2019)

Turville-Petre, Thorlac, *England the Nation: Language, Literature, and National Identity, 1290–1340* (Oxford: Clarendon Press, 1996)

Ussery, Huling E., *Chaucer's Physician: Medicine and Literature in Fourteenth-Century England* (New Orleans, LA: Tulane University, 1971)

Vaught, Jennifer C. (ed.), *Rhetorics of Bodily Disease and Health in Medieval and Early Modern England* (Farnham: Ashgate, 2010)

Verdon, Jean, *Night in the Middle Ages*, trans. George Holoch (Notre Dame, IN: University of Notre Dame Press, 2002)

Wakelin, Daniel, *Humanism, Reading, and English Literature 1430–1530* (Oxford: Oxford University Press, 2007)

Walker, Matthew, *Why We Sleep: The New Science of Sleep and Dreams* (London: Allen Lane, 2017)

Walker, Matthew, and E. van der Helm, 'Overnight Therapy? The Role of Sleep in Emotional Brain Processing', *Psychological Bulletin*, 135 (2009), 731–48

Wallace, David, *Premodern Places: Calais to Surinam, Chaucer to Aphra Behn* (Oxford: Blackwell, 2004)

Webb, Diana, *Privacy and Solitude in the Middle Ages* (London: Hambledon Continuum, 2007)

Weiss, Judith, '"The Courteous Warrior": Epic, Romance, and Comedy in *Boeve de Haumtone*', in Neil Cartlidge (ed.), *Boundaries in Medieval Romance* (Cambridge: D. S. Brewer, 2008), pp. 149–60

Weiss, Judith, 'Modern and Medieval Views on Swooning: The Literary and Medical Contexts of Fainting in Romance', in Rhiannon Purdie and Michael Cichon (eds), *Medieval Romance, Medieval Contexts* (Cambridge: D. S. Brewer, 2011), pp. 121–34

Wenzel, Siegfried, *The Sin of Sloth: Acedia in Medieval Thought and Literature* (Durham, NC: University of North Carolina Press, 1960)

White, Sarah M., 'Lancelot's Beds: Styles of Courtly Intimacy', in R. T. Pickens (ed.), *The Sower and His Seed: Essays on Chrétien de Troyes* (Lexington, KY: French Forum, 1983), pp. 116–26

Williams, Deanne, 'The Dream Visions', in Seth Lerer (ed.), *The Yale Companion to Chaucer* (London: Yale University Press, 2006), pp. 147–78

Williams, Deanne, *French Fetish from Chaucer to Shakespeare* (Cambridge: Cambridge University Press, 2004)

Wimsatt, James, *Chaucer and His French Contemporaries: Natural Music in the Fourteenth Century* (Toronto: University of Toronto Press, 1991)

Wimsatt, James, *Chaucer and the French Love Poets: The Literary Background of the* Book of the Duchess (Chapel Hill, NC: University of North Carolina Press, 1968)

Wimsatt, James, 'Machaut's *Lay de Confort* and Chaucer's French Inheritance', in Rossell Hope Robbins (ed.), *Chaucer at Albany* (New York: Burt Franklin, 1975), pp. 11–26

Wimsatt, James I., 'The Sources of Chaucer's "Seys and Alcyone,"' *Medium Aevum*, 36 (1967), 231–41

Windeatt, Barry, 'The Art of Swooning in Middle English', in Christopher Cannon and Maura Nolan (eds), *Medieval Latin and Middle English Literature: Essays in Honour of Jill Mann* (Cambridge: D. S. Brewer, 2011), pp. 211–30

Windeatt, Barry, 'Towards a Gestural Lexicon of Medieval English Romance', in Elizabeth Archibald, Megan G. Leitch and Corinne Saunders (eds), *Romance Rewritten: The Evolution of Middle English Romance* (Cambridge: D. S. Brewer, 2018), pp. 133–51

Windeatt, Barry, '"Troilus" and the Disenchantment of Romance', in Derek Brewer (ed.), *Studies in Medieval English Romances: Some New Approaches* (Cambridge: D. S. Brewer, 1988), pp. 129–47

Wittgenstein, Ludwig, *Philosophical Investigations*, trans. G. E. M. Anscombe (Oxford: Blackwell, 1953)

Wolfthal, Diane, *In and Out of the Marital Bed: Seeing Sex in Renaissance Europe* (New Haven, CT: Yale University Press, 2010)

Wright, Glenn, '"Other Wyse Then Must We Do": Parody and Popular Narrative in *The Squyr of Lowe Degre*', *Comitatus*, 27 (1996), 14–41

Wright, Neil, 'Geoffrey of Monmouth and Gildas', *Arthurian Literature*, 2 (1982), 1–40

Zeeman, Nicolette, 'Medieval Dreams', in *A Concise Companion to Literary Criticism and Psychoanalysis*, ed. Laura Marcus and Ankhi Mukherjee (Oxford: Blackwell, 2014), pp. 137–50

Zeeman, Nicolette, *Piers Plowman and the Medieval Discourse of Desire* (Cambridge: Cambridge University Press, 2006)

Index

appetite 2–5, 17, 30, 56, 68, 77, 91–130, 159–62, 198, 212, 229
   see also dangers of sleep; digestion
Aquinas, Thomas 24, 49, 54, 76, 210
Aristotle 12, 49–50, 54–5, 74–7, 162, 218, 252
Augustine 54–5, 75–7
Avicenna 49–51, 54–5, 76–7, 100

bedchambers 6, 10, 13–14, 31, 152–4, 167–80, 182–3, 212
beds 8–10, 13–15, 18, 31, 59, 63, 96–101, 111–13, 121–31, 151–7, 162–7, 171–8, 181–9, 210–11, 216, 225–30
   bedsheets 14, 147 n. 54, 180–9, 211
Bernard of Clairvaux 24
Bevis of Hampton 145 n. 118
biphasic sleep 99–100, 138 n. 34
Boccaccio, Giovanni 24, 179
Boethius 226, 229, 240 n. 126
Book of the Courtier 116–17
Bourchier, John
   Huon of Burdeux 145 n. 118
Borde, Andrew 96–8, 101

Capgrave, John 60
Caxton, William
   Blanchardyn and Eglantine 115
   Book of Fayttes of Armes and of Chivalry 102

Book of the Knight of the Tower 17, 102
Book of the Ordre of Chyualry 25, 116
Game and Playe of the Chesse 100
Golden Legend 47
Gouernayle of Helthe 56, 97–100
Chardri 22, 47–9, 58–60, 69, 204, 227, 245
chastity 17, 100, 103, 109–13, 179
Chaucer, Geoffrey
   Book of the Duchess 2–3, 6–9, 21, 27, 32, 50, 60, 69, 75–8, 135, 163–5, 198–231, 244–5
   'General Prologue' to the *Canterbury Tales* 48, 70
   House of Fame 165, 200, 218–19
   'Knight's Tale' 70, 117, 221, 243
   Legend of Good Women 8, 32, 156–8, 165–7, 199–200, 218–20, 225–9
   'Miller's Tale' 101, 121–2, 163, 167, 209
   'Nun's Priest's Tale' 77, 220–1
   'Pardoner's Tale' 121, 250
   Parliament of Fowls 8–9, 32, 59–60, 78, 165, 199–200, 218–29
   'Parson's Tale' 92, 119, 244
   'Reeve's Tale' 33, 121–4, 167, 209
   'Second Nun's Tale' 164
   'Shipman's Tale' 99
   'Squire's Tale' 54, 78–9, 138

'Tale of Sir Thopas' 221, 230–1
Troilus and Criseyde 70, 163–5, 167, 191, 220, 223, 229
'Wife of Bath's Tale' 80 n. 10, 157
Chrétien de Troyes
  Erec and Enide 141
  Le Chevalier de la charrette 117, 167, 181–2, 185
  Yvain 58, 84 n. 61, 104, 140 n. 53, 153
churches 6, 18, 32, 35 n. 13, 98, 119, 124–5, 135, 138 n. 33, 151, 155, 158–62, 191 n. 31
class 2, 7, 13, 56, 67, 94, 101, 121–6
Cogan, Thomas 57, 69
comedy 7, 122, 148 n. 162, 245
consolation *see* emotions

dangers of sleep 91–135
  gendered dimensions 16–18, 30–1, 93, 101–2, 113, 154–7, 180–7
  incubi 17–18, 106, 112–13, 157
  noon-day demon 5, 110
  sin 5, 10, 24, 30, 62–5, 91–9, 105, 108, 118–35
  social reputation 1–8, 16–26, 30, 62–7, 79, 91–135, 180–7
  see also appetite; daytime sleep; illness; temperance
Dante Alighieri 24, 44 n. 87
daytime sleep 1–2, 30, 44 n. 82, 91–135
  see also dangers of sleep
desire 1–5, 15, 151–89
  for sex 167–87
  for sleep 1–2, 27, 31, 49, 91, 104, 114, 135, 151–62, 201–17
  for truth 49, 67–73, 152
digestion 14–15, 19, 29–32, 49, 51–6, 96, 100–1, 140 n. 53, 204
  see also appetite; Galen; medicine

dreams 2–11, 14–15, 21, 24–5, 27–33, 49–54, 59–60, 64–7, 72–9, 118, 123–7, 131–45, 152–62, 164–5, 198–231, 243–8, 251–2
  see also Aristotle; Macrobius

Elyot, Thomas 137 n. 18, 139 n. 41, 254 n. 30
emotions 14, 19–20, 47–79, 162–7, 206–17
  anger 8, 14, 29, 48–54, 57–8, 63–6
  consolation for 3, 8, 33, 151, 200, 205–17, 224, 226, 230
  sorrow *or* melancholy 8, 14, 25, 29, 32, 48–9, 55–69, 72, 76, 79, 119, 158, 165–6, 176, 200, 208–29, 235 n. 38
  see also humours; mental health
Everyman 72

first sleep *see* biphasic sleep
Froissart, Jean 203–7, 212, 216

Galen 10, 13–14, 19, 23, 27, 32, 47–70, 76–7, 154, 201, 204, 207, 215, 224–7, 247, 252
gardens *see locus amoenus*; trees
Gawain-poet 22, 30, 92–5, 128–34, 242, 245, 249–50
  Cleanness 93, 128–32, 245, 249
  Patience 60, 128–9
  Pearl 8–9, 32, 66, 128, 131–2
  Sir Gawain and the Green Knight 7, 53, 57–8, 93–5, 106, 128, 130–2, 153, 163, 167, 172–5, 178, 243–5, 249–50
Geoffrey of Monmouth 151, 154–5, 242
Gildas 189 n. 1
Glyndwr, Owain 72
Gottfried von Strassburg 181–2
Gower, John 38, 72, 92, 120–1, 146 n. 130, 191 n. 26

Gregory the Great 23, 35 n. 13, 70–1, 75, 87 n. 116
Guy of Warwick 86 n. 88

habitus 5, 13, 16, 21, 23, 94, 102
halls (of castles) 6, 14, 31, 131, 171, 177–8, 187–8
Havelok the Dane 71
Hippocrates 50–1, 201, 215
Hoccleve, Thomas 80 n. 6
Horn Childe 167, 171–4
humours 8–9, 13–14, 19–20, 27, 28–9, 32, 48–78, 95, 119, 132, 166, 204–8, 216, 219–27, 247, 254
 see also emotions
Humphrey, Duke of Gloucester *see* Kymer, Gilbert

idleness *see* sloth
Idley, Peter 71, 119
illness 2, 11, 26, 76, 206–17
 see also dangers of sleep; emotions; Galen
incubi *see* dangers of sleep
insomnia 2, 7, 19, 24, 49, 67–70, 164, 198–230, 247–50
 see also sleep deprivation

Kempe, Margery 5, 17, 59, 74, 84 n. 63, 191 n. 31
King Horn 153, 167, 170–1, 174
King Ponthus and the Fair Sidone 221
Knyghthode and Bataile 115
Kymer, Gilbert 2, 22–3, 52, 56–7, 63–4, 68, 95–7, 99

Langland, William
 Piers Plowman 8, 14, 24, 30, 32, 66–7, 73, 92–4, 121, 123–5, 134–5
Last Supper, The 25, 58
locus amoenus 5, 8, 67, 151, 154–8, 165, 227
 see also trees

Lydgate, John
 Dietary 52, 56, 97–8
 Fall of Princes 119
 Troy Book 100

Machaut, Guillaume de 203–14
Macrobius 9, 74–7, 201–2, 218–20
Malory, Sir Thomas
 Morte Darthur 1–3, 6, 16–18, 21, 27, 31, 53, 60–6, 92–3, 103–9, 116, 157–7, 166–7, 175–89, 204, 216, 246–7
Mandeville's Travels 114, 144 n. 99
Mankind 7, 25, 91–5, 121, 125–7, 209, 243
Mannyng, Robert 98
Marlowe, Christopher
 Dr Faustus 14, 125, 244
medicine *see* Galen; humours; illness
melancholy *see* emotions
Melusine 6–7, 22, 25, 93, 105, 114–15, 138, 178–9, 250
mental health 8, 18, 26–9, 48, 49–67, 91, 132, 204, 216, 250–1
 see also emotions; humours
monasteries 19, 23, 99, 138
Morpheus 163, 198, 204, 206, 209–12
Mum and the Sothsegger 66, 149 n. 191

Nebuchadnezzar 160
noon-day demon *see* dangers of sleep; daytime sleep

Octavian 143 n. 88
Ovid 38 n. 31, 120, 203, 206, 209, 217

Peterborough Chronicle 4, 138
Plato 12, 76, 81, 108
Prik of Conscience 72
Prose *Lancelot* 103, 184–6
Prose *Merlin* 17, 112–13
Pseudo-Turpin Chronicle 191 n. 27

Rhodes, Hugh 99
Robert of Cisyle 158–61
Roman de la Rose 155, 165, 202, 208, 214–15

Seven Sleepers of Ephesus 47–8, 121, 251
    see also Chardri
sex 4–5, 7, 15, 30–1, 56, 68, 92, 99, 104, 112, 118, 151–3, 162–4, 167–89
    see also desire
Shakespeare, William
    Cymbeline 179–80
    Hamlet 33, 72, 247
    Henry IV Part I 122, 247
    Henry IV Part II 69, 247
    Henry V 247
    Henry VI Part I 117
    Macbeth 33, 69–70, 95, 242–50
    Midsummer Night's Dream, A 242–6
    Richard III 4, 33, 245–50
    Taming of the Shrew 244
    The Tempest 72, 151, 242, 245
    Troilus and Cressida 246
Sidney, Sir Philip 108, 245
siesta *see* daytime sleep
Sir Degaré 93, 110–14, 156, 243
Sir Isumbras 107–8
Sir Orfeo 7, 16–17, 63, 93, 102, 109–12
Skelton, John 108
sleep deprivation 27, 68, 99, 127
    see also insomnia
sleeping postures 15, 21, 94, 96, 100–1, 121, 209–10
sloth 2, 5, 10–11, 13, 23–4, 27, 30, 91–2, 98–102, 116, 118–29, 134, 157, 162, 209–10, 243–7, 251
    see also temperance
snoring 5, 7, 30, 33, 93, 118–29, 145, 201–10
Spenser, Edmund 13, 108, 158
spiritual perception 2, 18, 24, 105
Squire of Low Degree 153, 167–72
Stanzaic *Morte Arthur* 62
Surrey (Henry Howard) 108
swooning 11, 29, 49, 58, 60–5, 187

temperance 2, 13, 18, 91–2, 96–9, 102–3, 108–15, 128, 131, 158–62, 229
    see also sloth
trees 6, 17, 31, 63, 108–11, 151, 154–7, 160, 216, 243, 247
    see also locus amoenus
Trevisa, John 15, 48, 50, 54–7, 60, 68, 74–8, 245
Tuke, Sir Bryan 242

Vaughan, William 57
vigil 94, 103, 113–15
Virgil 71, 92

Wakefield Mystery Plays 71
Watson, Henry
    Valentine and Orson 106–7
Worde, Wynkyn de 55, 98, 106, 169
Wynnere and Wastoure 122

York Cycle Plays 17, 30, 59, 66, 93, 126–7, 157, 204, 216, 227
Ywain and Gawain 7, 53, 58–9, 93–5, 103–5, 117–18, 131, 141 n. 53, 216

EU authorised representative for GPSR:
Easy Access System Europe, Mustamäe tee 50,
10621 Tallinn, Estonia
gpsr.requests@easproject.com

www.ingramcontent.com/pod-product-compliance
Lightning Source LLC
Chambersburg PA
CBHW051604230426
43668CB00013B/1976